AF321581

We'd like to introduce you to this year's group of illustrators. While you may have seen directories before you'll notice quite a few differences from the typical directory here.

The major difference, we're very selective on who gets in. And who doesn't. We avoid the typical high fees to be in our directory, in fact just the opposite, our page rates are so low everyone can afford a page. But again only the best get in.

We've also made it easier for you by dividing our directory into categories.

We have designed a directory that's more handsome to look at by limiting each artist to one image per page.

Plus the size is portable, drop it in your briefcase, carry it on the subway, take it with you on your lunch break.

Do we have every good artist? No, but we do have artists who have met the high standards of 3x3, the only international magazine and annual of contemporary illustration. Artists from all over the world. Artists who we are confident will always deliver a great job.

As a former advertising agency art director and creative director I realize the challenges of hiring an illustrator. Finding them. Hiring them. Getting a client to accept a sketch of an idea. And the absolute trust that must exist between the art director and the artist.

I have been fortunate to work with both great photographers and great illustrators in New York and across the globe. And I'm convinced illustrators have made me look better and smarter.

To me commissioning an artist is like adding a new face to the creative team. While we art directors think both visually and verbally, illustrators concentrate on pure visual solutions and will add a new dimension to a concept. Just pick up any newspaper or magazine and see how illustrators bring interesting ideas to life. Notice how much more life there can be in a drawn portrait or how easily a map can be read.

Working with illustrators is really not all that difficult. But I think there is a secret on how best to work with one. Give them the a general direction, the reproduction size and then step back and let them shine. Don't treat them like a pair of hands, add their brain to the equation and you'll always come out ahead. They'll appreciate the freedom. You'll applaud the results.

If you're using illustrators now you'll know what I'm talking about; if you're new to illustration, now is a great time to explore just how impactful illustration can be. And what a pleasure it is to work with an illustrator.

So get started. Each page has the illustrator's url, our index their email and phone. Or log on to 3x3Directory.com for direct links to each artist's site.

So the next time your visual idea needs a solution consider speaking with an illustrator, chances are illustration could be the answer. Enjoy.

THREE *by* THREE ILLUSTRATION DIRECTORY 2016

CURATED BY
Charles Hively
Design Director
3x3 Magazine

DESIGNED BY
Charles Hively

ART DIRECTOR
Sarah Munt

COORDINATORS
Skye Bolluyt
Jacob Berry

PUBLISHED BY
Artisanal Media LLC

COVER ART
Joey Guidone
www.joeyguidone.com

PRINTED BY
Allen Press, USA

THREE *by* THREE ILLUSTRATION DIRECTORY 2016

CURATED *by*

CHARLES HIVELY *Design Director*

3X3 THE ANNUAL *of* CONTEMPORARY ILLUSTRATION

Bill Mayer

Mark McGinnis

Marco Melgrati

Jose Alé Mercado

René Milot

Julia Minamata

Ian Murray

Alex Nabaum

Toby Thane Neighbors

Gary Neill

Robert Neubecker

Lauren Newburg

Xiangdi Nie

Shaw Nielsen

Chelsea O'Byrne

Melda Oncu Yildiz

Jim Paillot

Katie Pak

Curtis Parker

Daron Parton

Shiho Pate

Filip Peraic

Valeria Petrone

Denise Plauche

Emmanuel Polanco

Emiliano Ponzi

Andy Potts

Charlie Powell

Somya Raju

Fatinha Ramos

Jacob Reeves

Angela Rio

Luisa Rivera

Kathrin Roedl

Elyse Salazar

Stephan Schmitz

Rick Sealock

Boris Séméniako

Paul Shipper

Steve Simpson

Lasse Skarbövik

Mark Smith

Molly Snee

Dave Szalay

Ken Tackett

Benoit Tardif

Daria Theodora

Brenna Thummler

Sue Todd

Man-Tsun Tsang

Jean Tuttle

Kirsten Ulve

Tim Van Den Broeck

João Vaz de Carvalho

Alexei Vella

Gary Venn

Klaas Verplancke

Michael Waraksa

Laura Weiszer

Taylor Wessling

Ian Whadcock

Patrick Widmer

Oli Winward

Gary Wright

Stephanie Wunderlich

James Yang

Xiaohua Yang

Moran Yogev

Heidi Younger

Yao Yu

Natalya Zahn

Natalia Zaratiegui

Tina Zellmer

Francesco Zorzi

THREE *by* THREE ILLUSTRATION DIRECTORY 2016

CATEGORIES

ANIMAL
Page 10

BUSINESS
Page 22

CHILDREN
Page 31

CONCEPTUAL
Page 49

DECORATIVE
Page 96

FOOD/BEVERAGE
Page 100

FIGURATIVE
Page 102

LANDSCAPE
Page 126

LETTERING/MAPS
Page 138

LIFESTYLE
Page 146

PORTRAITS
Page 158

SEASONAL
Page 179

WHIMSICAL
Page 183

INDEX
Page 202

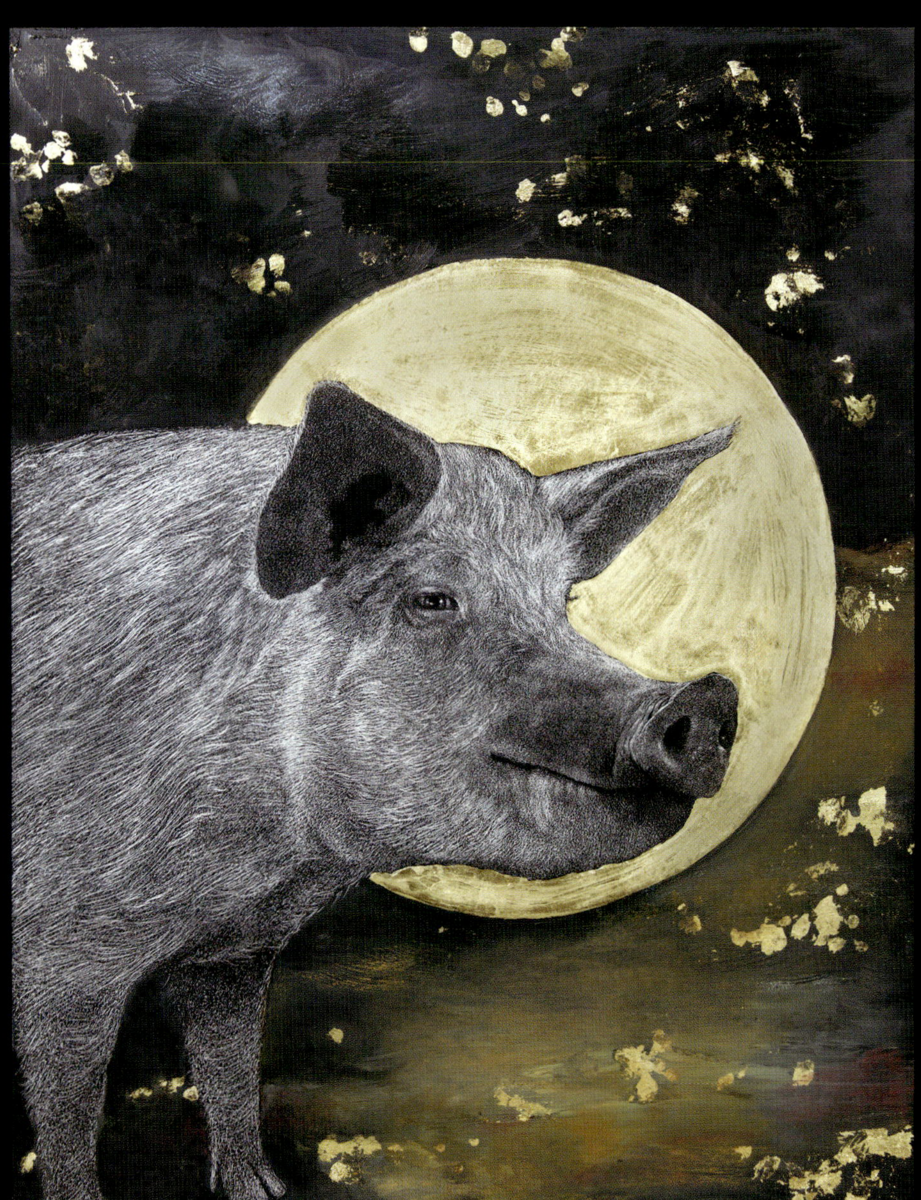

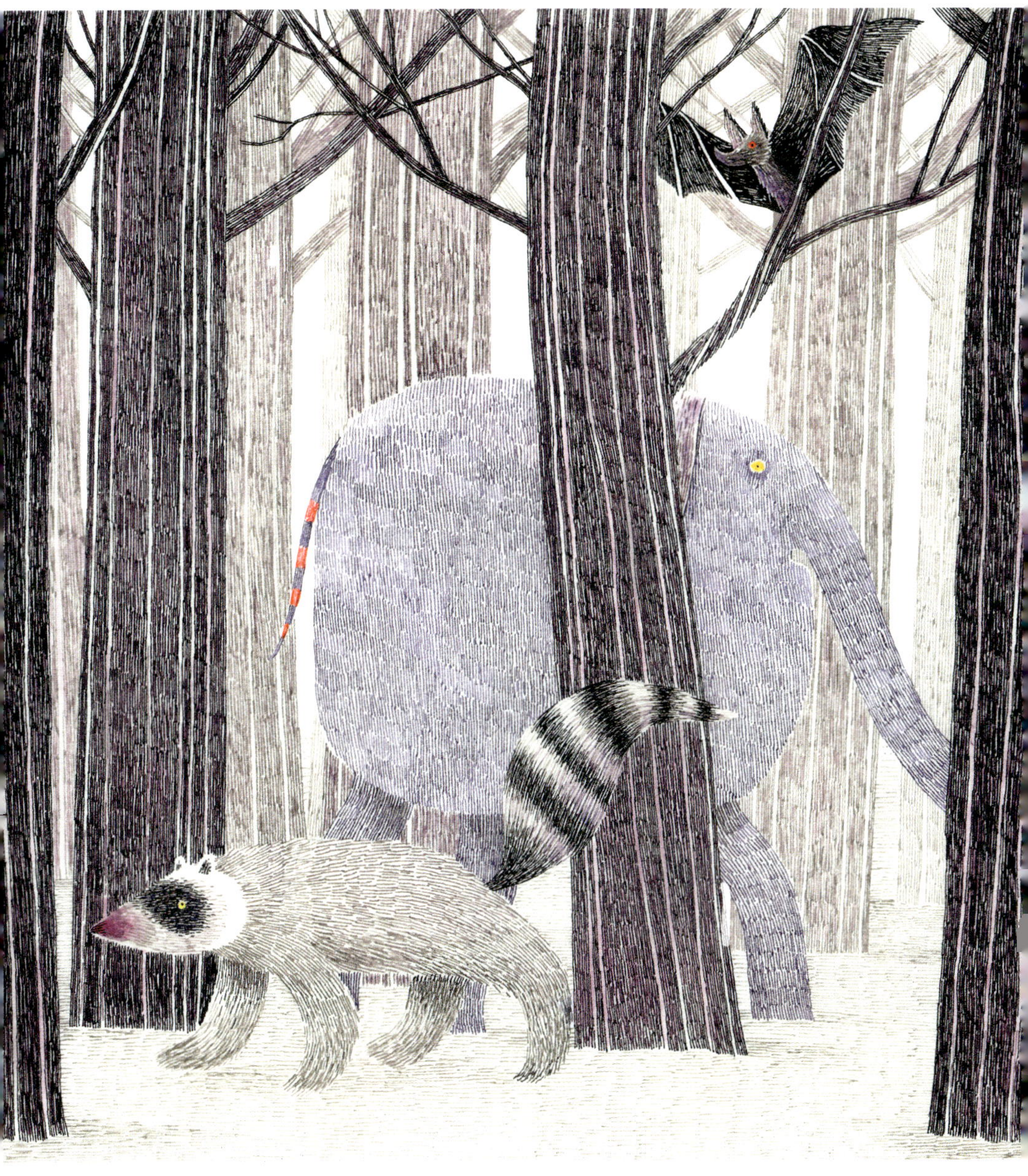

Sara Corbett *www.sarahcorbett.com*

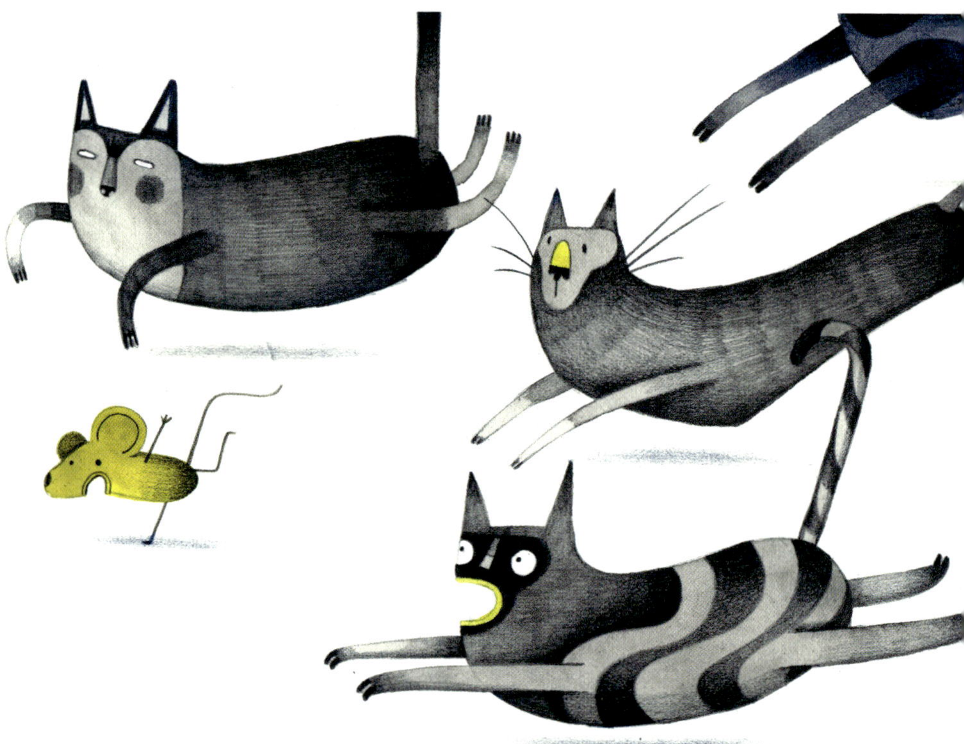

Marion Arbona *www.marionarbona.com*

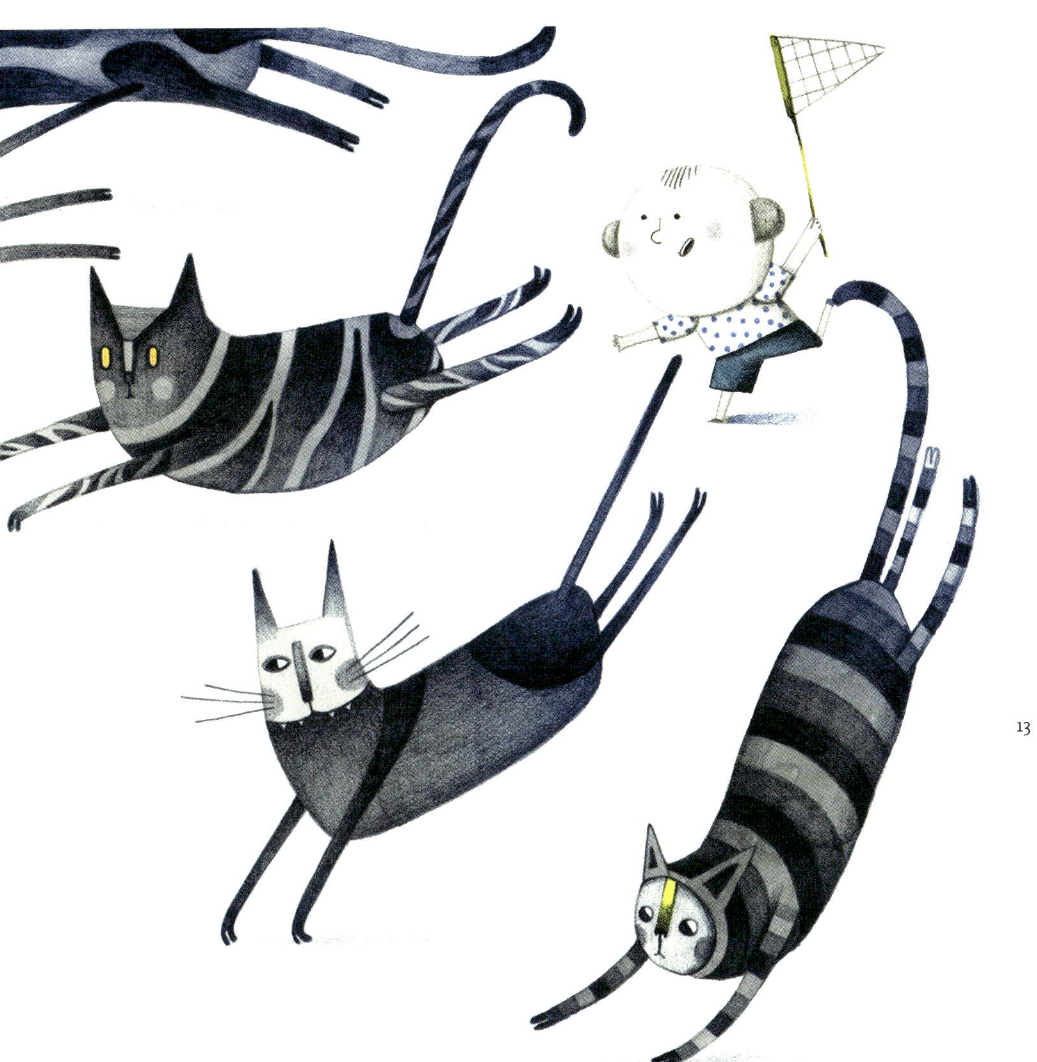

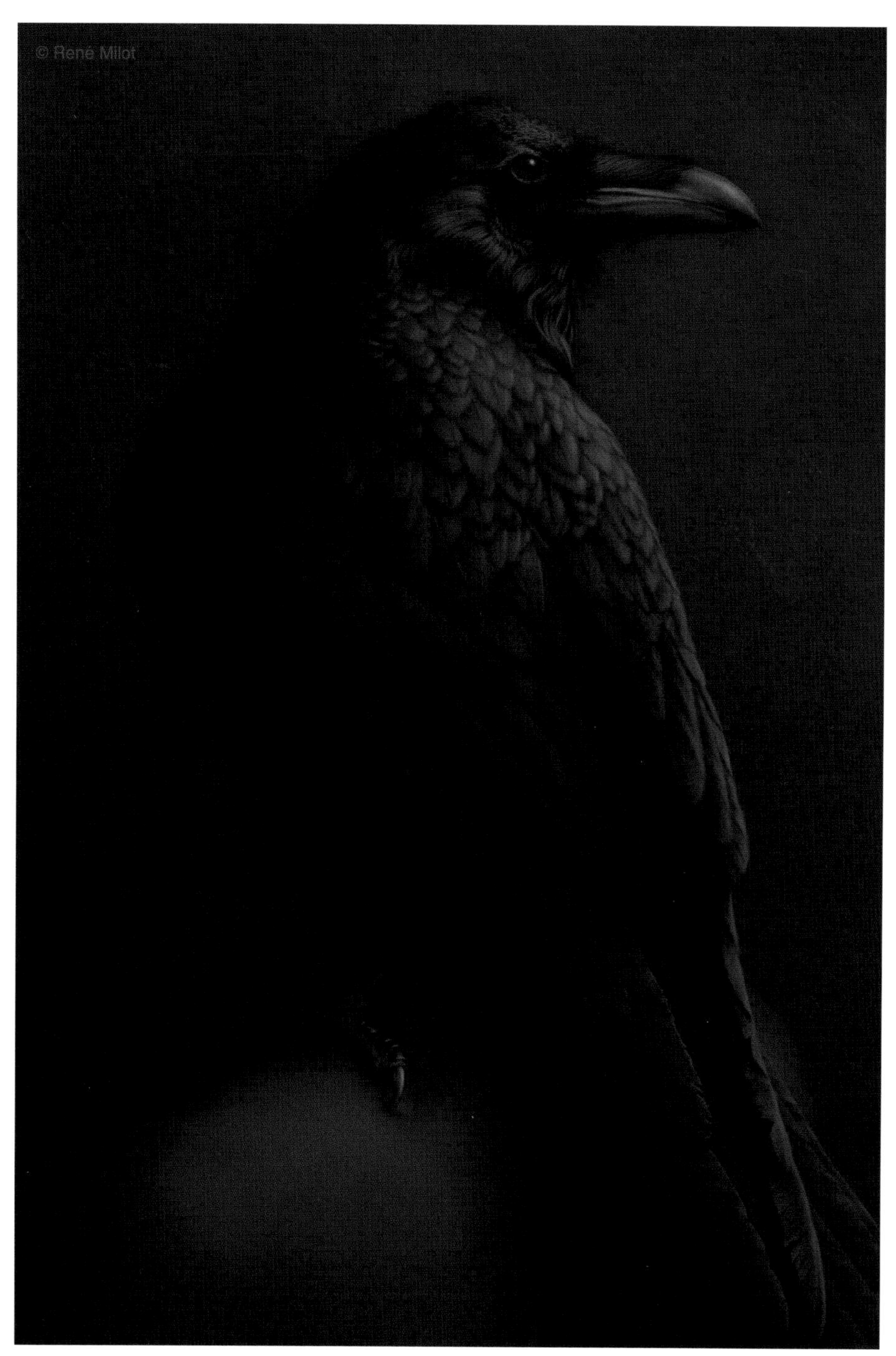

14

René Milot *www.renemilot.com*

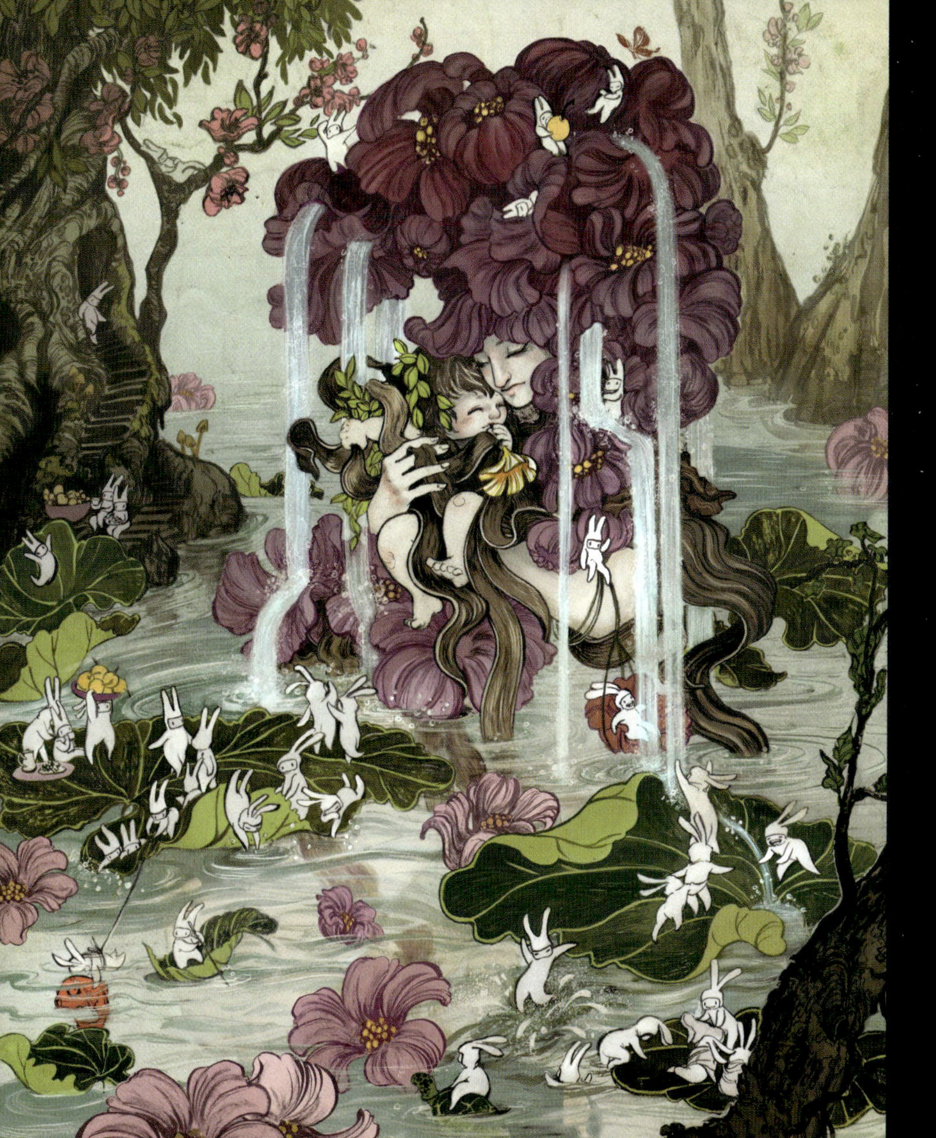

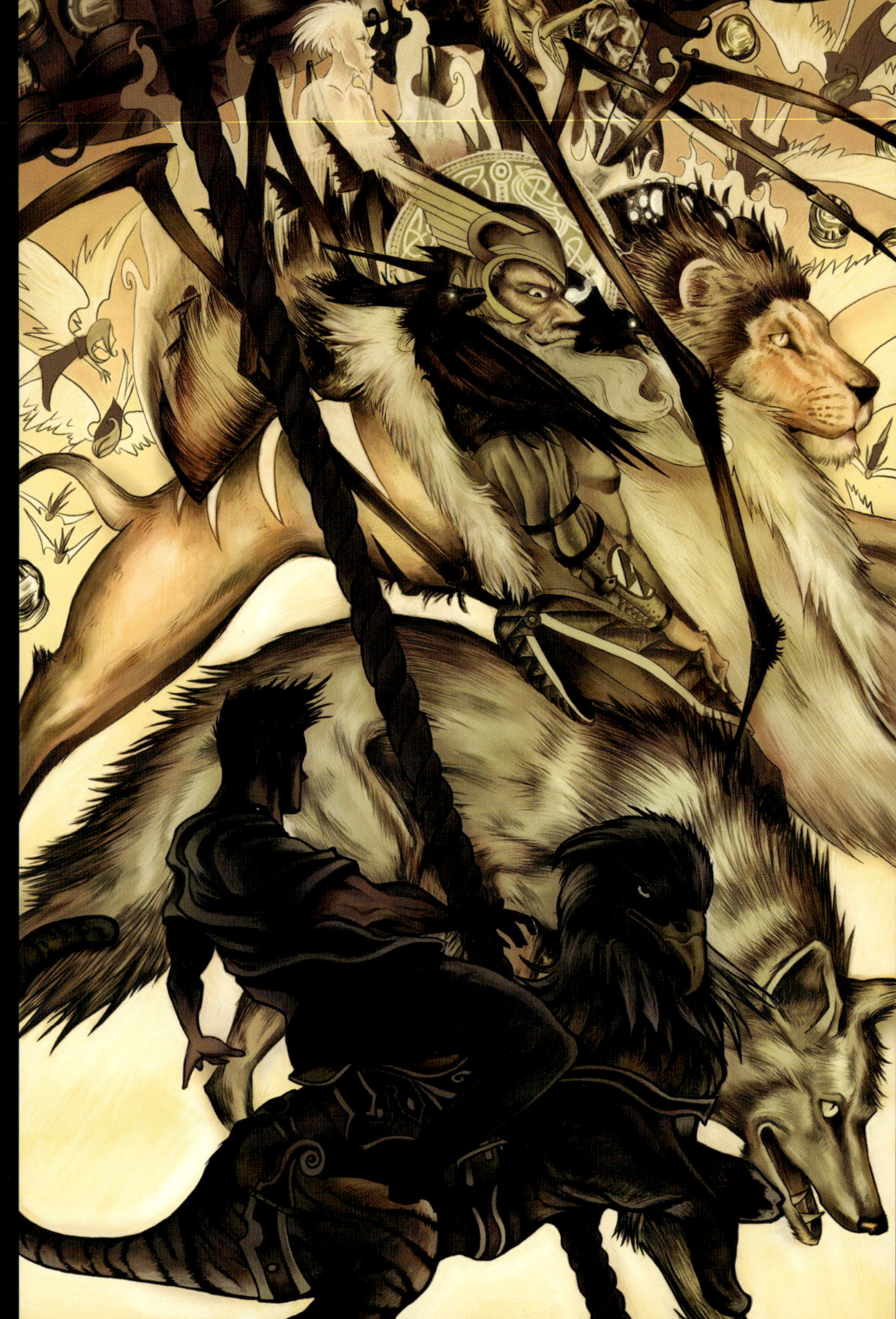

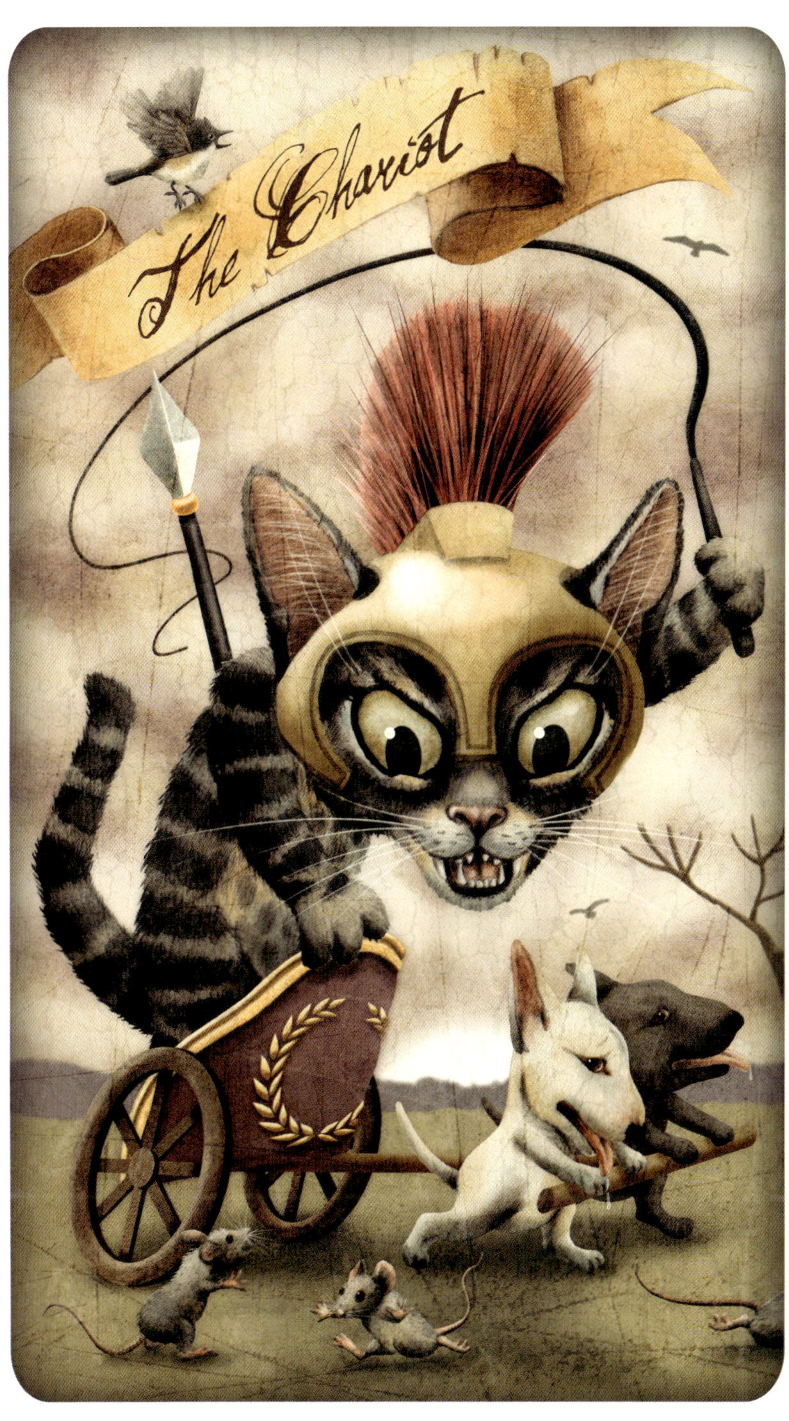

Denise Plauche *www.deniseplauche.com*

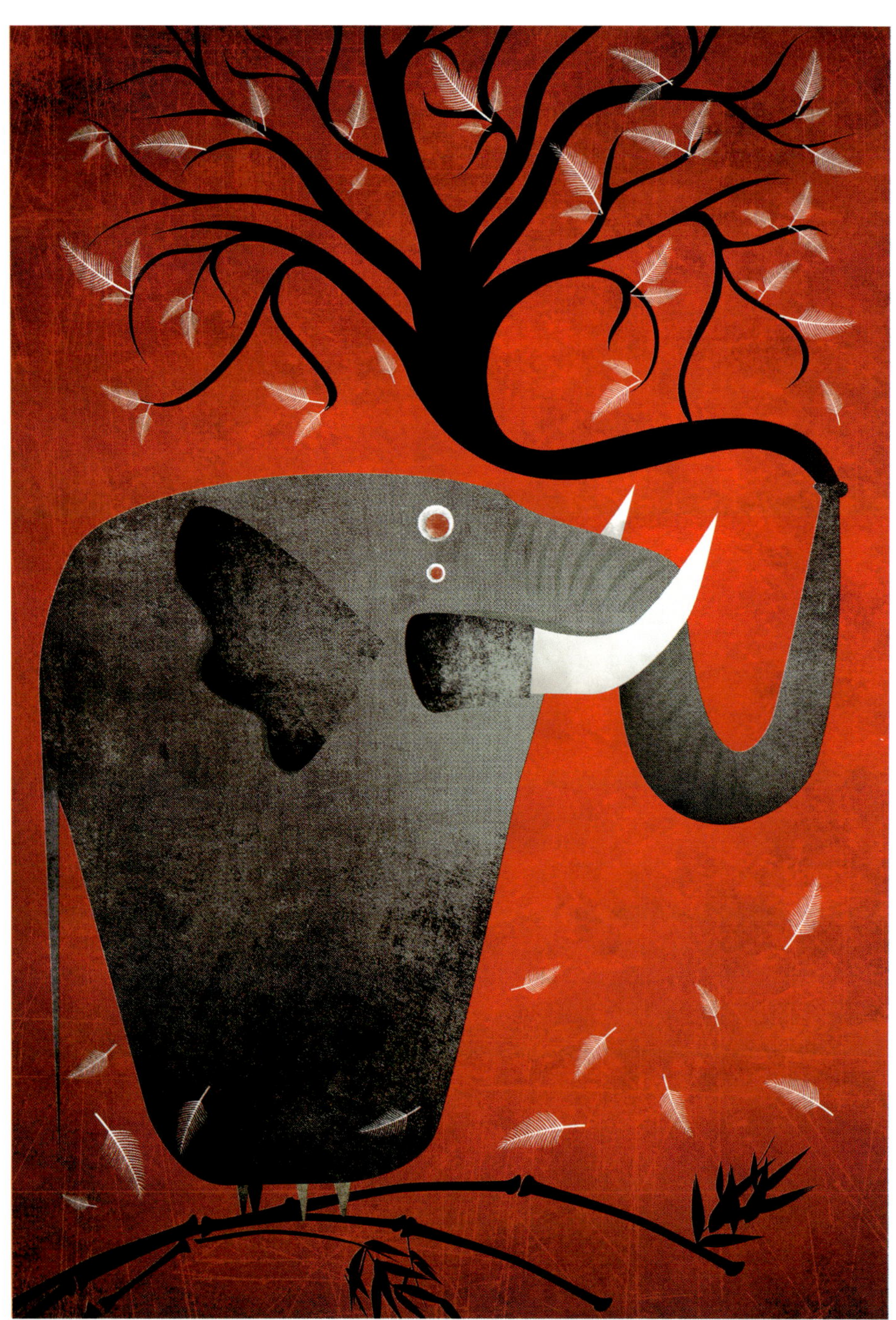

Fatinha Ramos *www.fatinha.com*

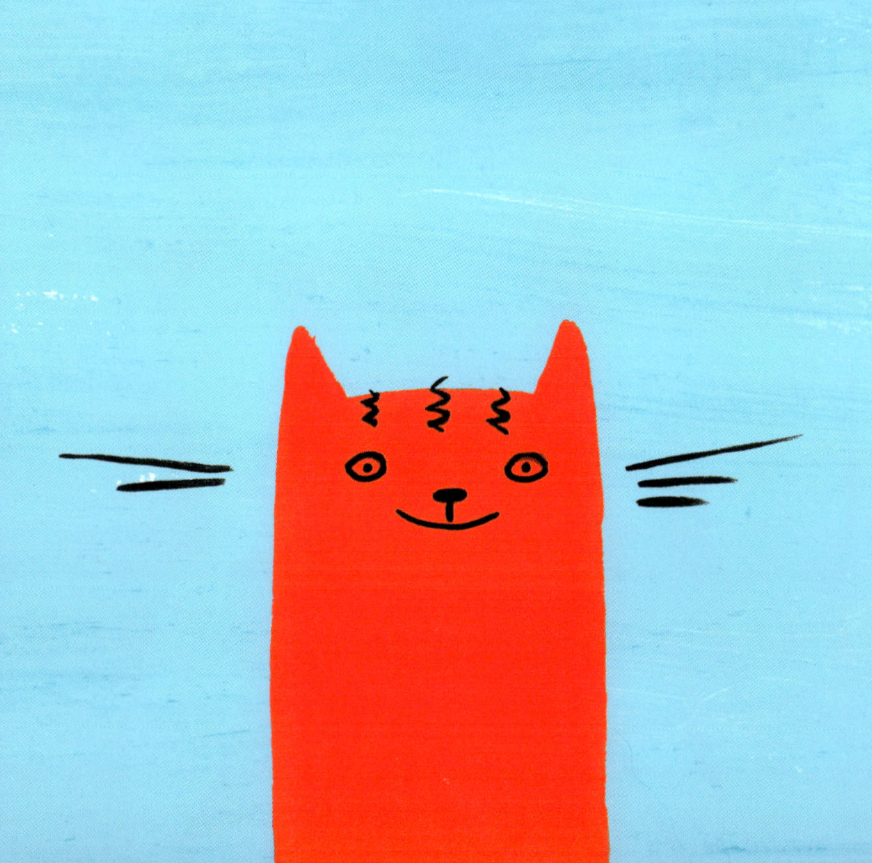

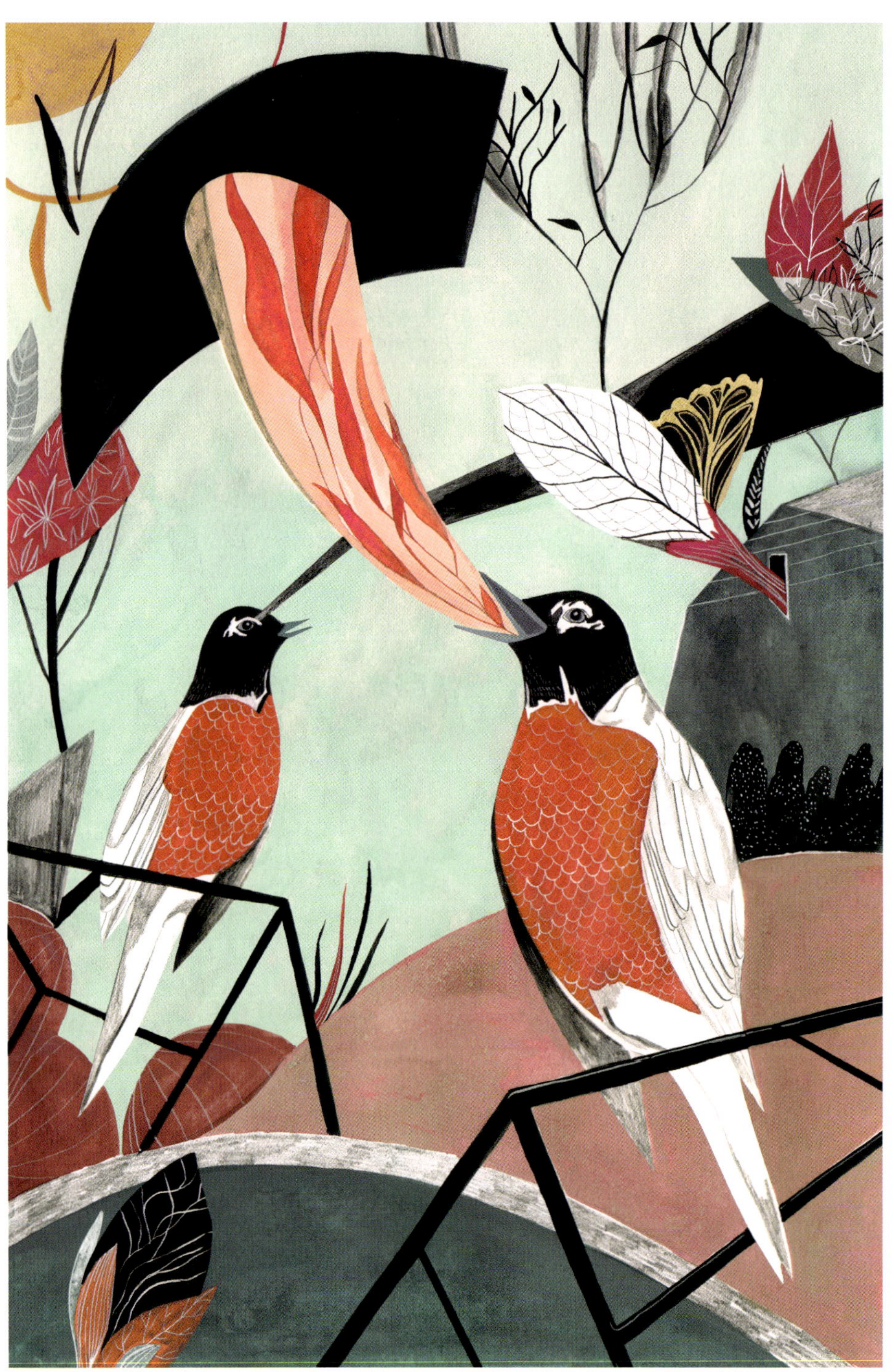

Luisa Rivera *www.luisarivera.cl*

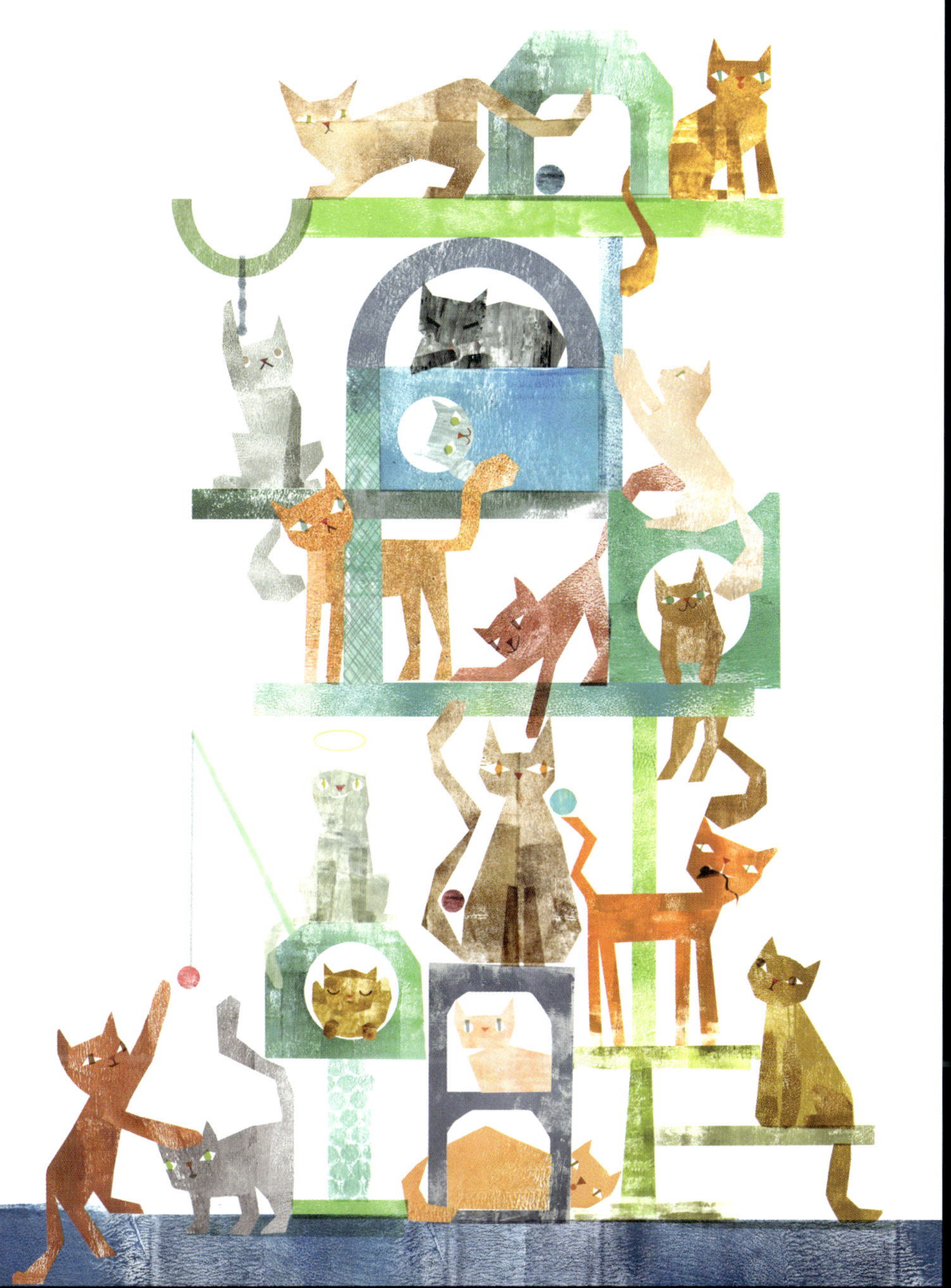

Maria Carluccio *www.mariacarluccio.com*

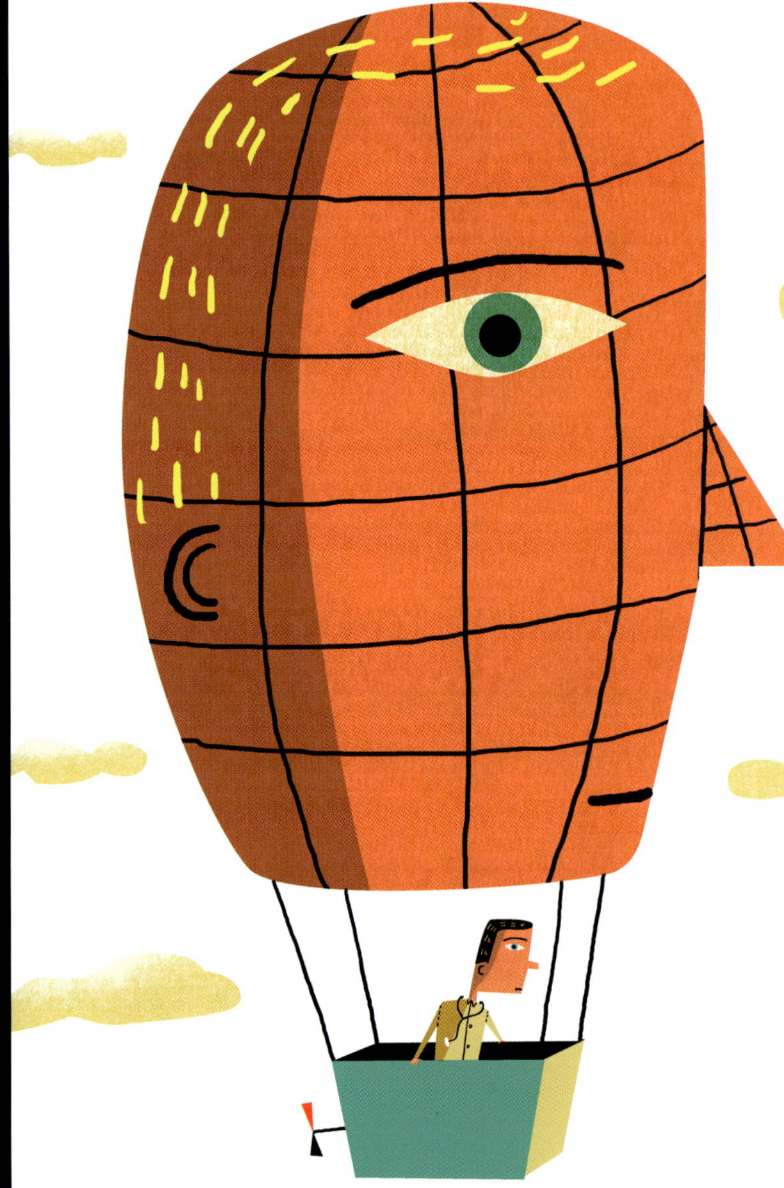

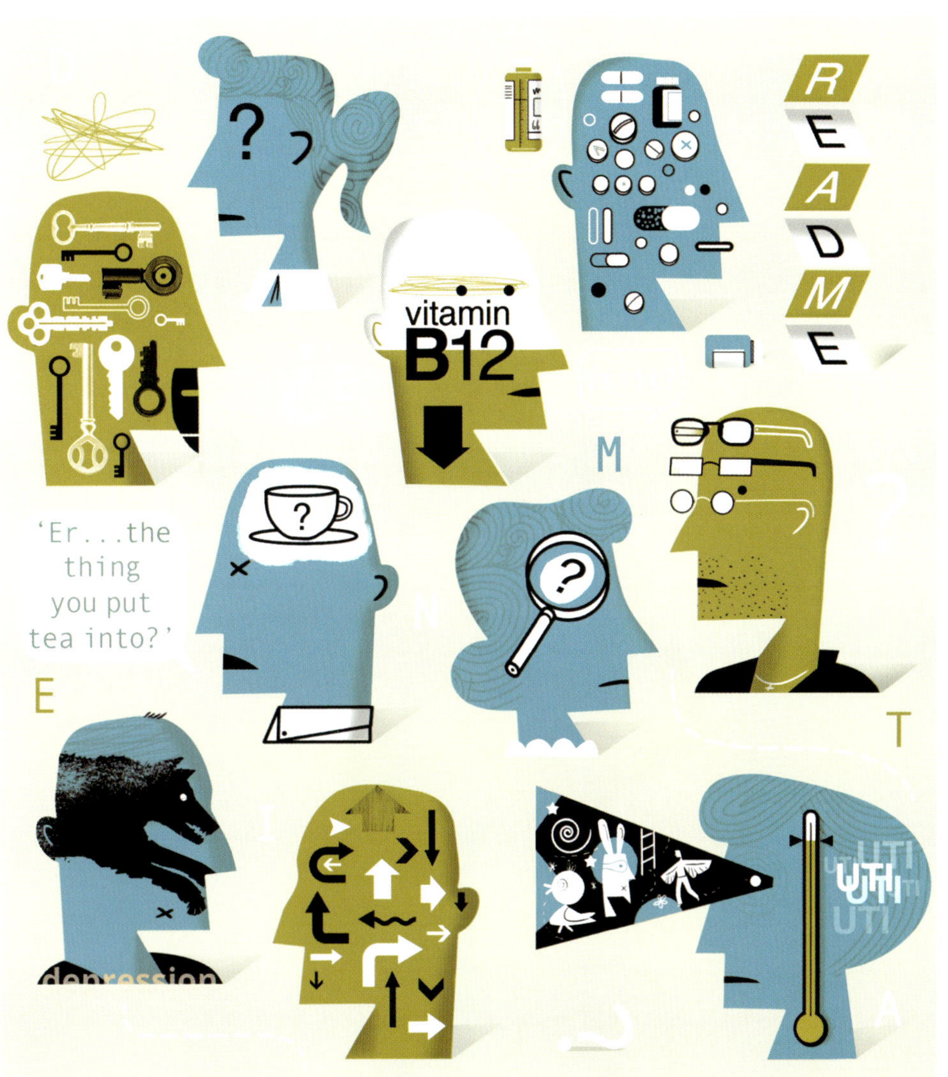

Ian Whadcock *www.ianwhadcock.com*

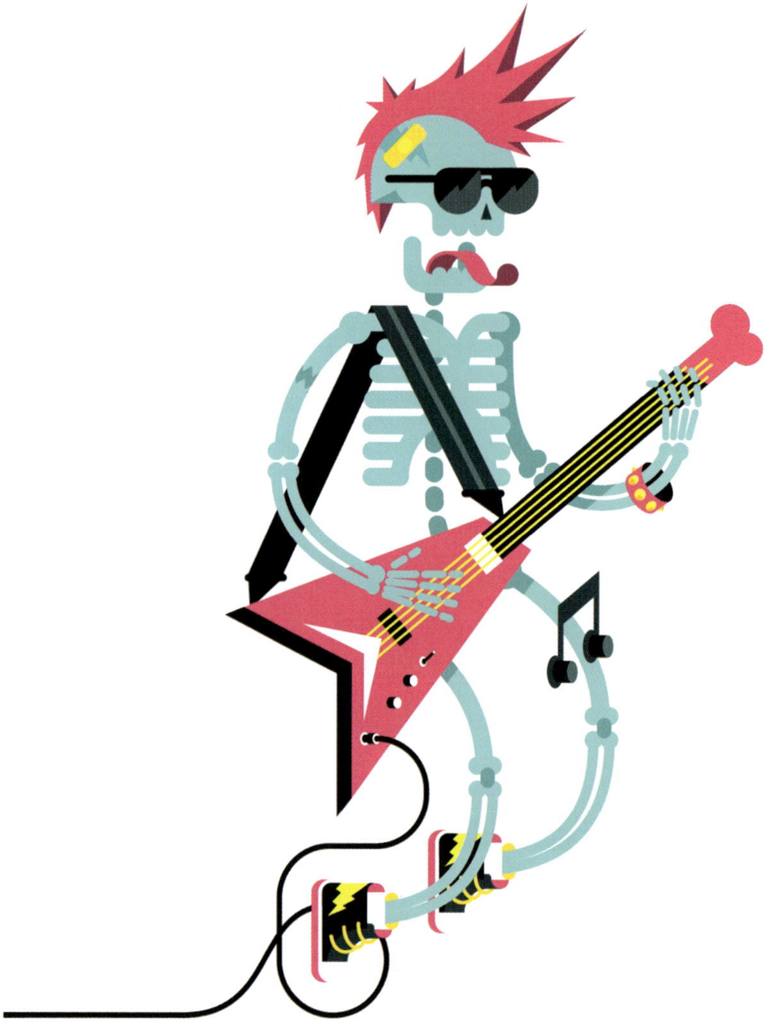

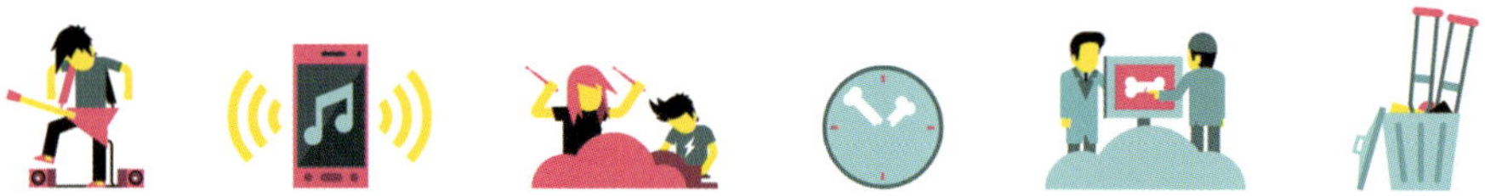

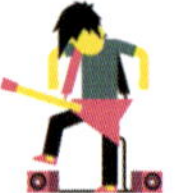 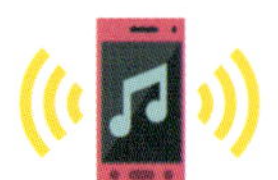  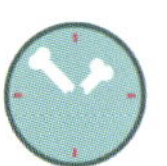 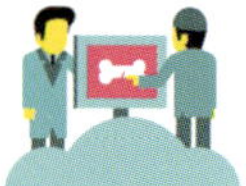 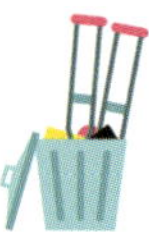

Tim Van Den Broeck *www.timvandenbroeck.com*

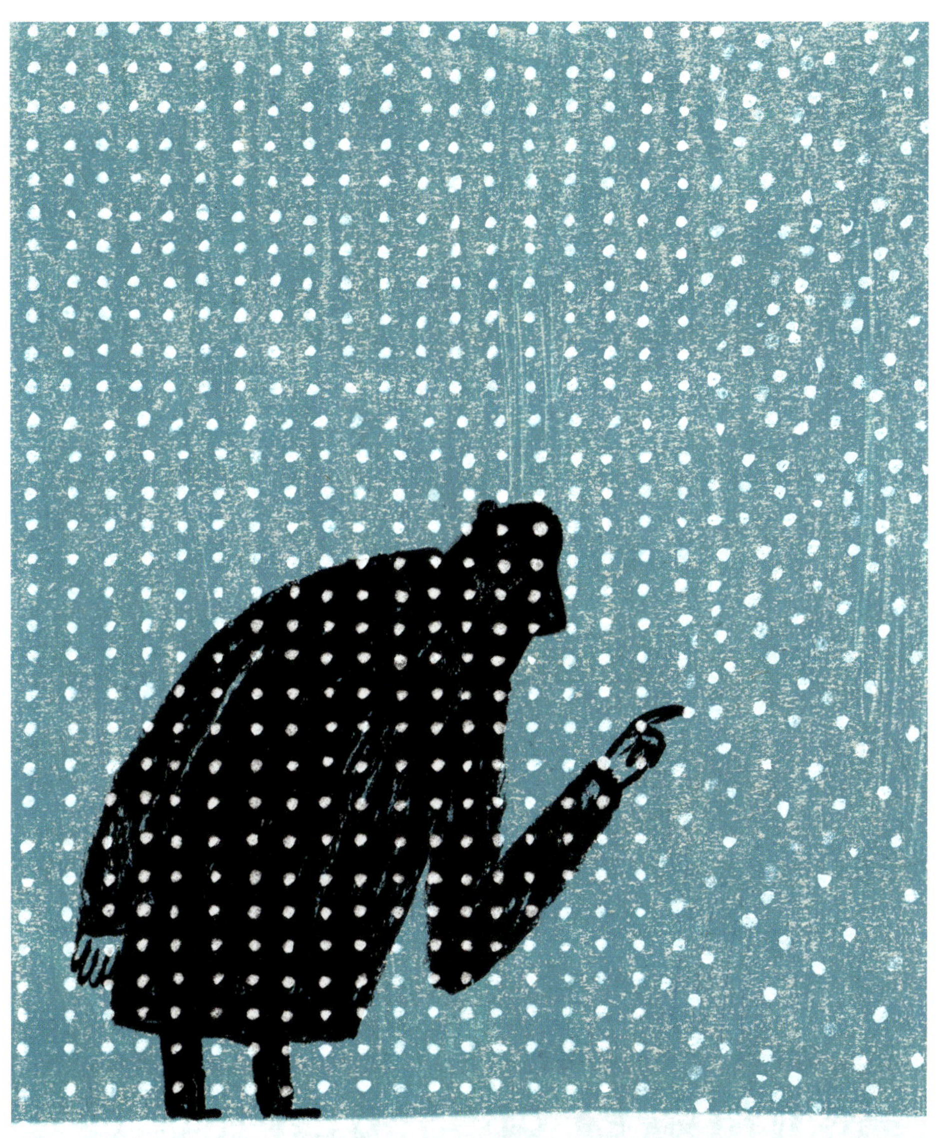

Klaas Verplancke *www.klaas.be*

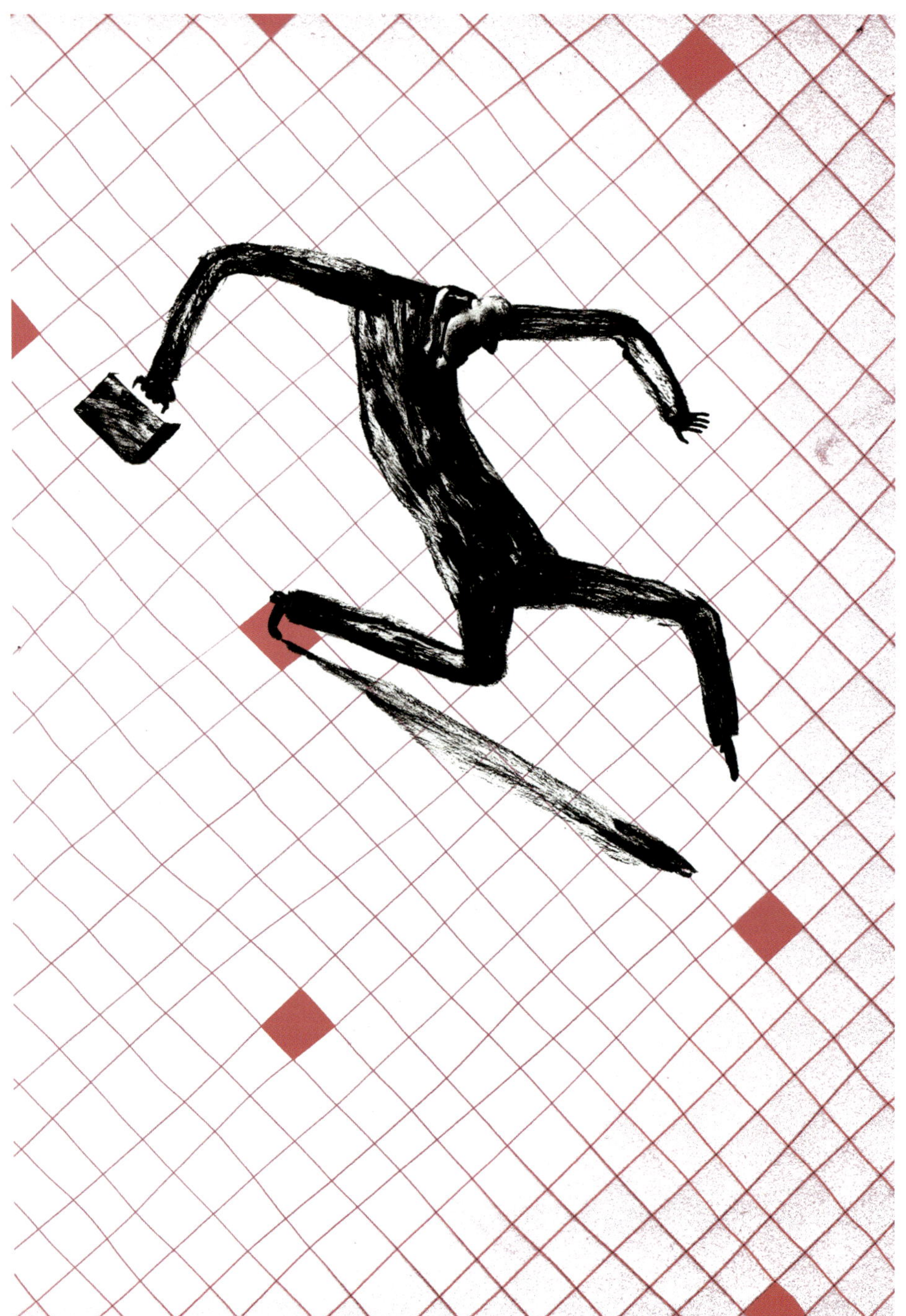

Klaas Verplancke *www.klaas.be*

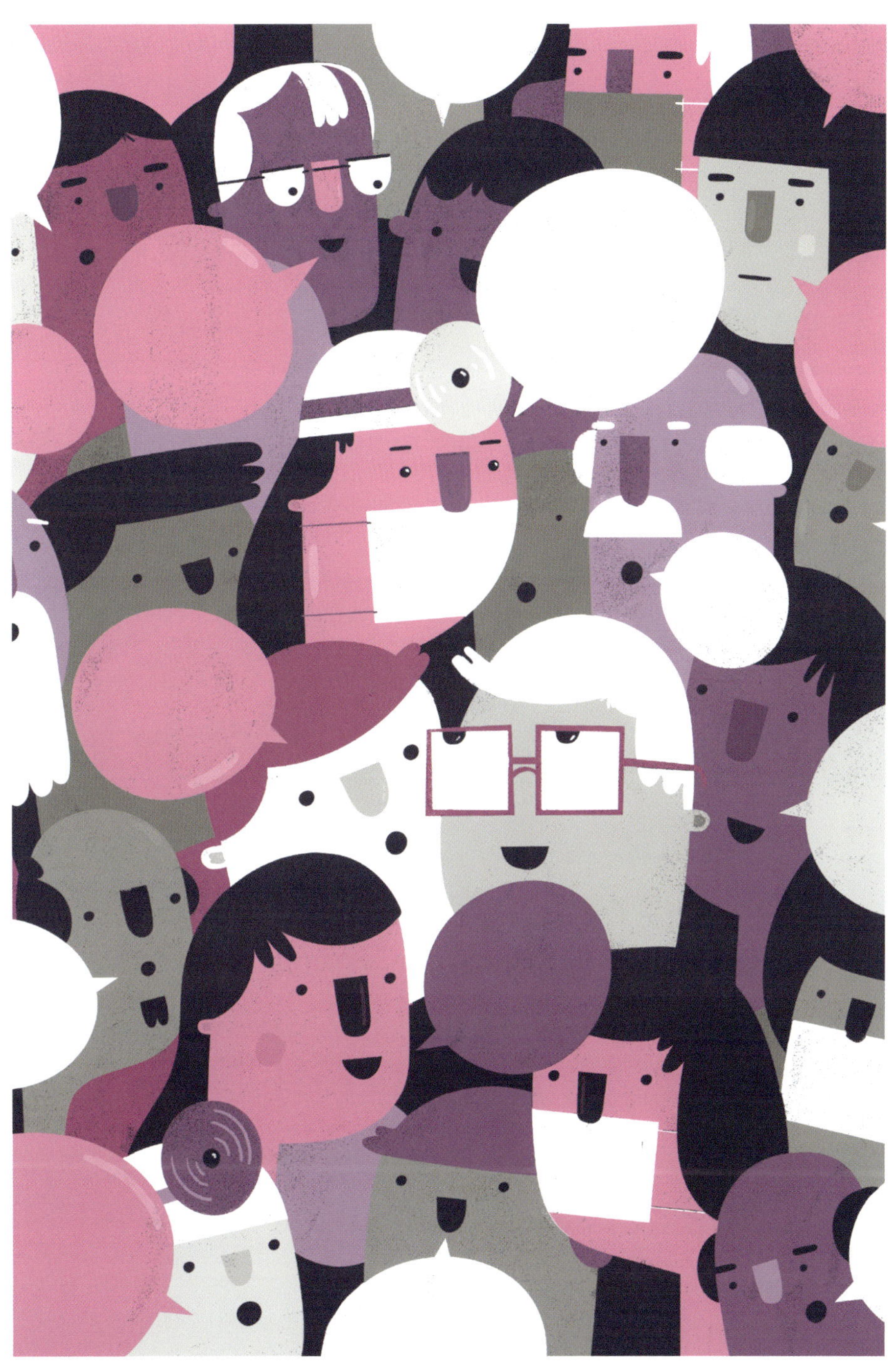

Shaw Nielsen *www.shawnielsen.com*

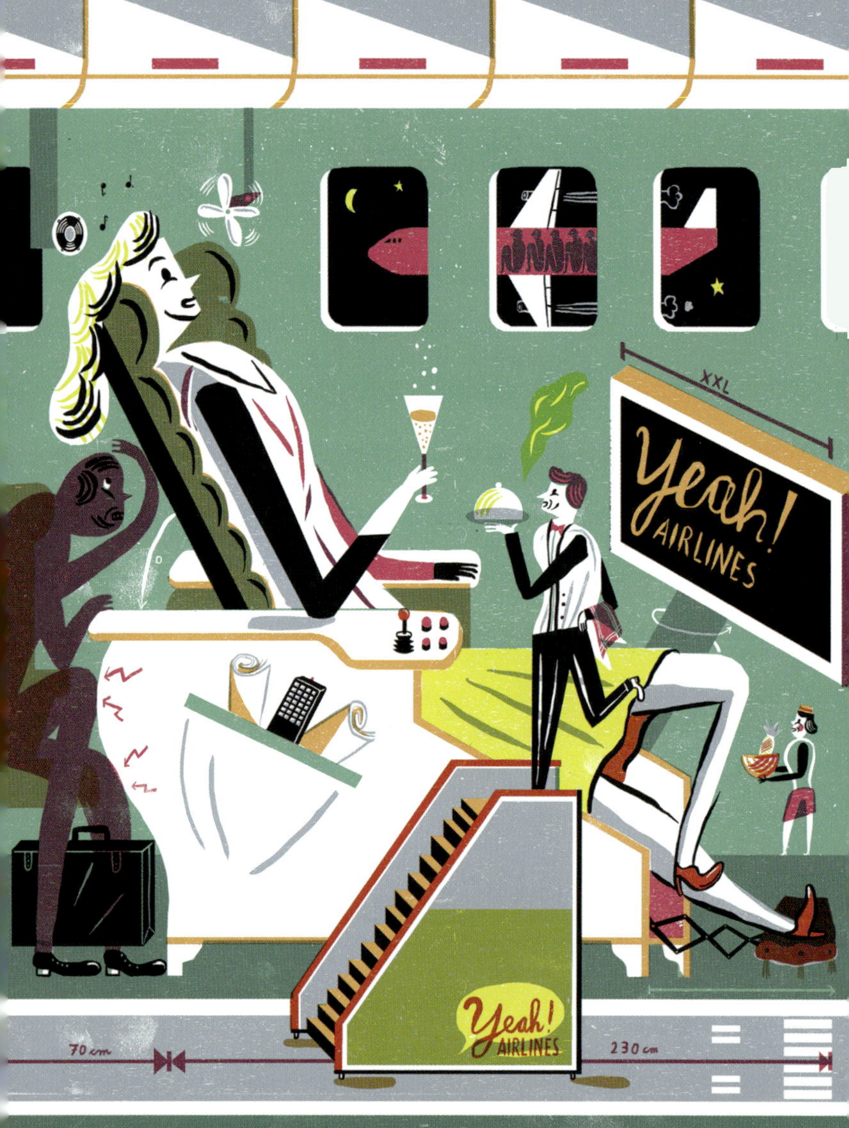

XXL
Yeah!
AIRLINES
Yeah!
AIRLINES
70 cm
230 cm

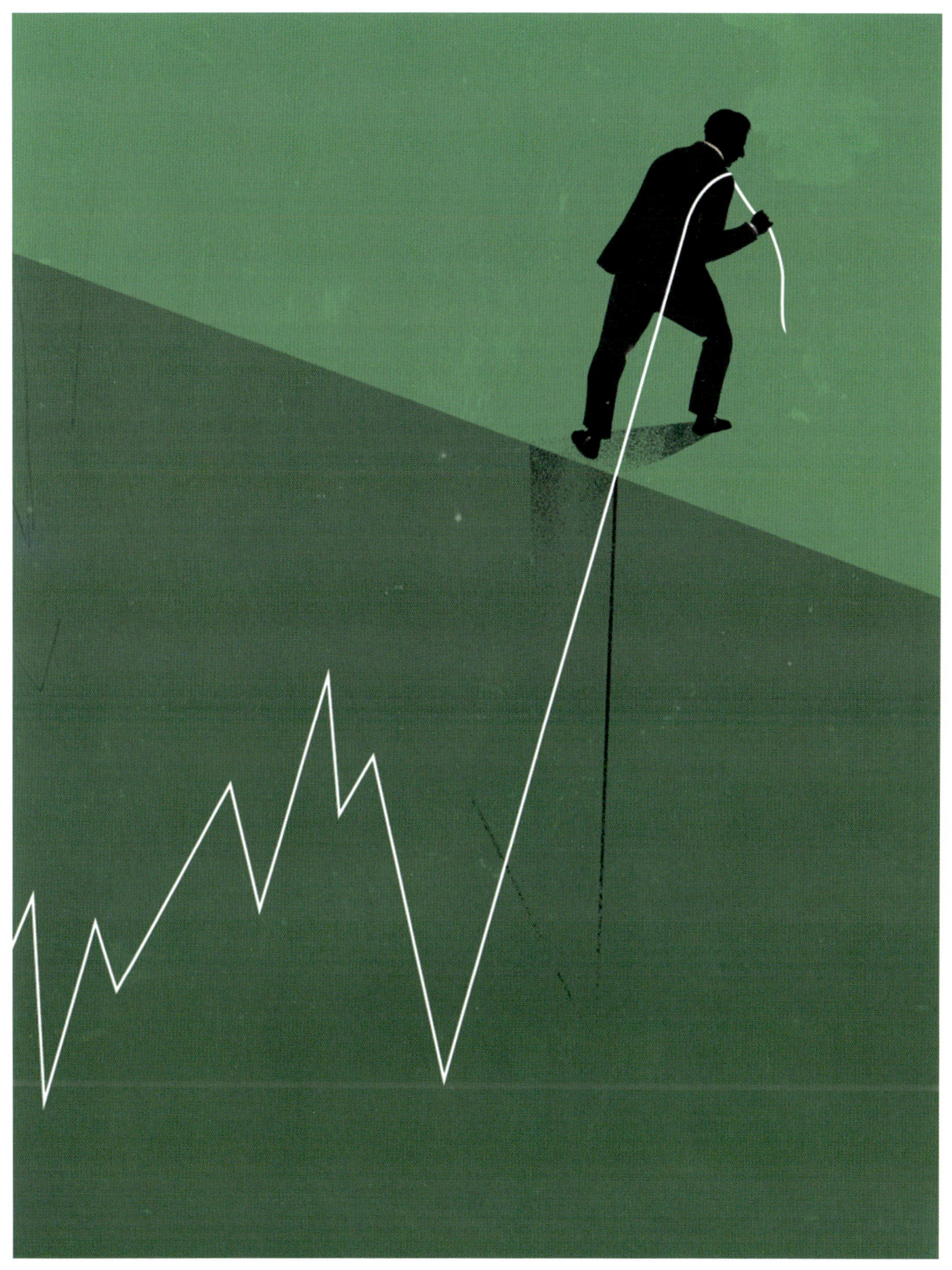

Emmanuel Polanco *www.colagene.com*

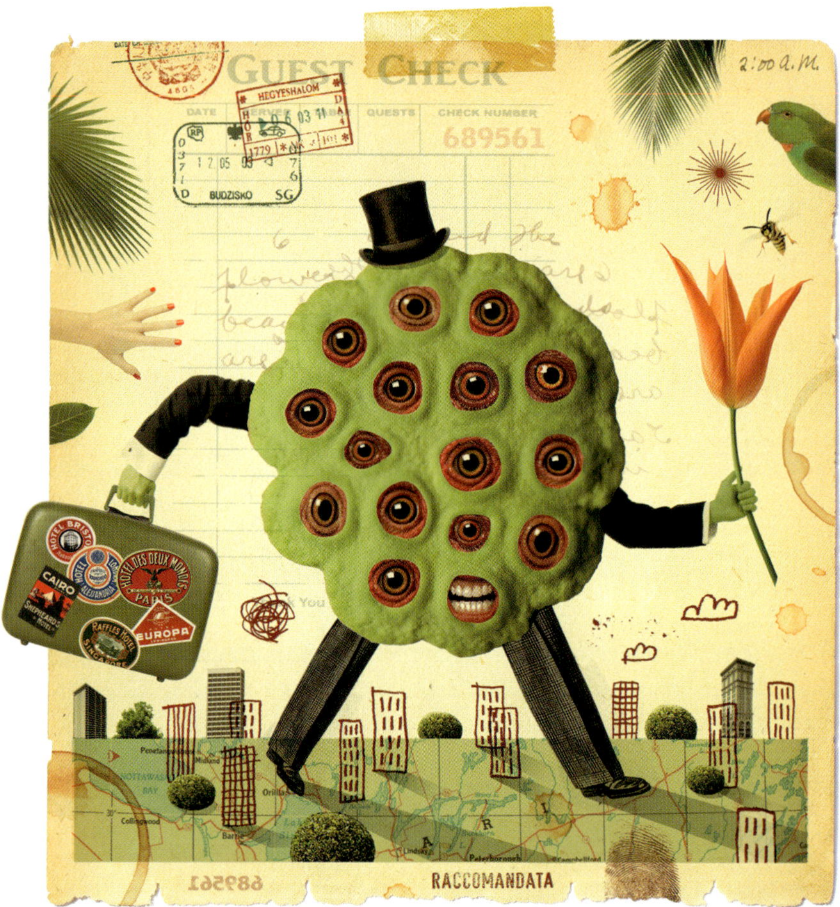

Michael Waraksa *www.michaelwaraksa.com*

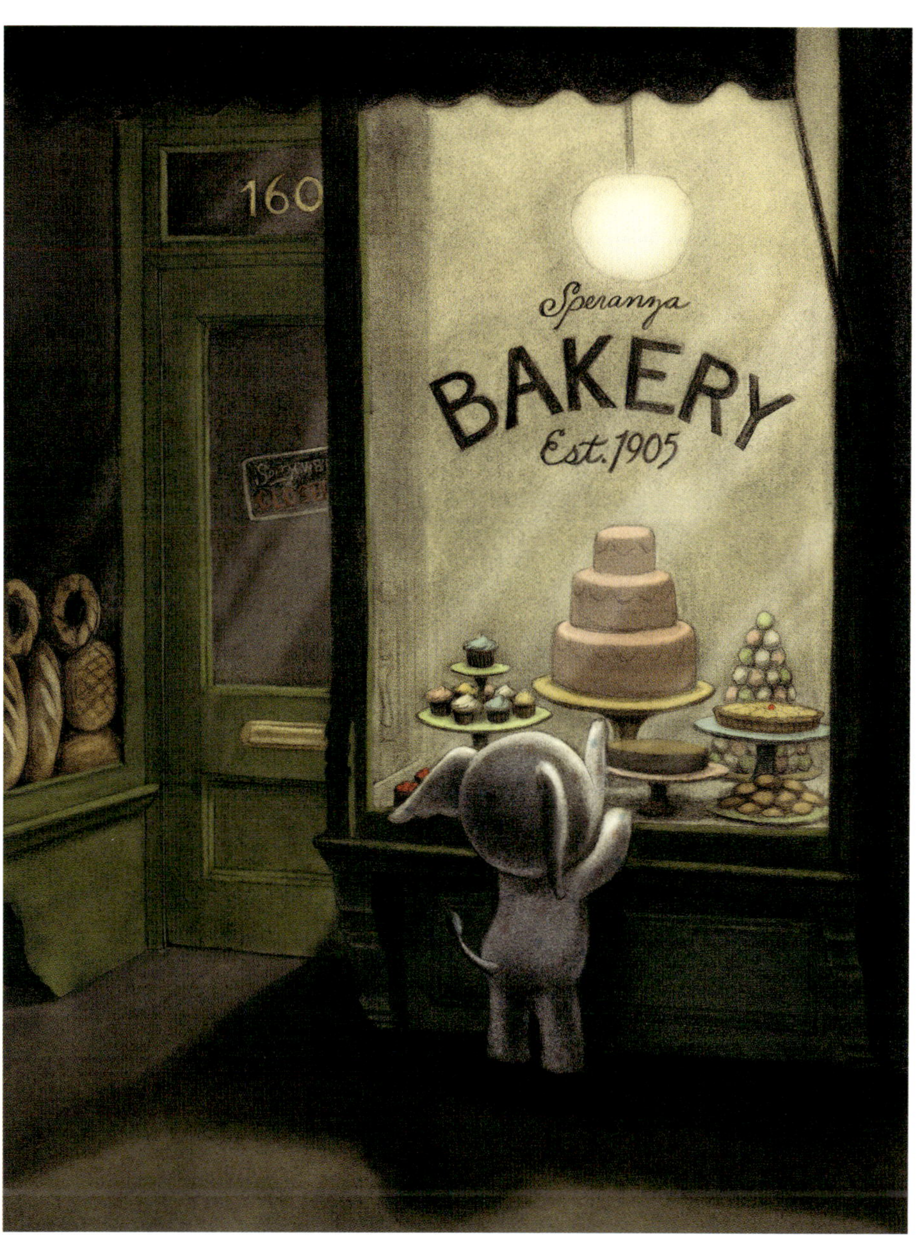

Mike Curato *www.mikecurato.com*

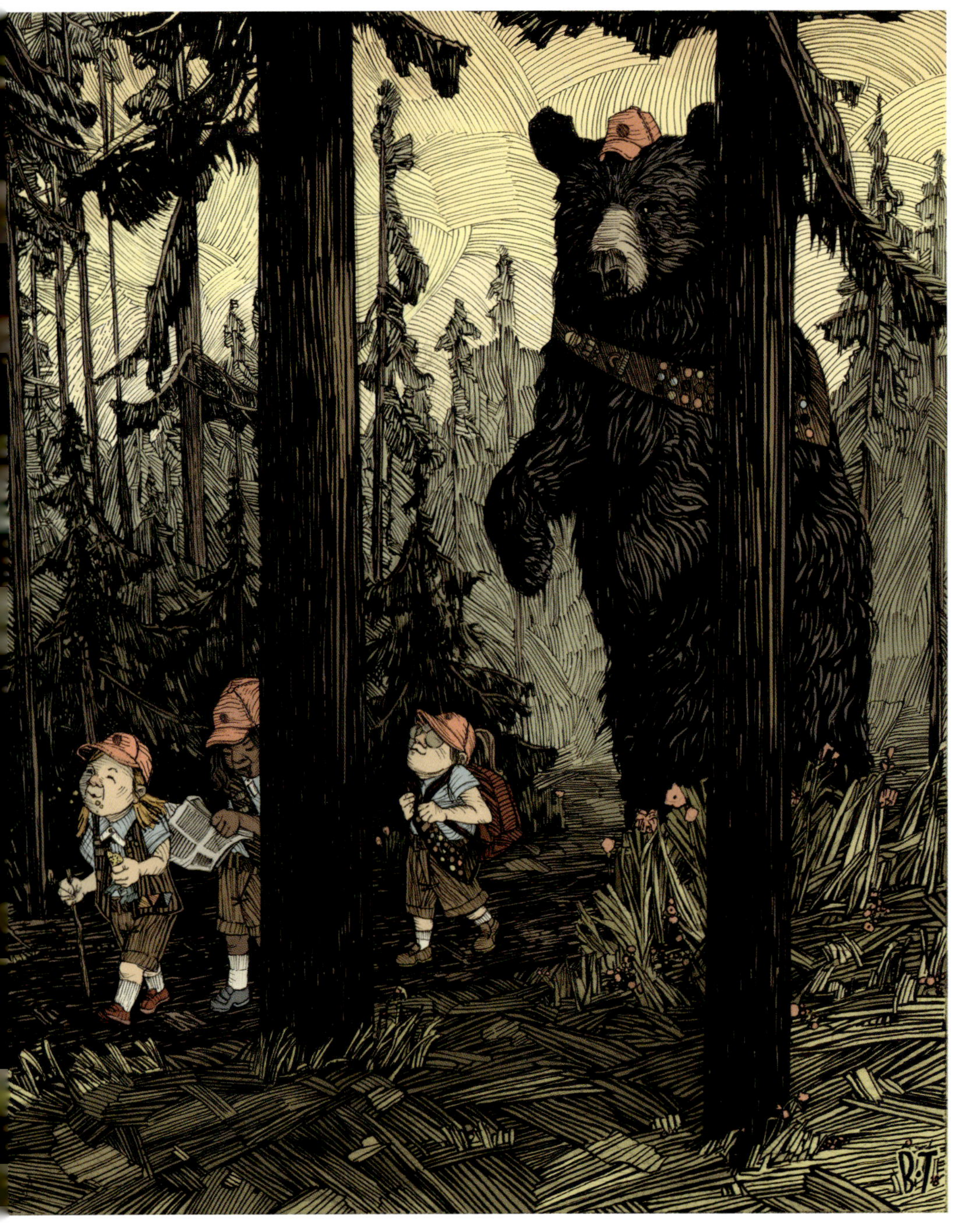

Brenna Thummler *www.brennathummler.com*

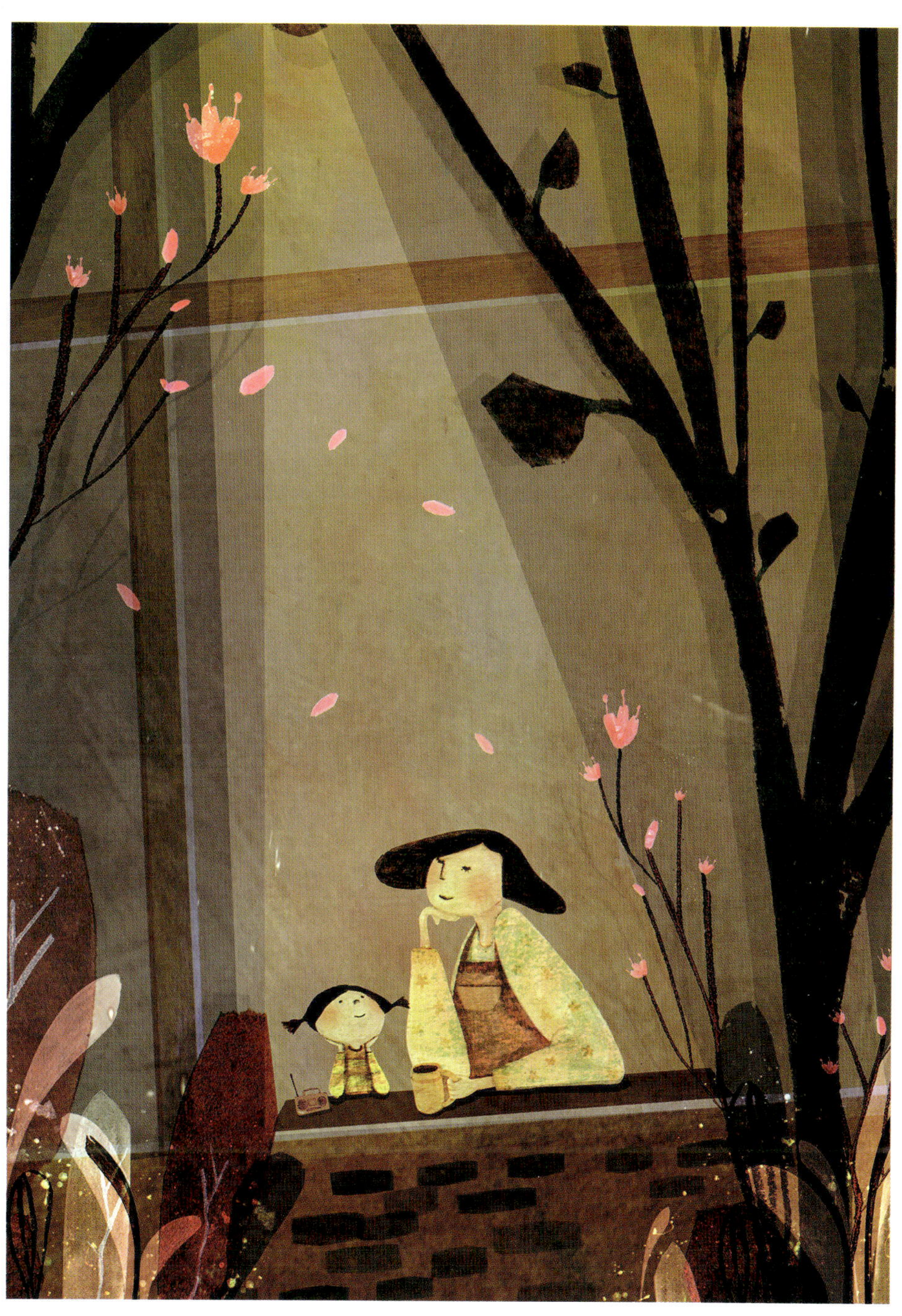

Jaime Kim *www.jaimekim.com*

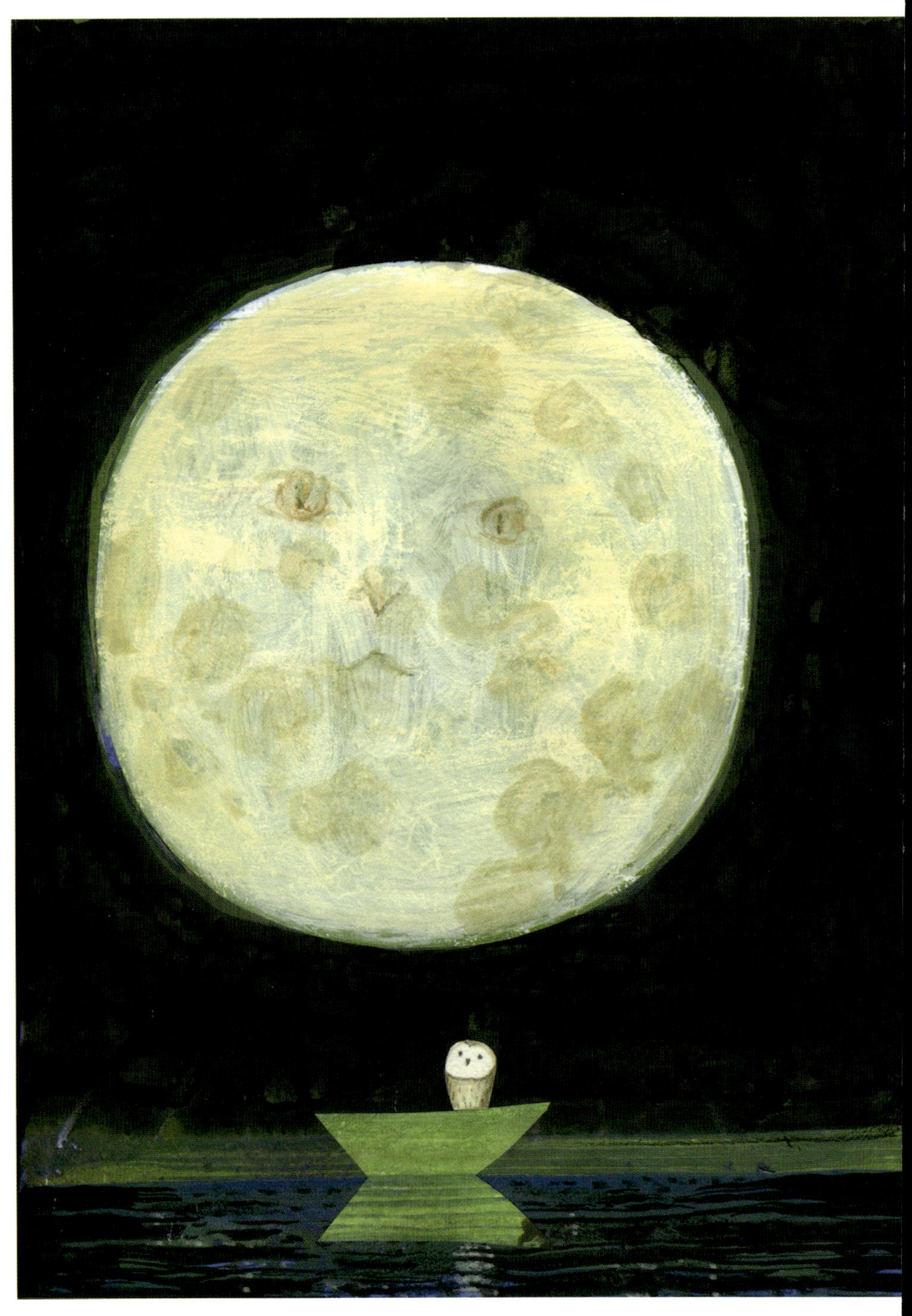

Rob Dunlavey *www.robd.com*

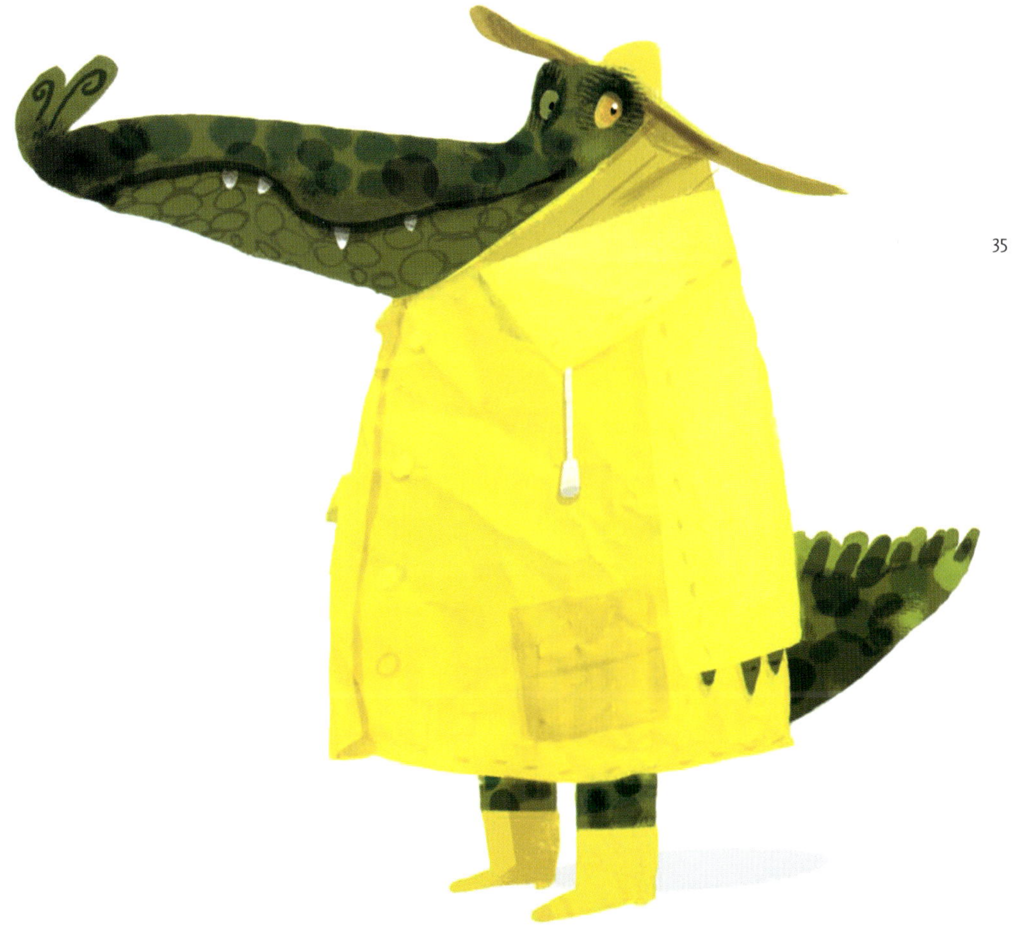

Daron Parton *www.watermarkltd.com/artists/daron-parton*

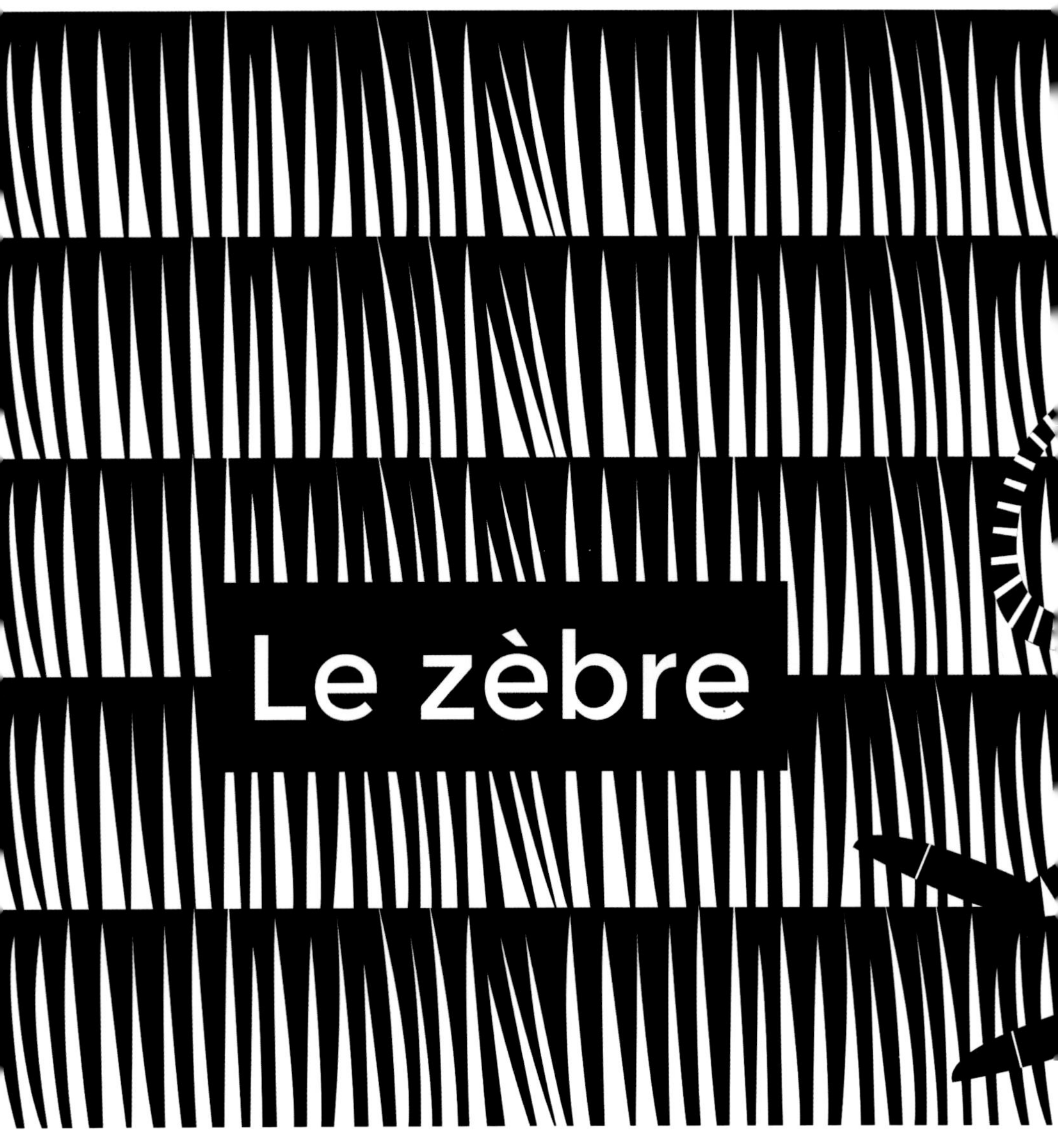

Julien Chung *www.julienchung.com*

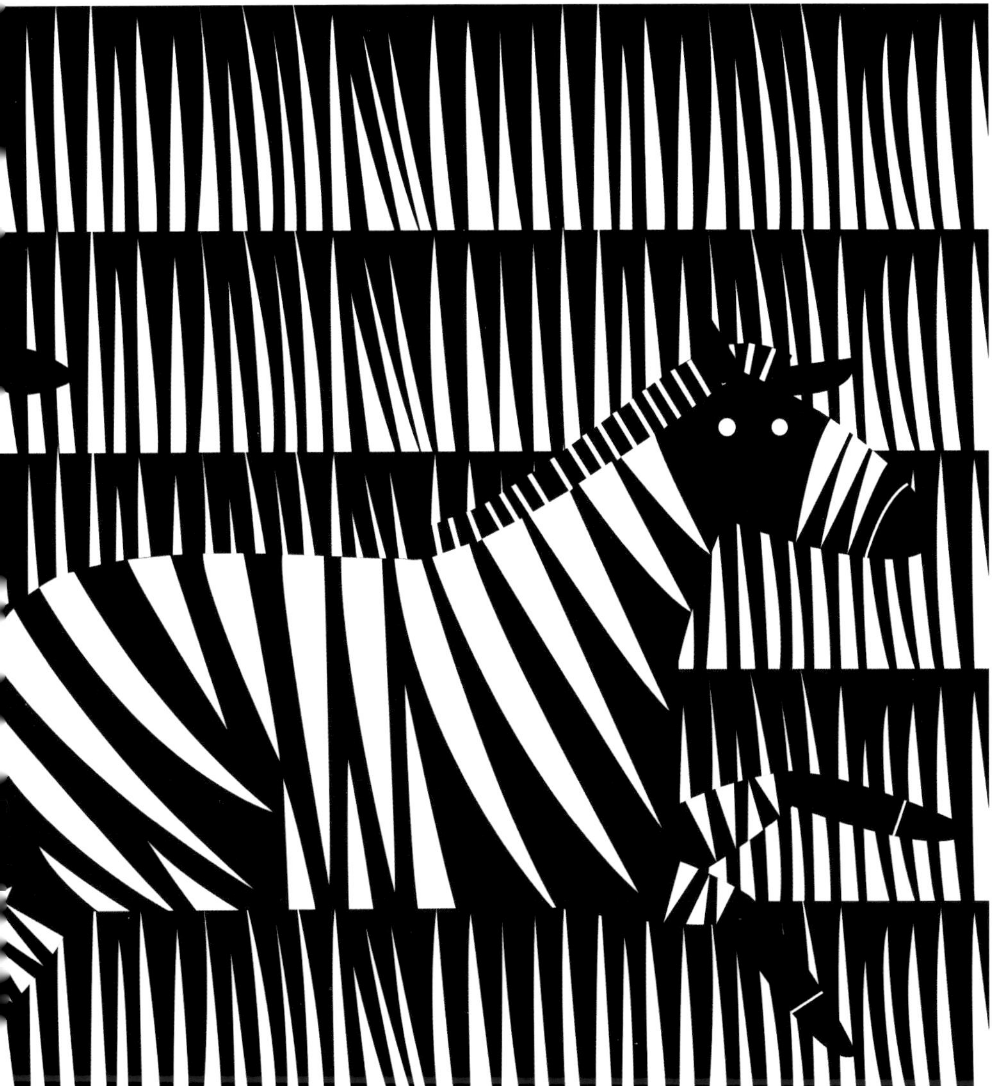

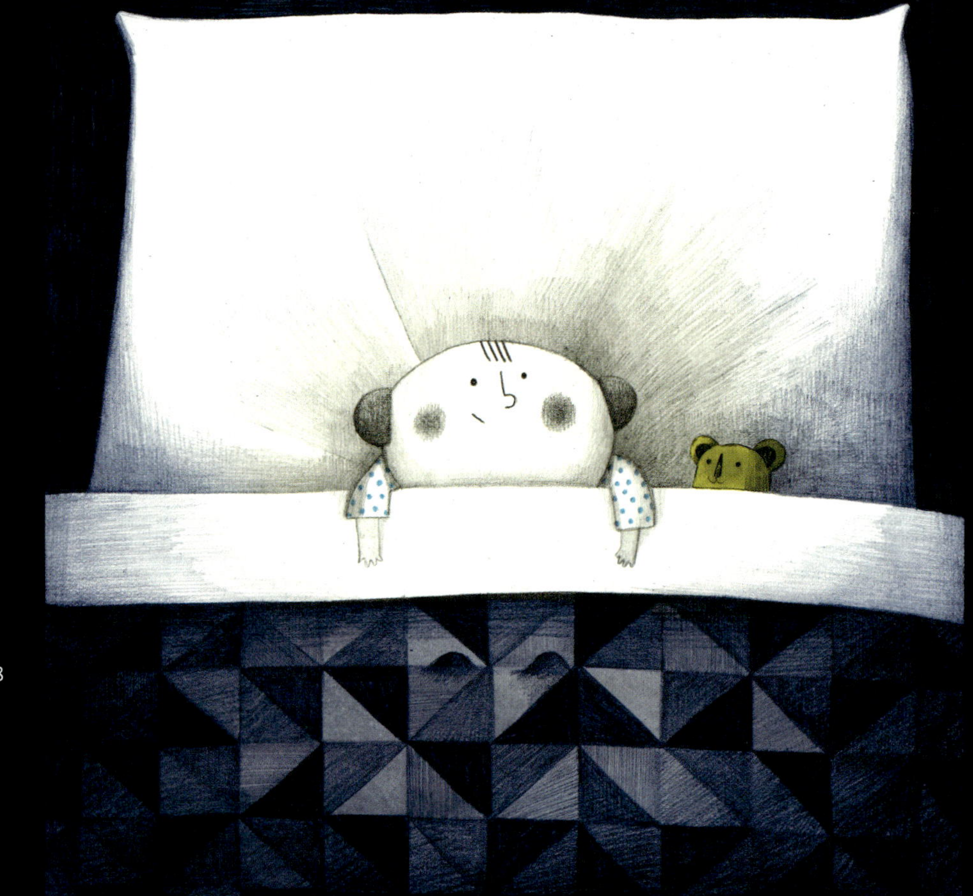

38

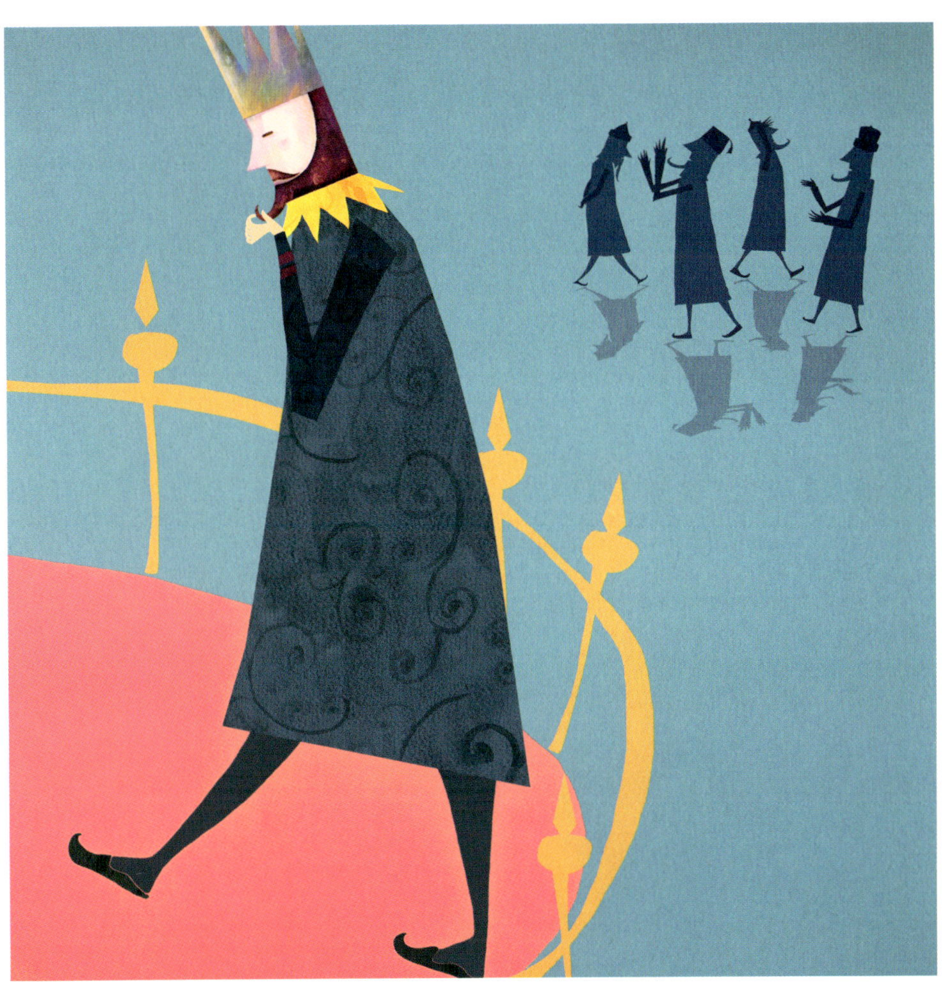

Melda Oncu Yildiz *www.meldaoncu.com*

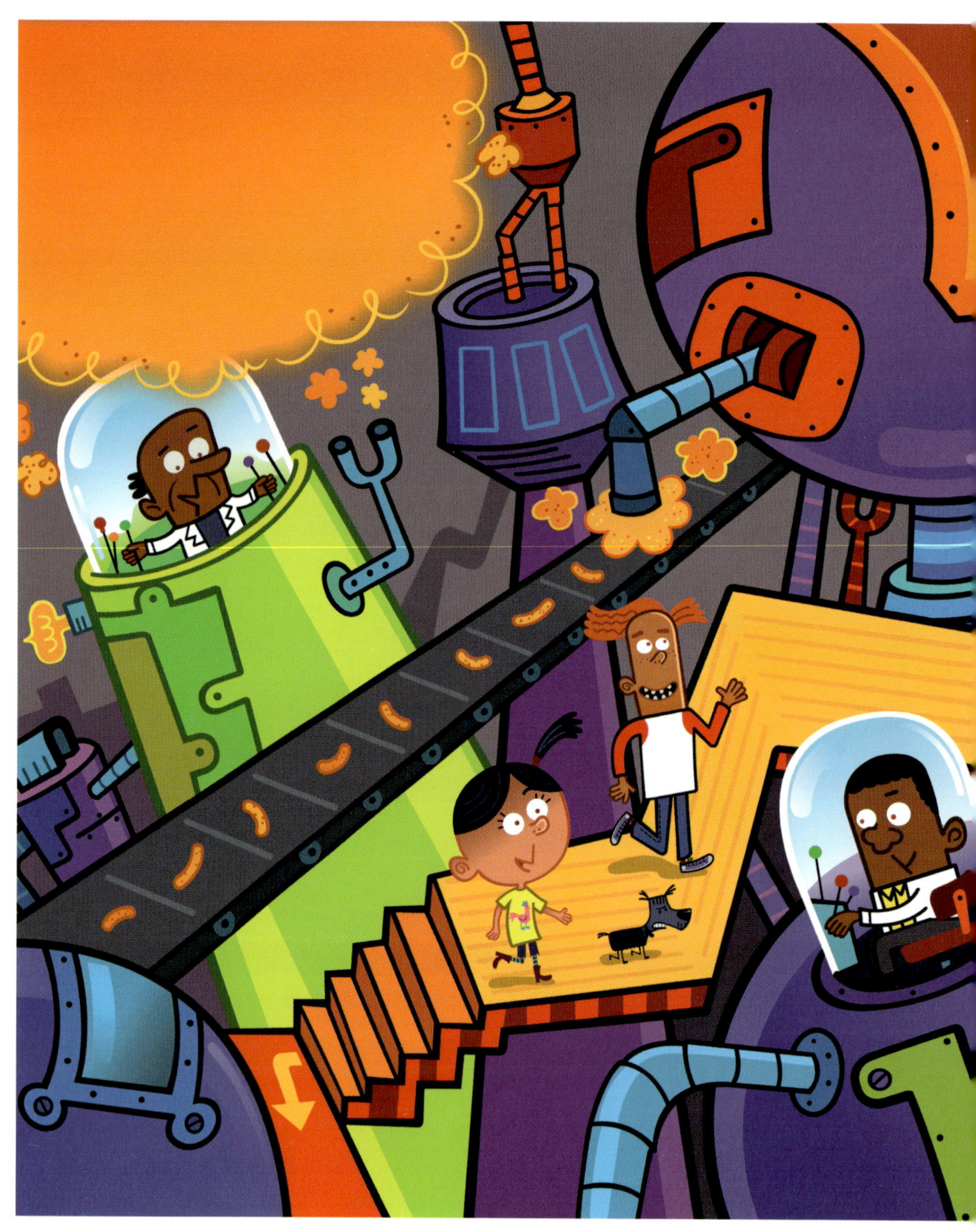

Jim Paillot *www.jimpaillot.com*

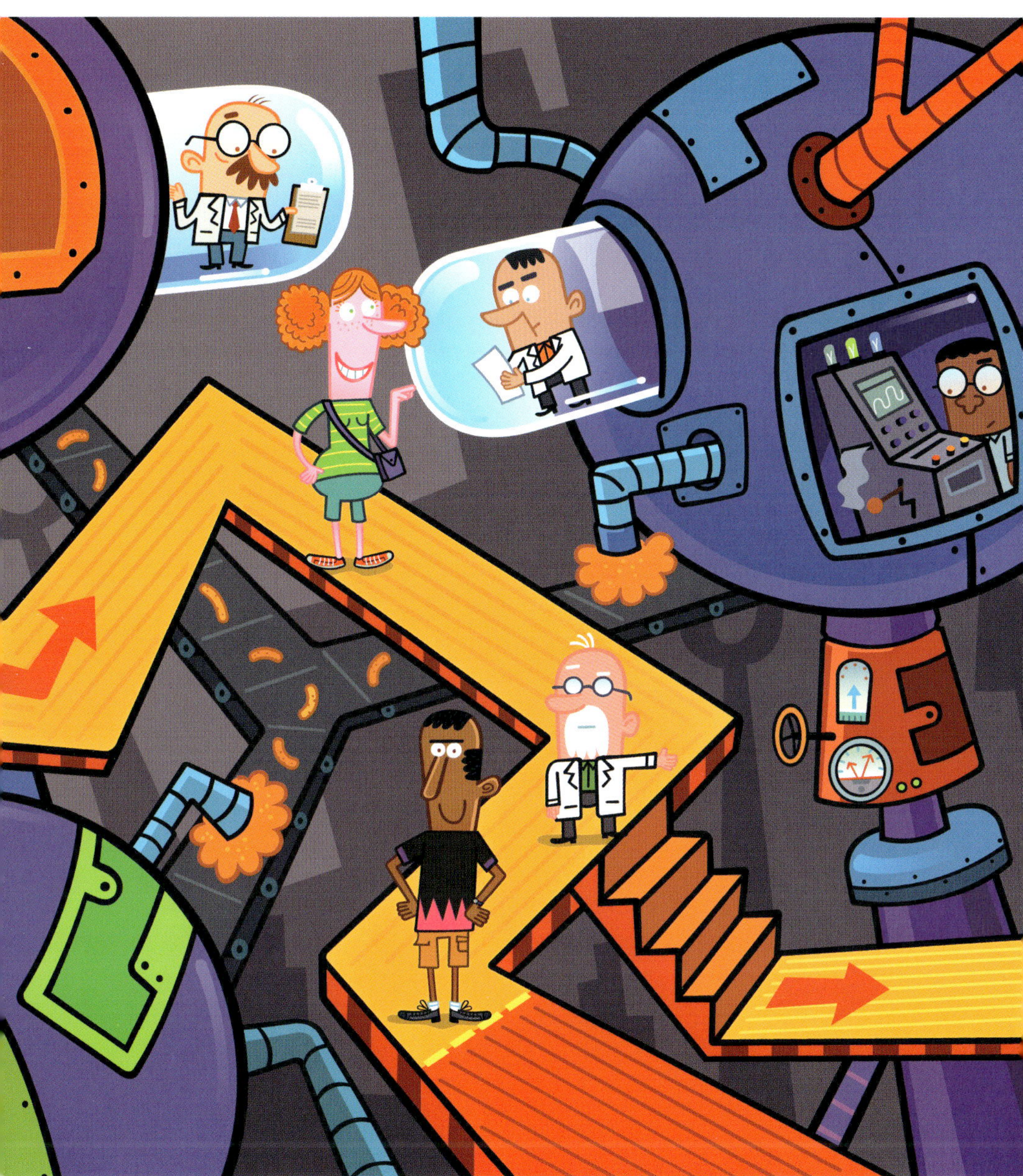

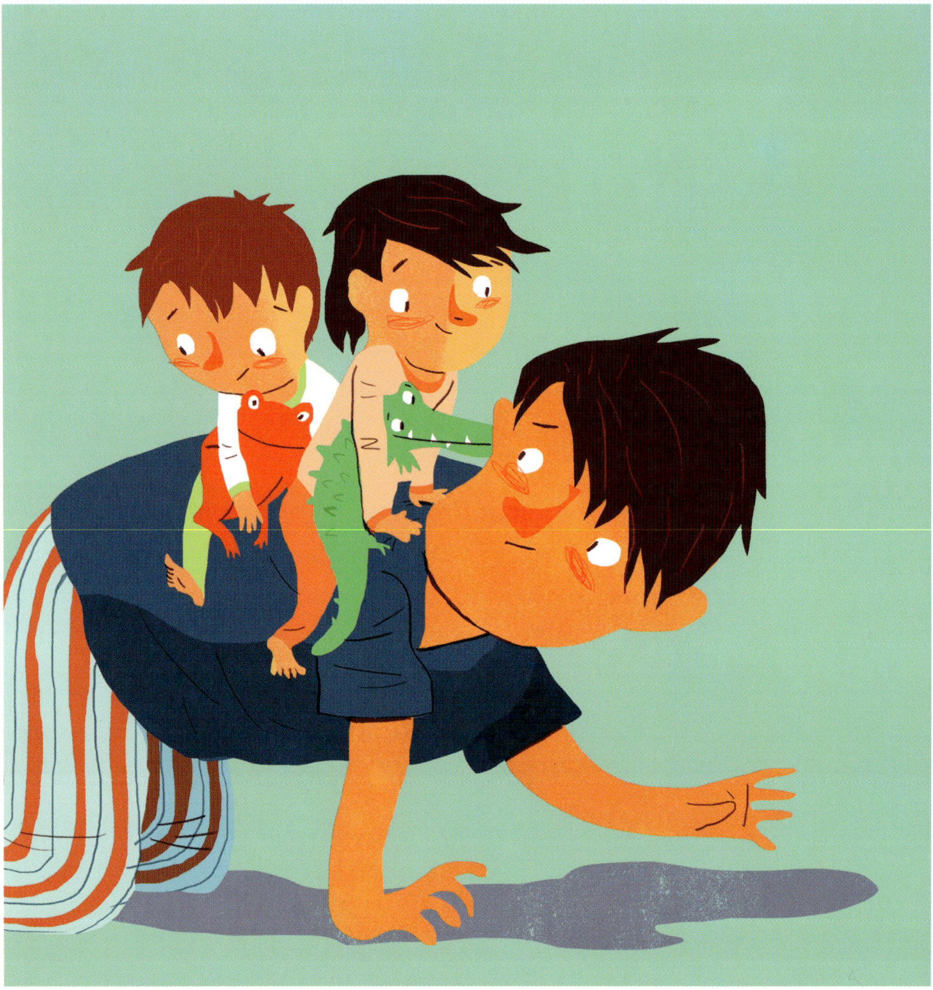

42

Tom Jellett *www.tomjellett.com*

43

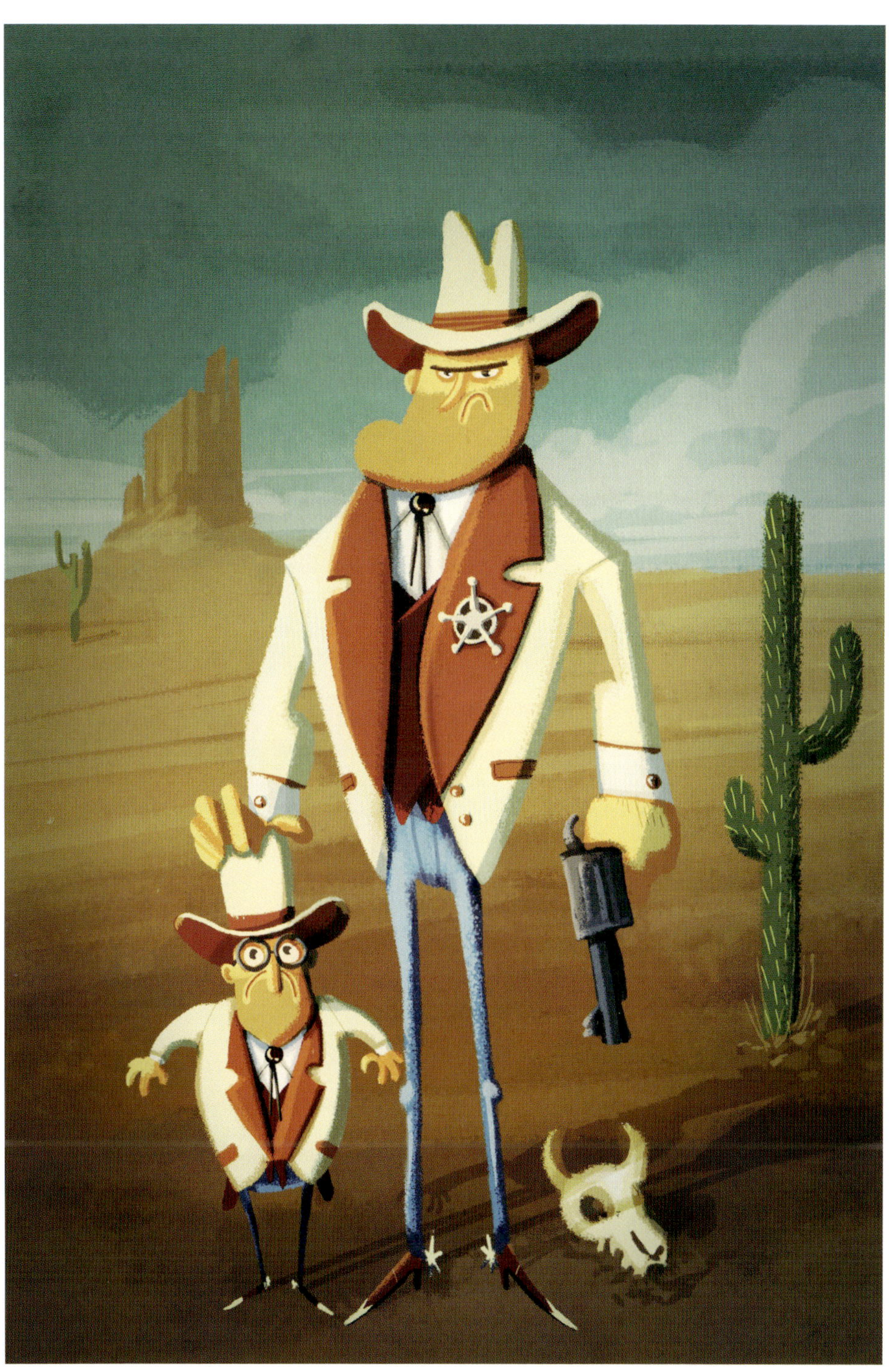

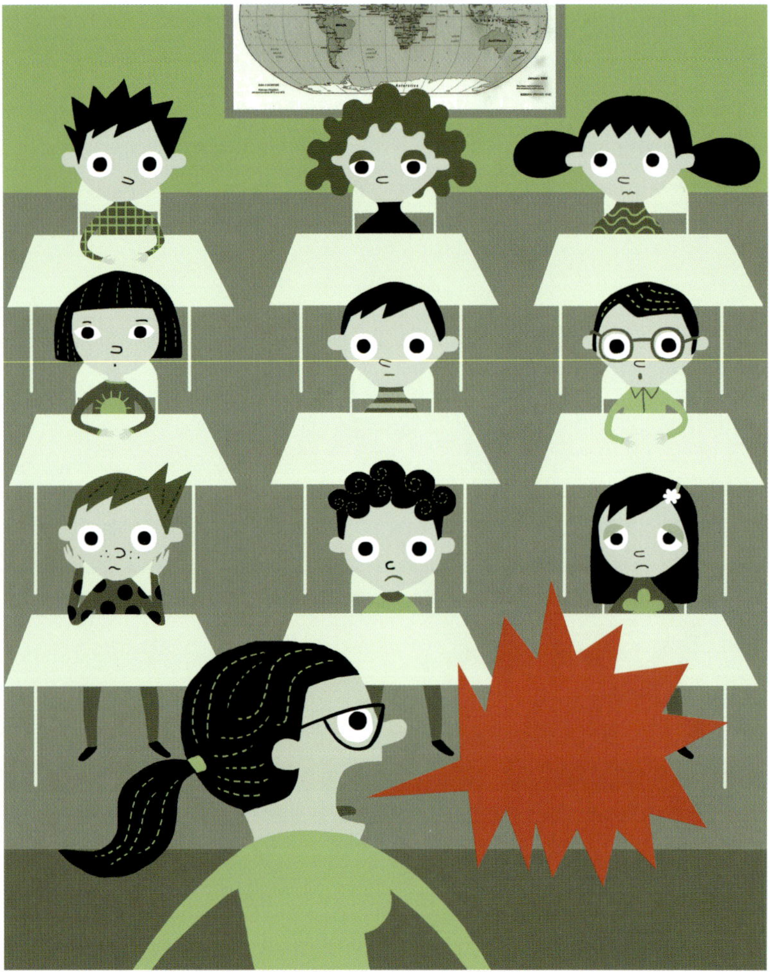

44

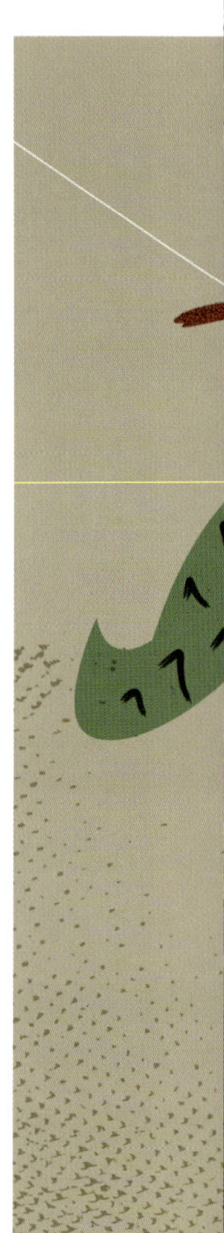

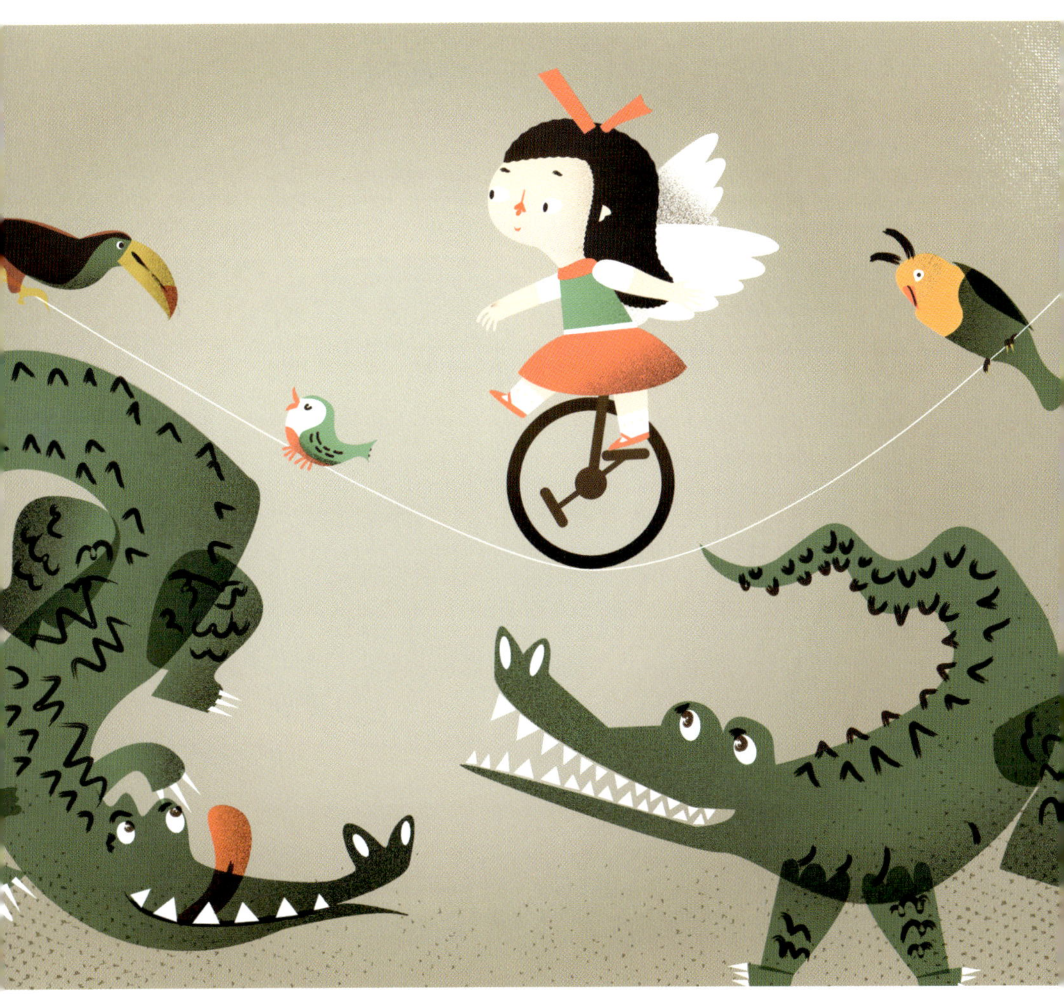

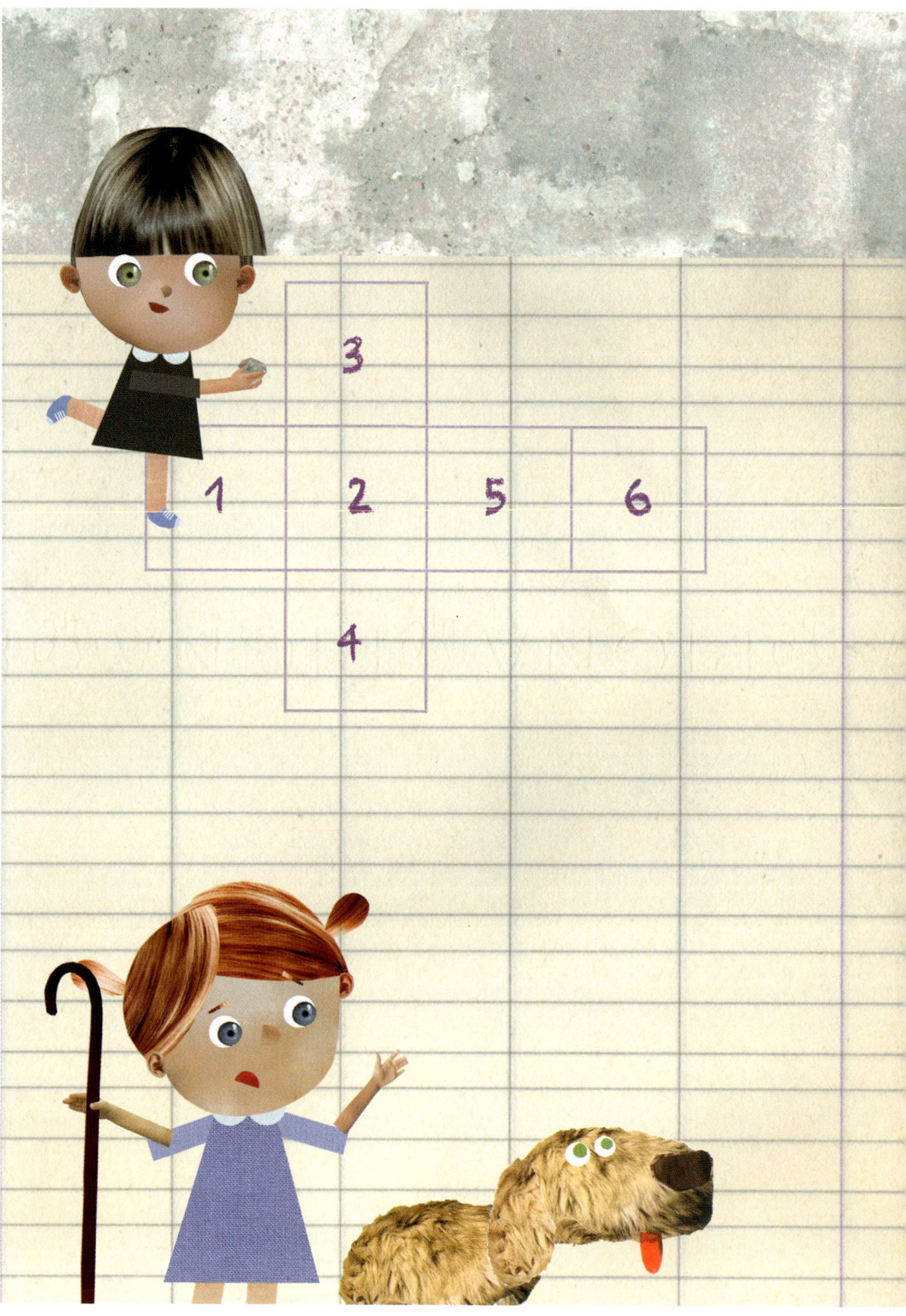

46

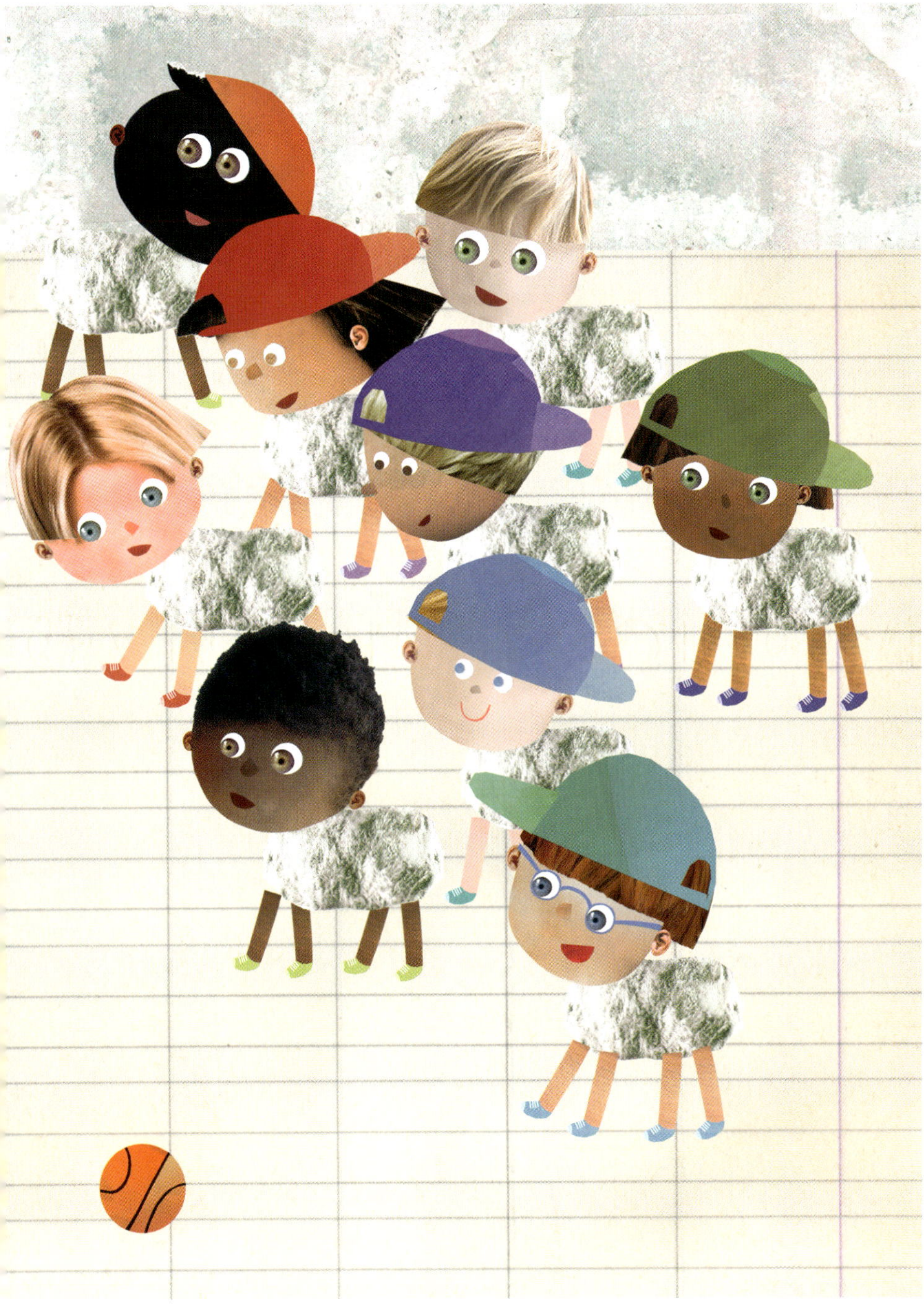

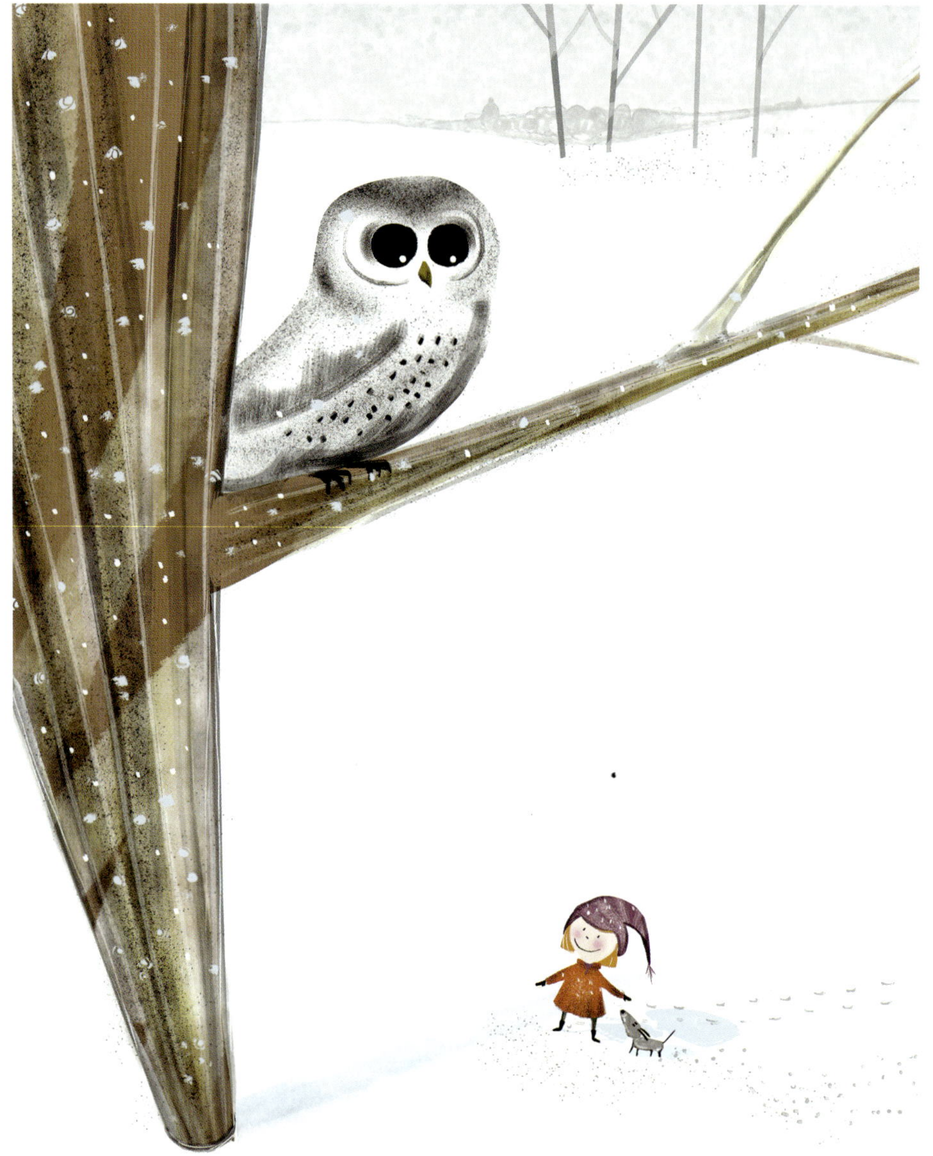

Dave Szalay *www.szalaydesign.com*

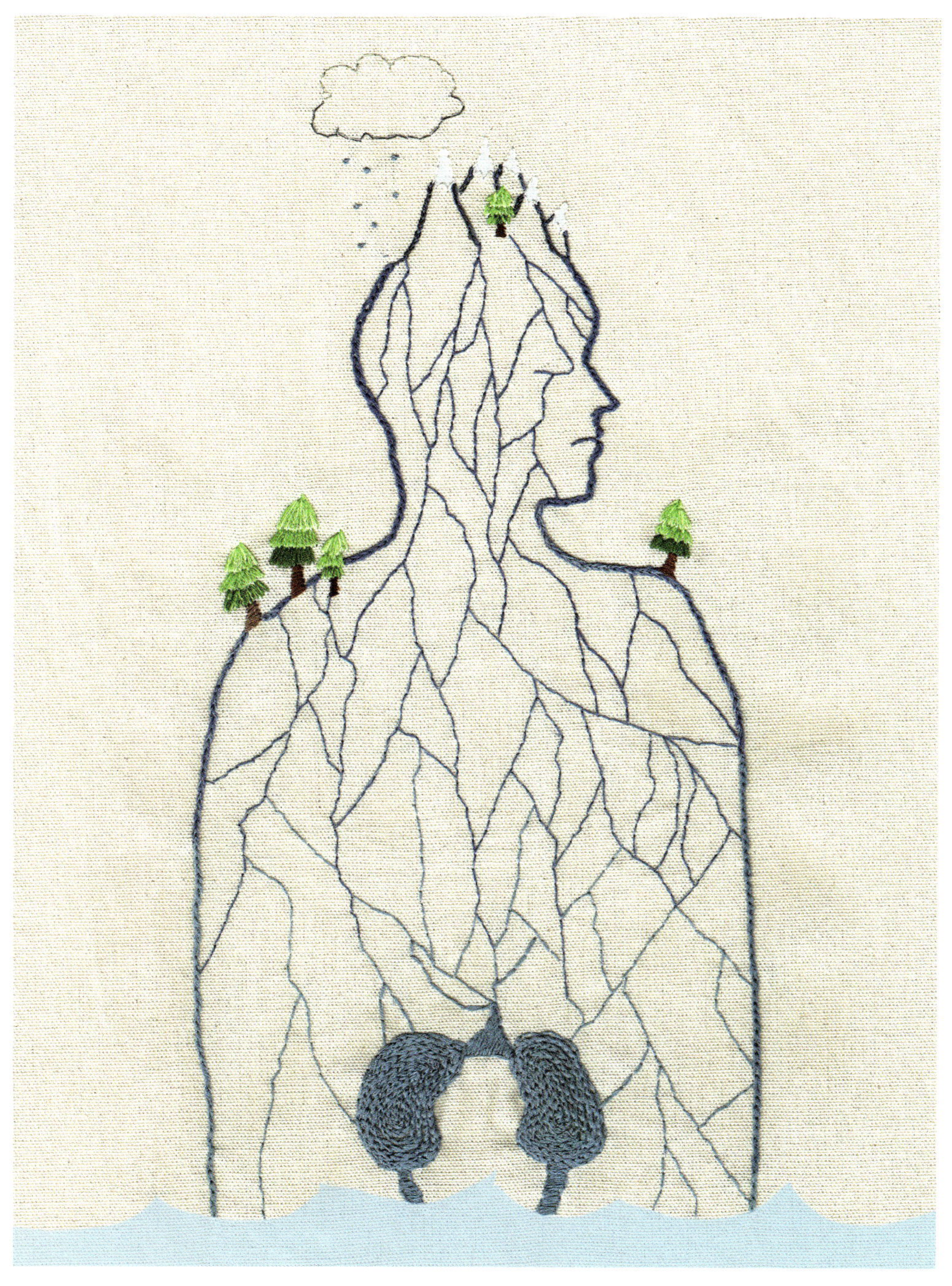

Katie Pak *www.katiepak.com*

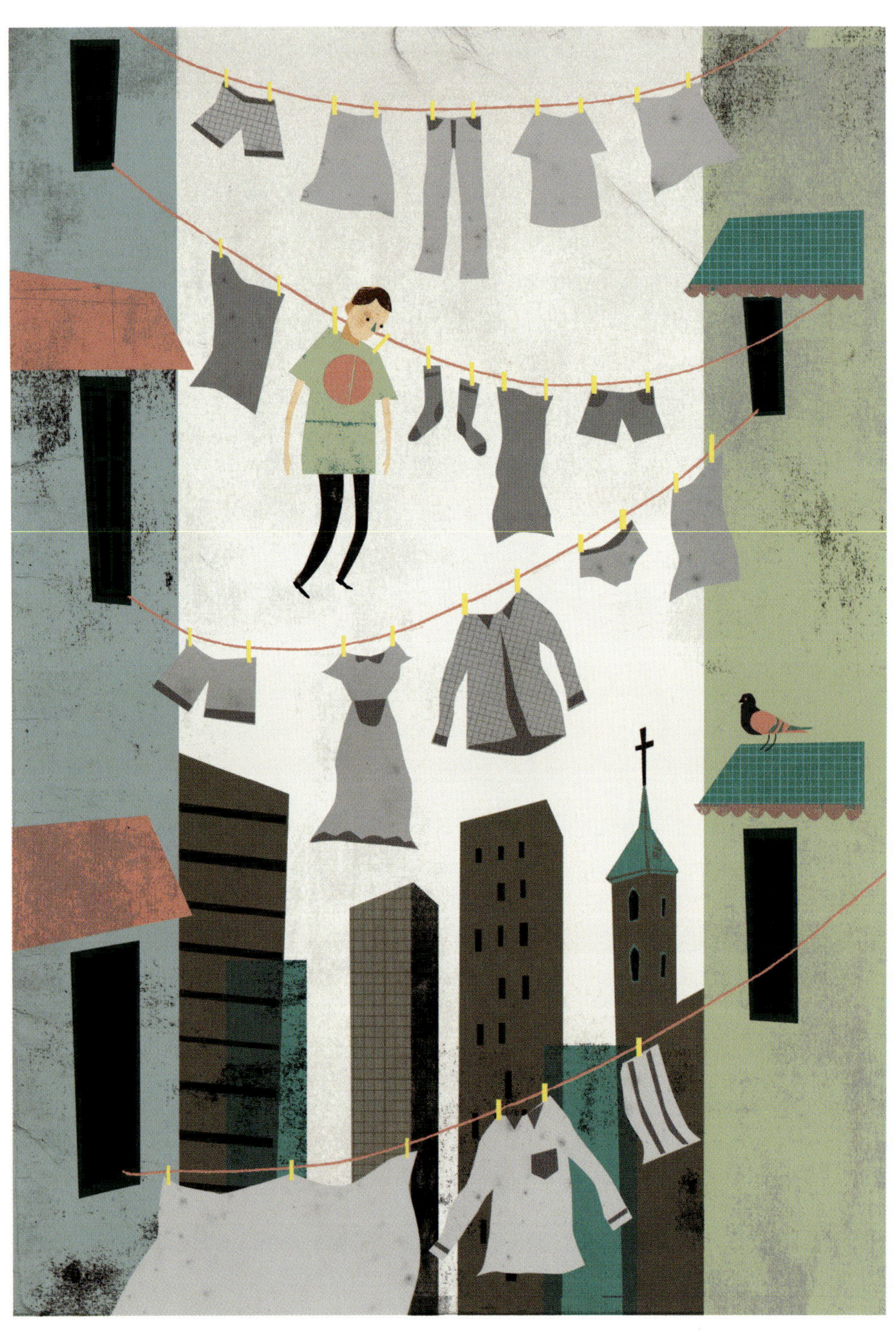

Gary Venn *www.garyvennillustration.com*

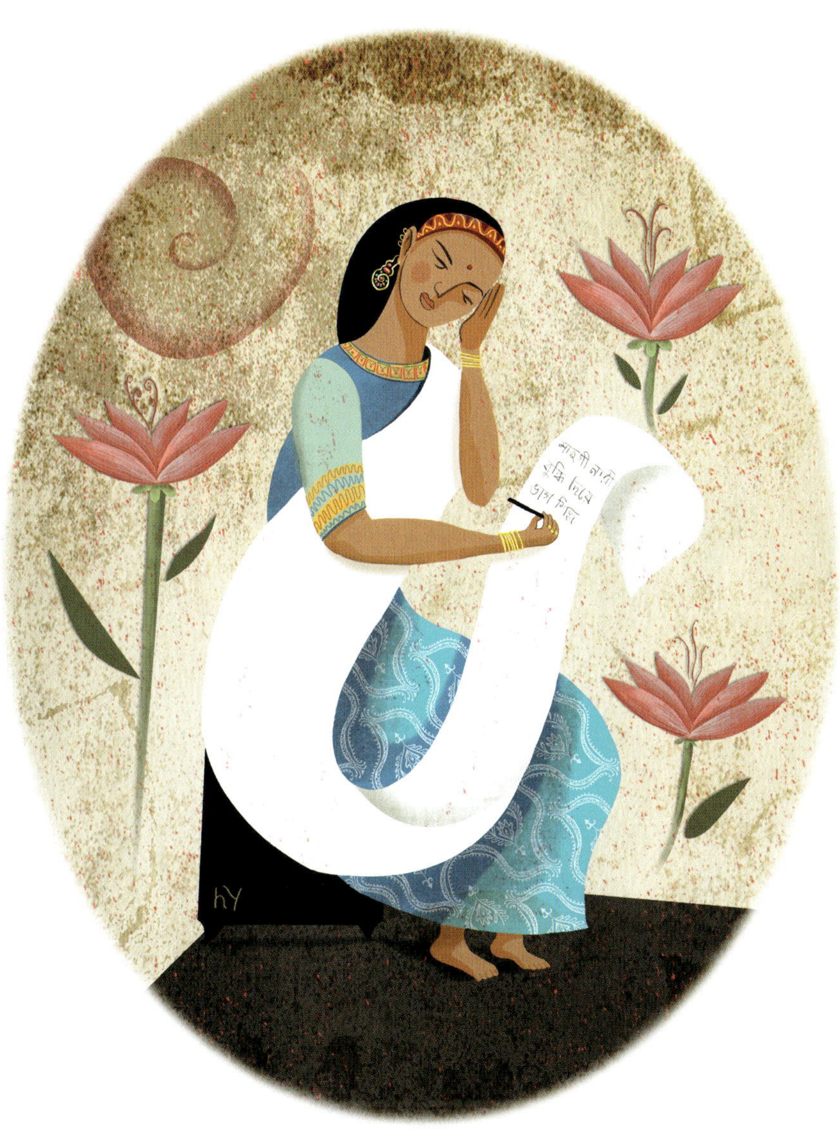

Heidi Younger *www.heidiyounger.com*

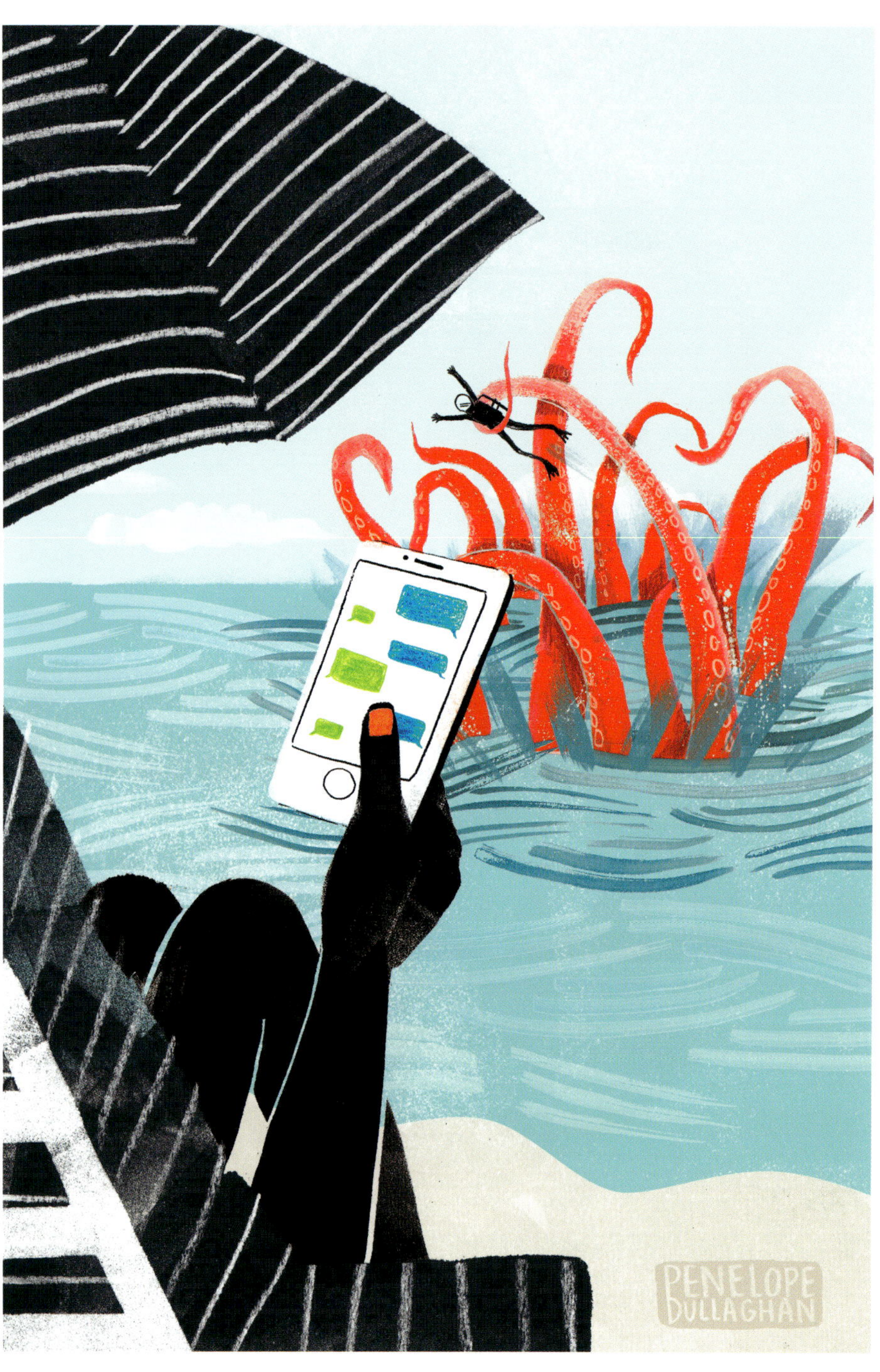

Penelope Dullaghan *www.scotthull.com*

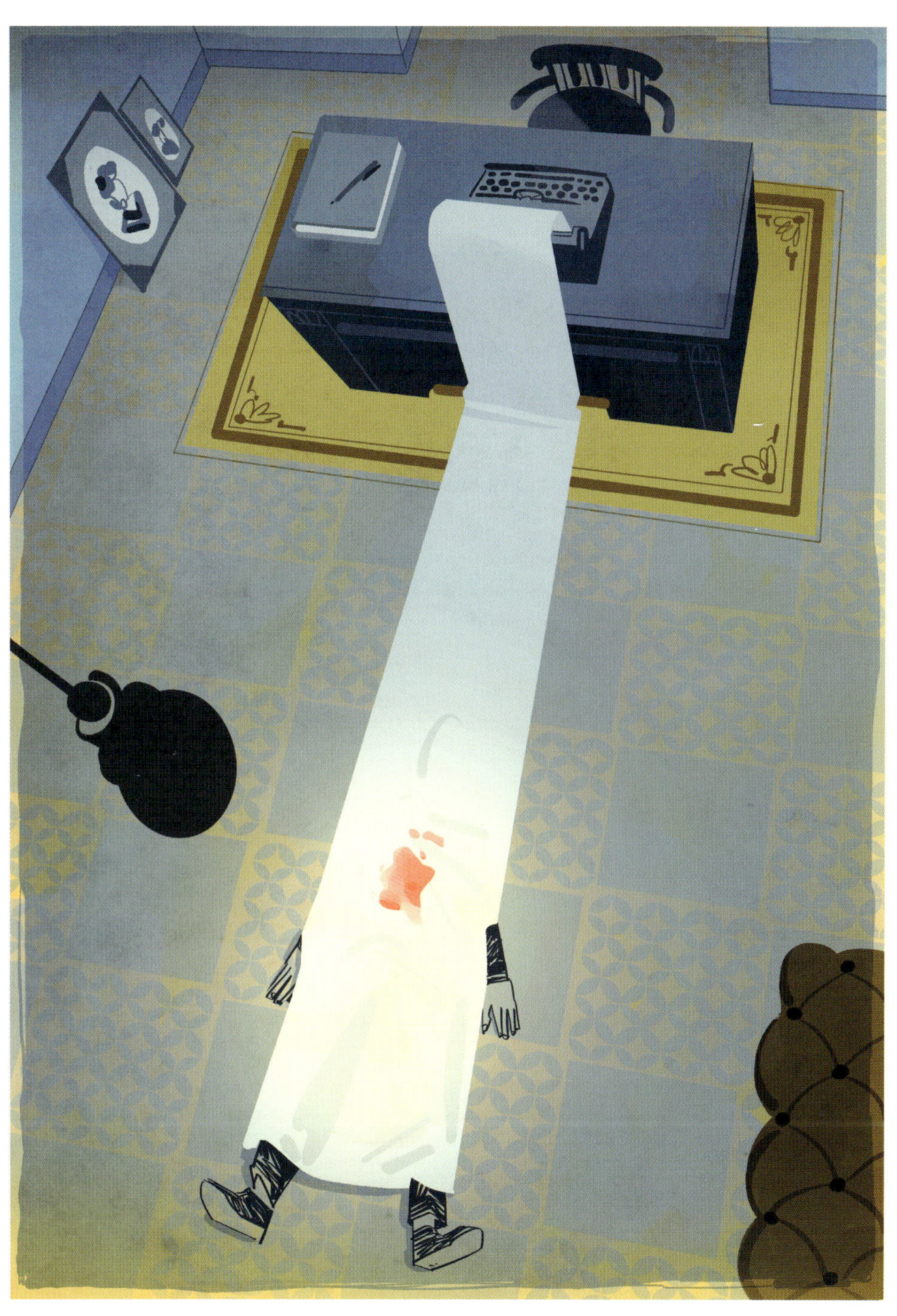

Giovanni Da Re *www.giovannidare.com*

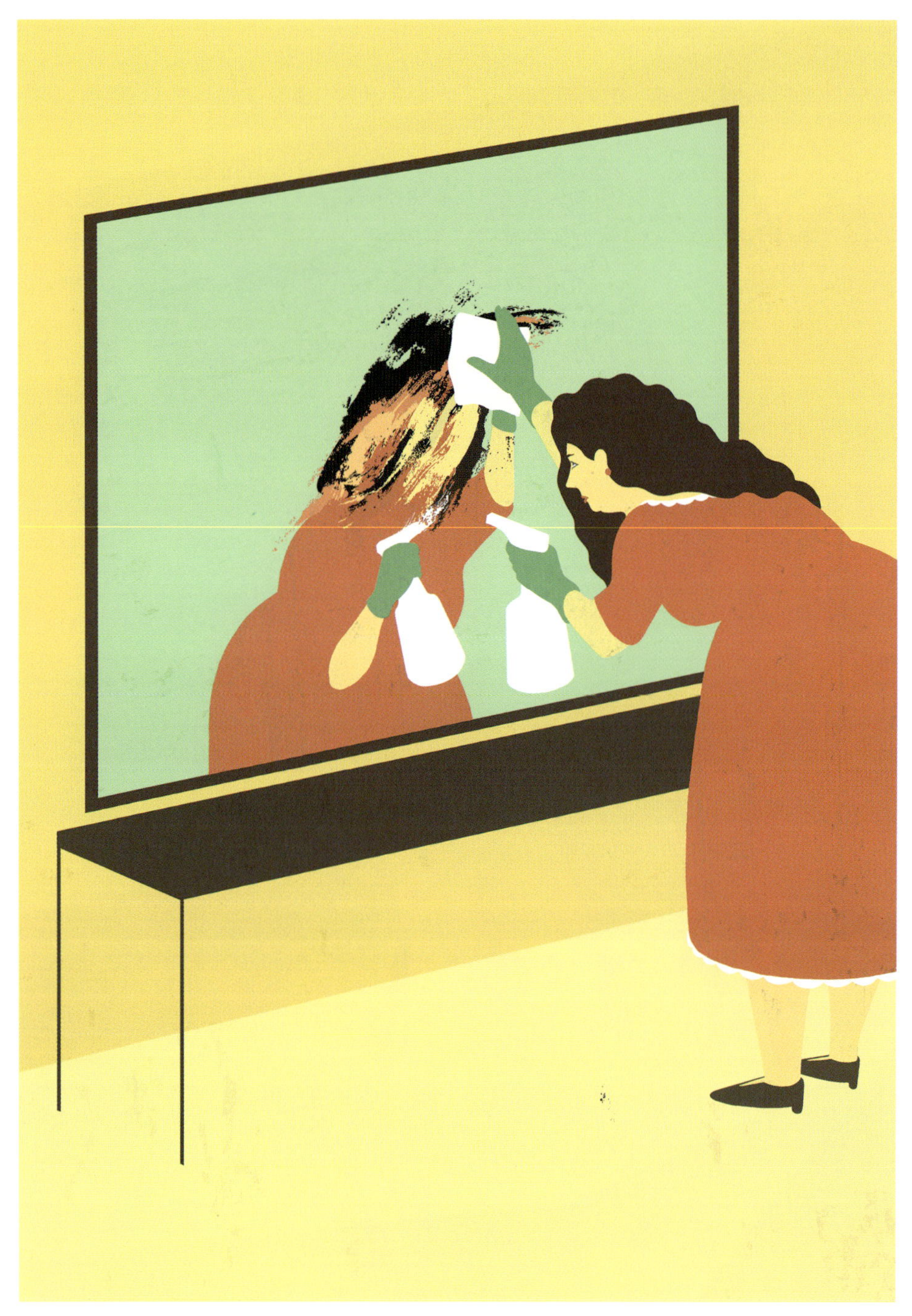

Stephan Schmitz *www.stephan-schmitz.ch*

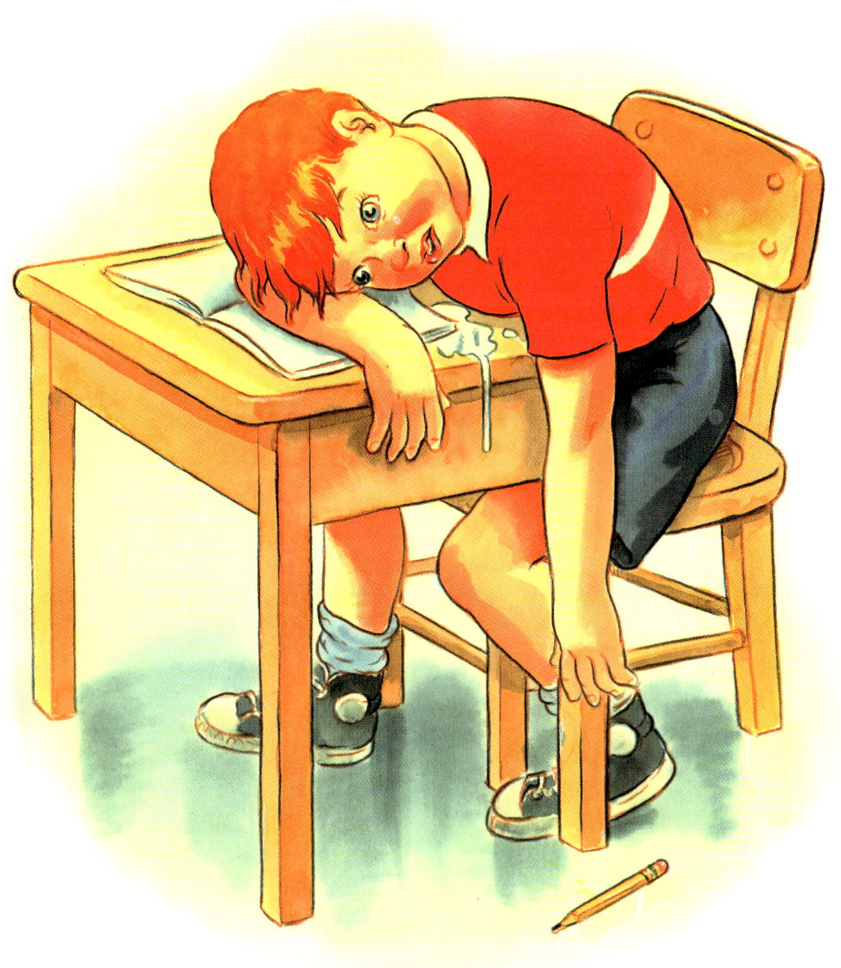

Ross MacDonald *www.ross-macdonald.com*

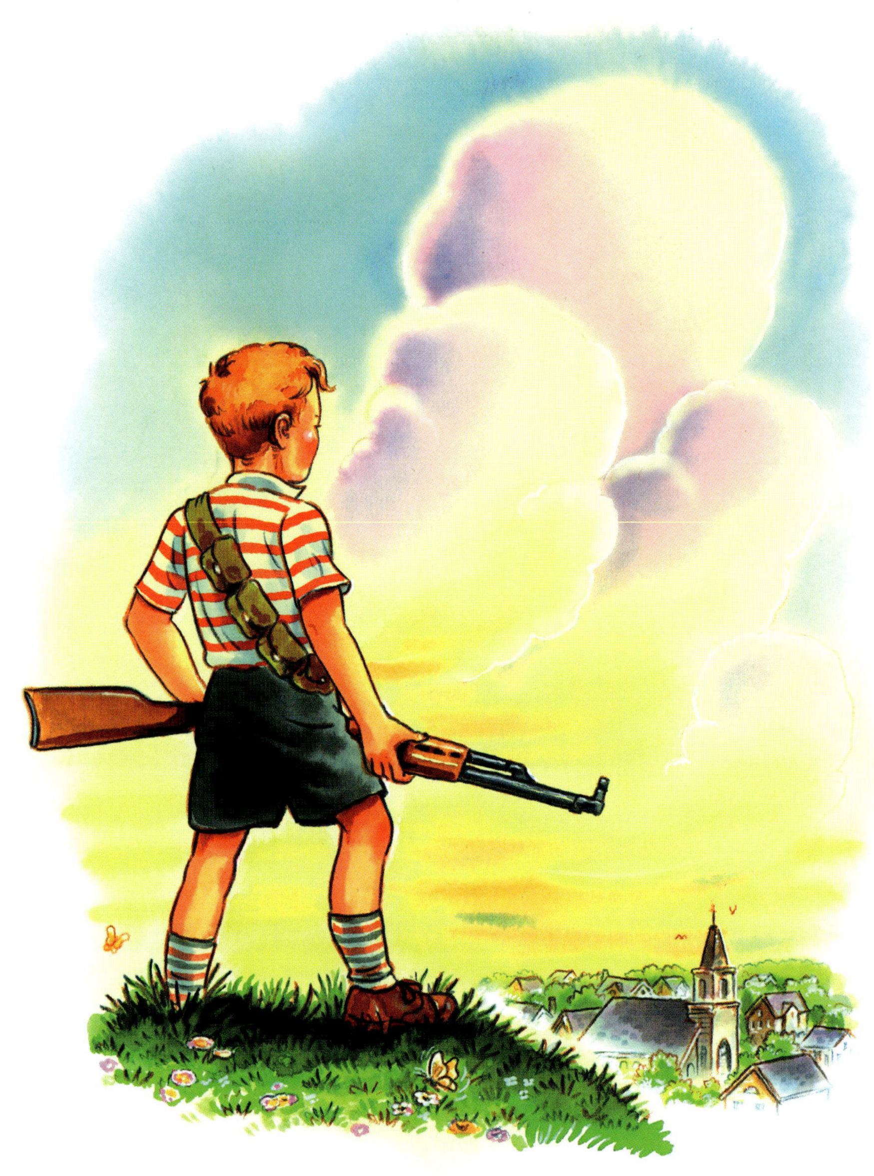

Ross MacDonald *www.ross-macdonald.com*

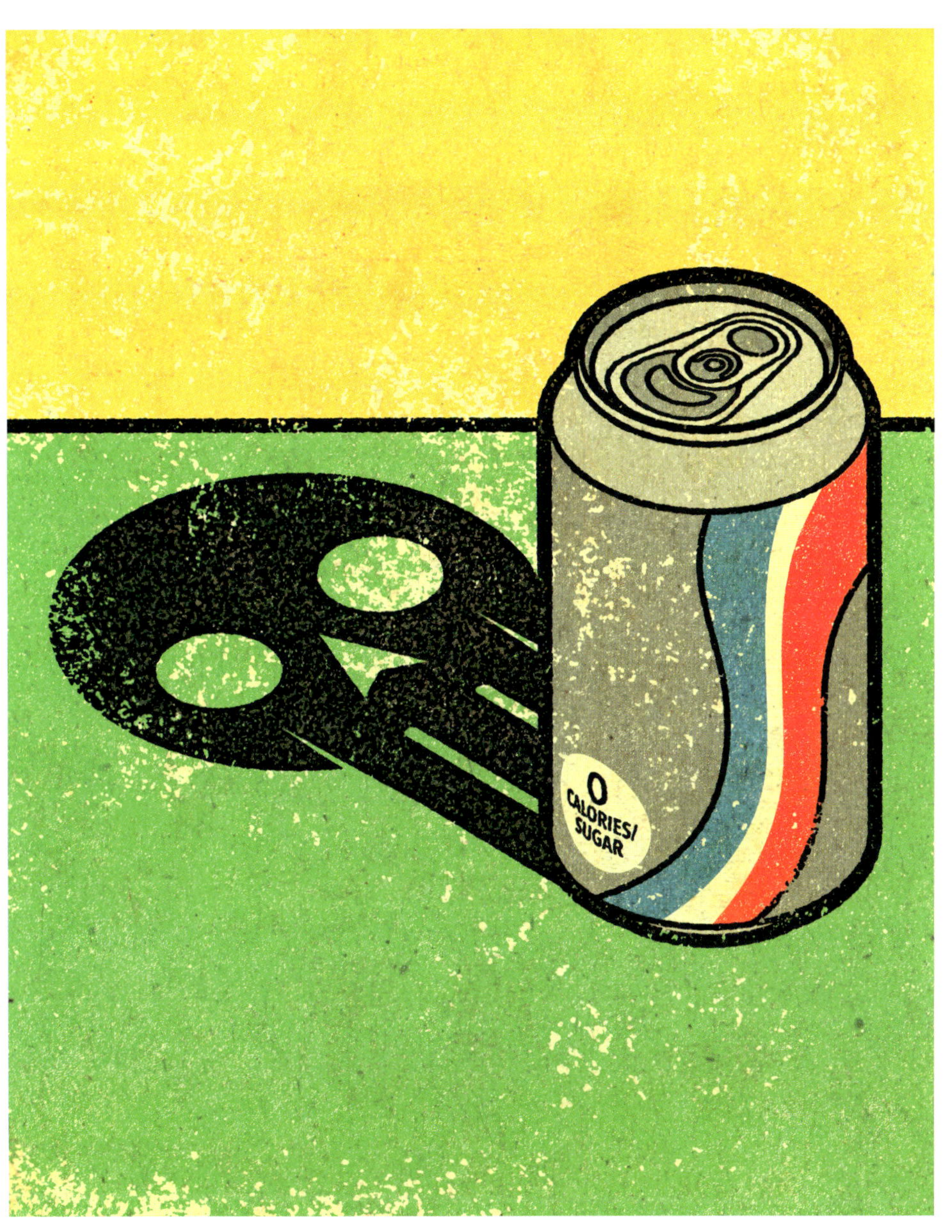

Alexei Vella *www.salzmanart.com*

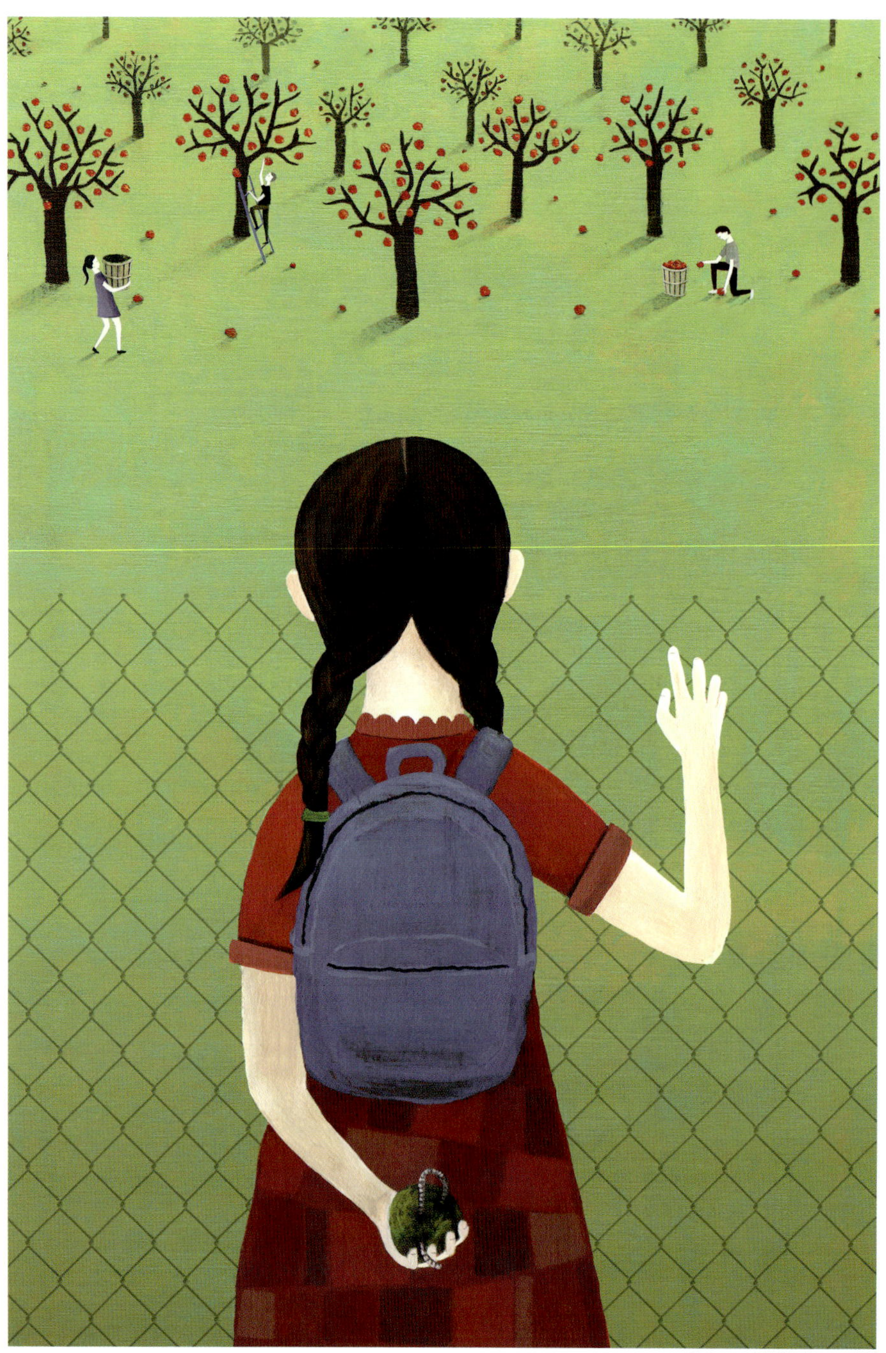

Laura Weiszer *www.lauraweiszer.com*

58

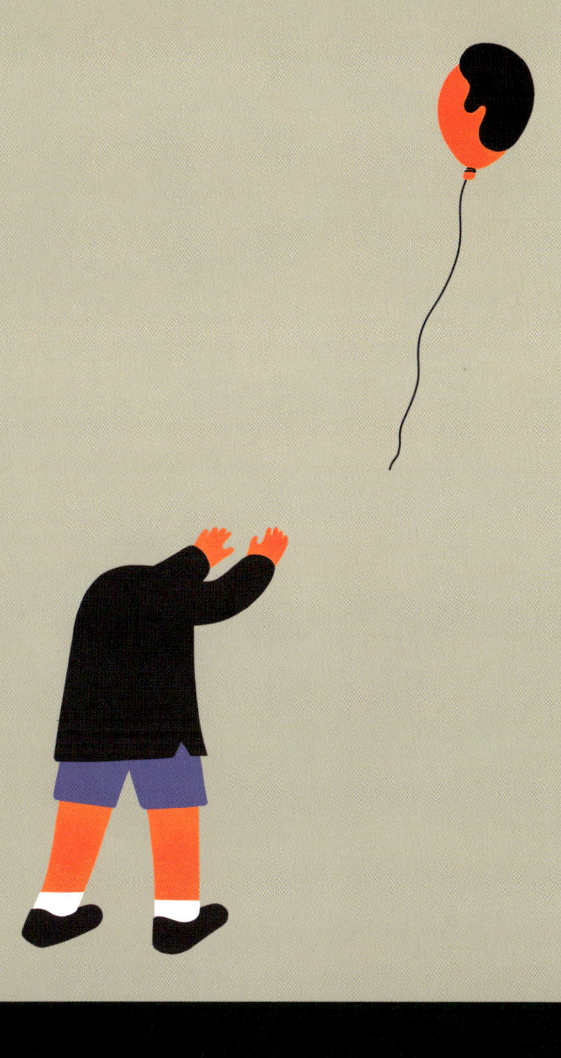

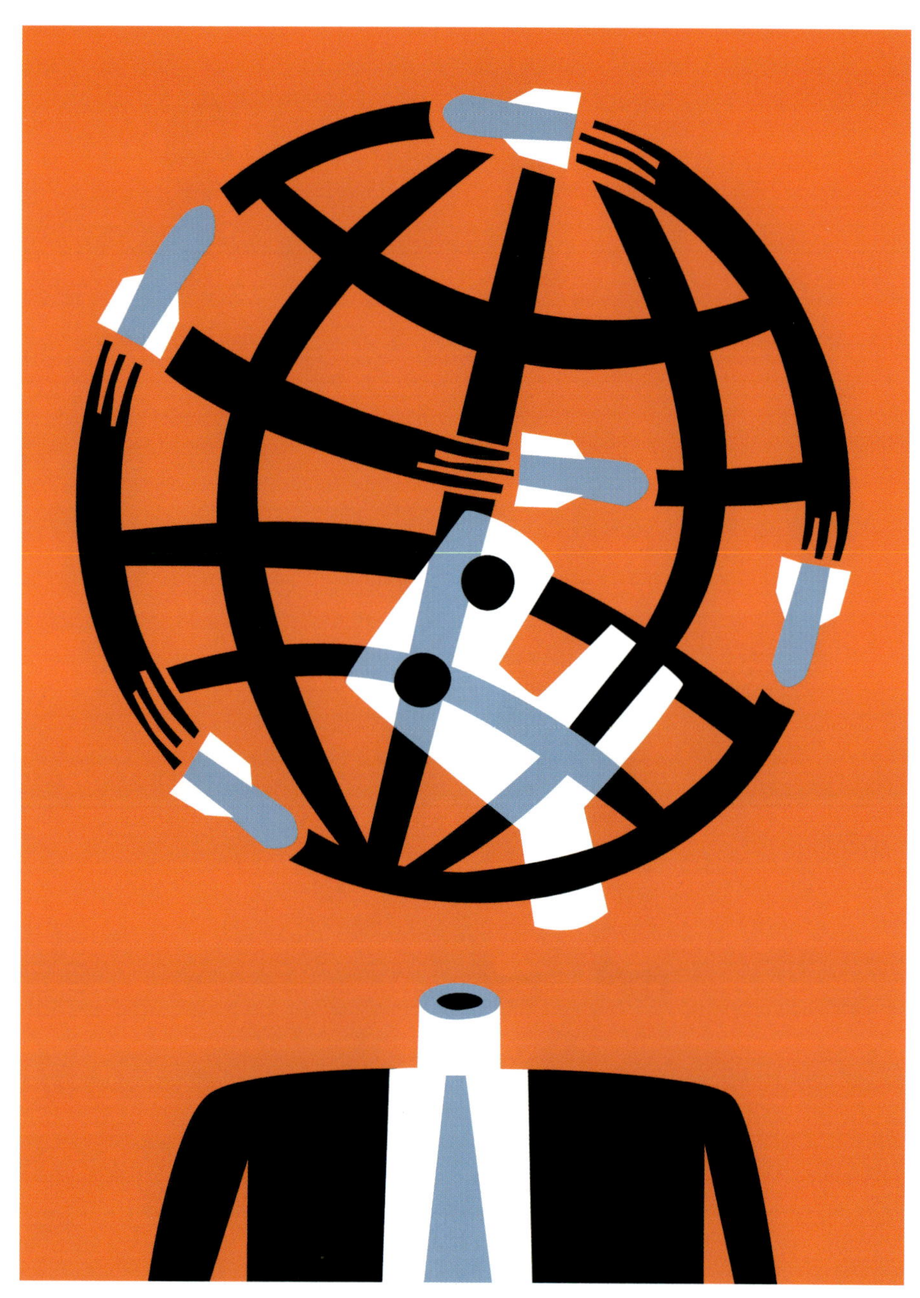

Lasse Skarbövik *www.lasseskarbovik.com*

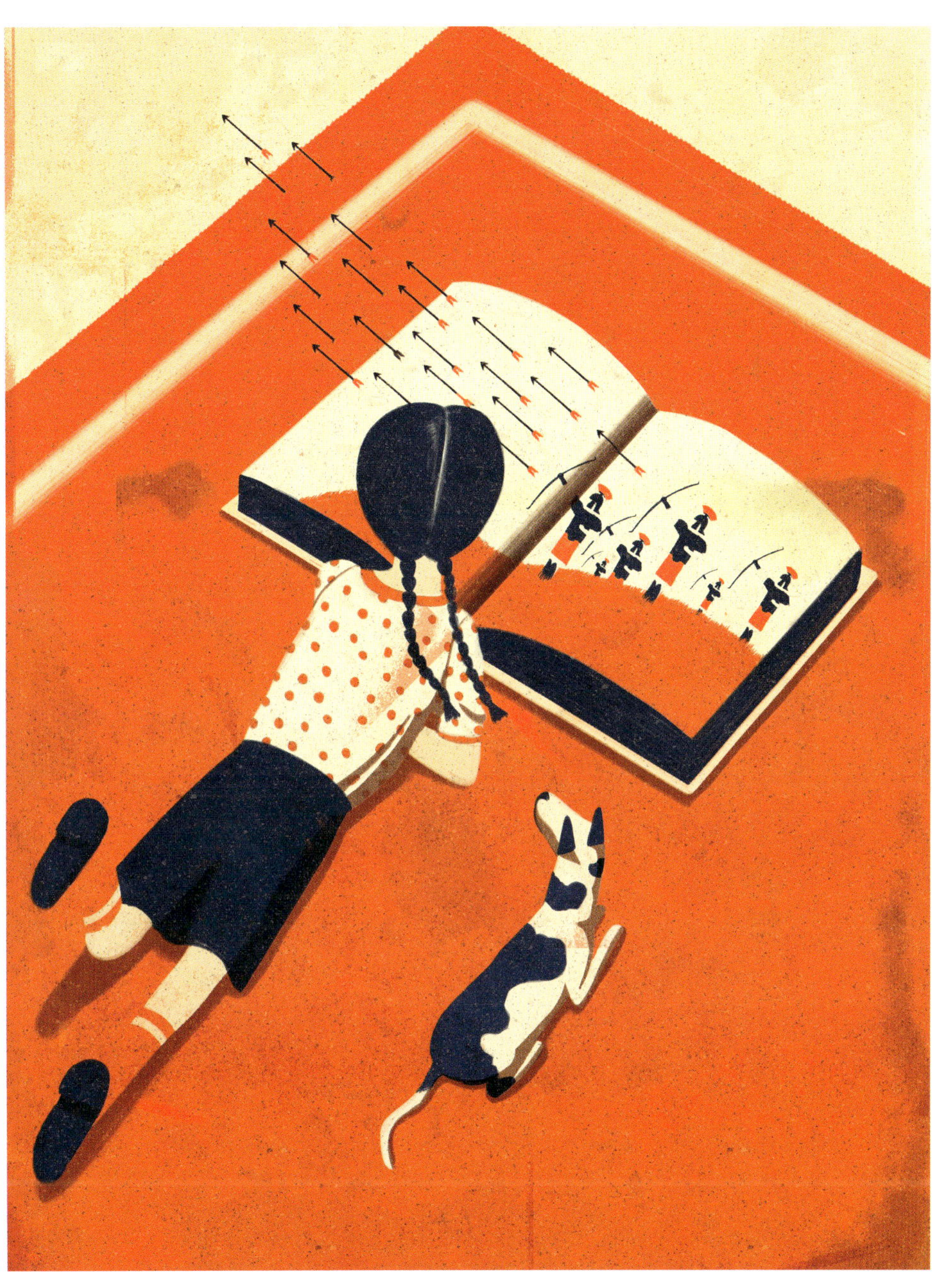

Emiliano Ponzi *www.emilianoponzi.com*

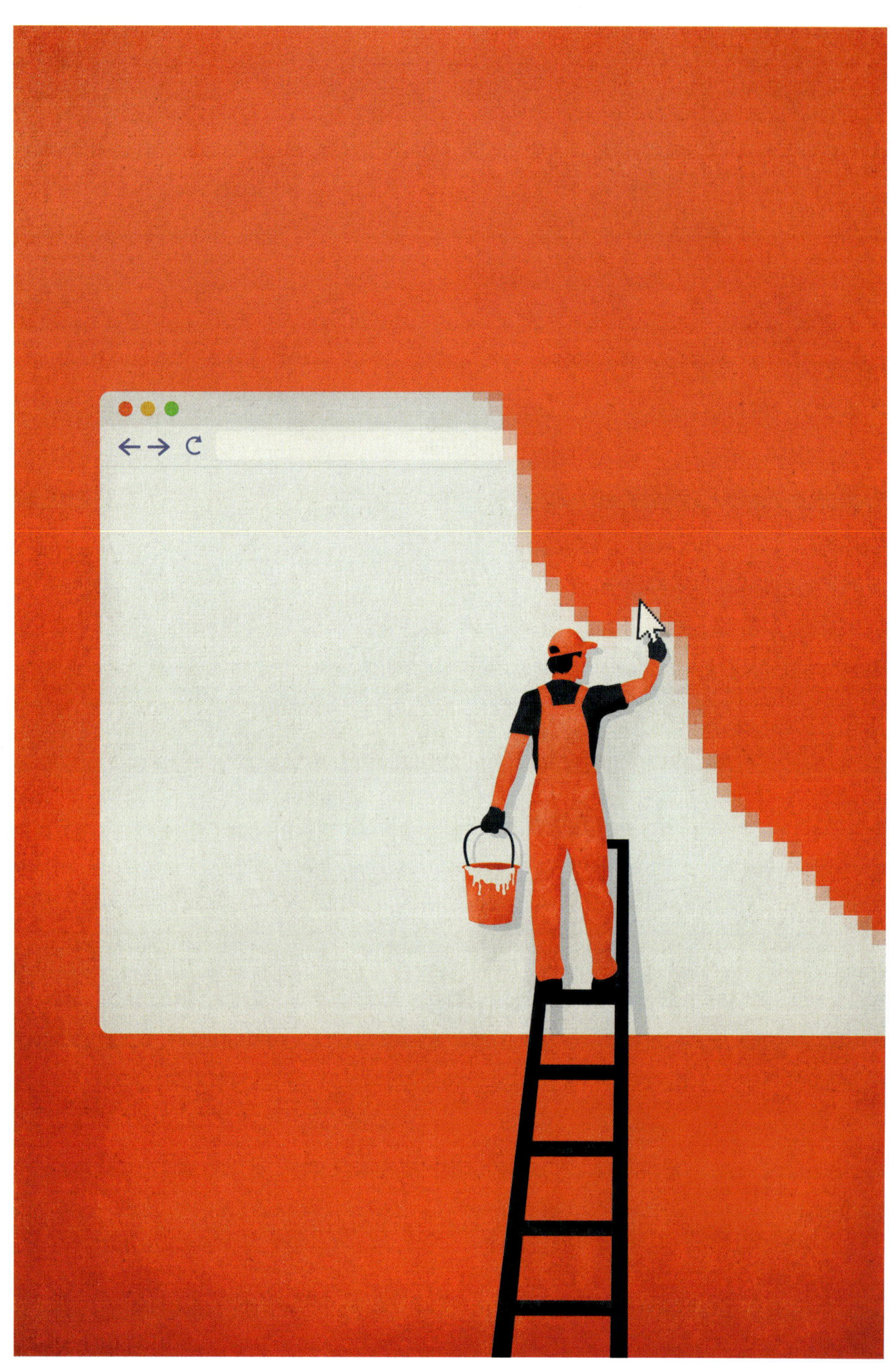

Benedetto Cristofani *www.salzmanart.com*

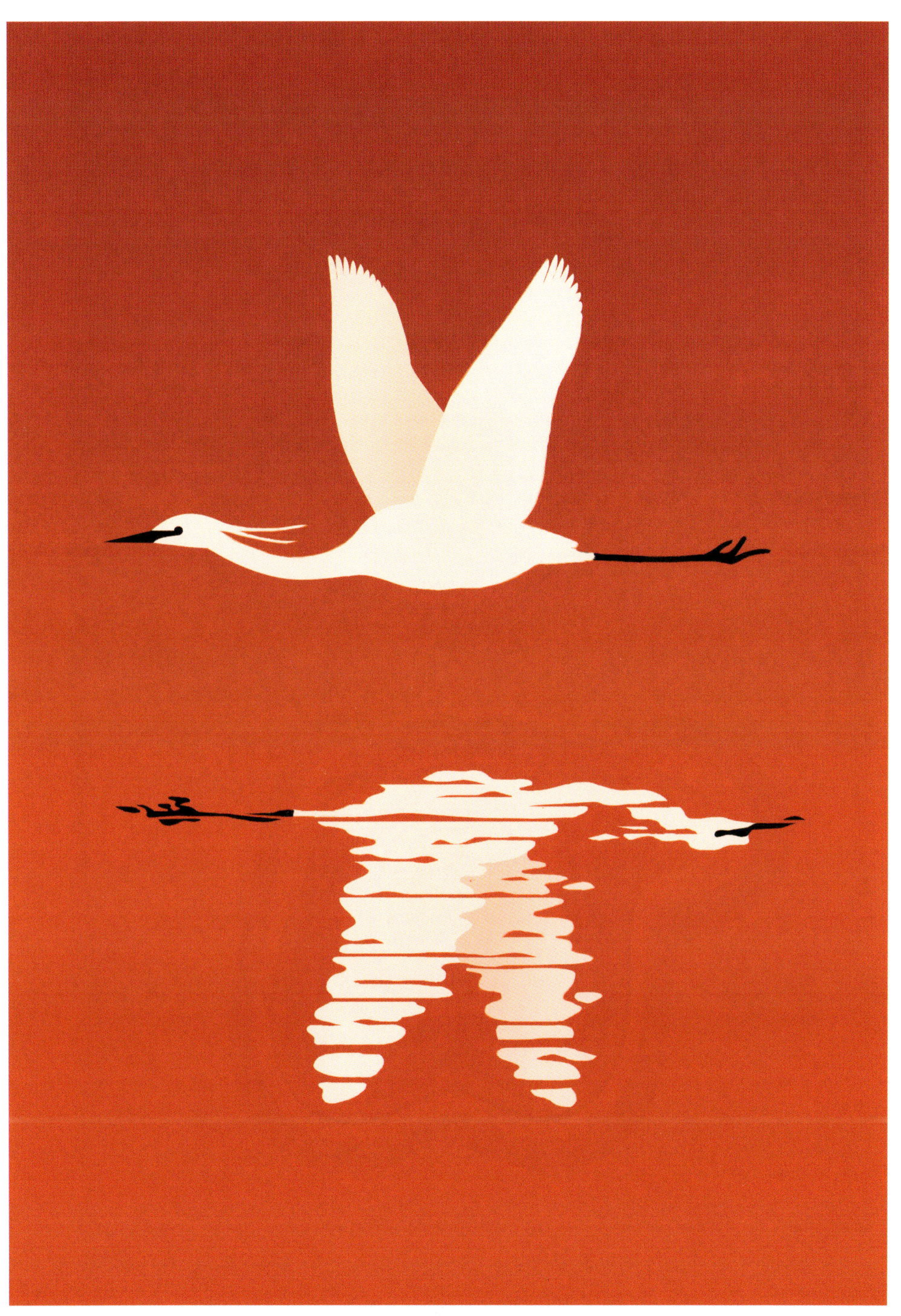

Joey Guidone *www.salzmanart.com*

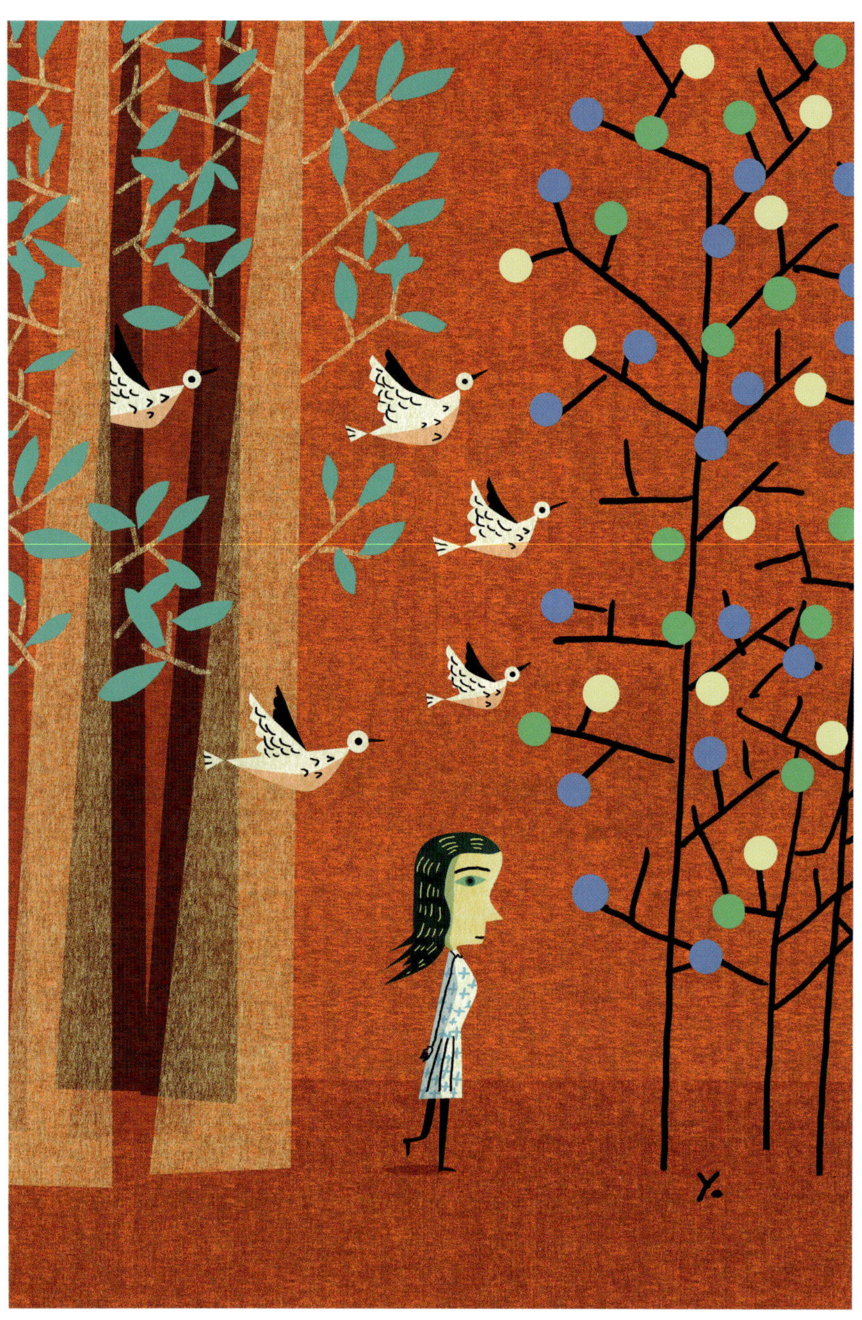

James Yang *www.jamesyang.com*

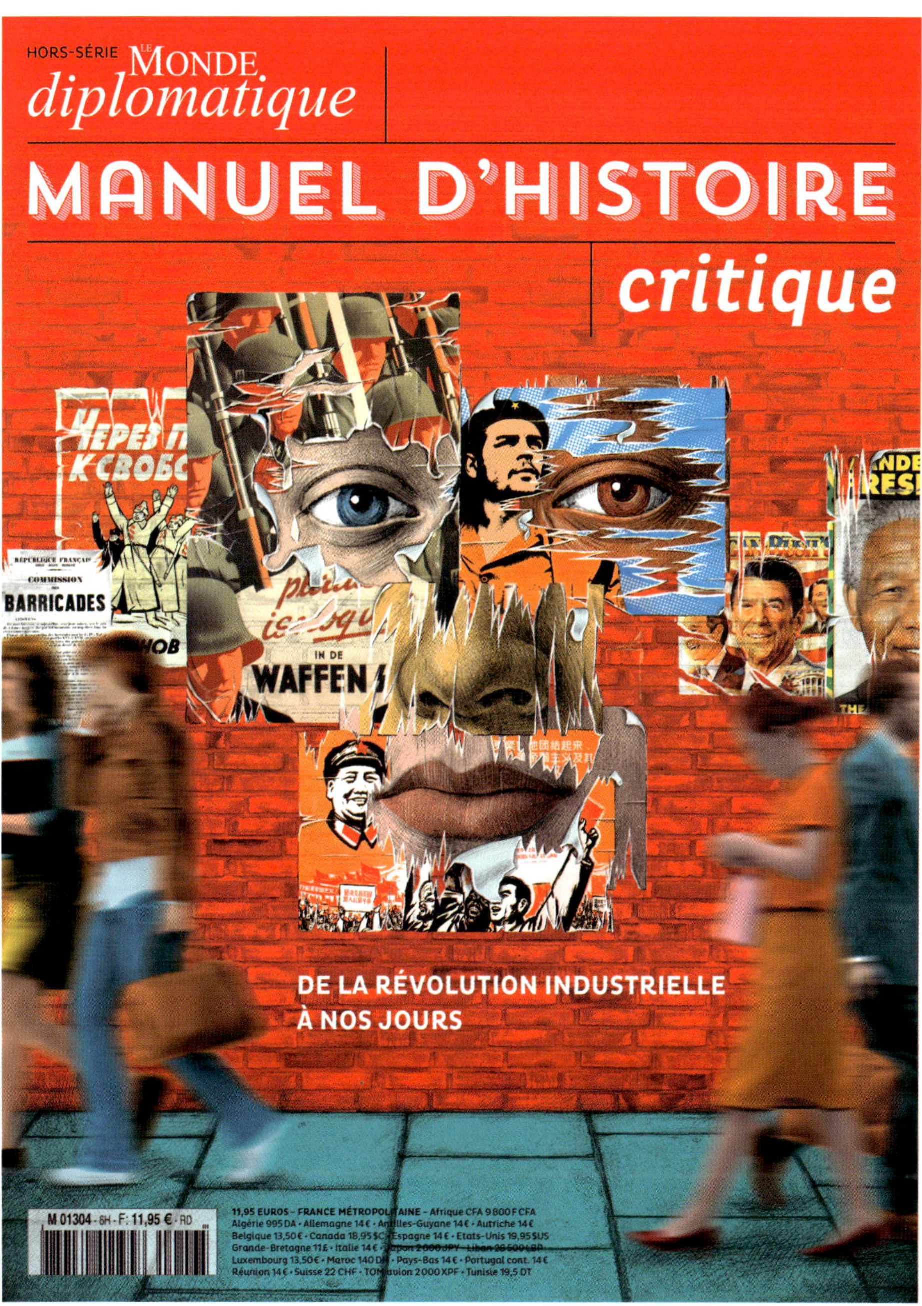

Boris Séméniako *www.borissemeniako.fr*

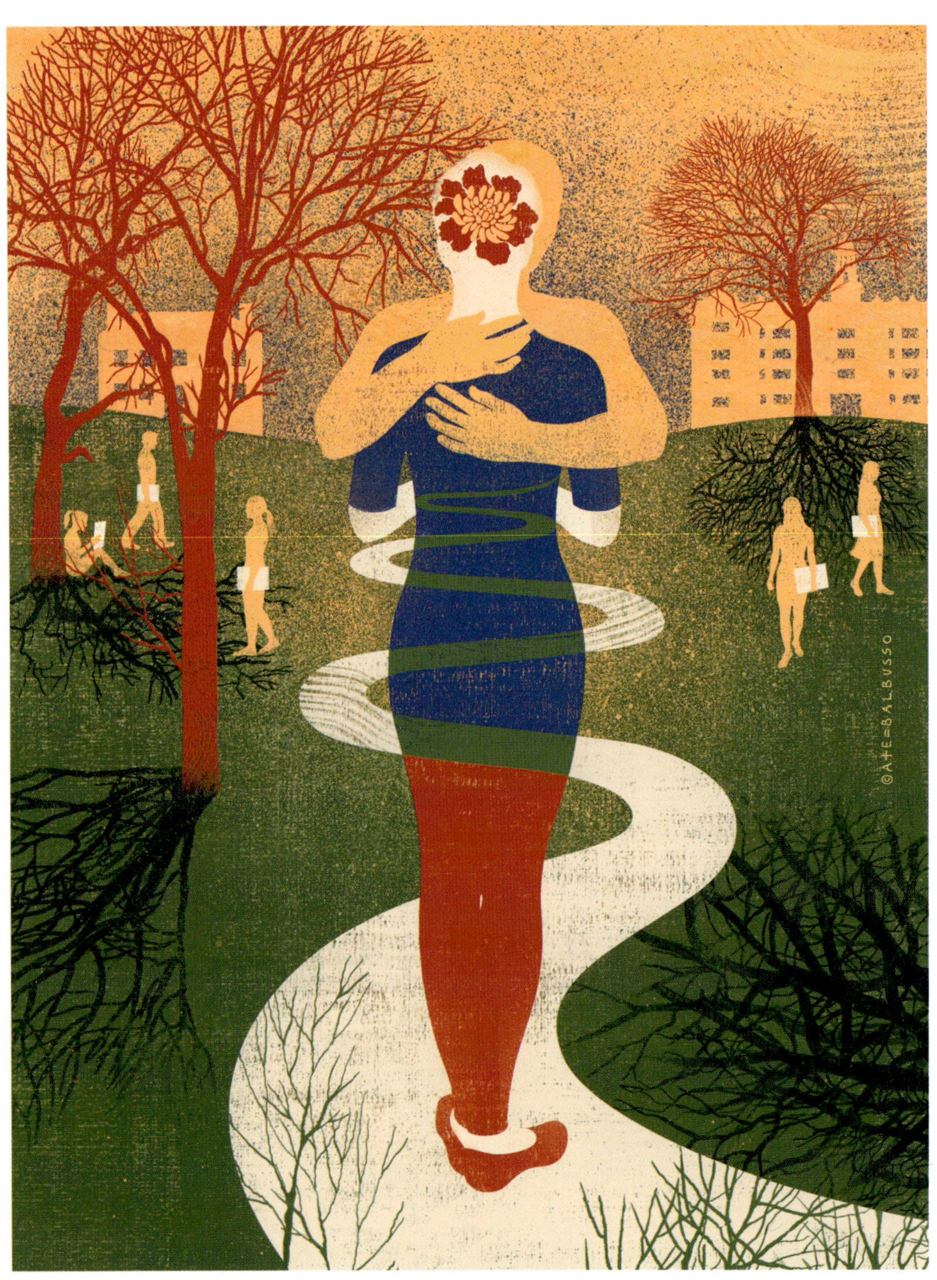

Anna & Elena Balbusso *www.balbusso.com*

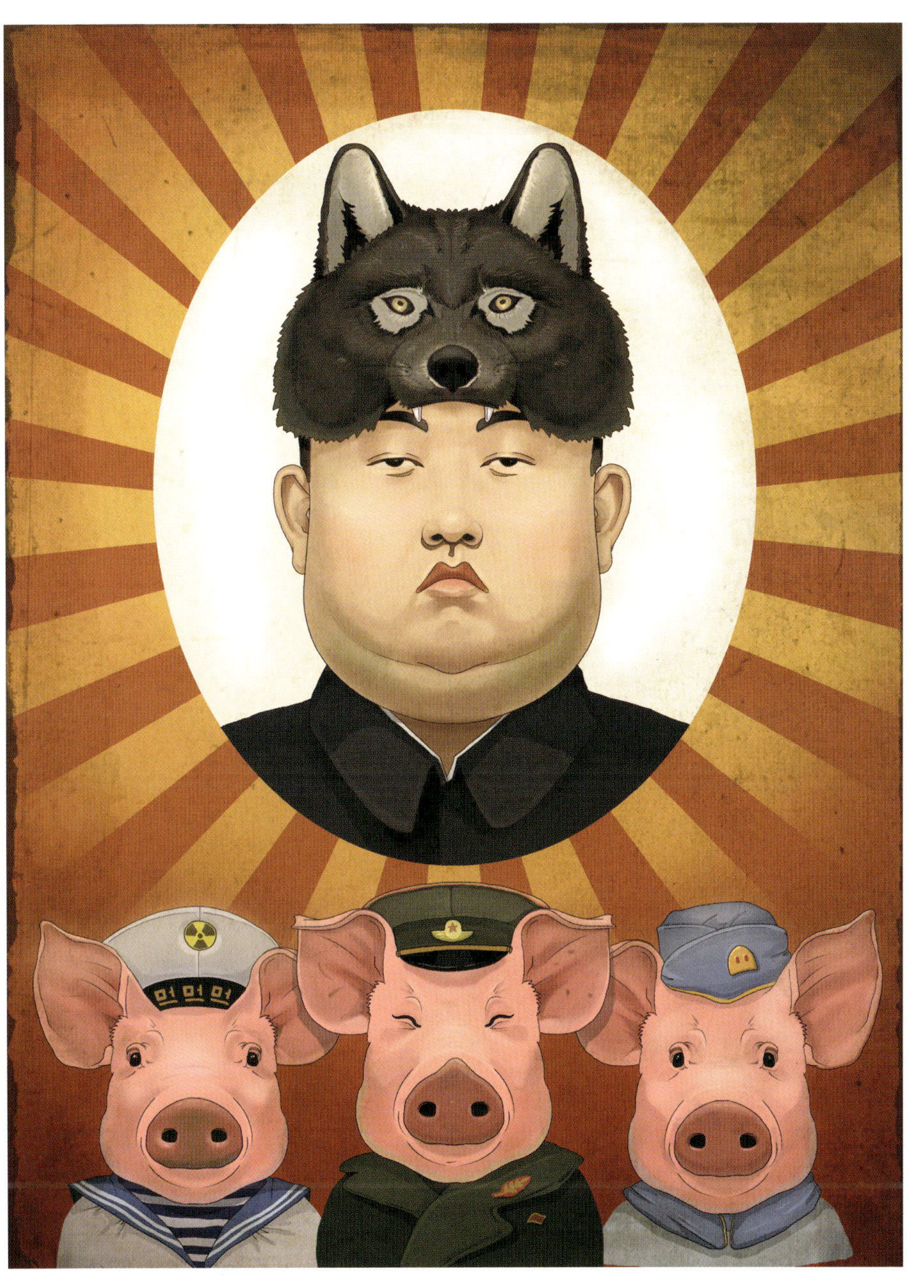

Jiale Kuang *www.lokkuang.com*

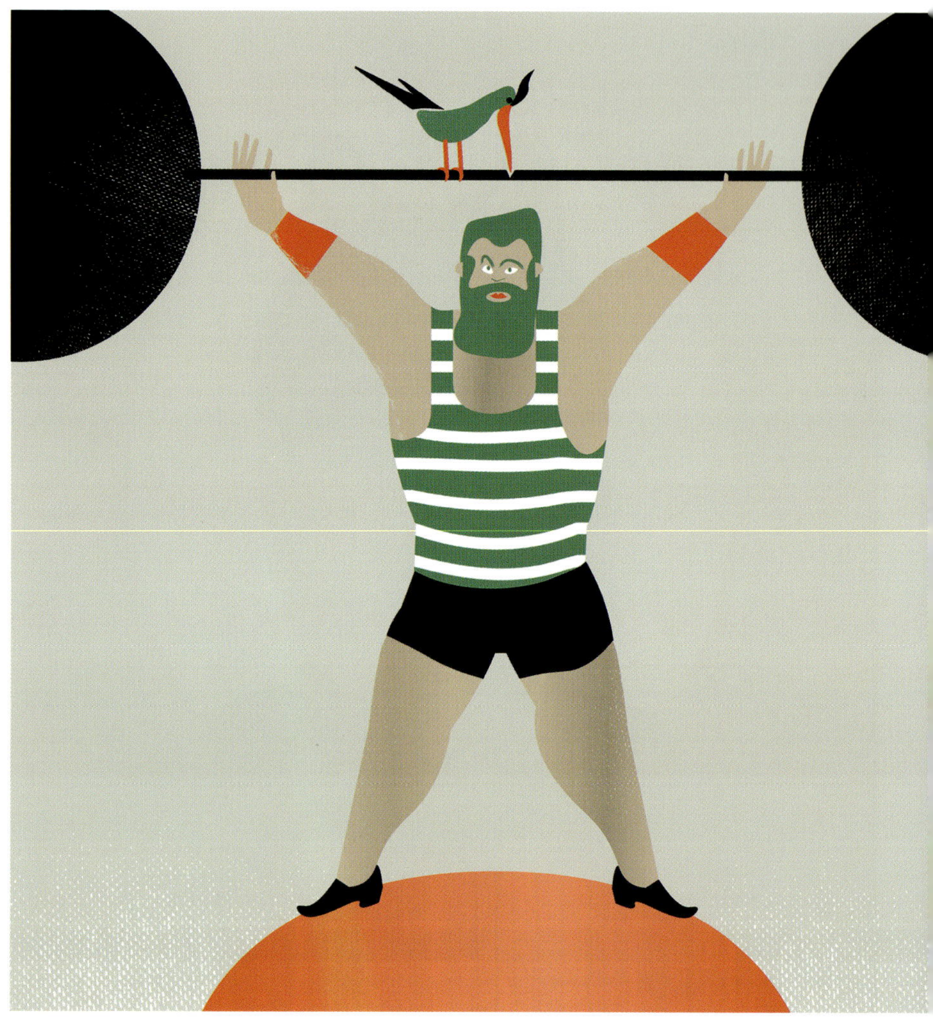

Francesco Zorzi *www.francescozorzi.it*

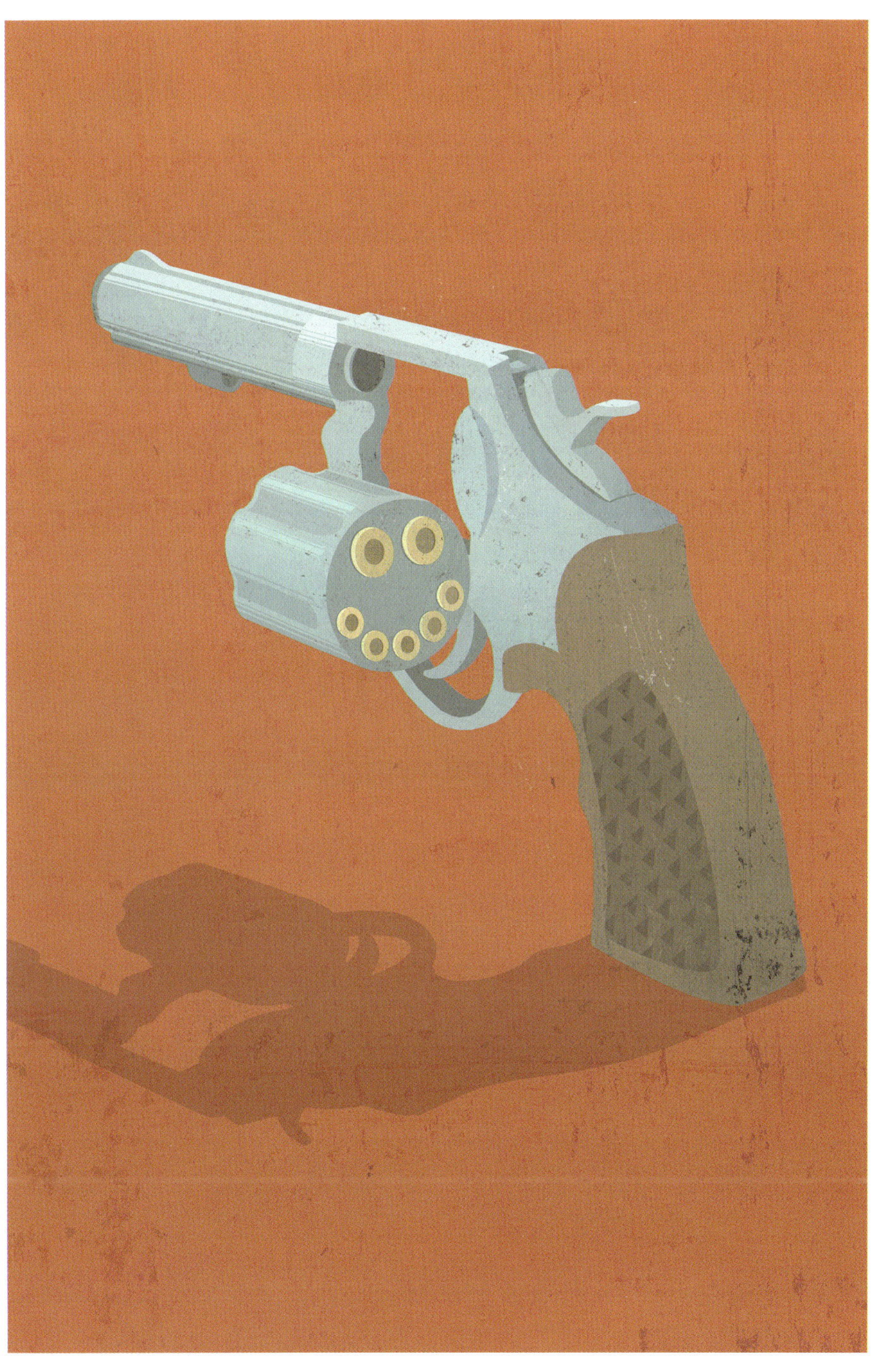

Stephan Schmitz *www.stephan-schmitz.ch*

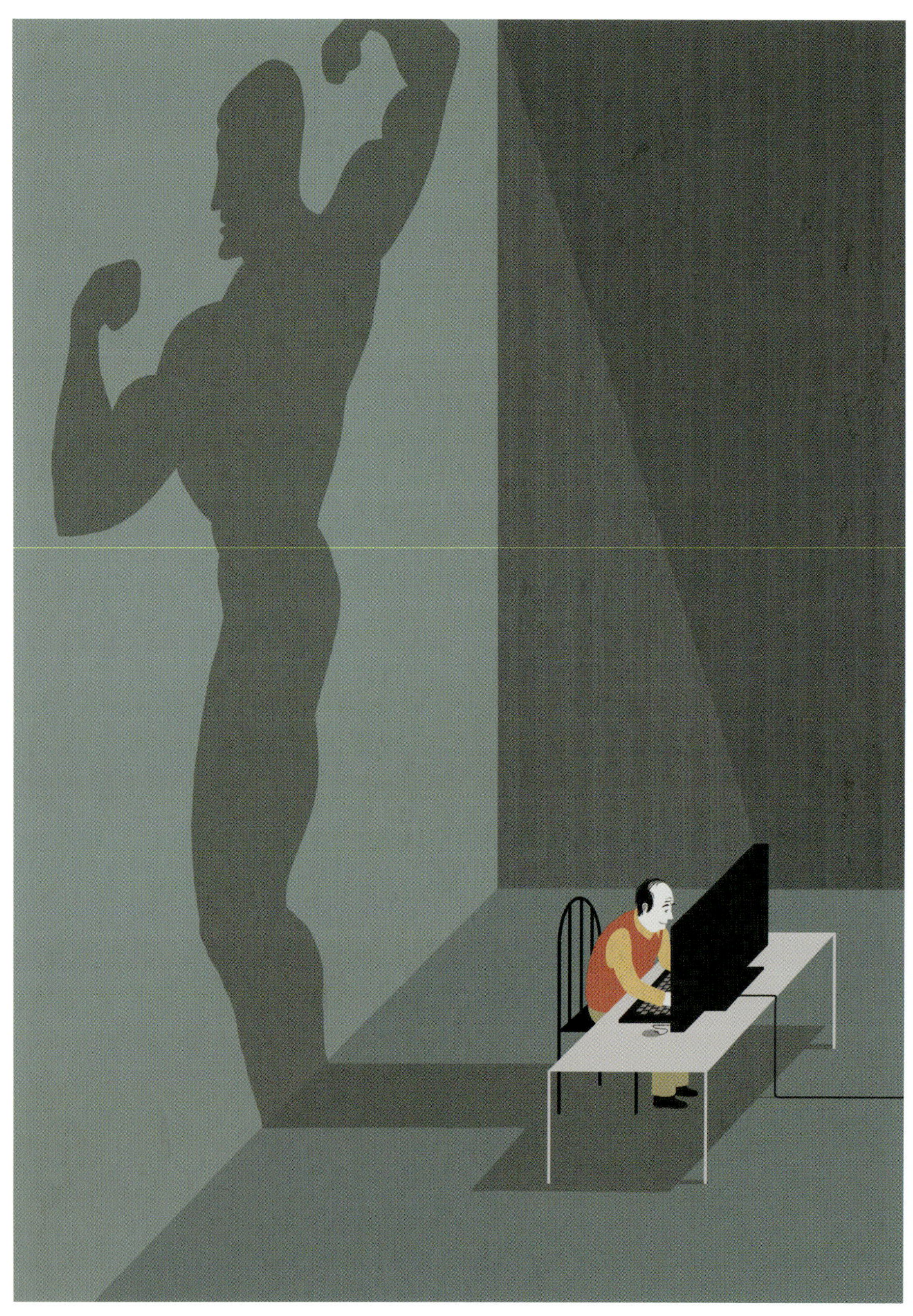

Stephan Schmitz *www.stephan-schmitz.ch*

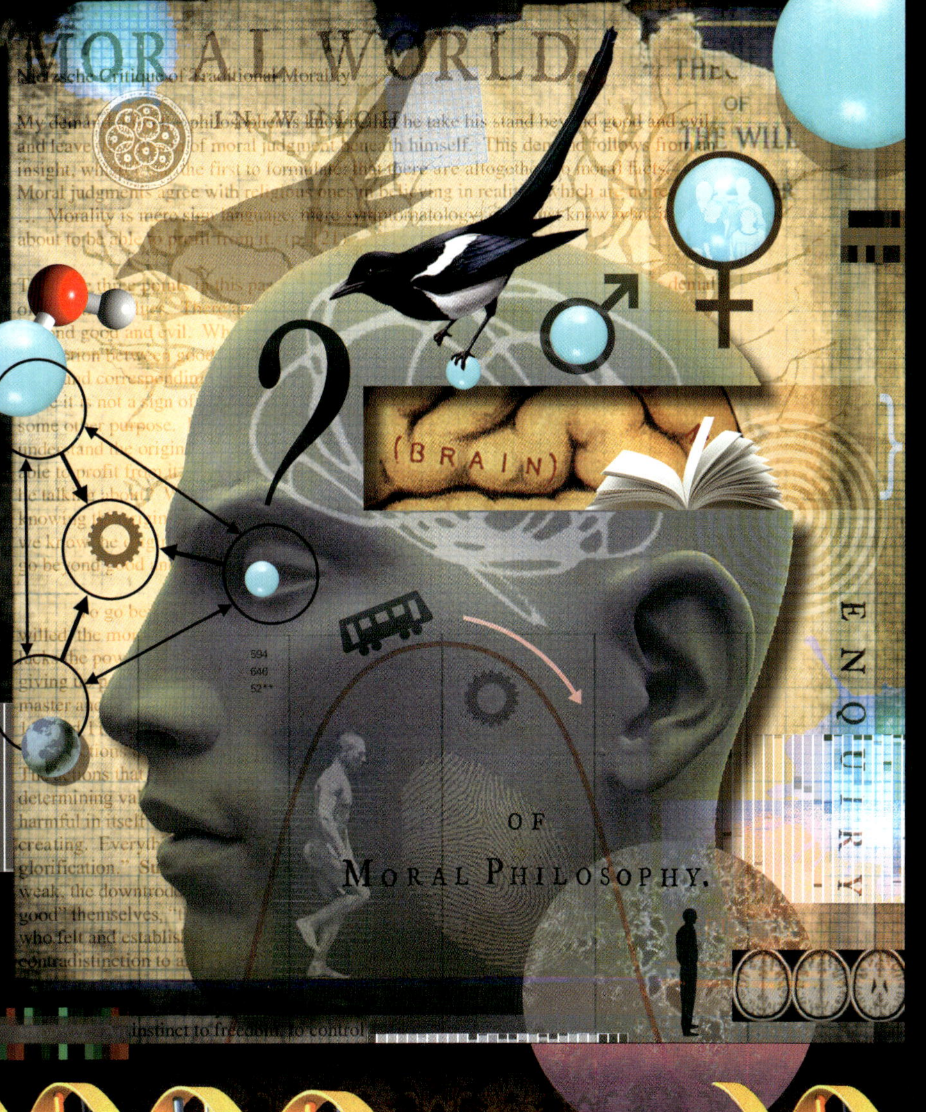

MORAL WORLD.
THE
OF
THE WILL
Nietzsche Critique of Traditional Morality
(BRAIN)
ENQUIRY
OF
MORAL PHILOSOPHY.
instinct to freedom, to control
594
646
52**
71

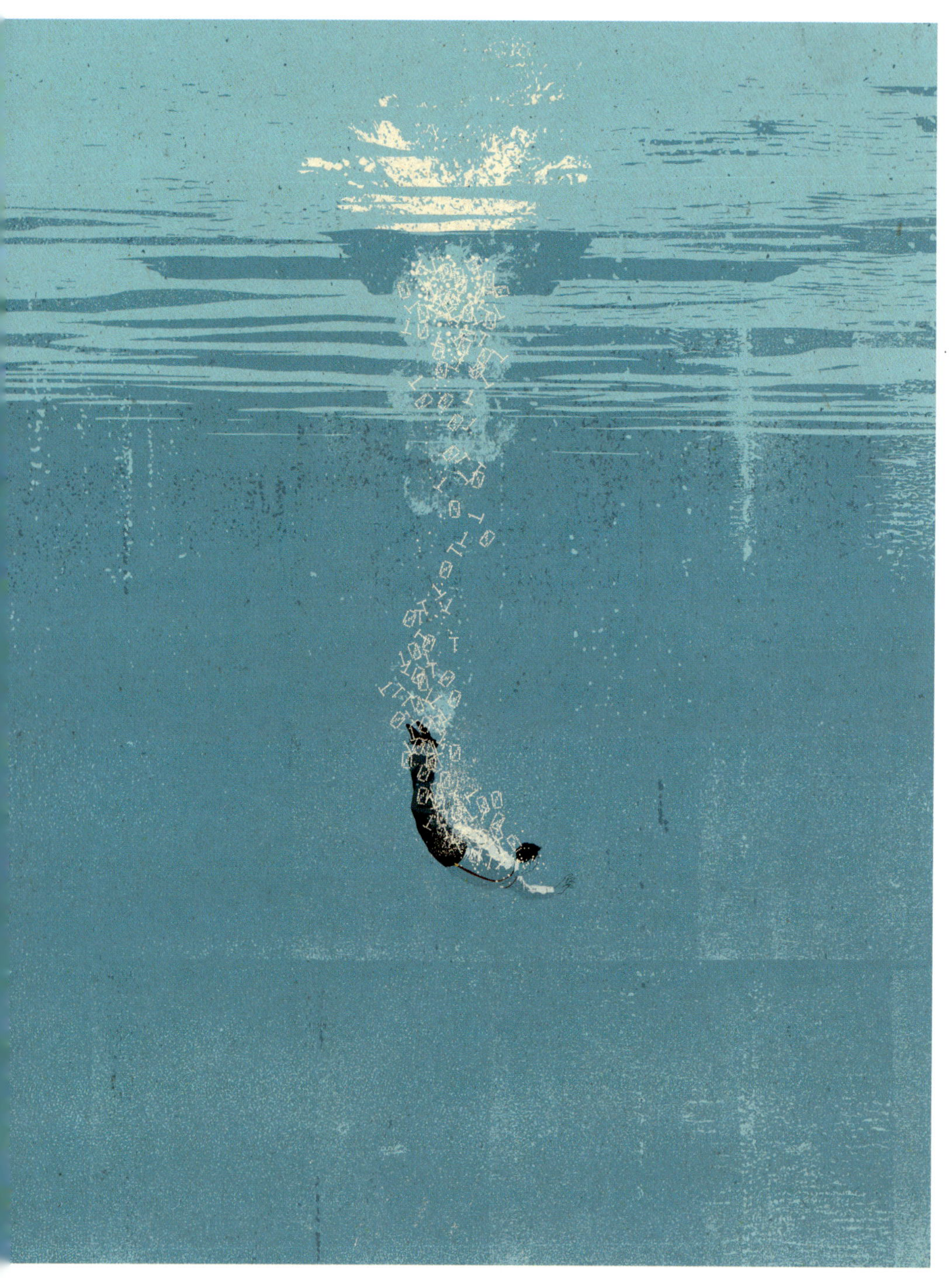

Mark Smith *www.salzmanart.com*

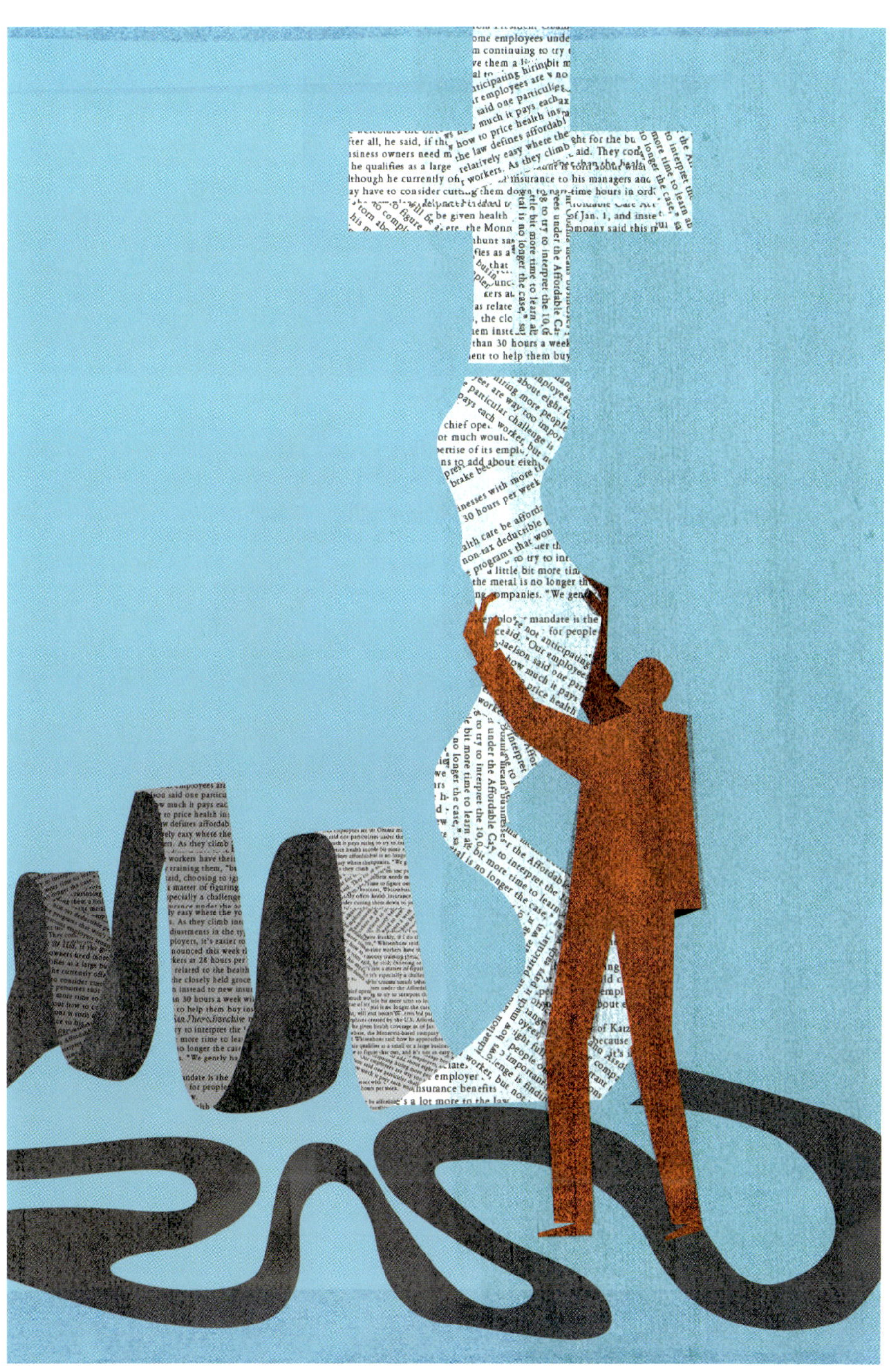

Mark McGinnis *www.mistermcginnis.com*

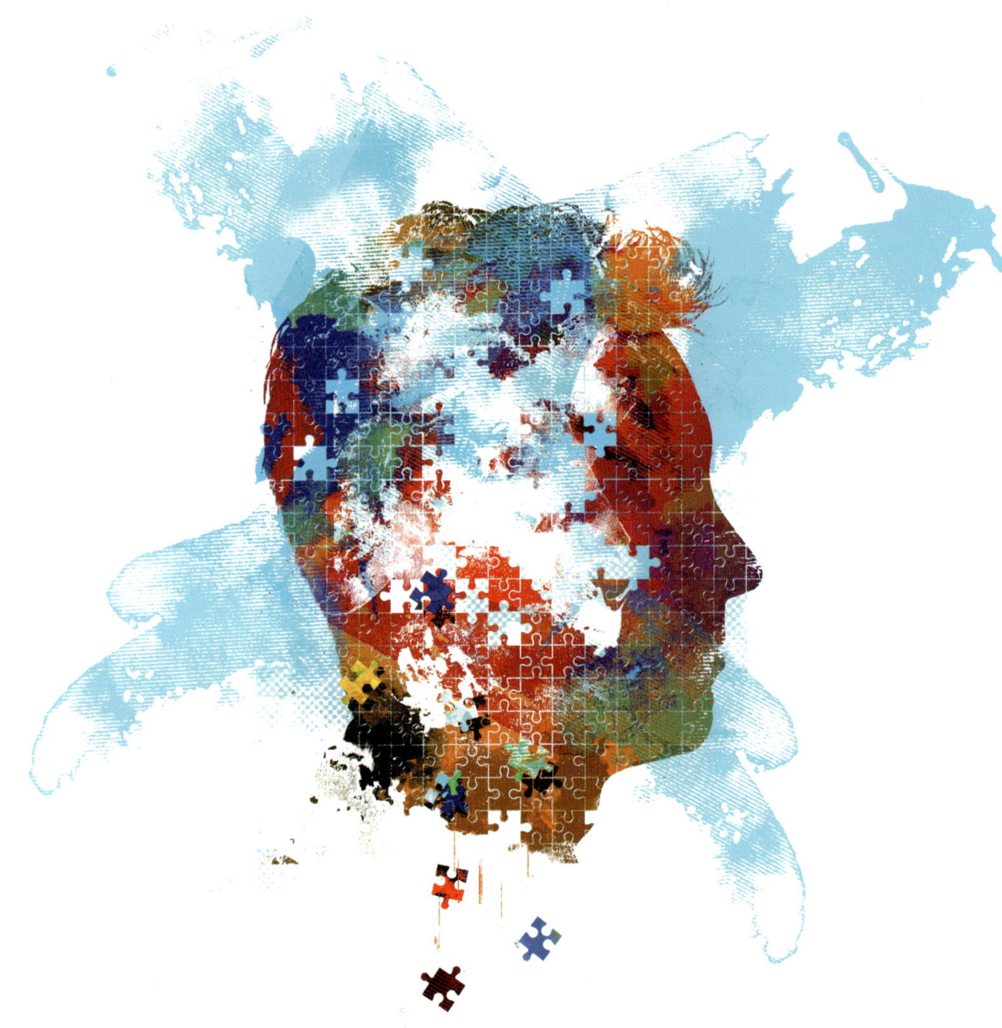

Gary Neill *www.agoodson.com*

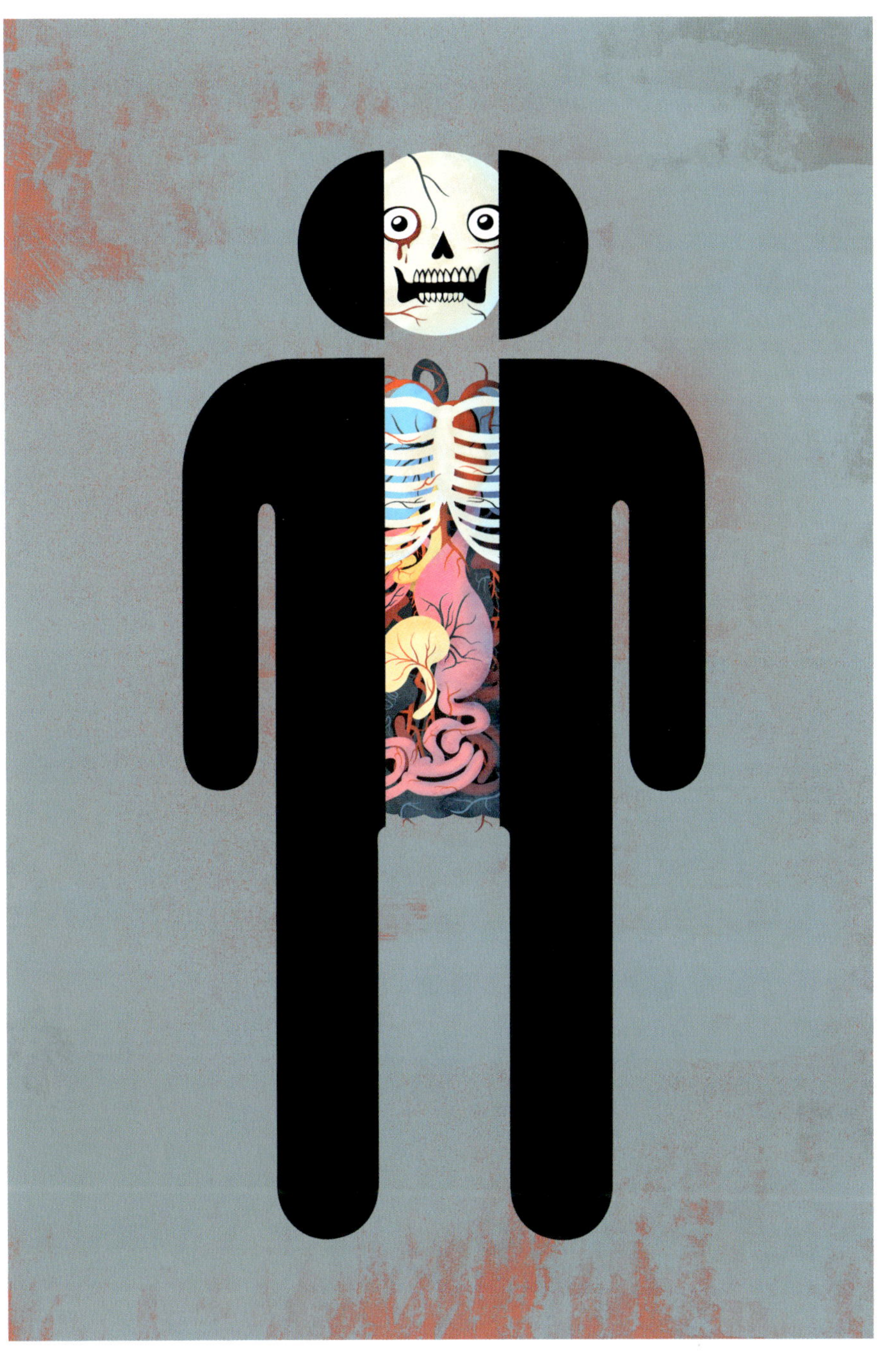

Ken Tackett *www.kentackettart.com*

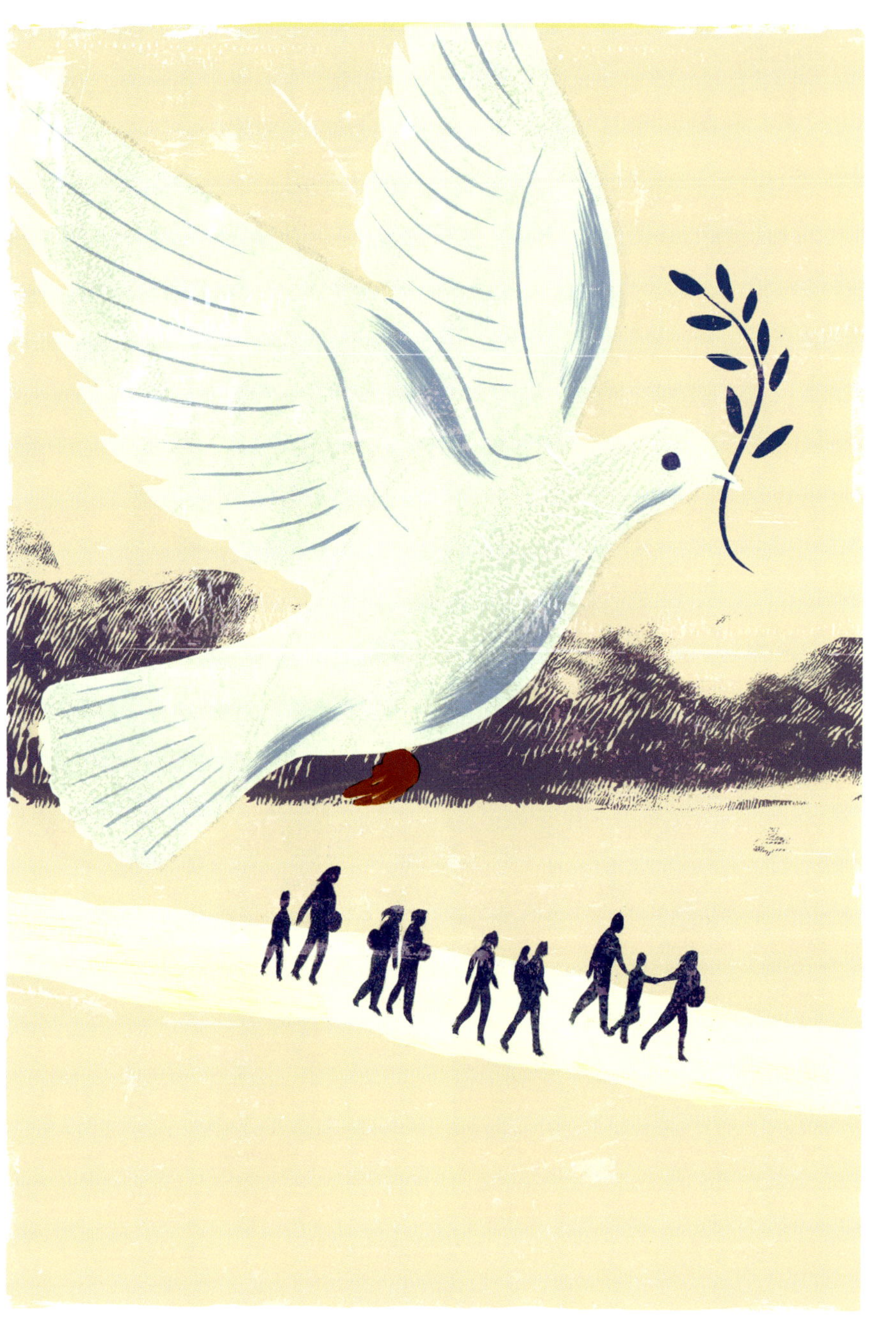

Curtis Parker *www.scotthull.com*

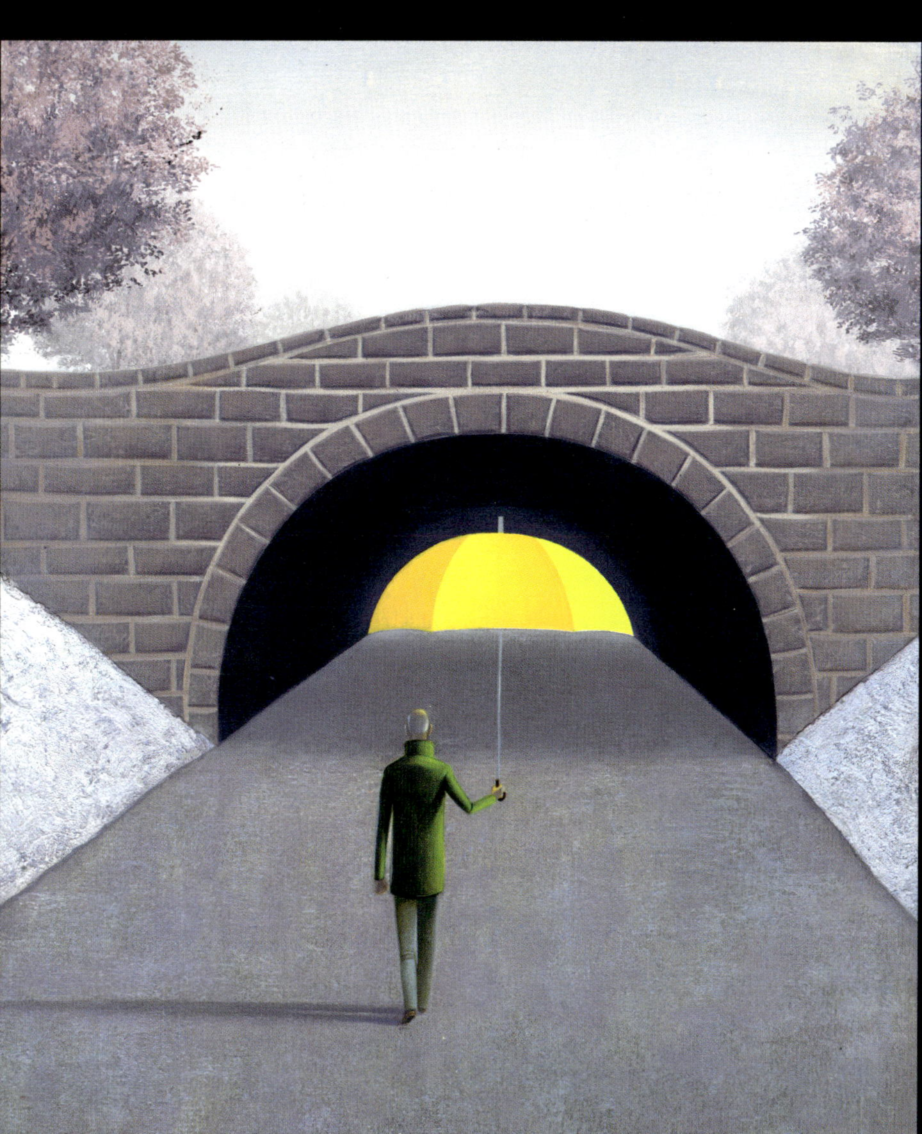

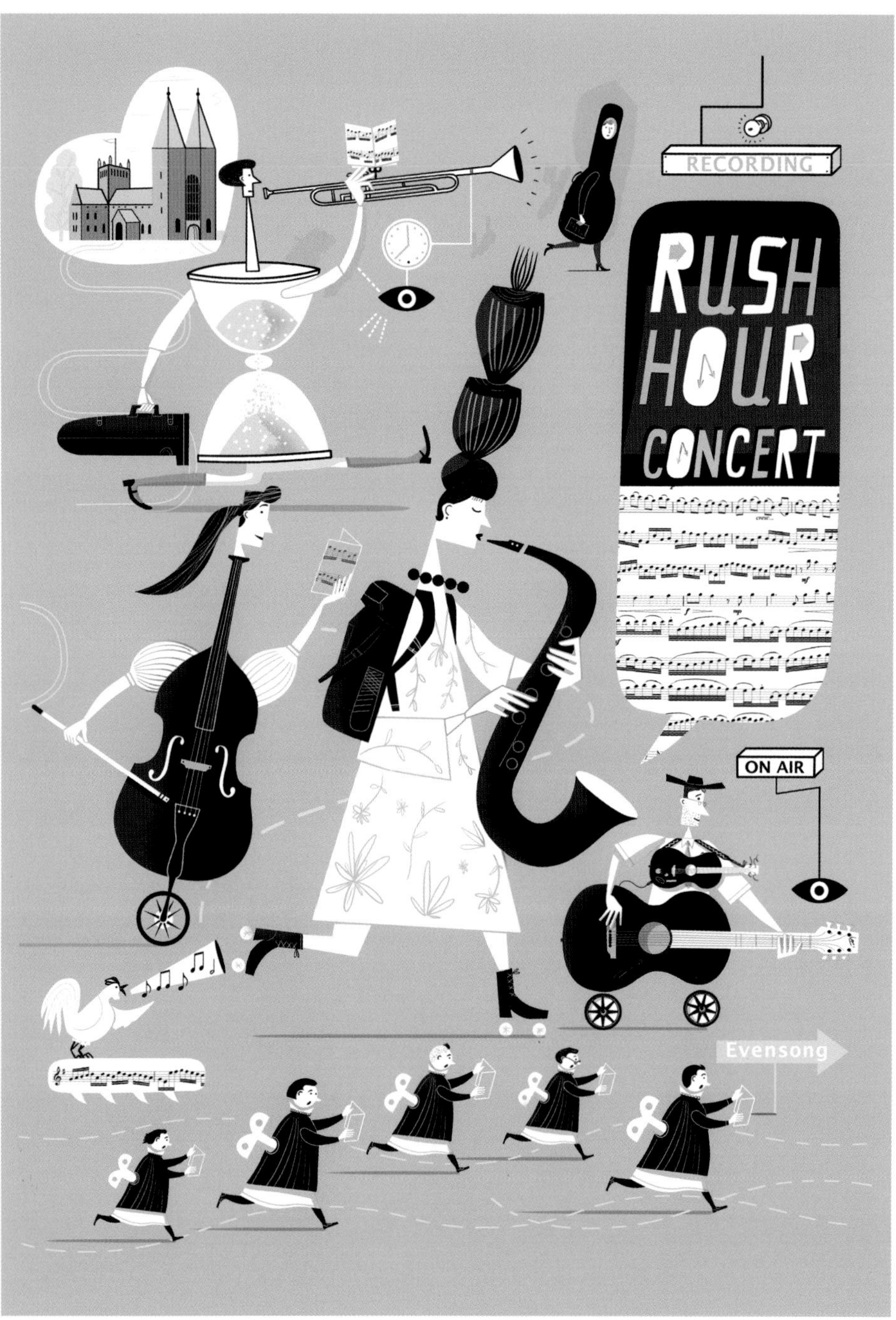

Ian Whadcock *www.ianwhadcock.com*

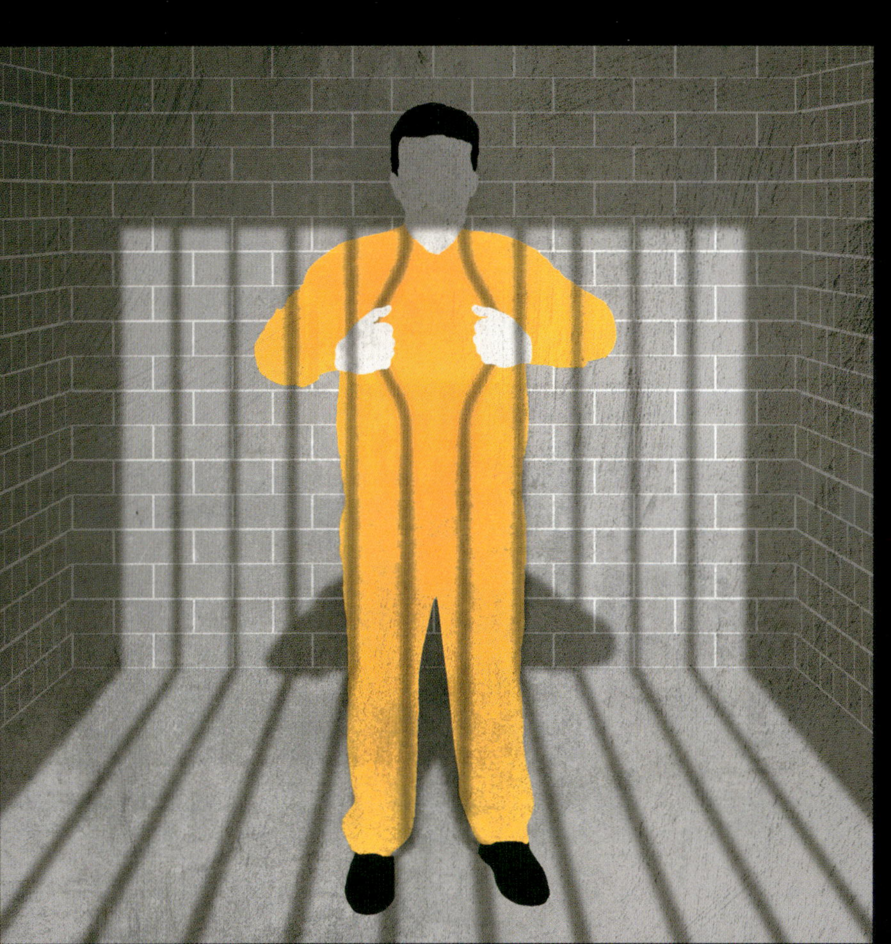

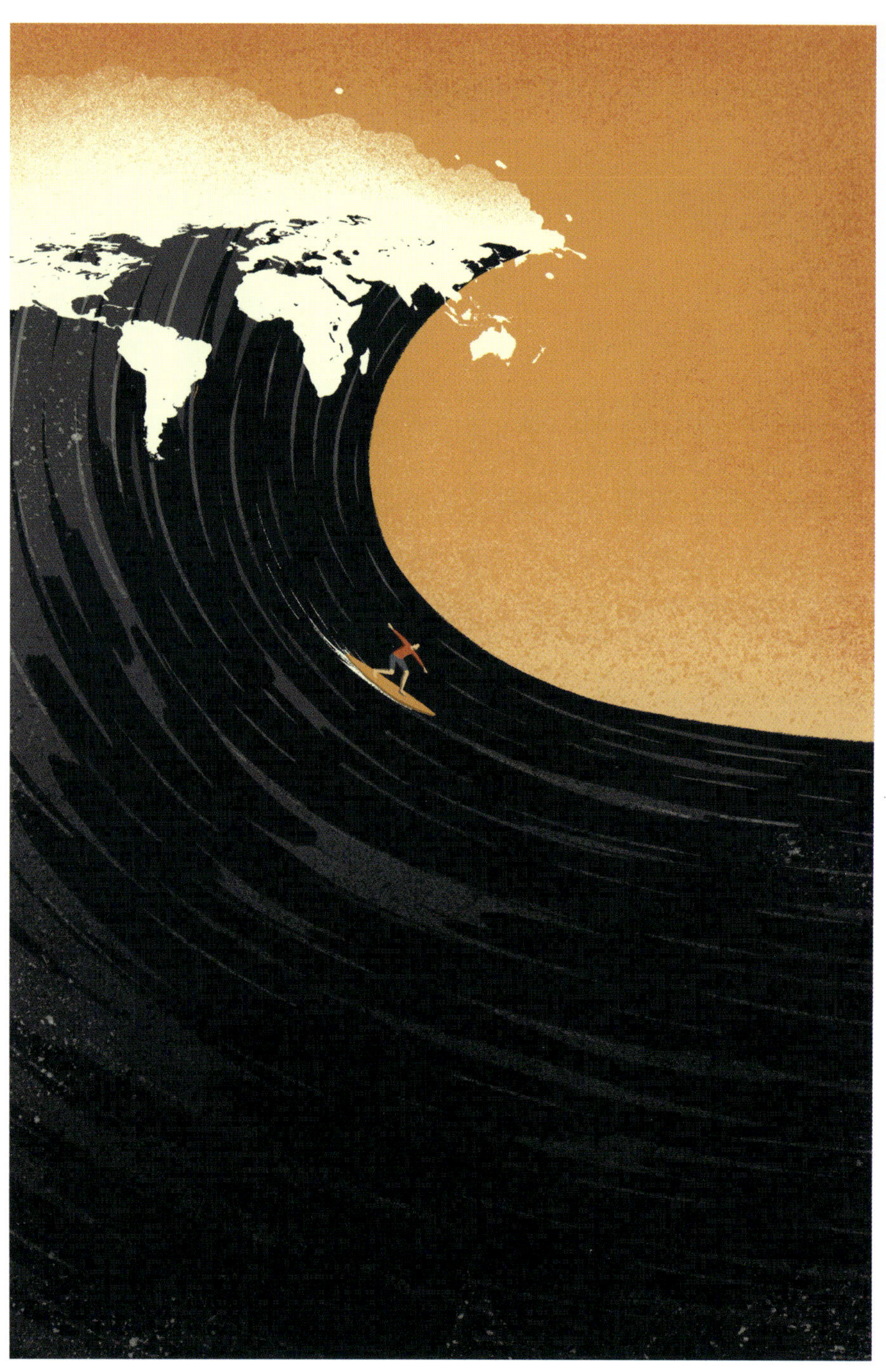

Davide Bonazzi *www.salzmanart.com*

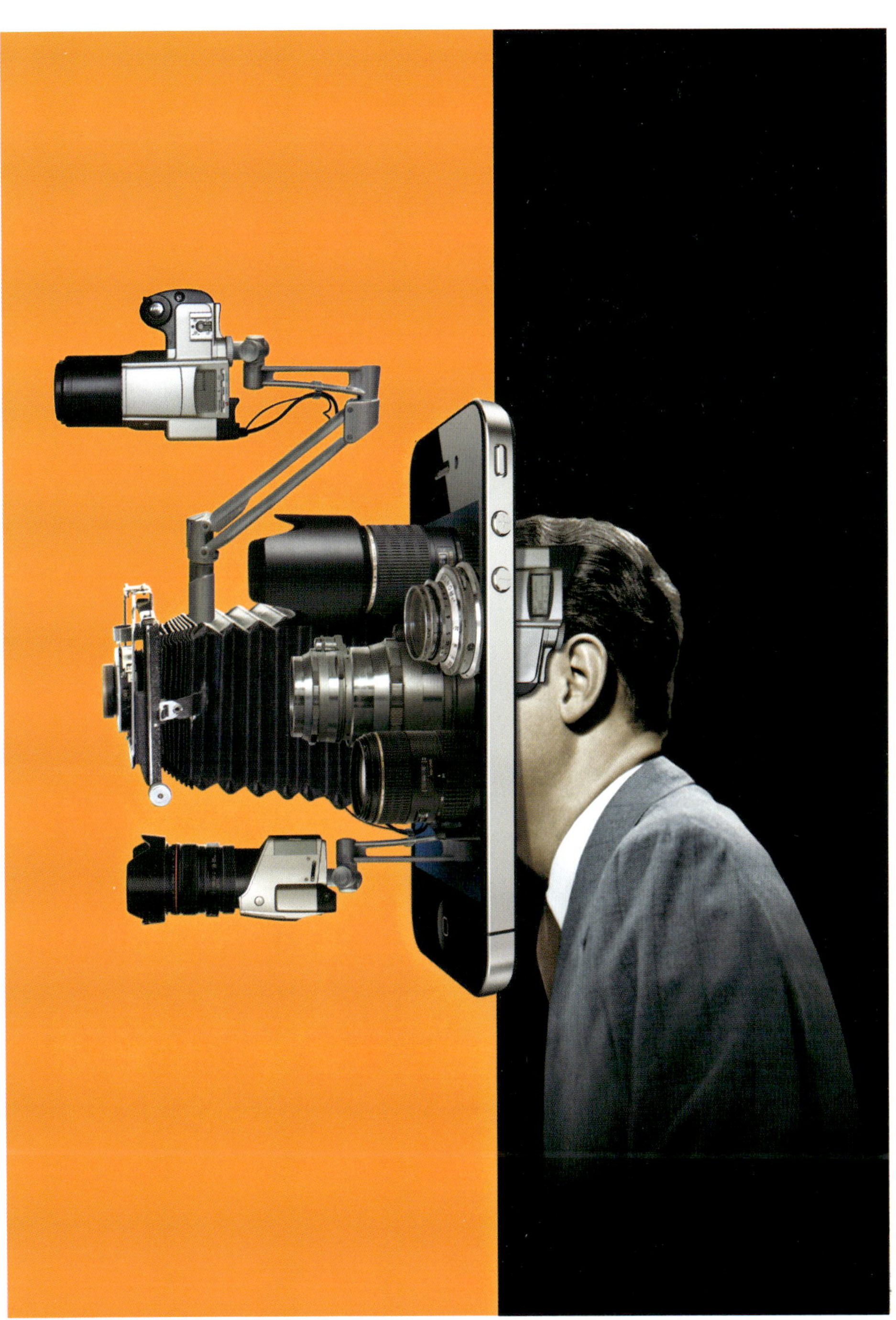

Viktor Koen *www.viktorkoen.com*

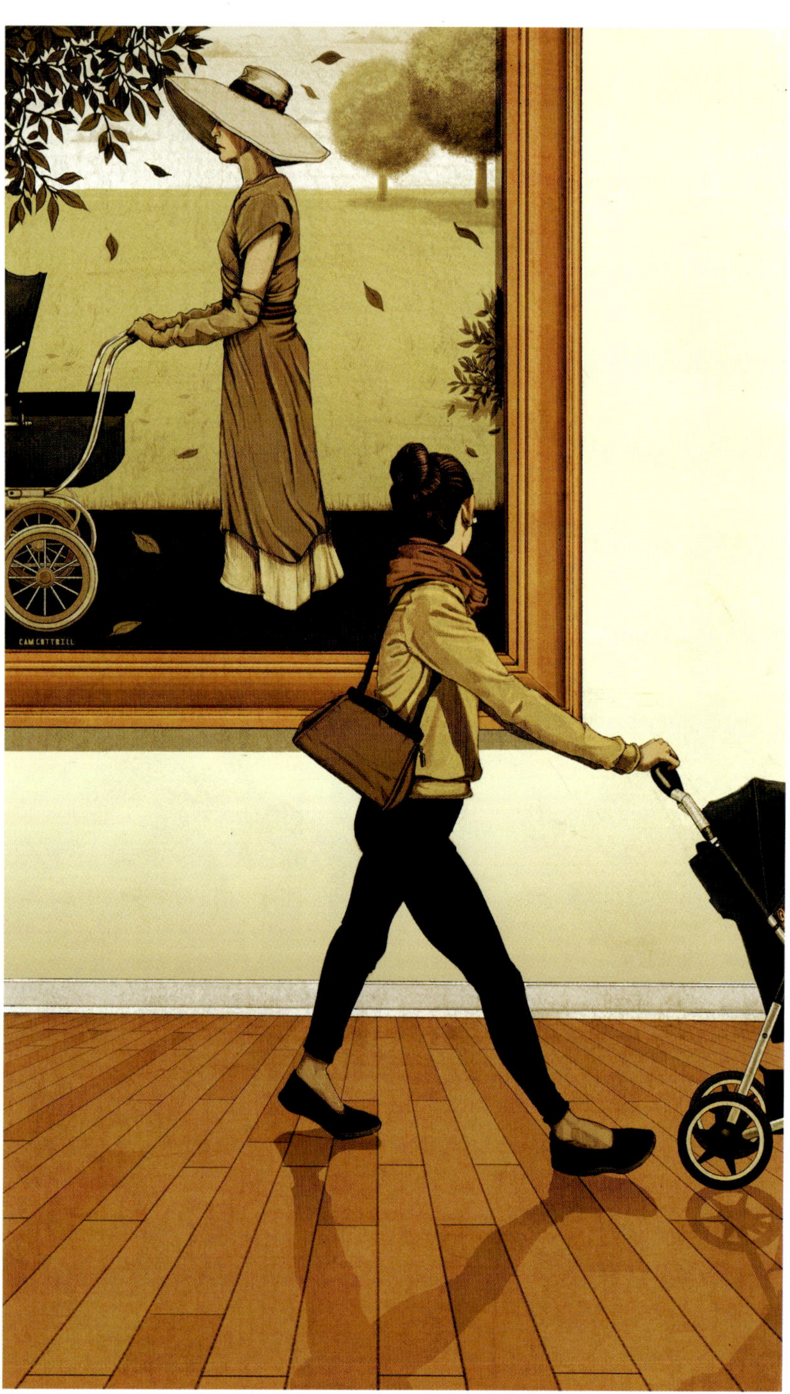

Cameron Cottrill *www.camcottrill.com*

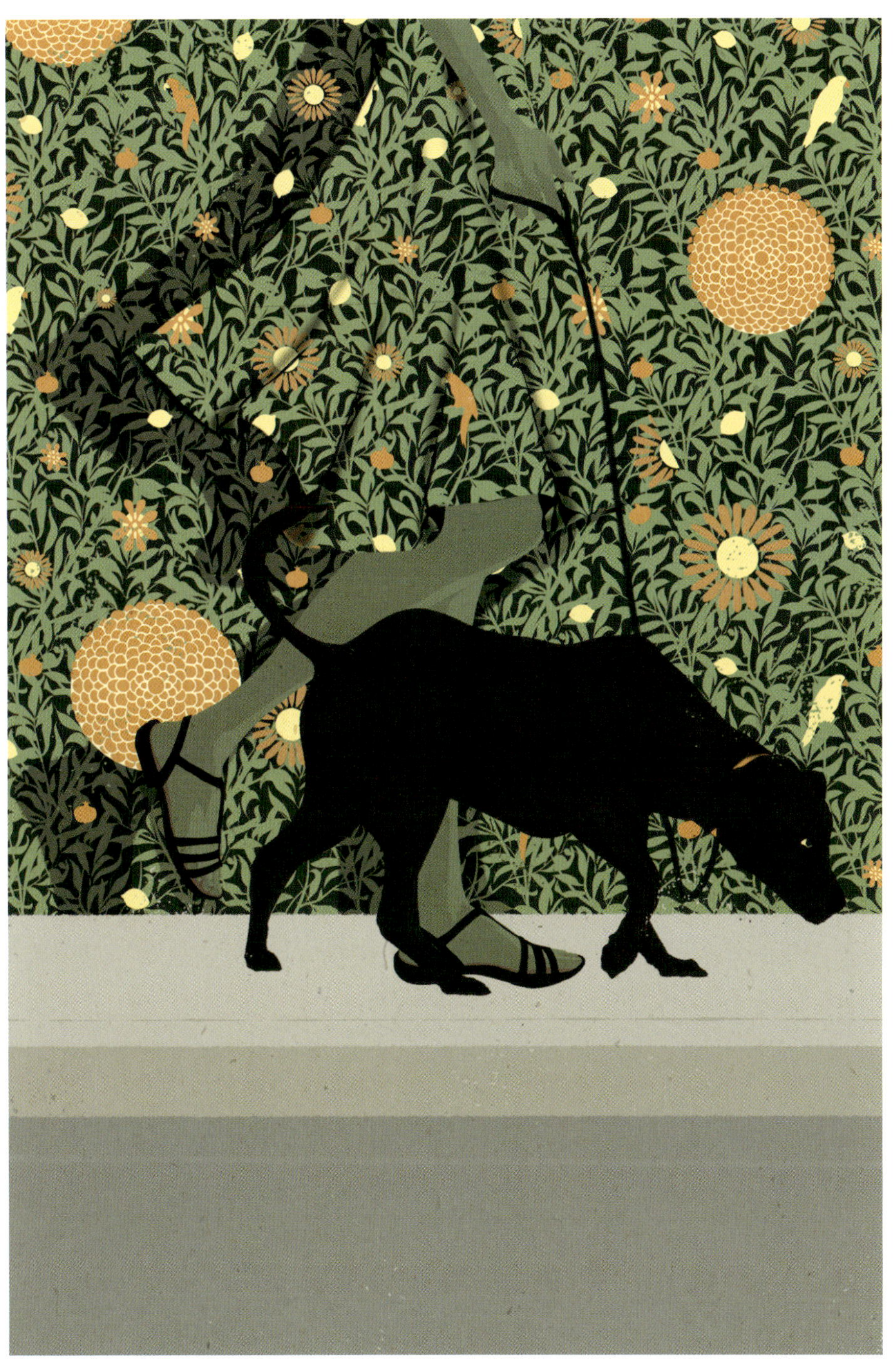

Oli Winward *www.salzmanart.com*

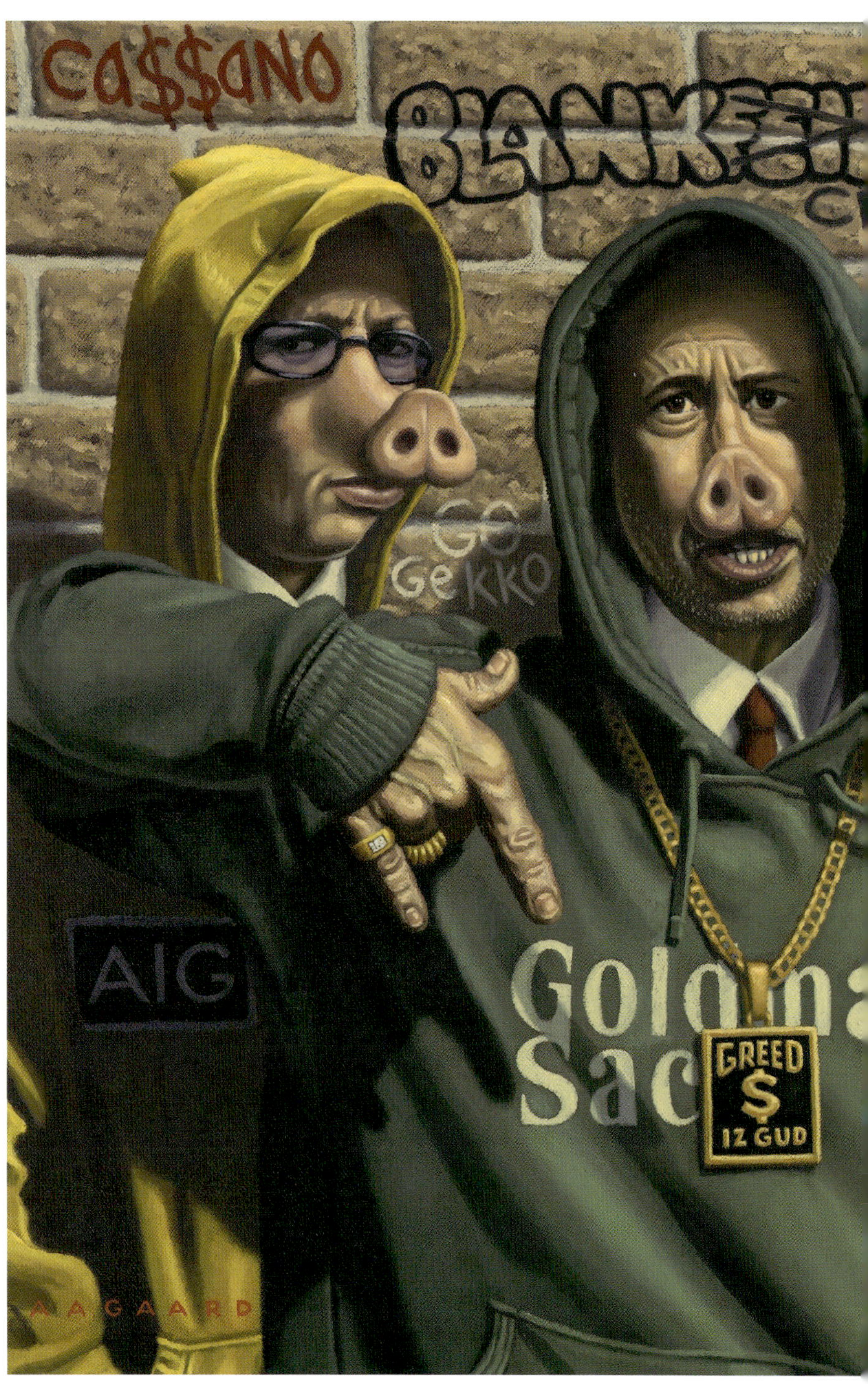

Gary Aagaard *www.garyaagaard.com*

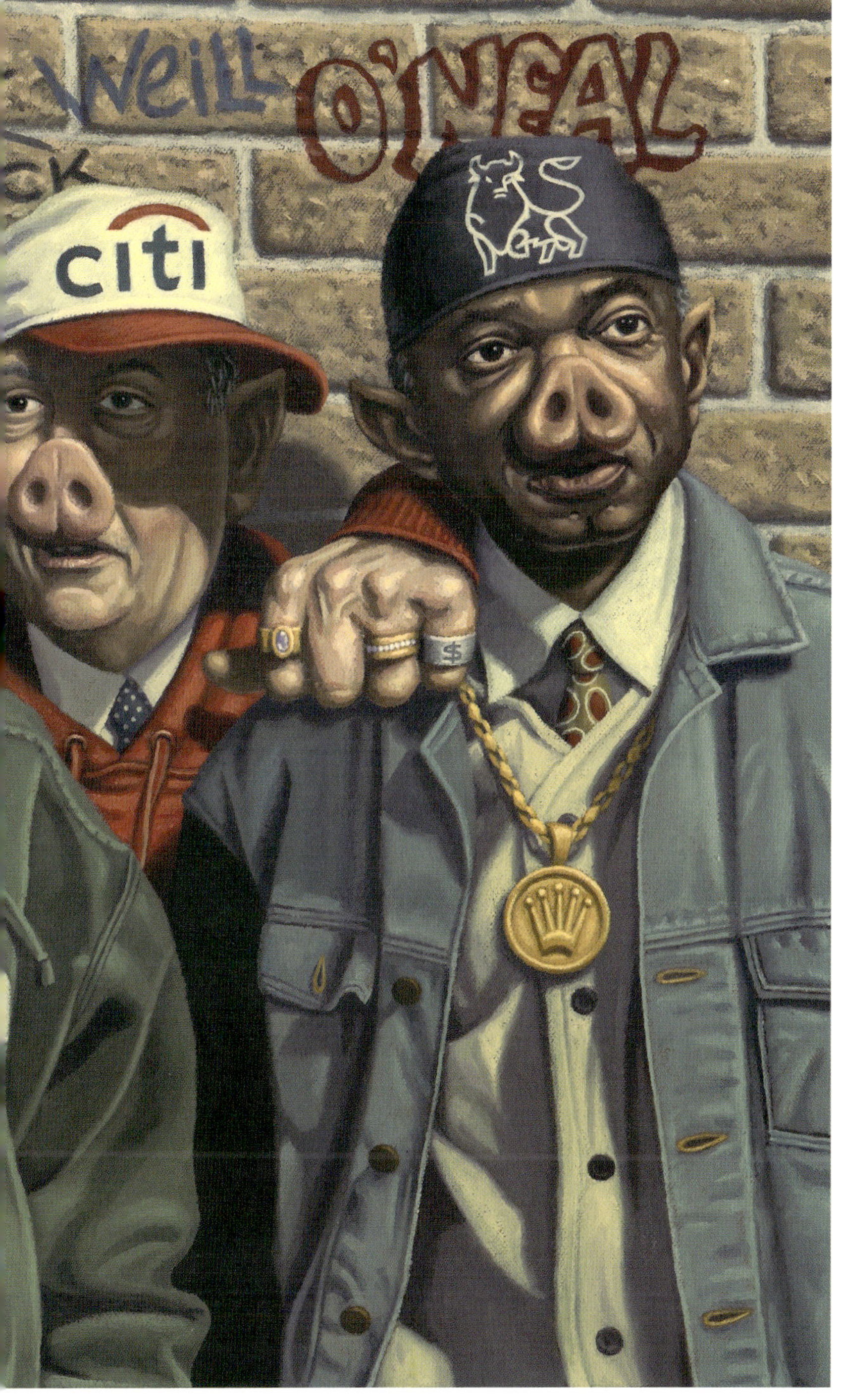
weill
O'NEAL
citi

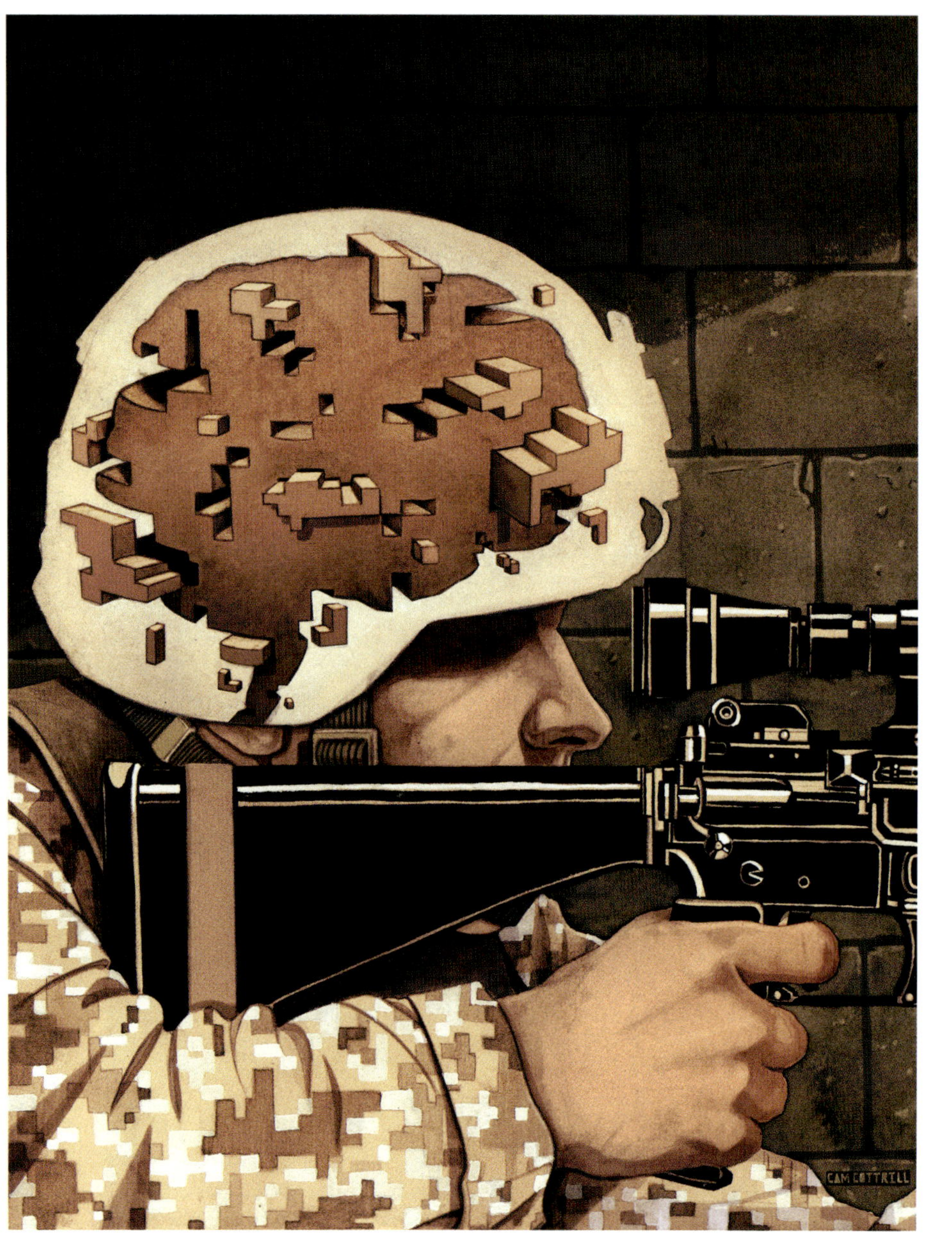

Cameron Cottrill *www.camcottrill.com*

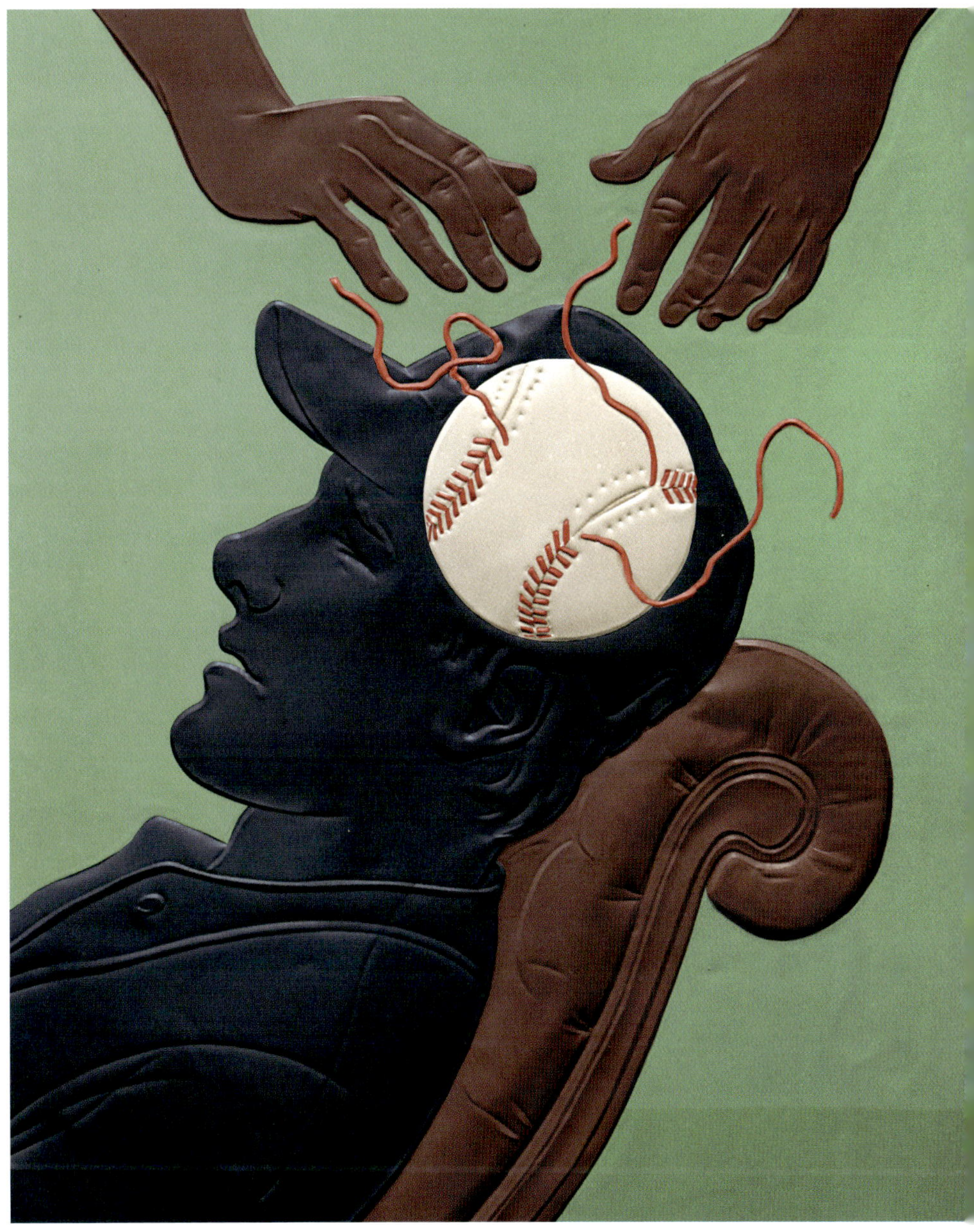

Alex Nabaum *www.alexnabaum.com*

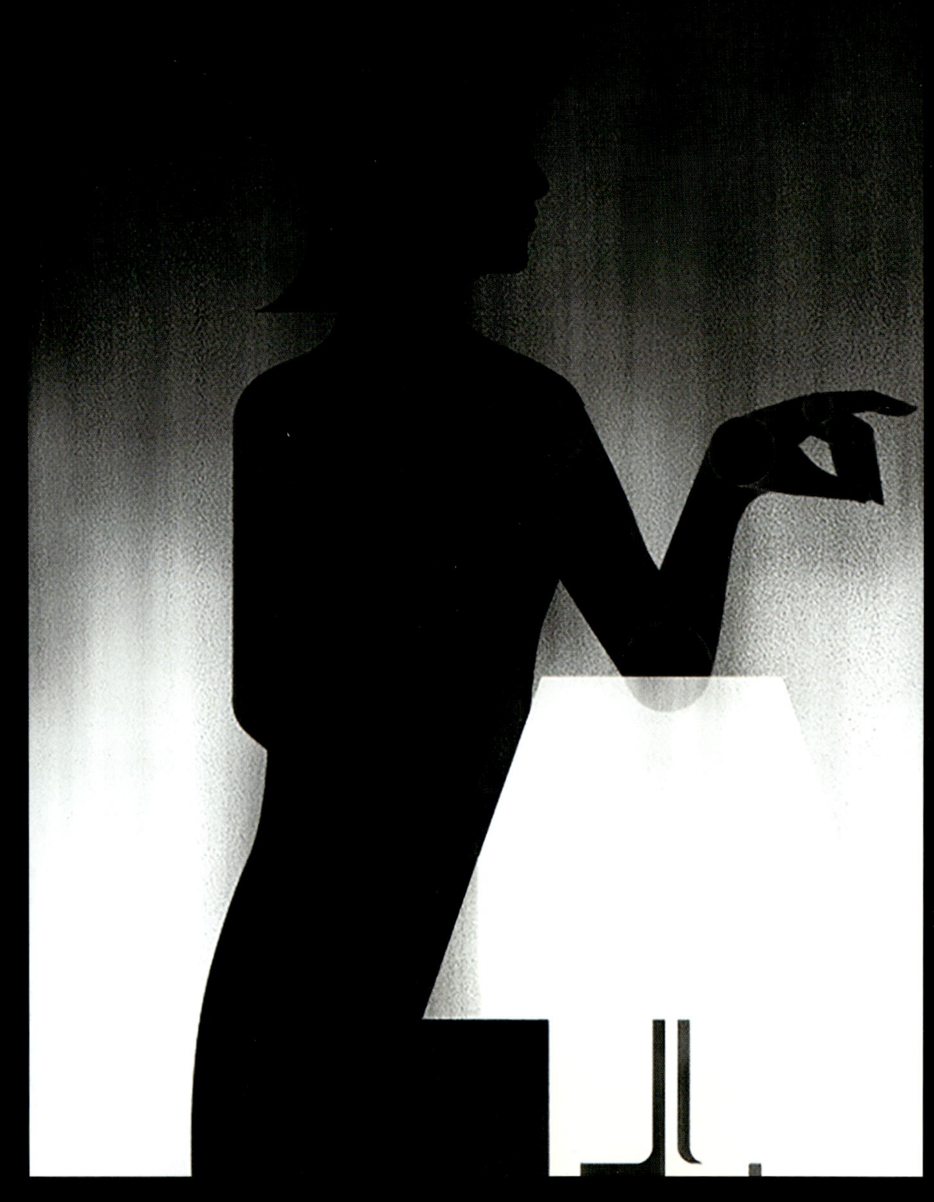

Giulio Bonasera *www.giuliobonasera.com*

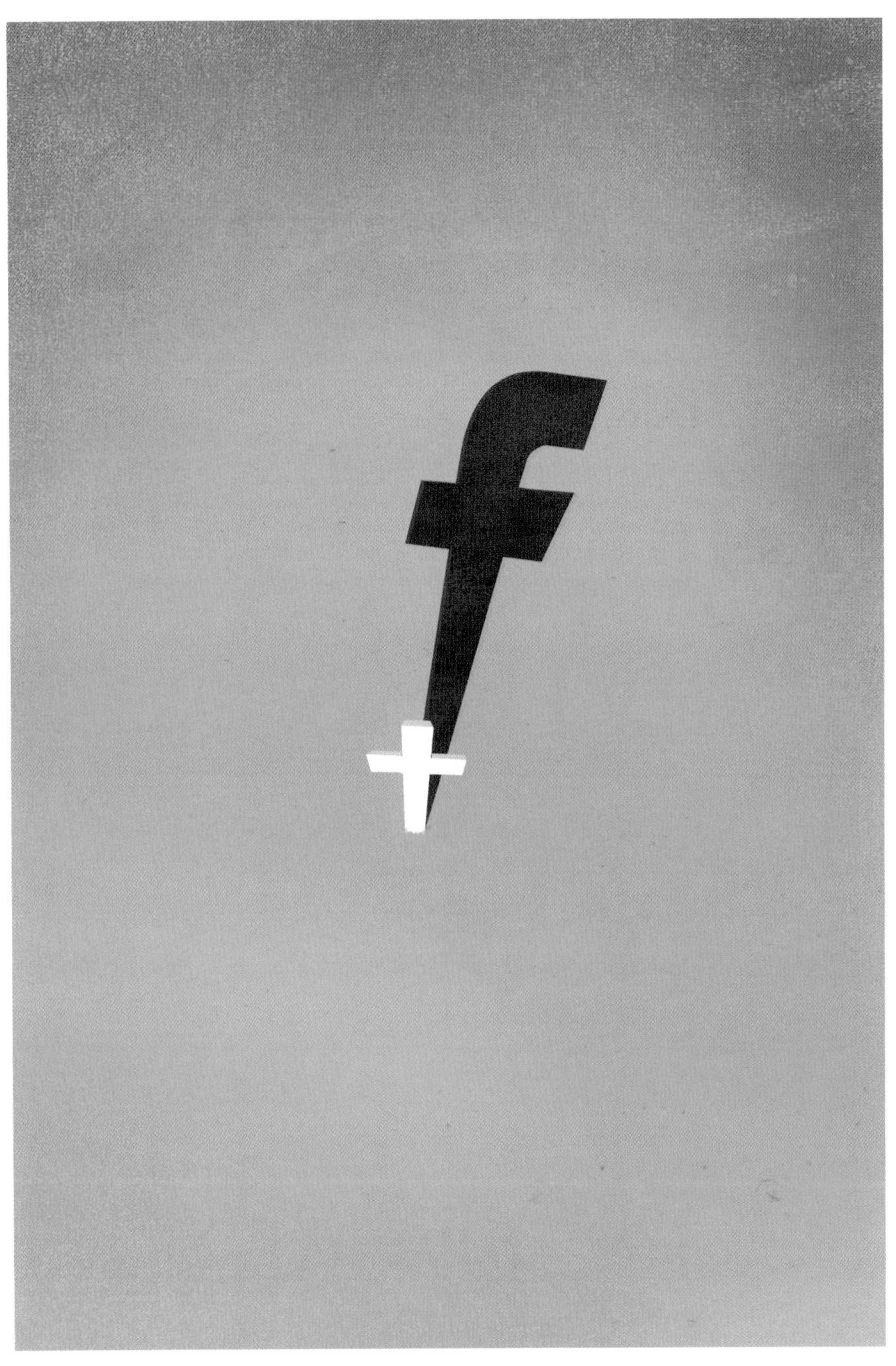

Marco Melgrati *www.salzmanart.com*

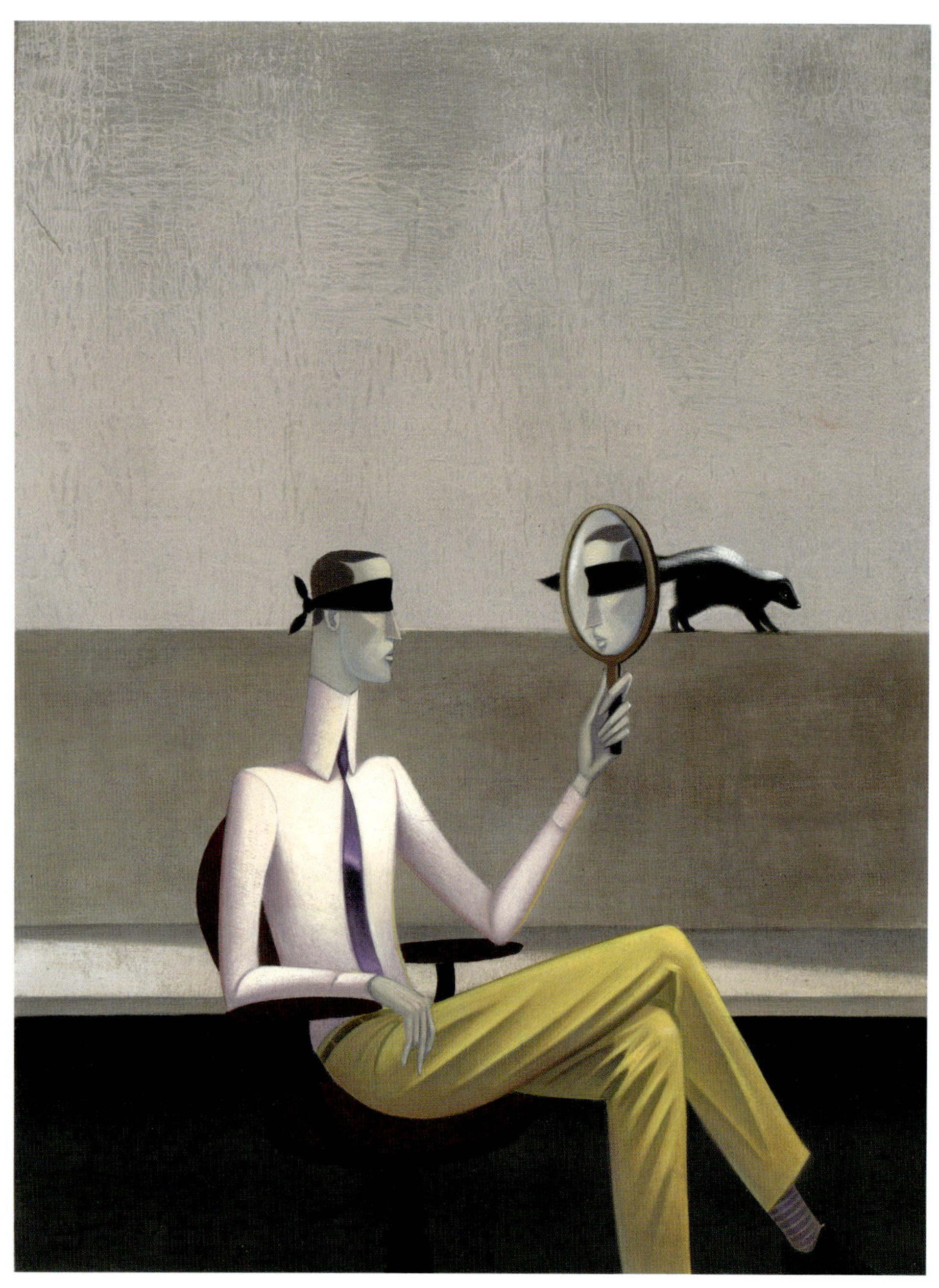

Jon Krause *www.jonkrause.com*

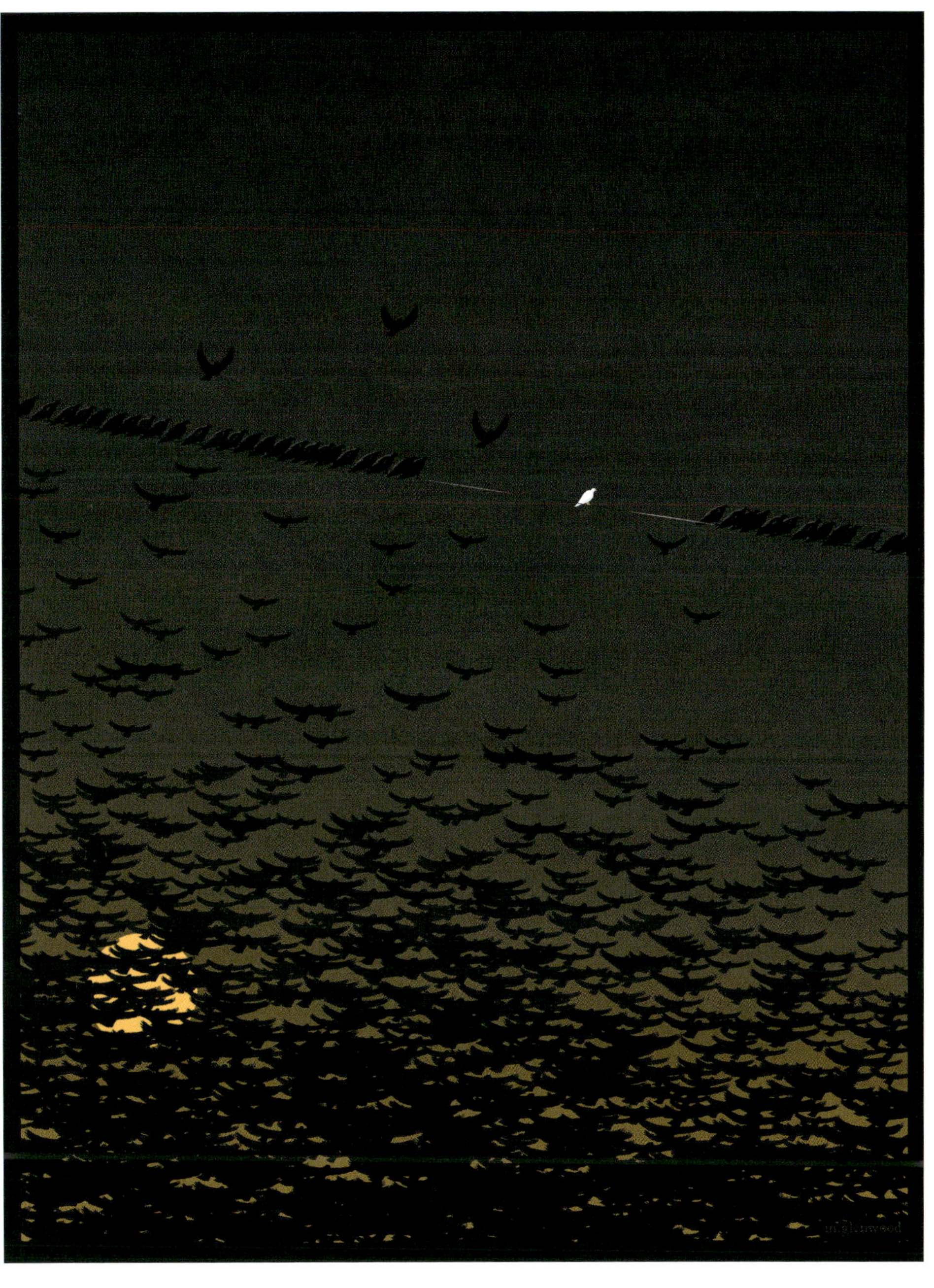

Michael Glenwood *www.mglenwood.com*

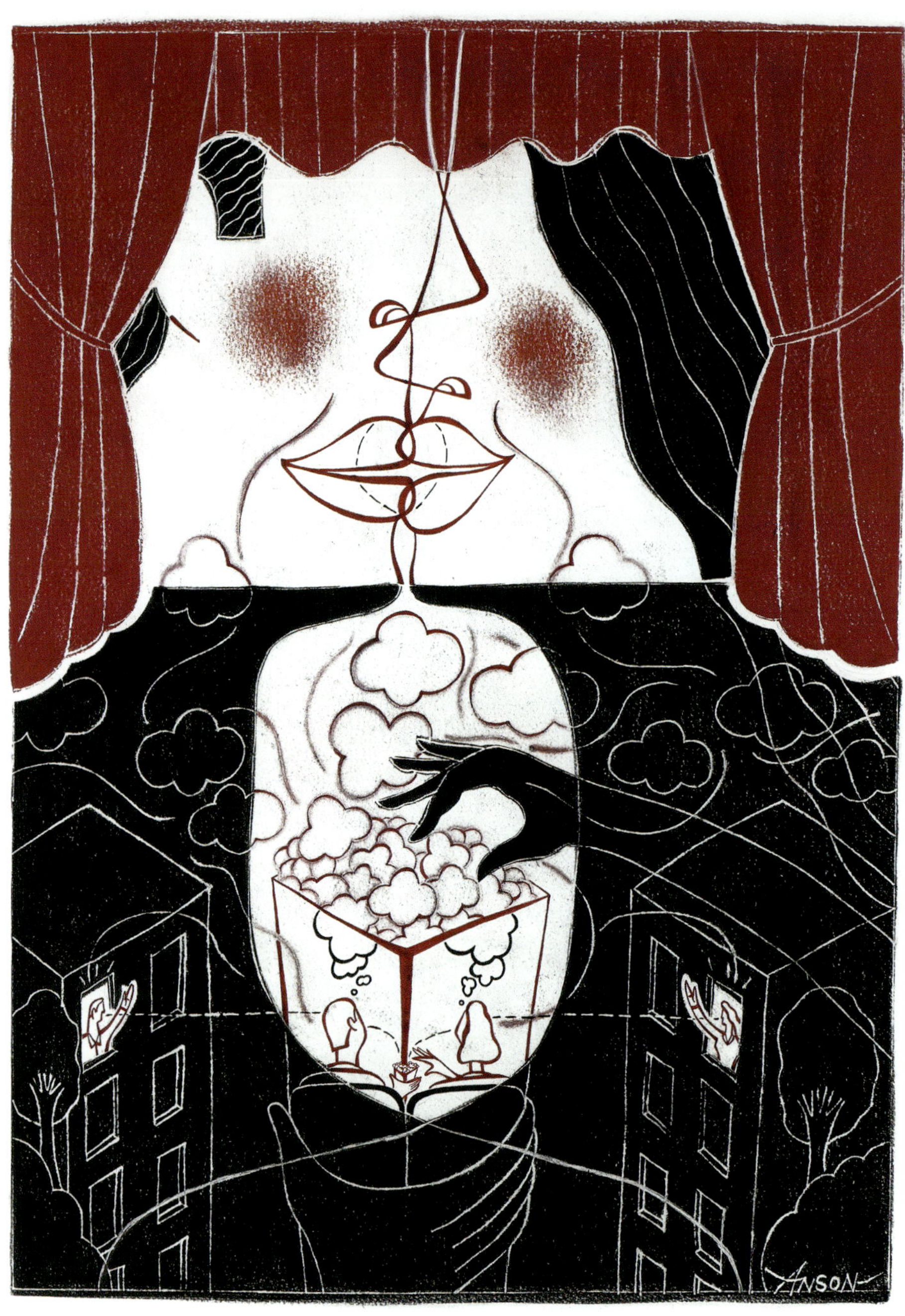

Anson Liaw *www.illoz.com/liaw*

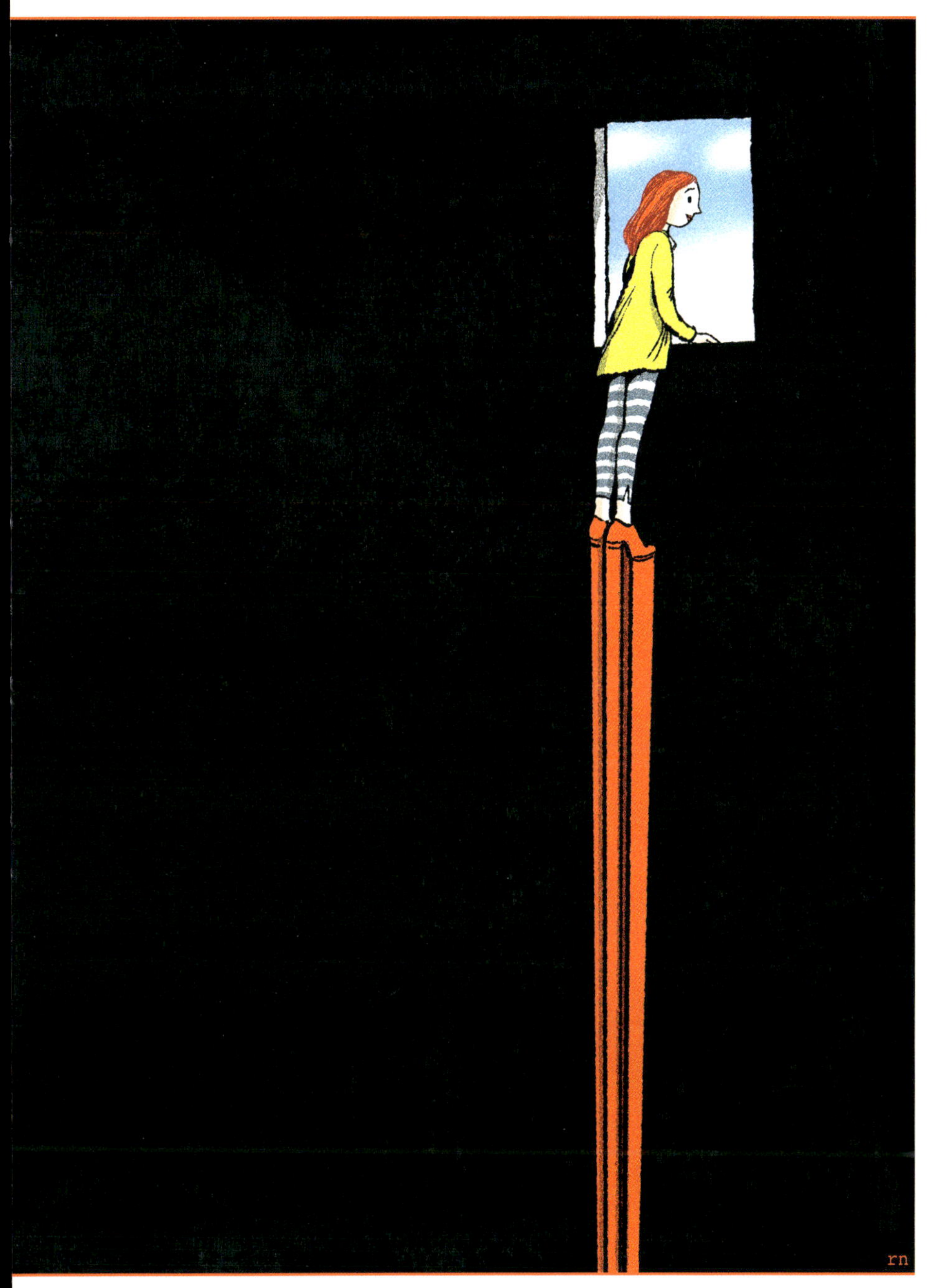

Robert Neubecker *www.neubecker.com*

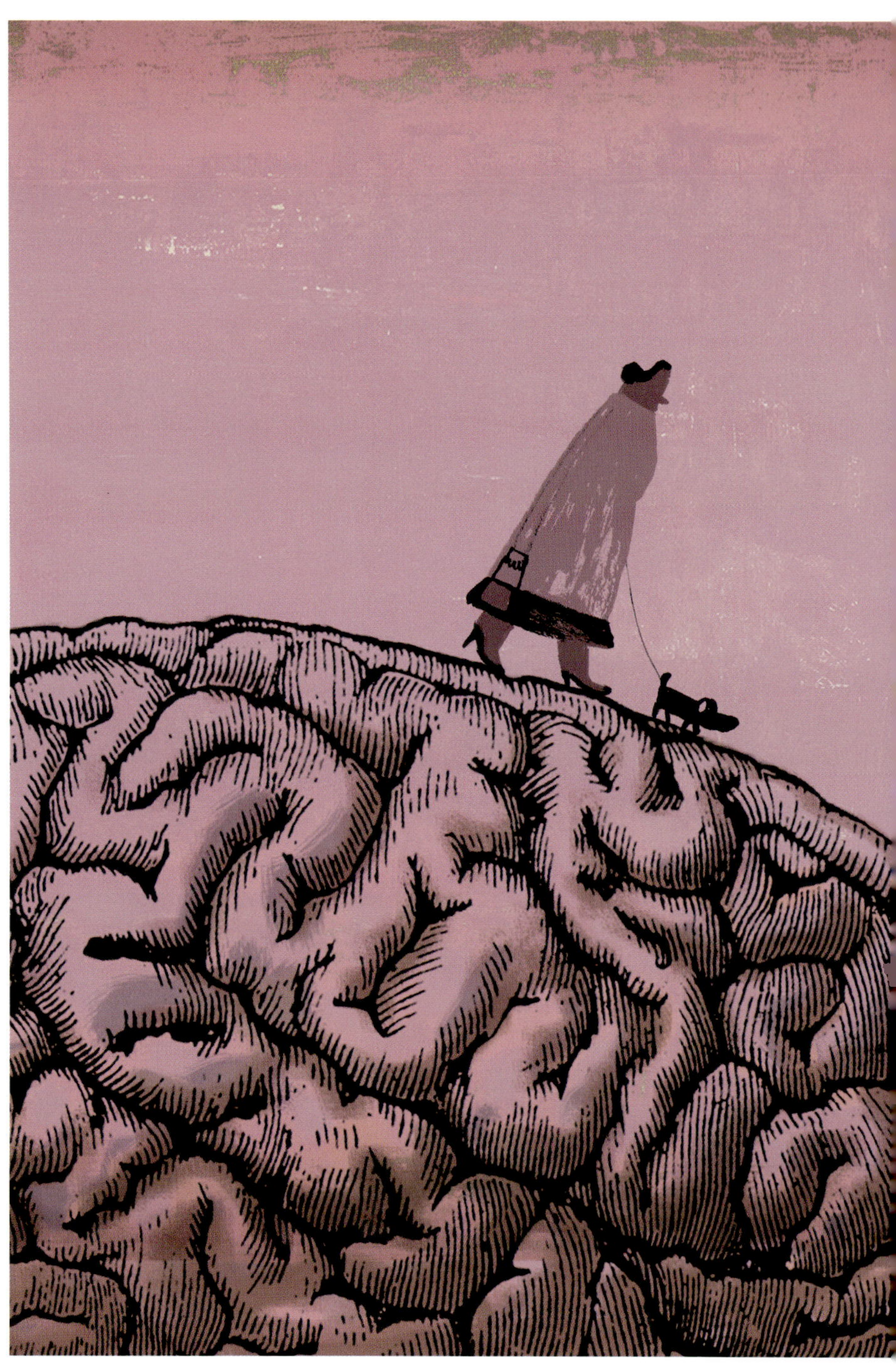

Klaas Verplancke *www.klaas.be*

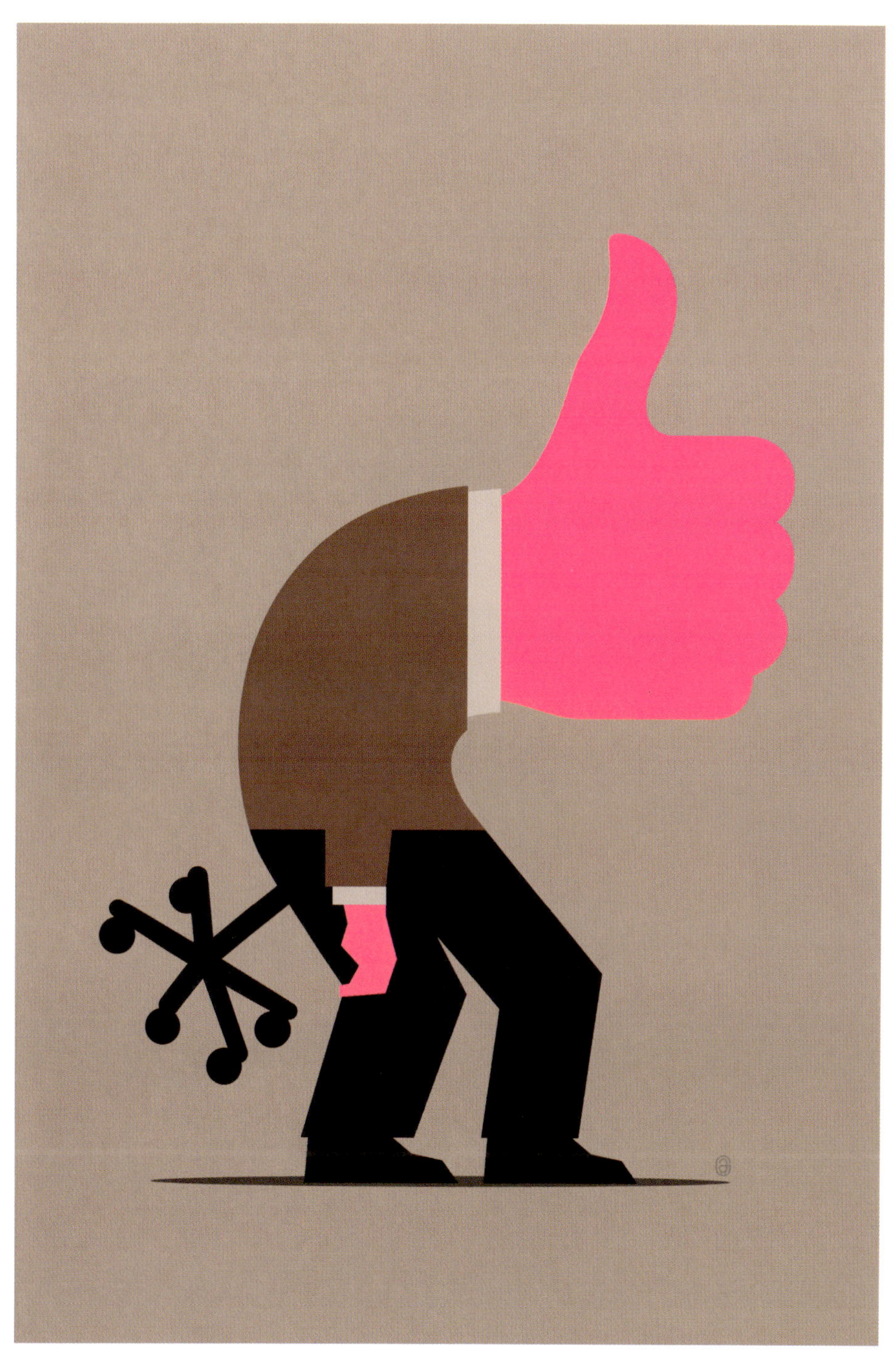

Aad Goudappel *www.aadgoudappel.com*

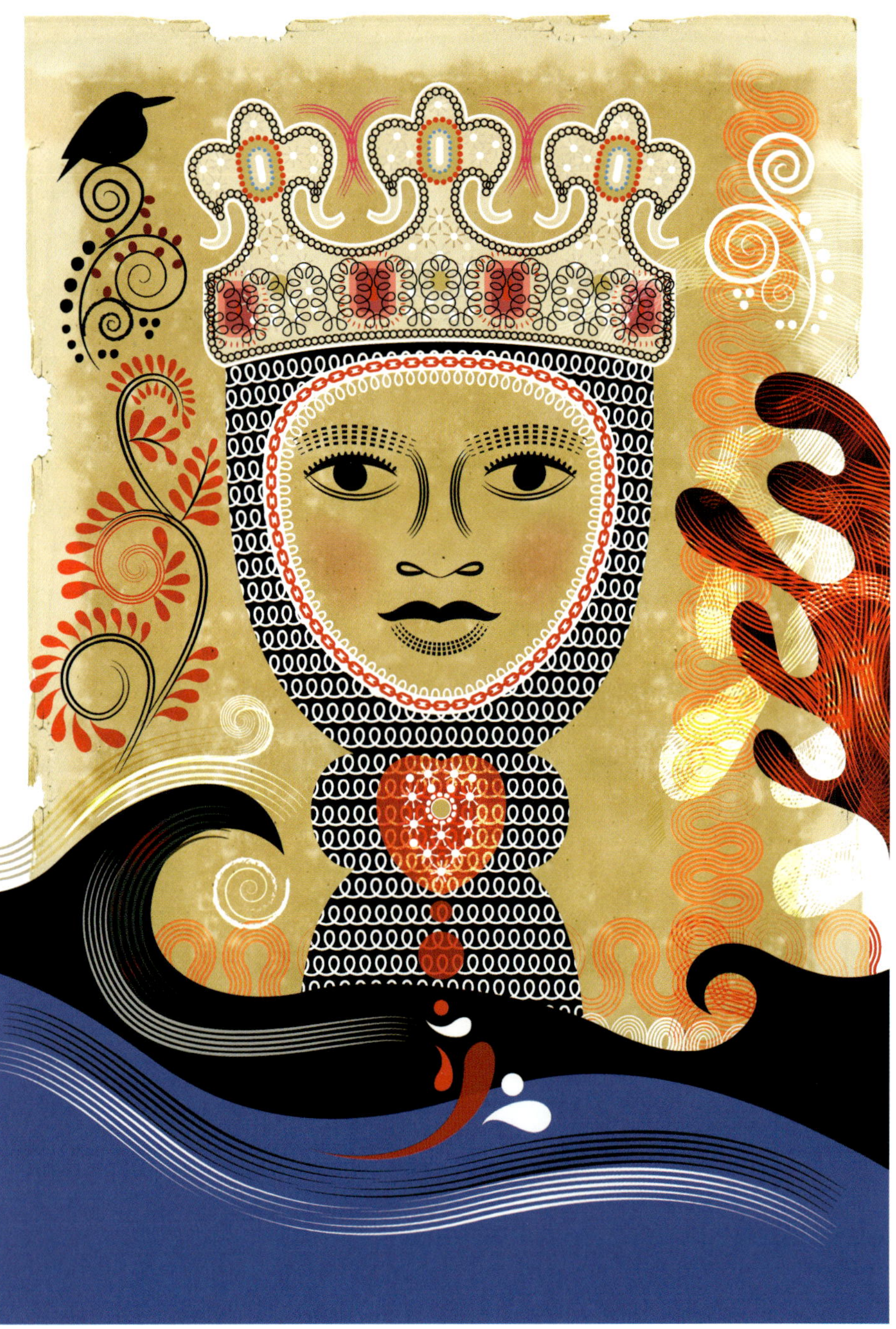

Jean Tuttle *www.jeantuttle.com*

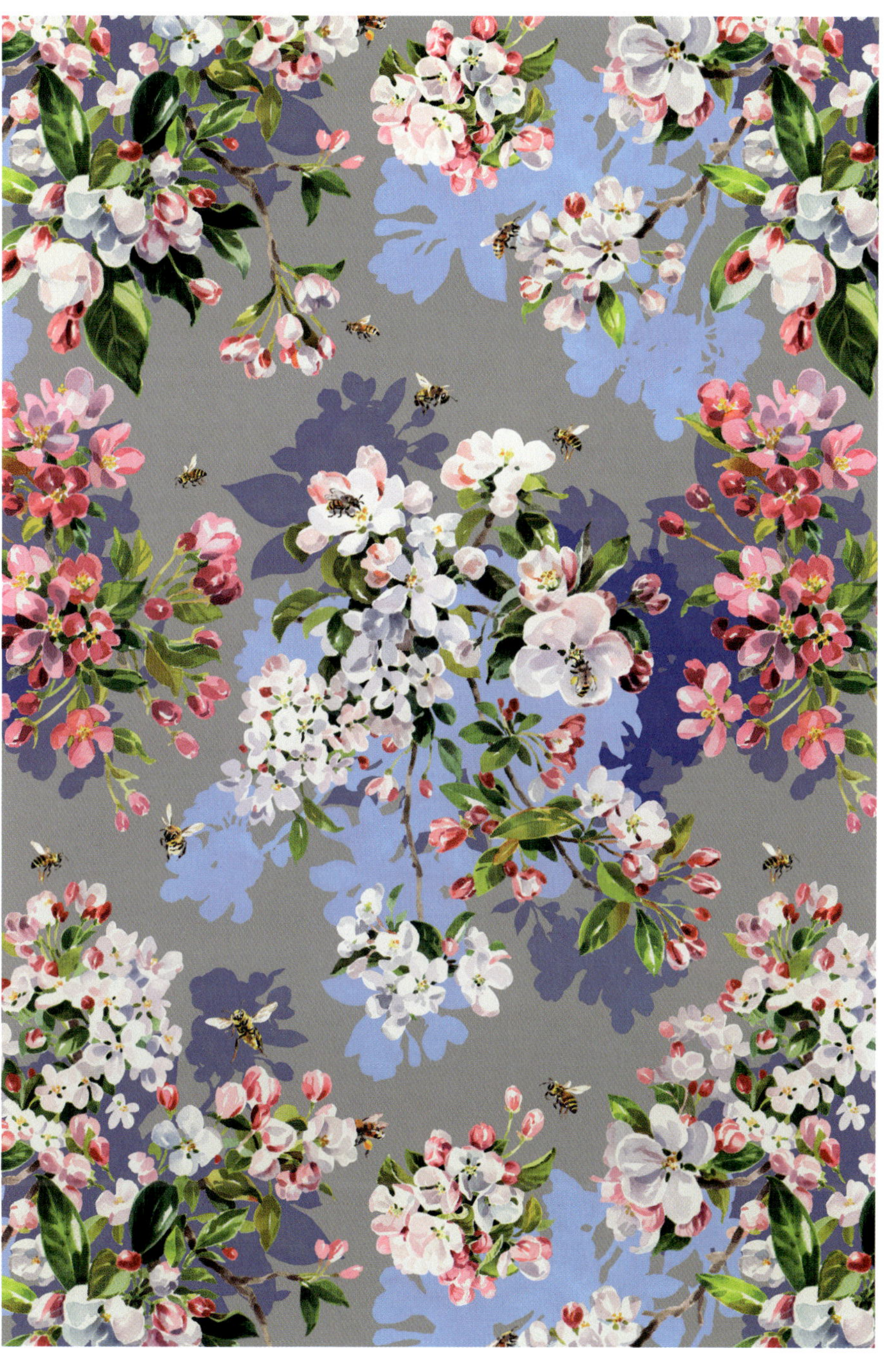

Natalya Zahn *www.natalya.com*

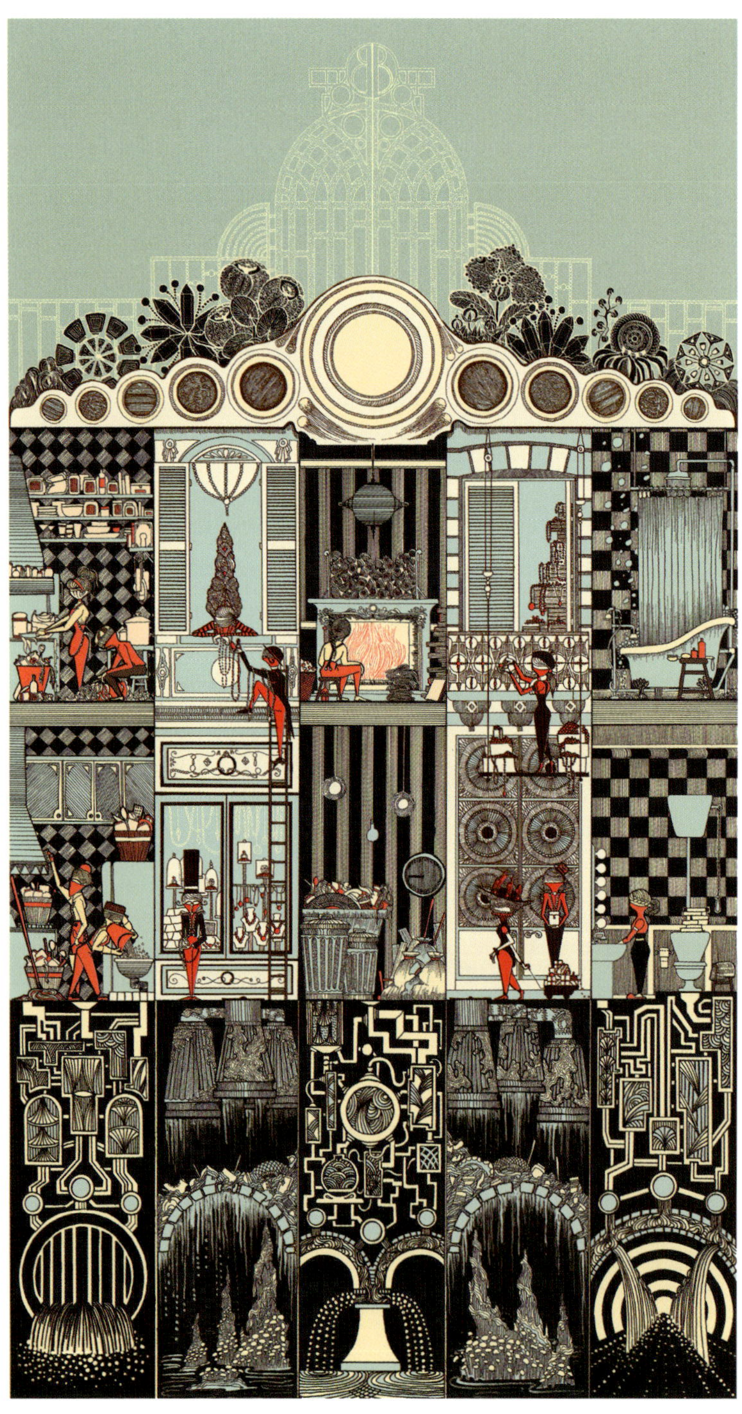

Liisa Aaltio *www.liisaaaltio.com*

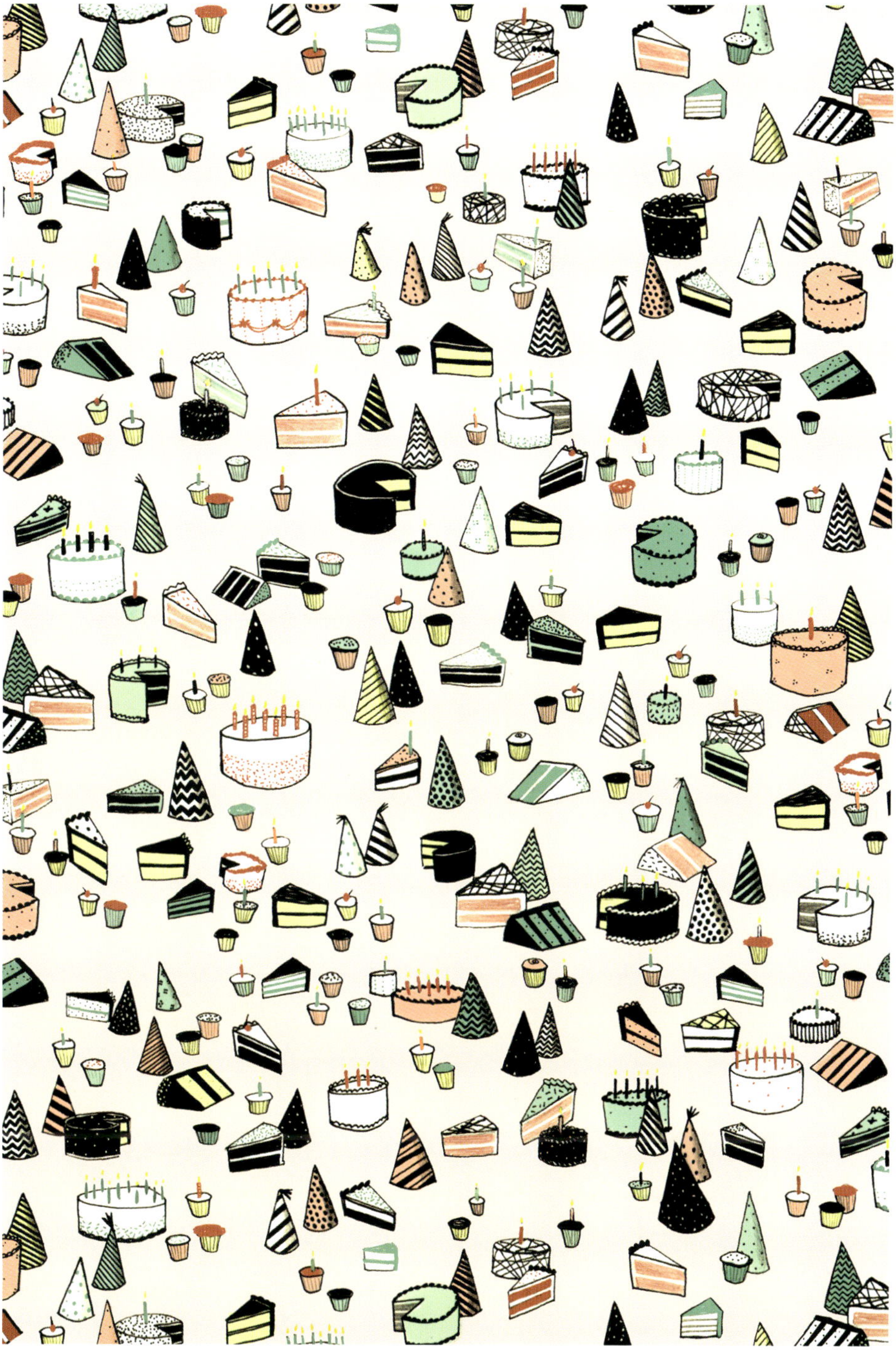

Mai Ly Degnan *www.mailydegnan.com*

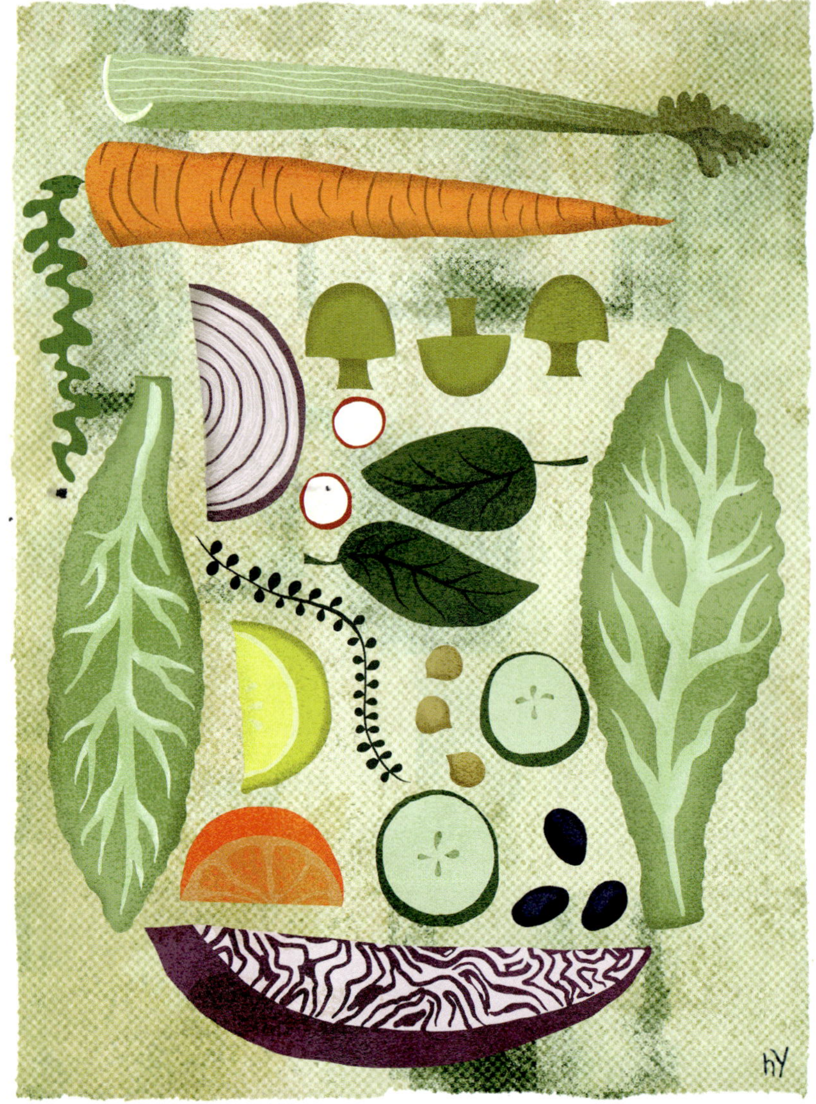

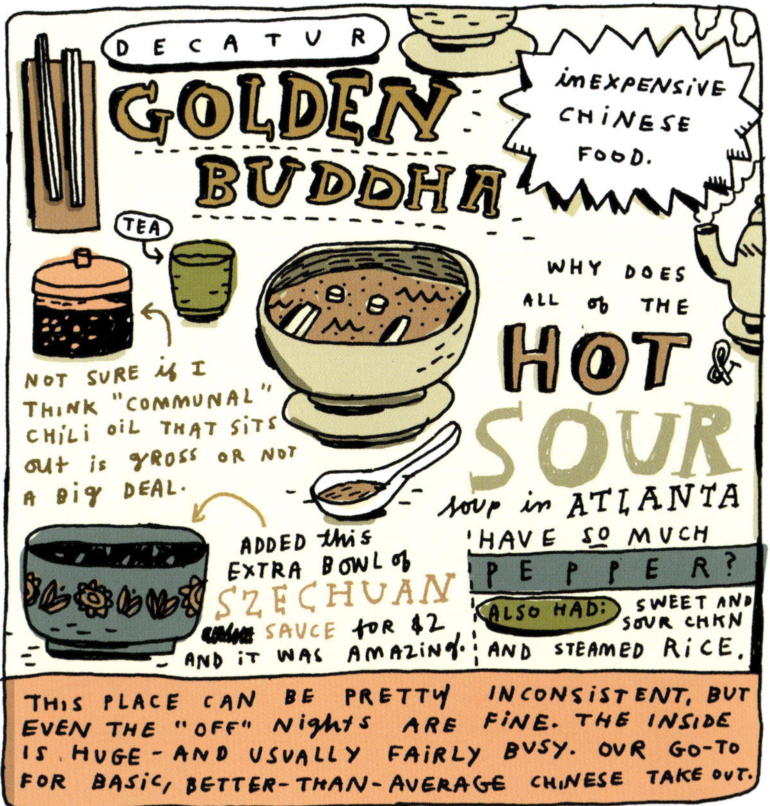

Mike Lowery *www.argyleacademy.com*

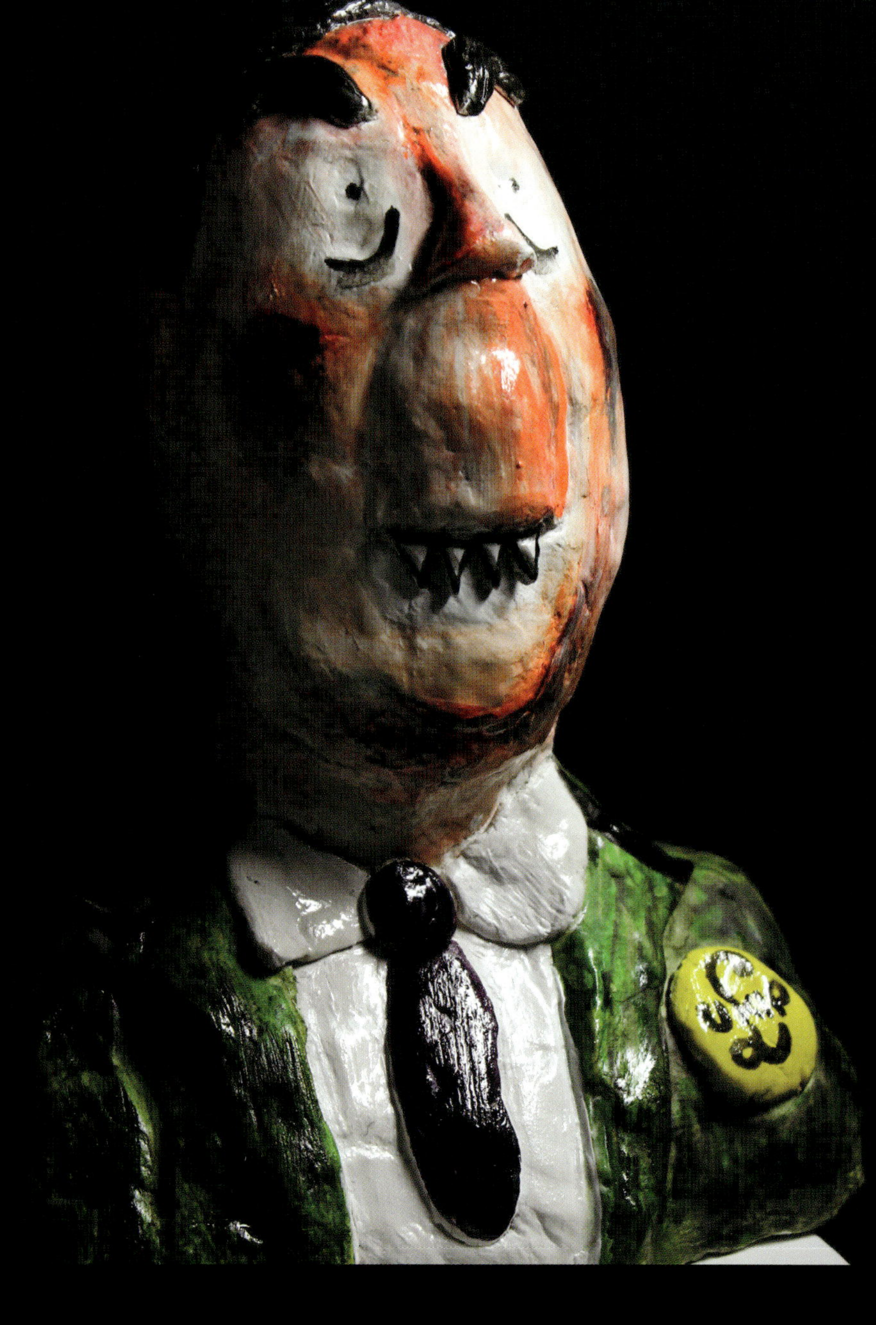

Holly Macdonald *www.hollymacdonald.co.uk*

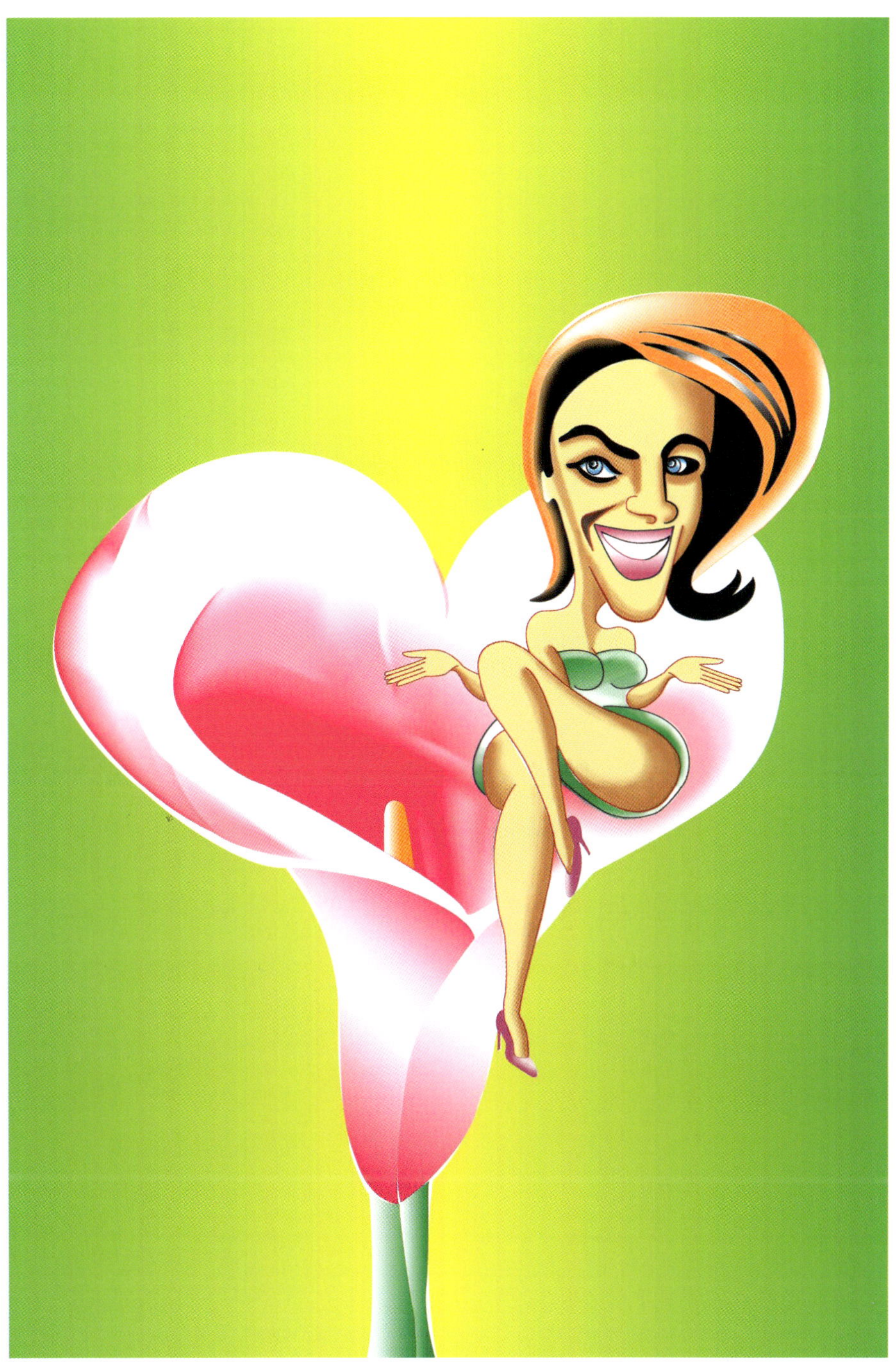

Urs J. Knobel *www.ursjknobel-art.ch*

104

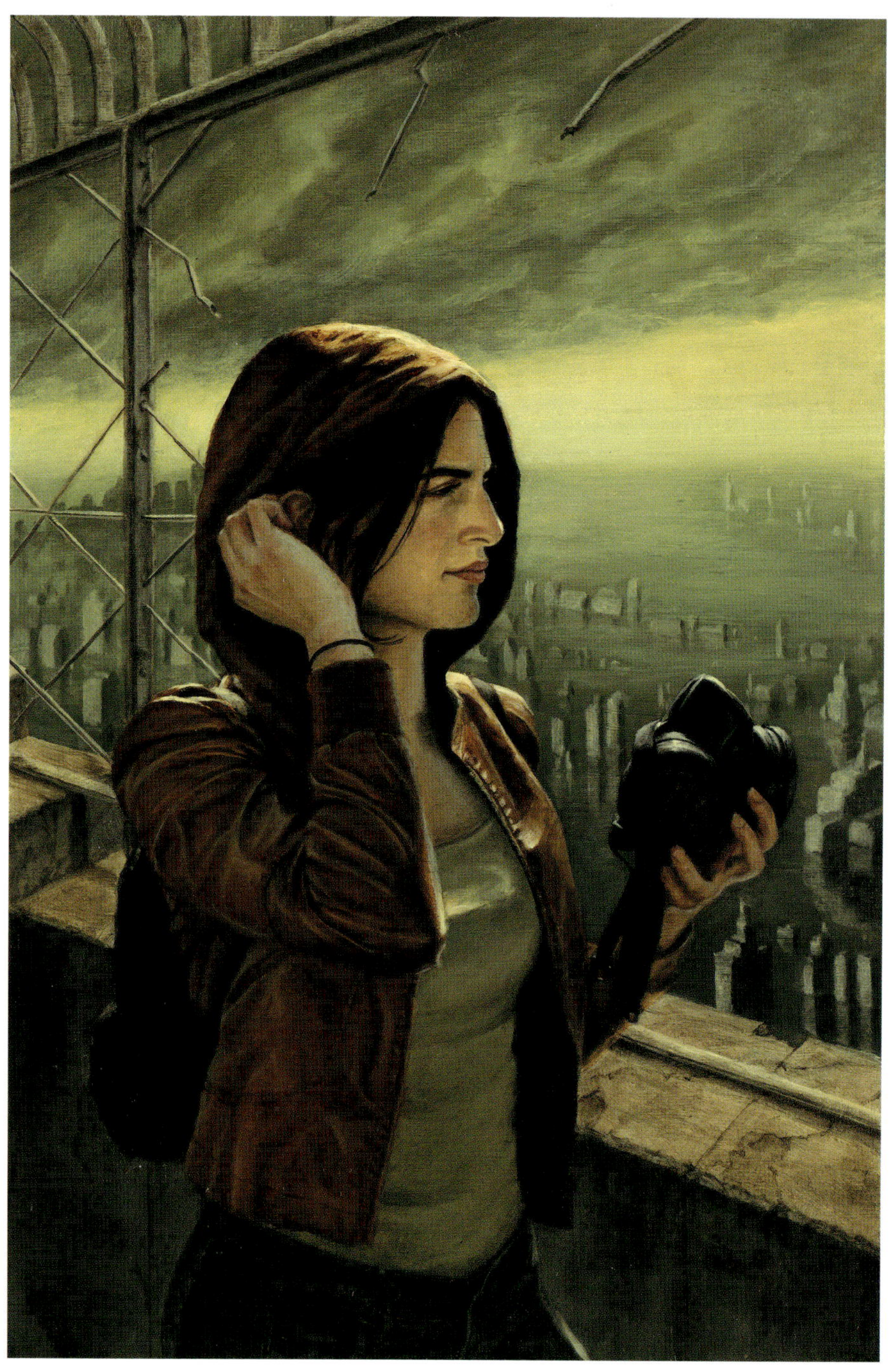

Nicholas Elias *www.eliasartstudio.com*

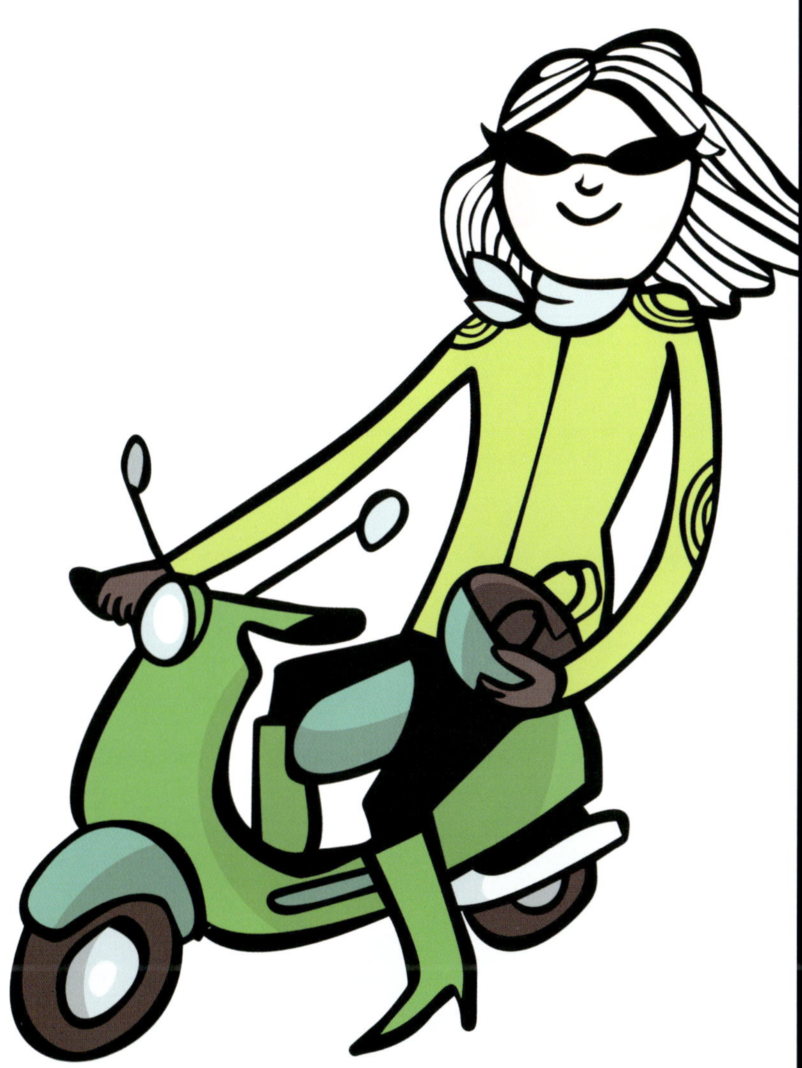

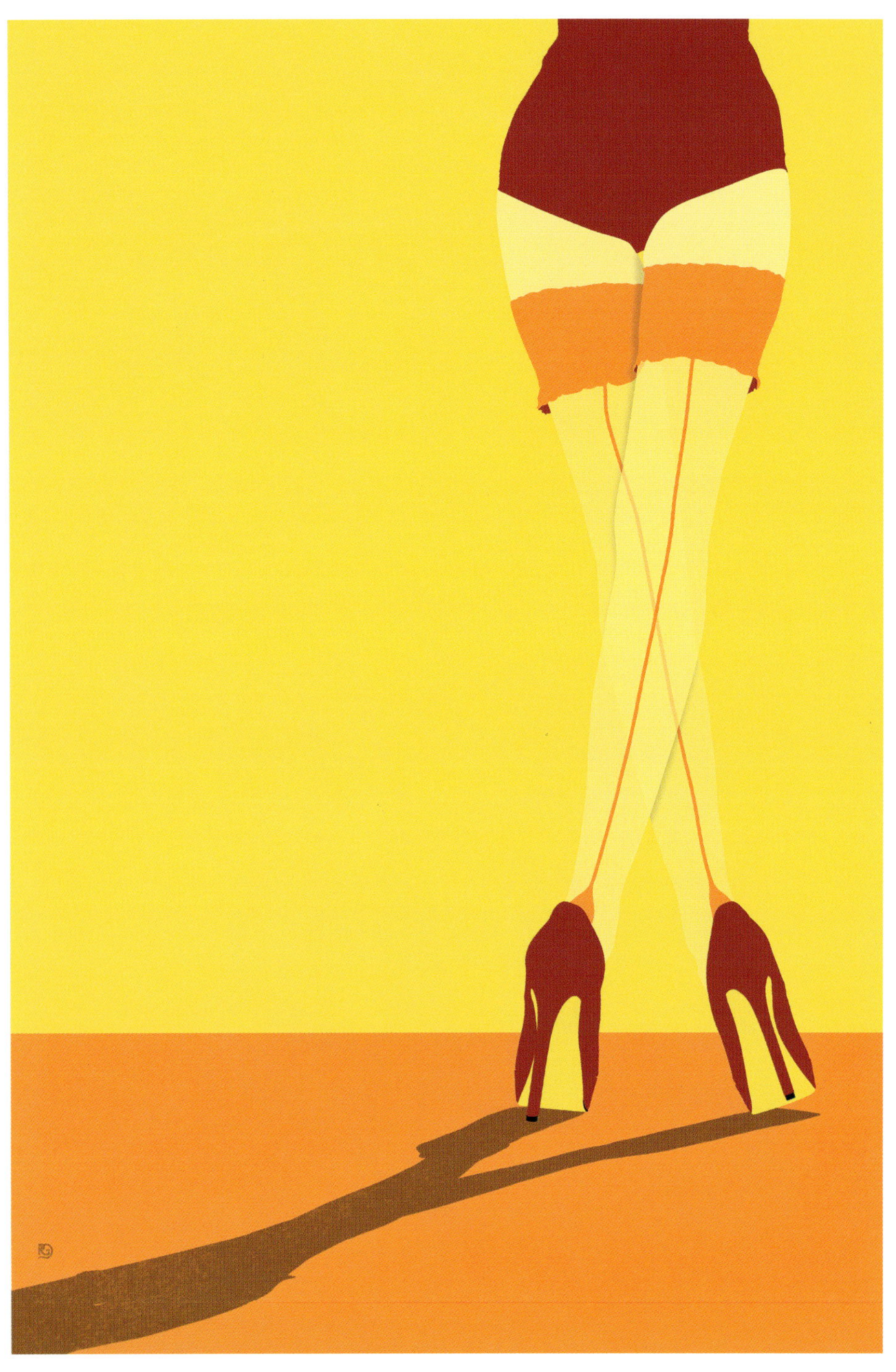

Paul Garland *www.paul-garland.com*

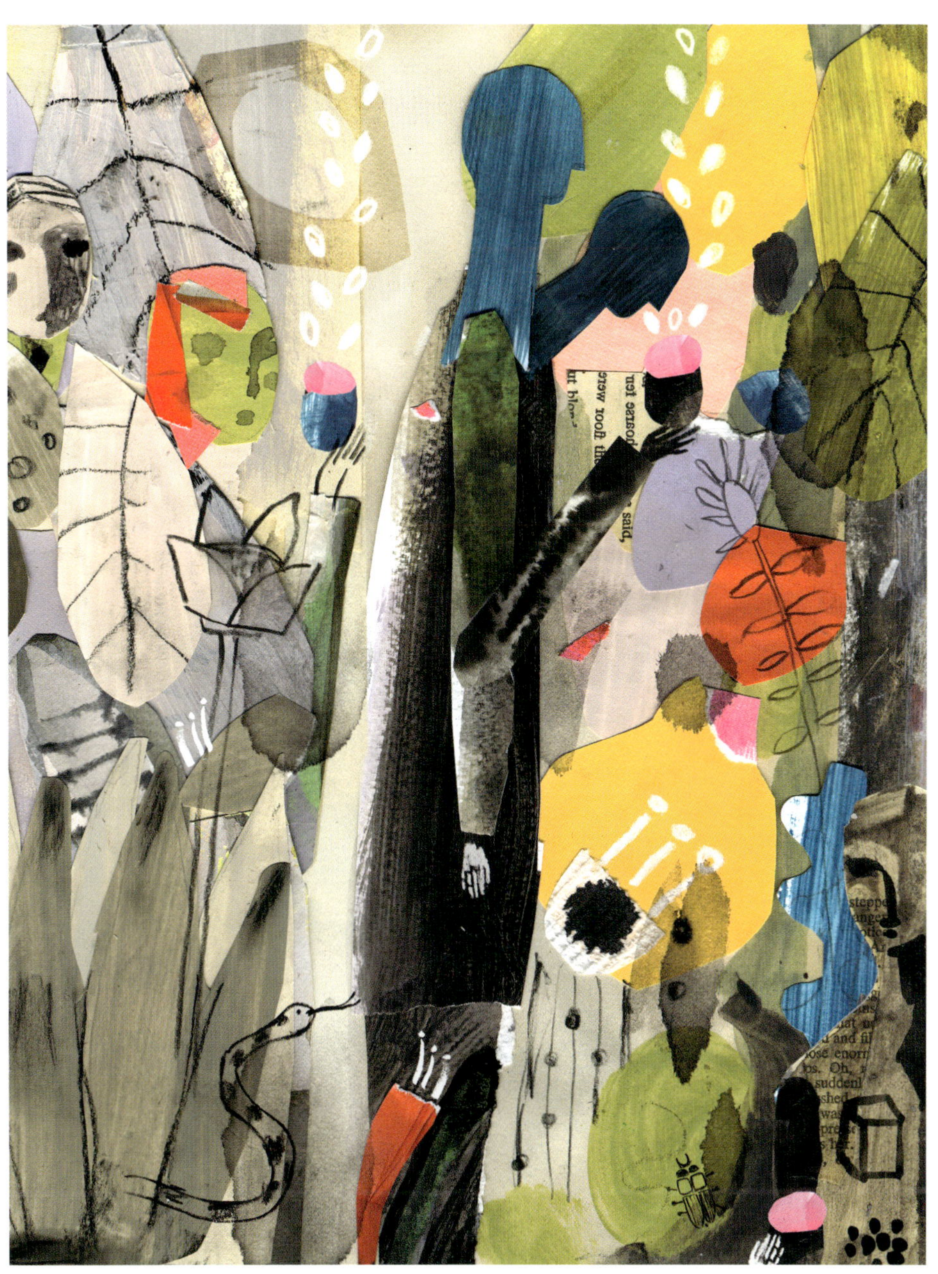

Andrea D'Aquino *www.andreadaquino.com*

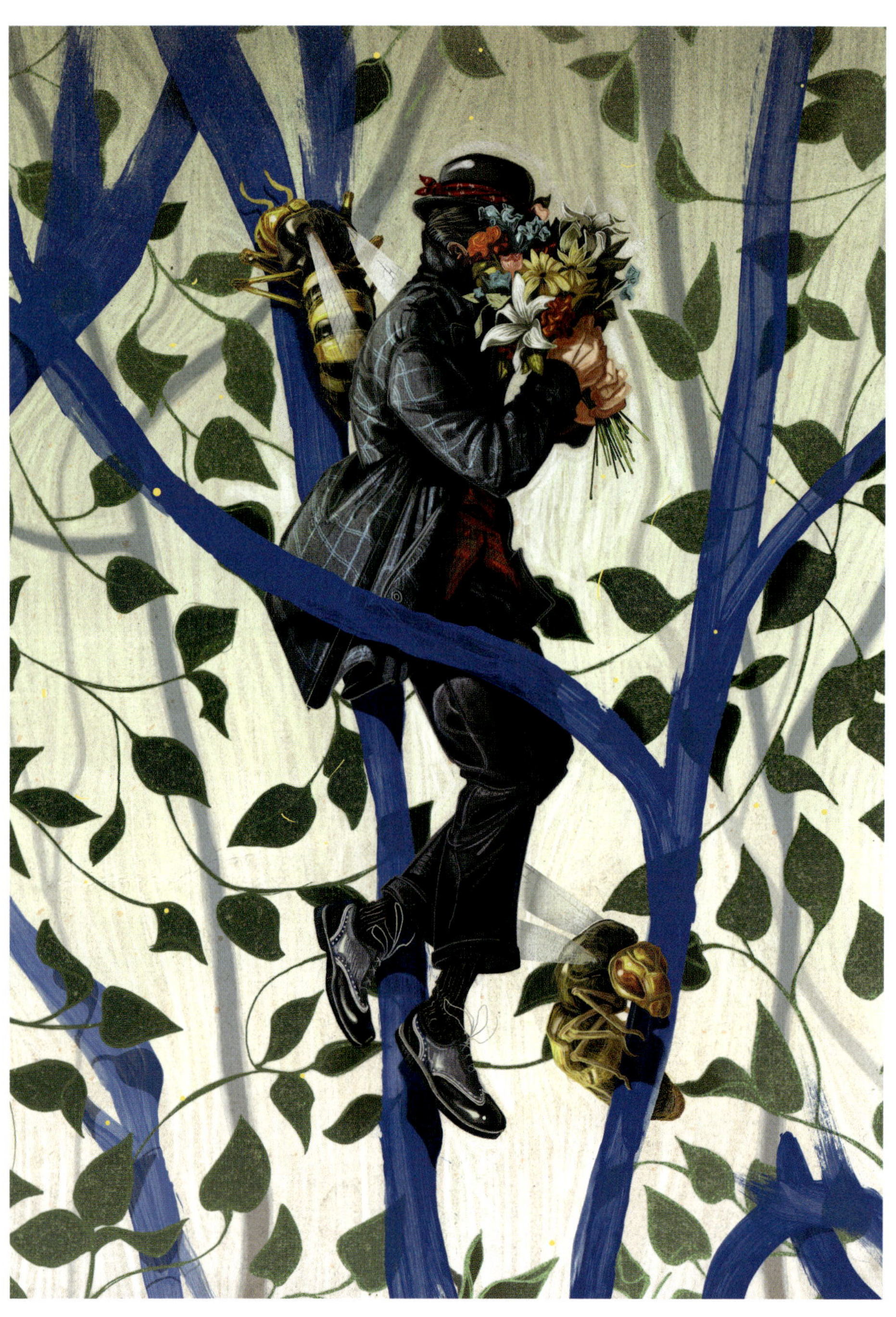

Jonathan Bartlett *www.bartlettstudio.com*

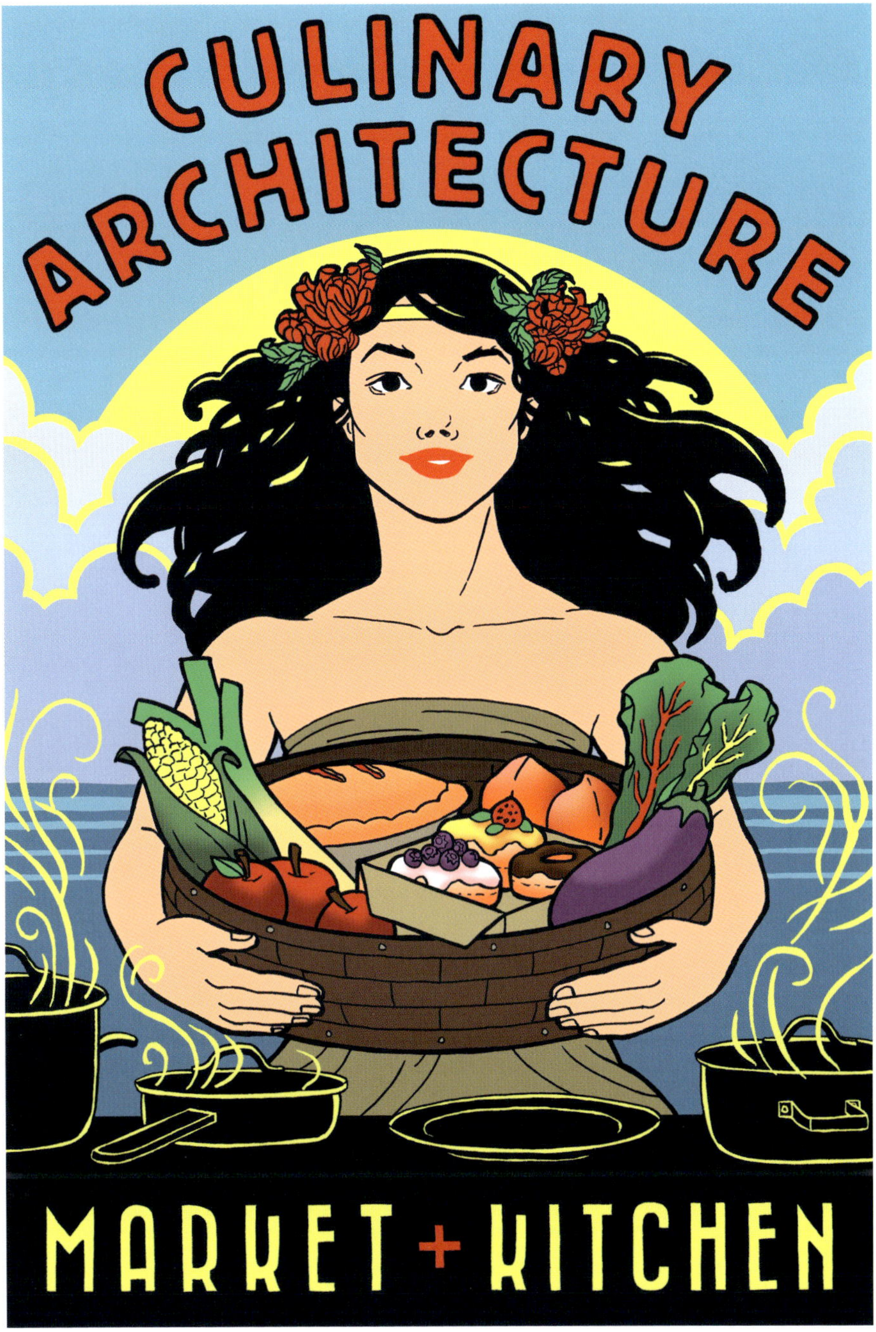

Julia Minamata *www.juliaminamata.com*

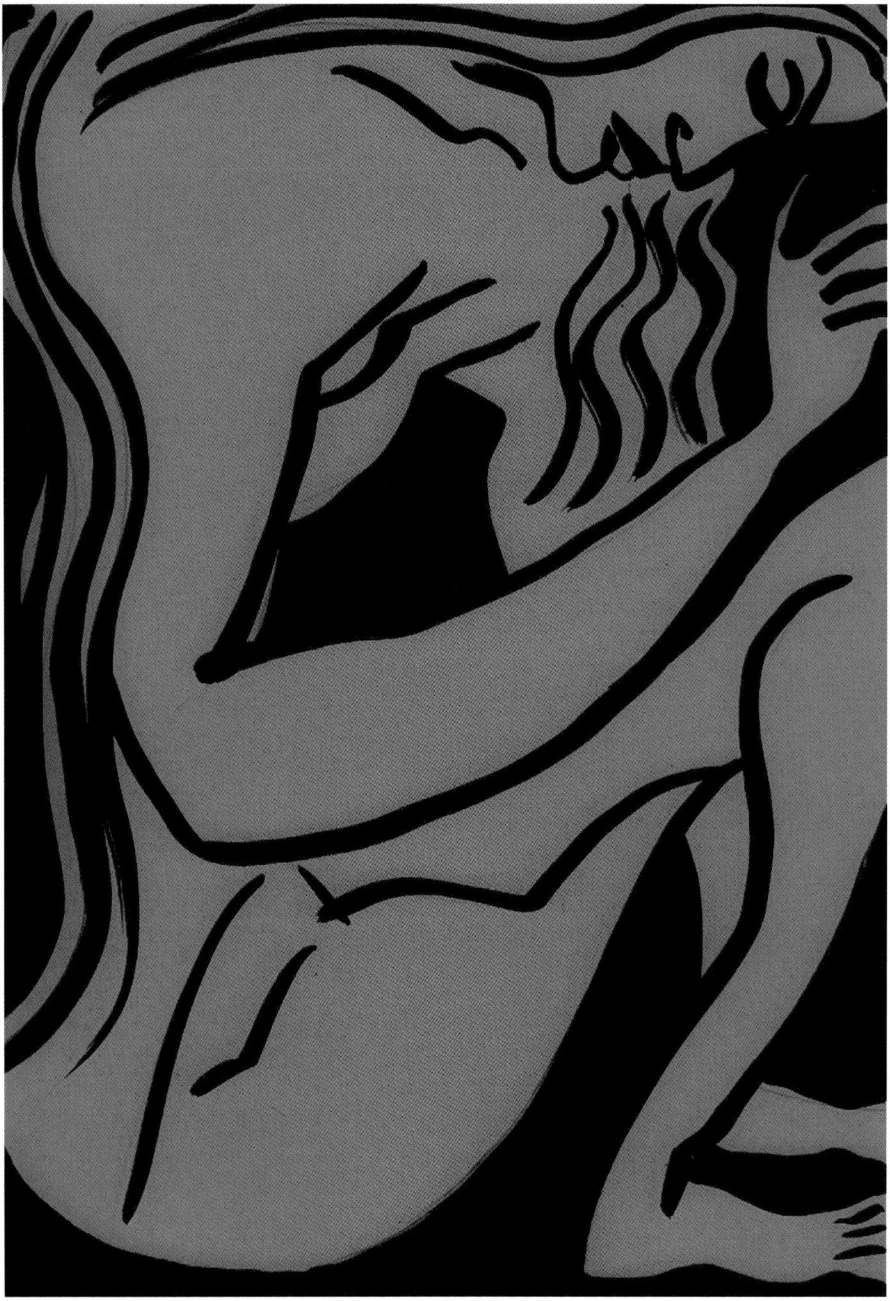

Gary Wright *www.supera4illustration.dunked.com*

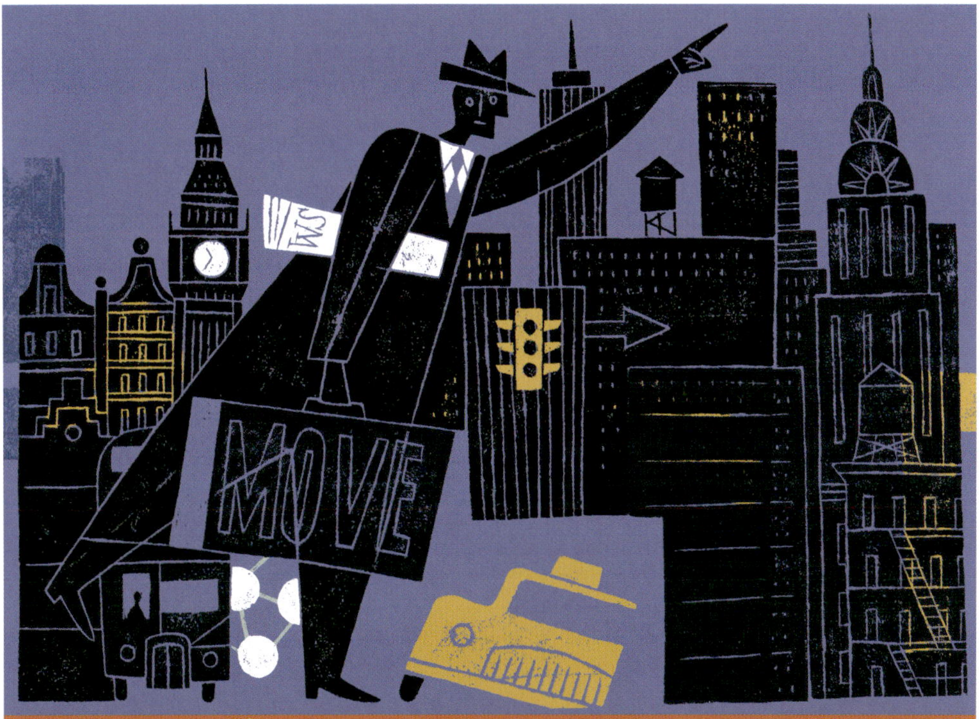

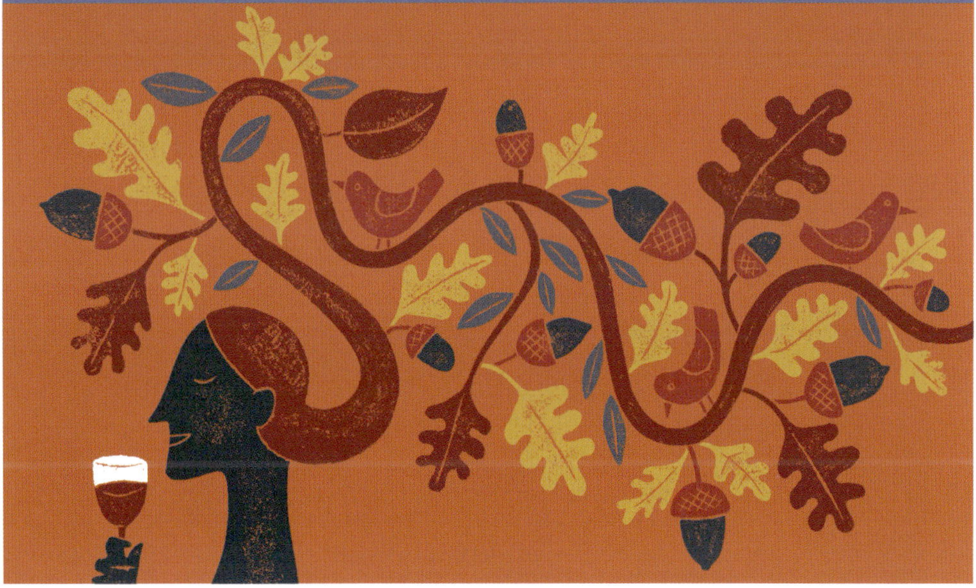

Jean-Manuel Duvivier *www.jmduvivier.com*

112

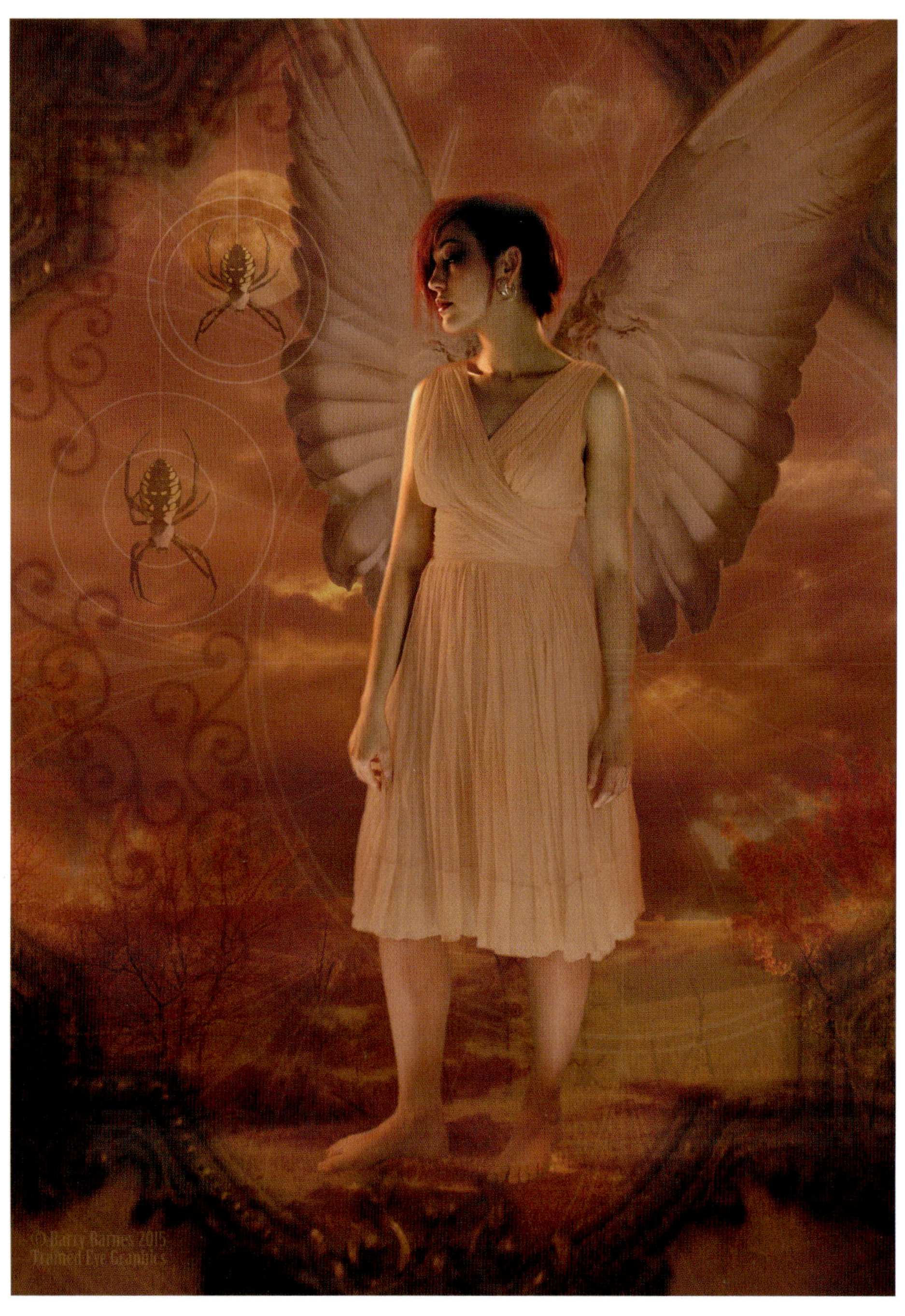

Barry Barnes *www.trainedeyegraphics.com*

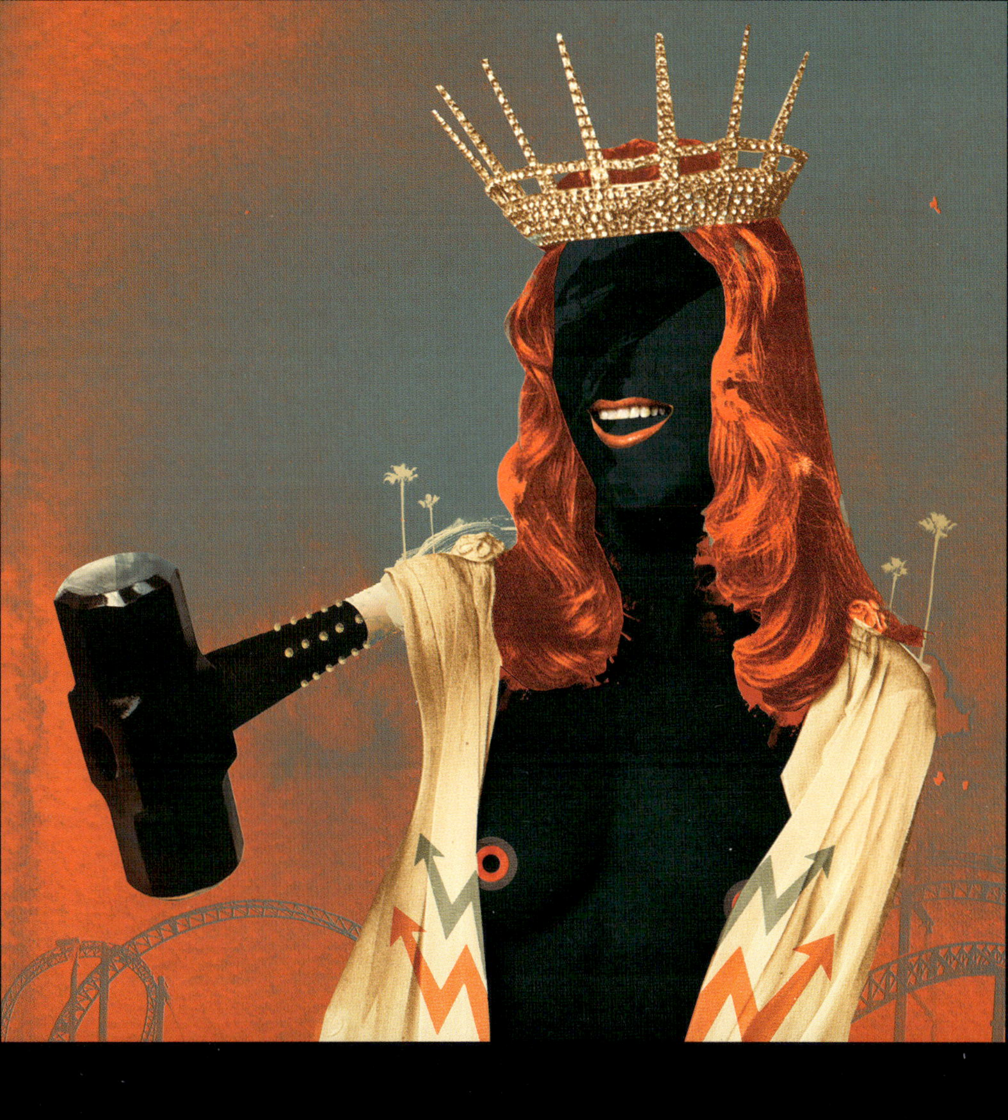

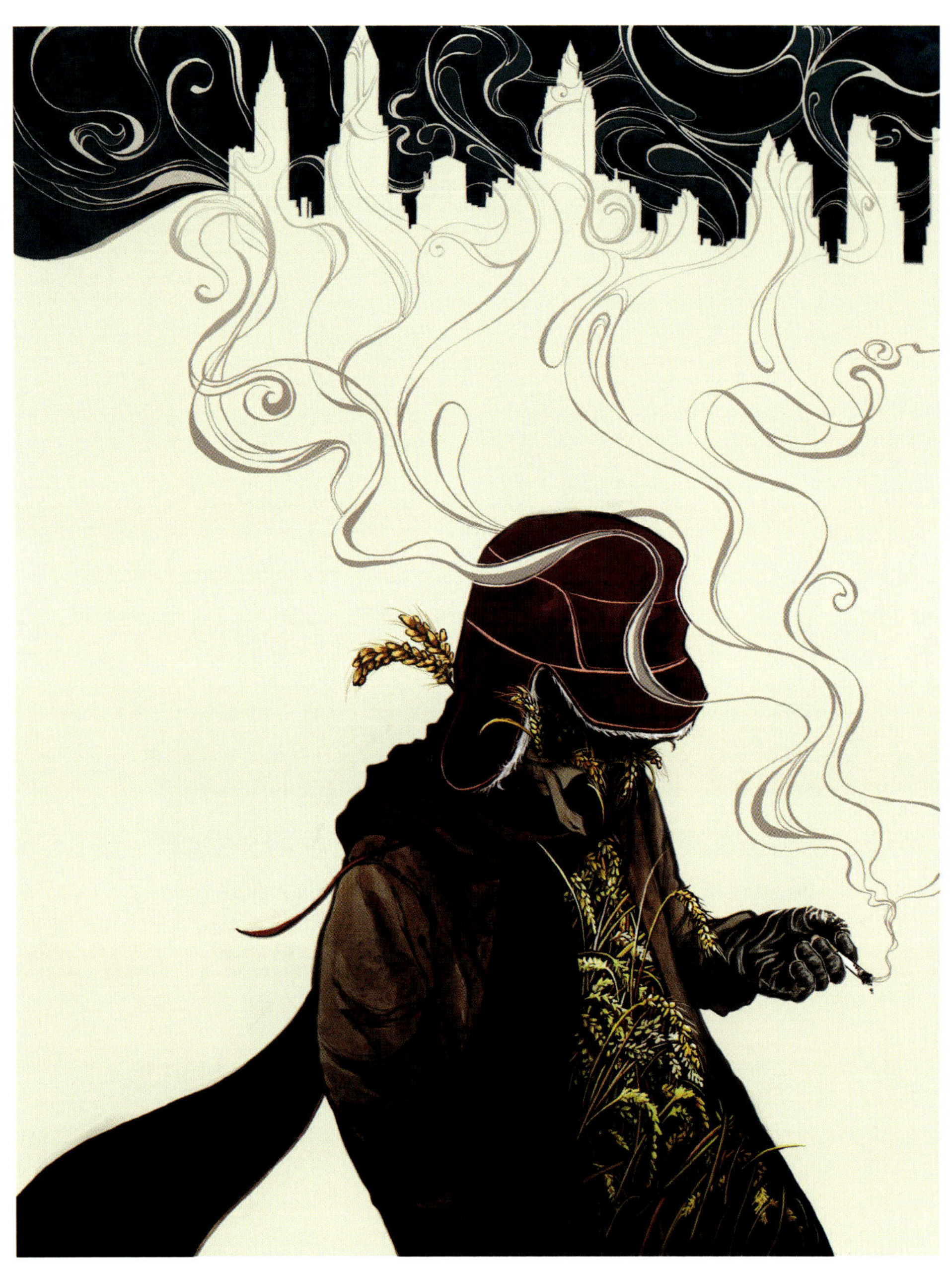

Daria Theodora *www.xintheodora.com*

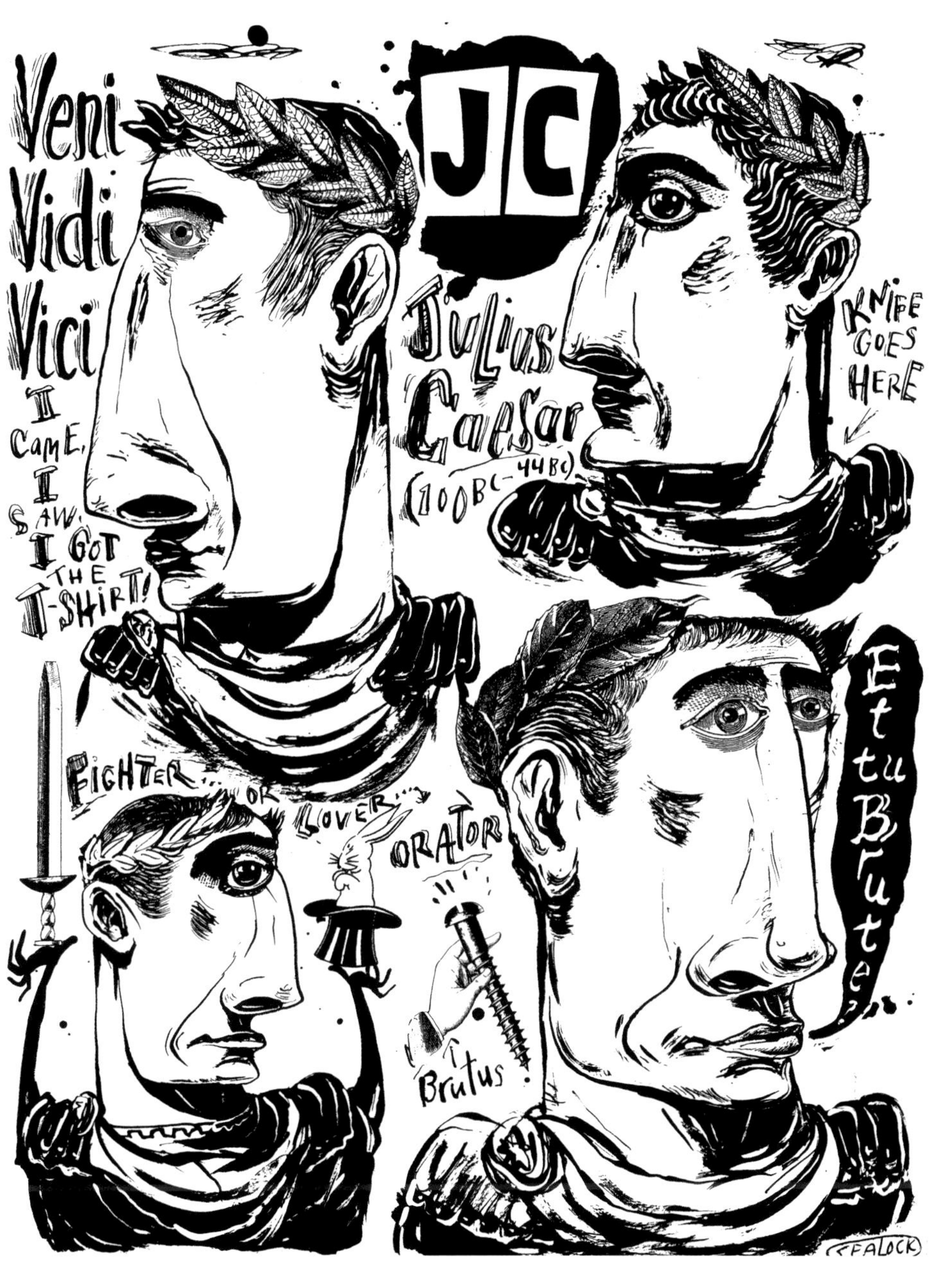
Veni
Vidi
Vici
I CAME, I SAW, I GOT THE T-SHIRT!
JC
Julius Caesar
(100BC - 44BC)
KNIFE GOES HERE
FIGHTER... OR LOVER...
ORATOR
Brutus
Et tu Brute...
SEALOCK

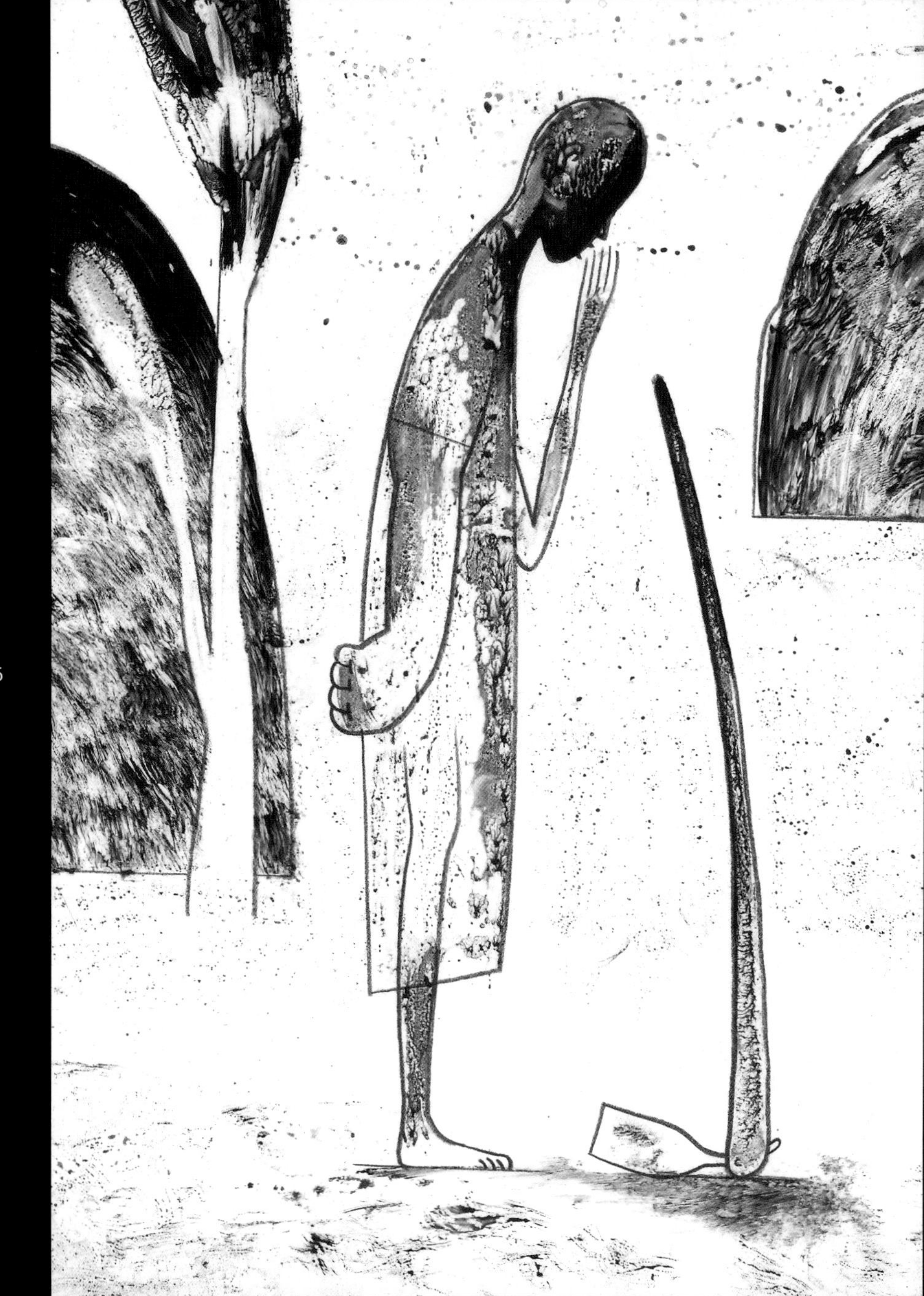

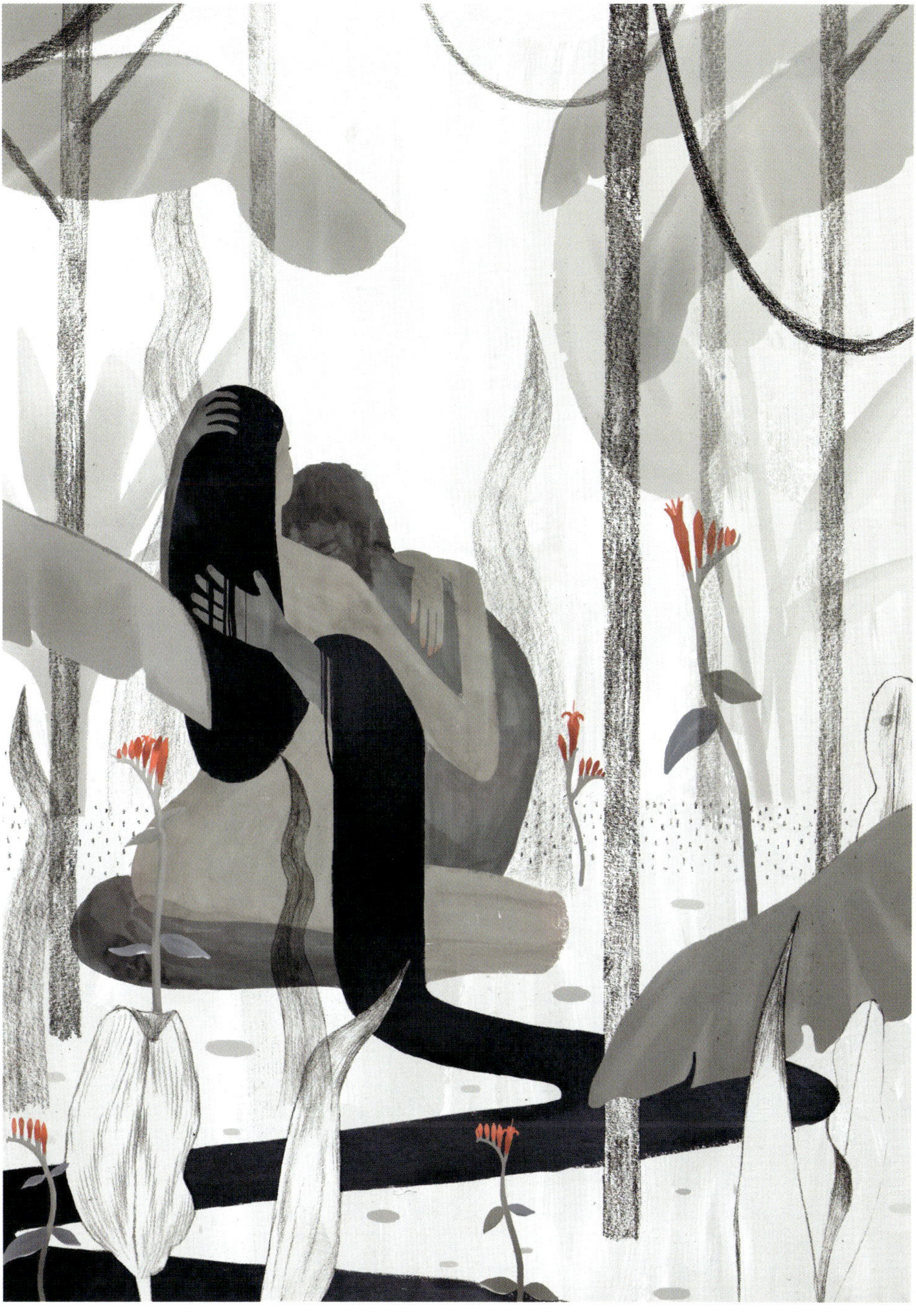

Xiaohua Yang *www.yxhart.me*

Man-Tsun Tsang *www.manxtsun.com*

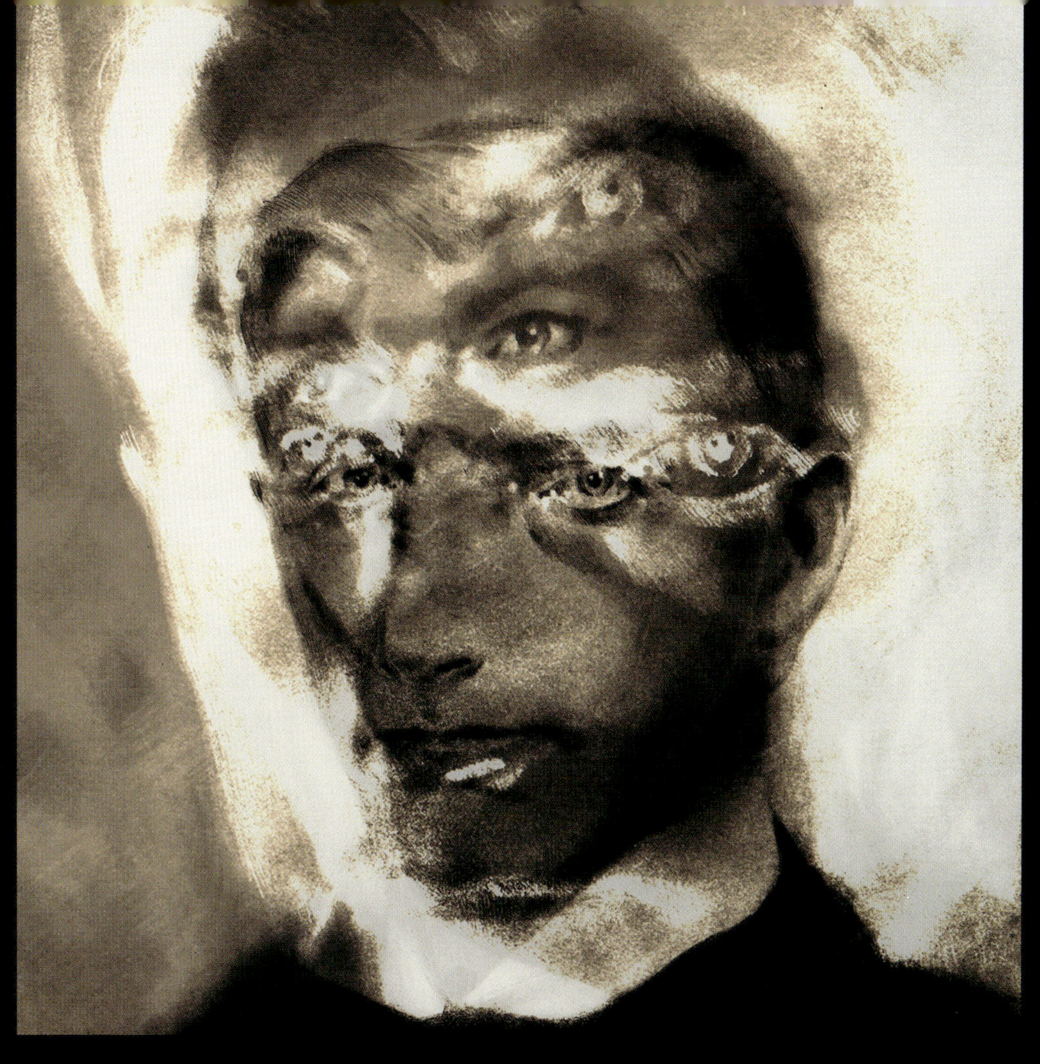

Taylor Wessling *www.taylorwessling.com*

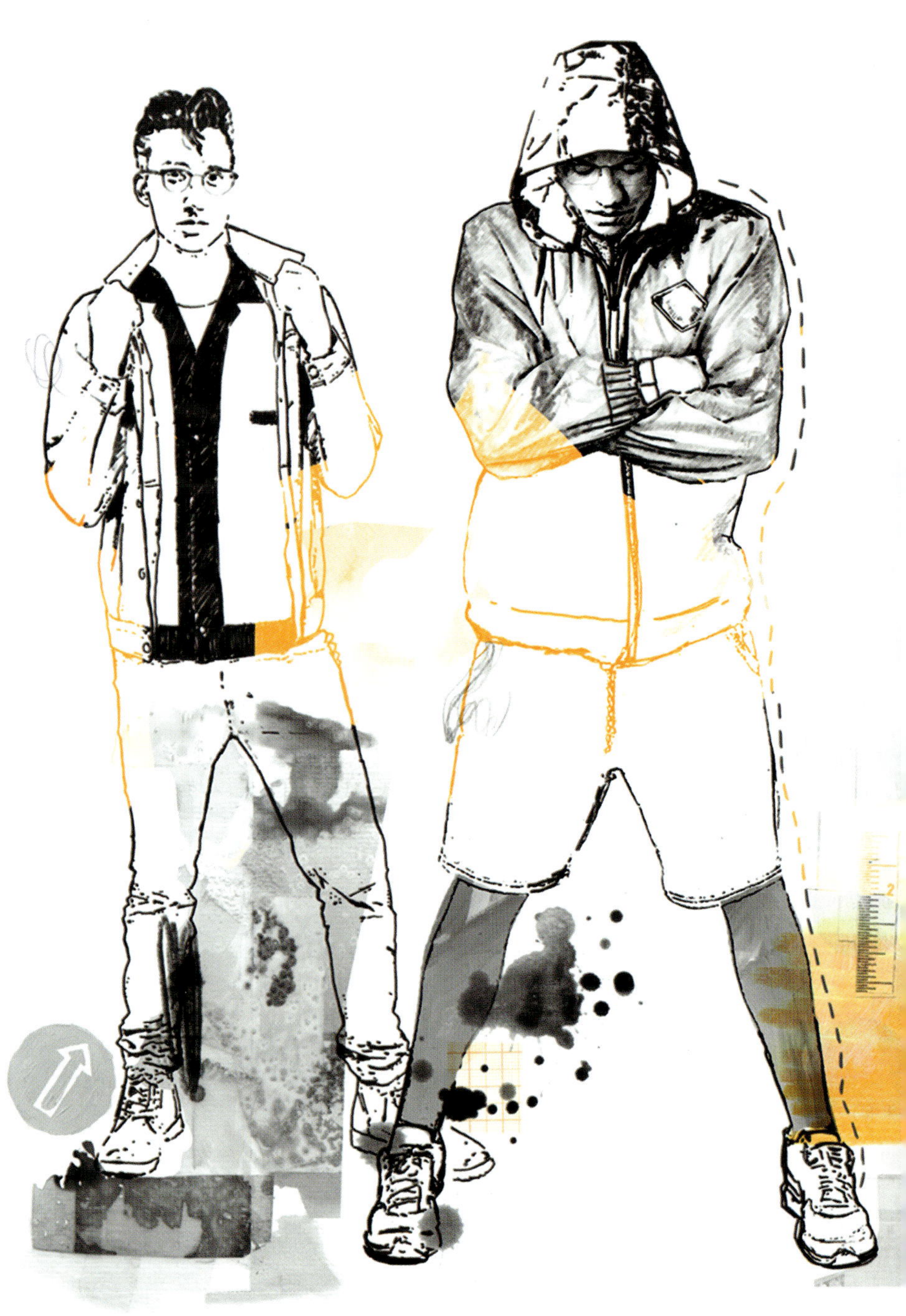

Tina Zellmer *www.tinazellmer.com*

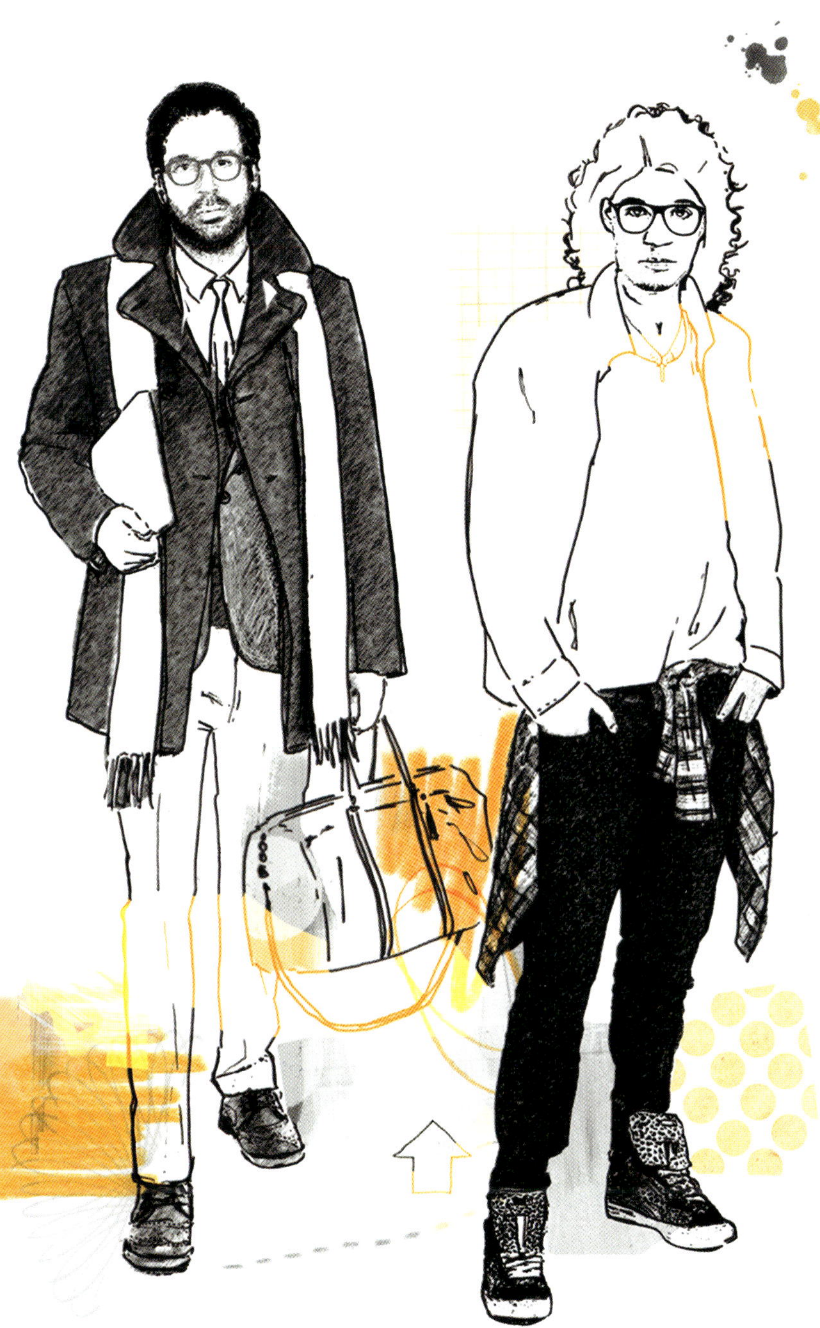

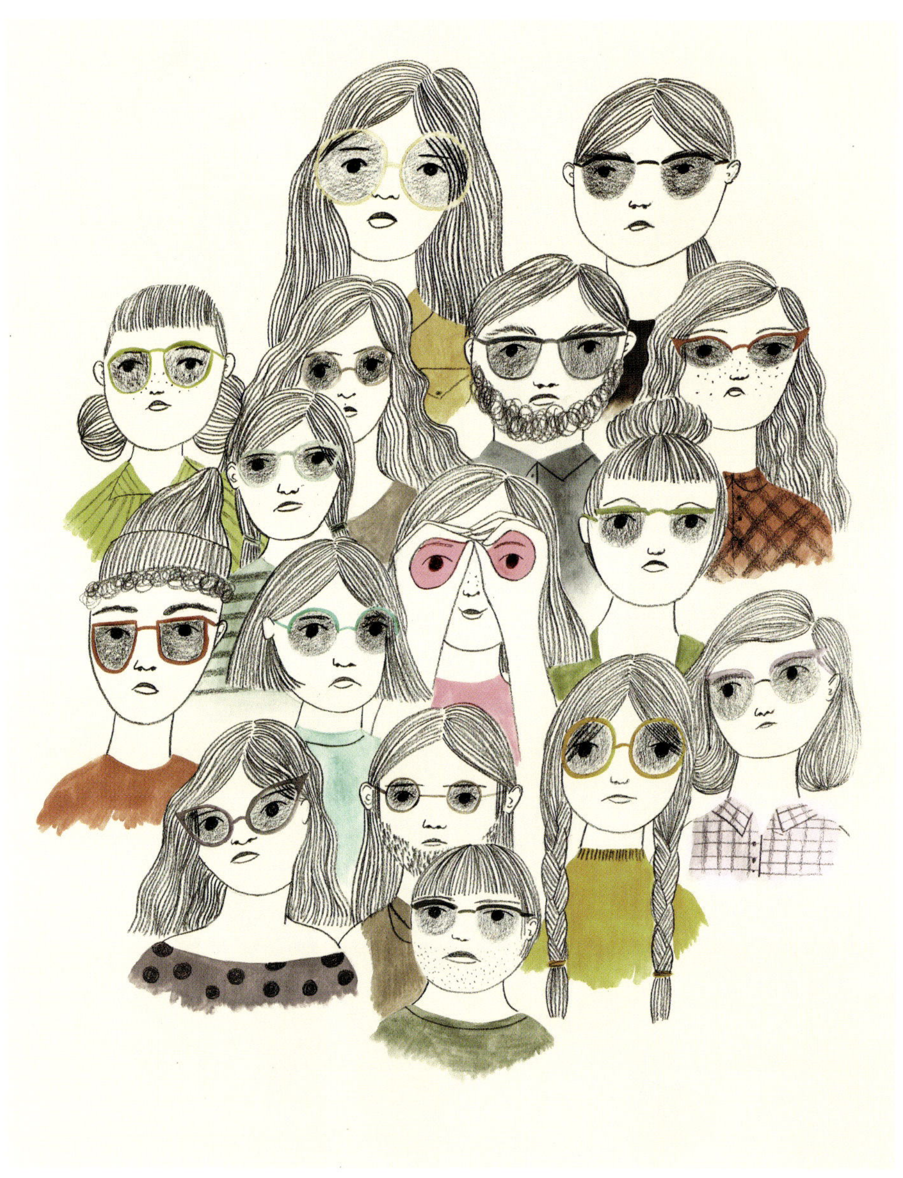

Chelsea O'Byrne *www.chelseaobyrne.com*

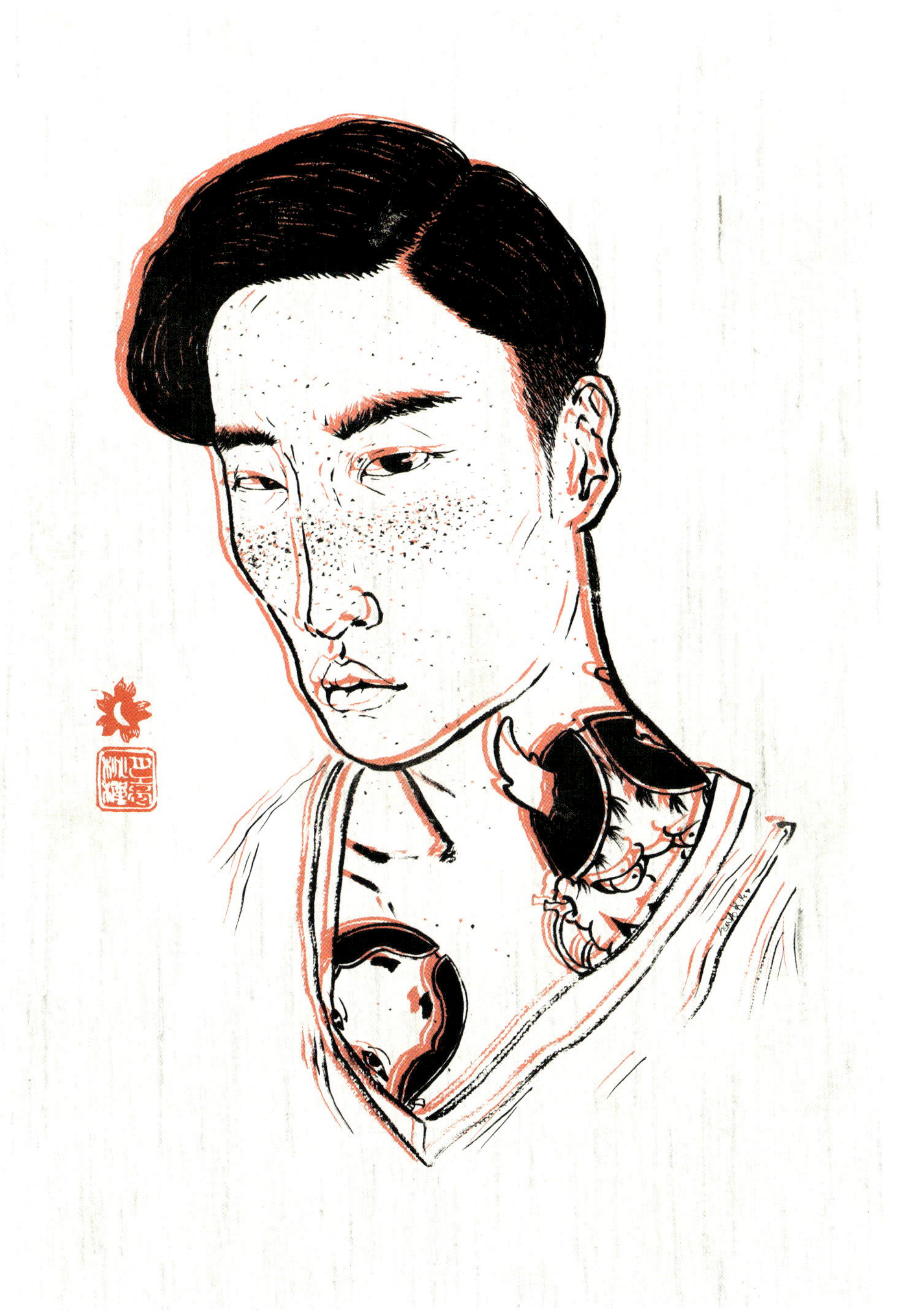

Luna Kirsche *www.mariadasideias.com*

124

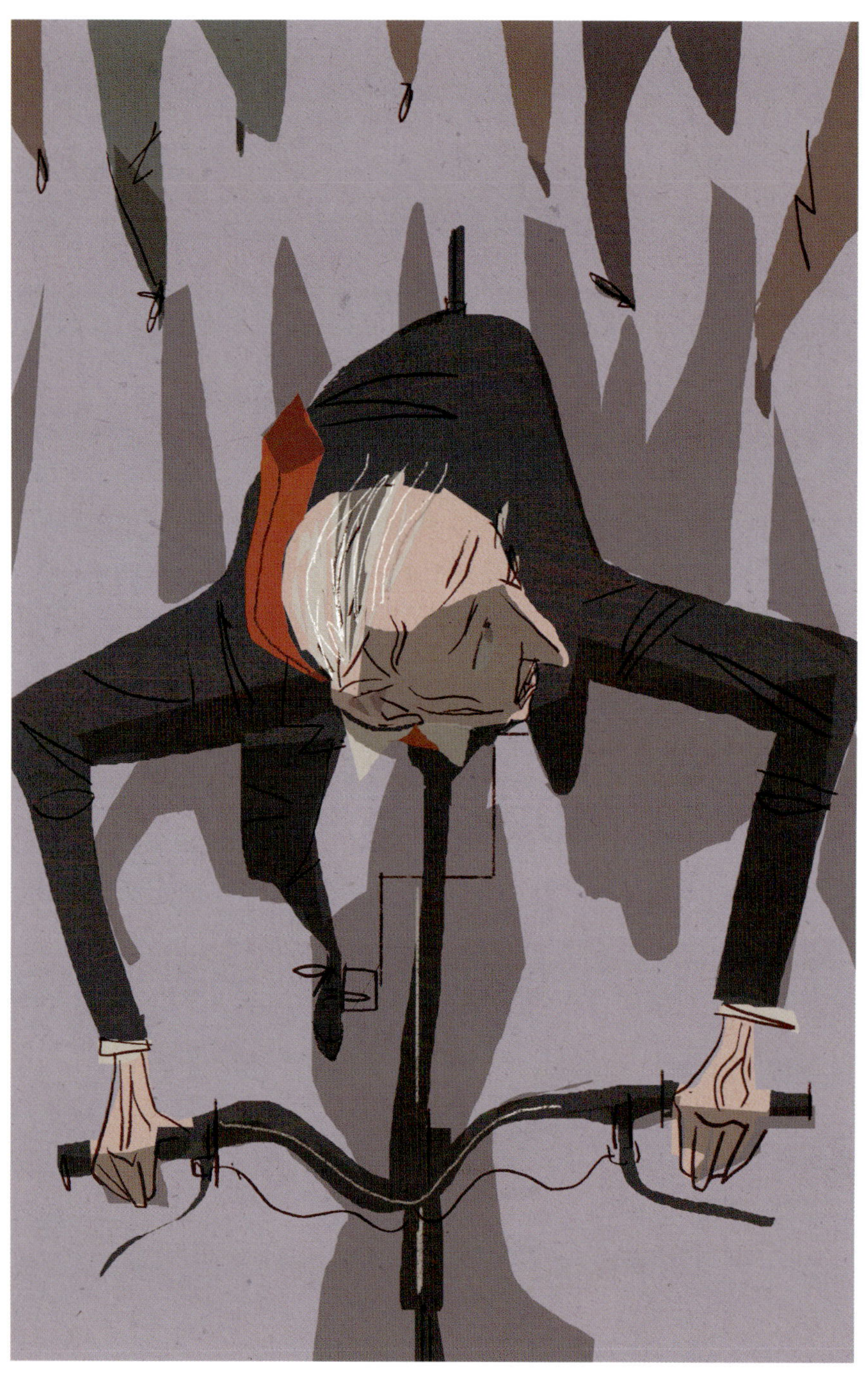

A.Richard Allen *www.arichardallen.com*

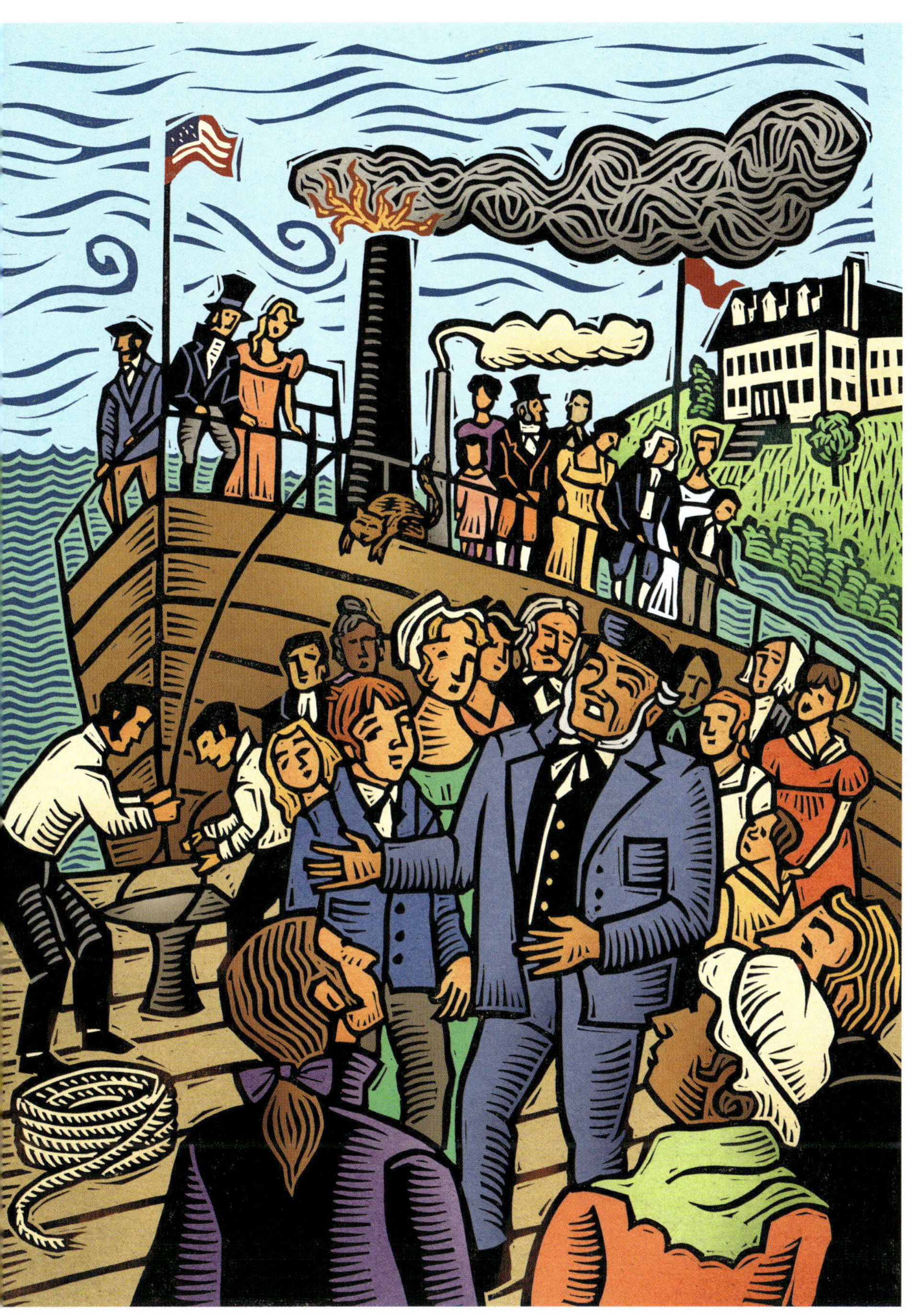

Sue Todd *www.suetodd.com*

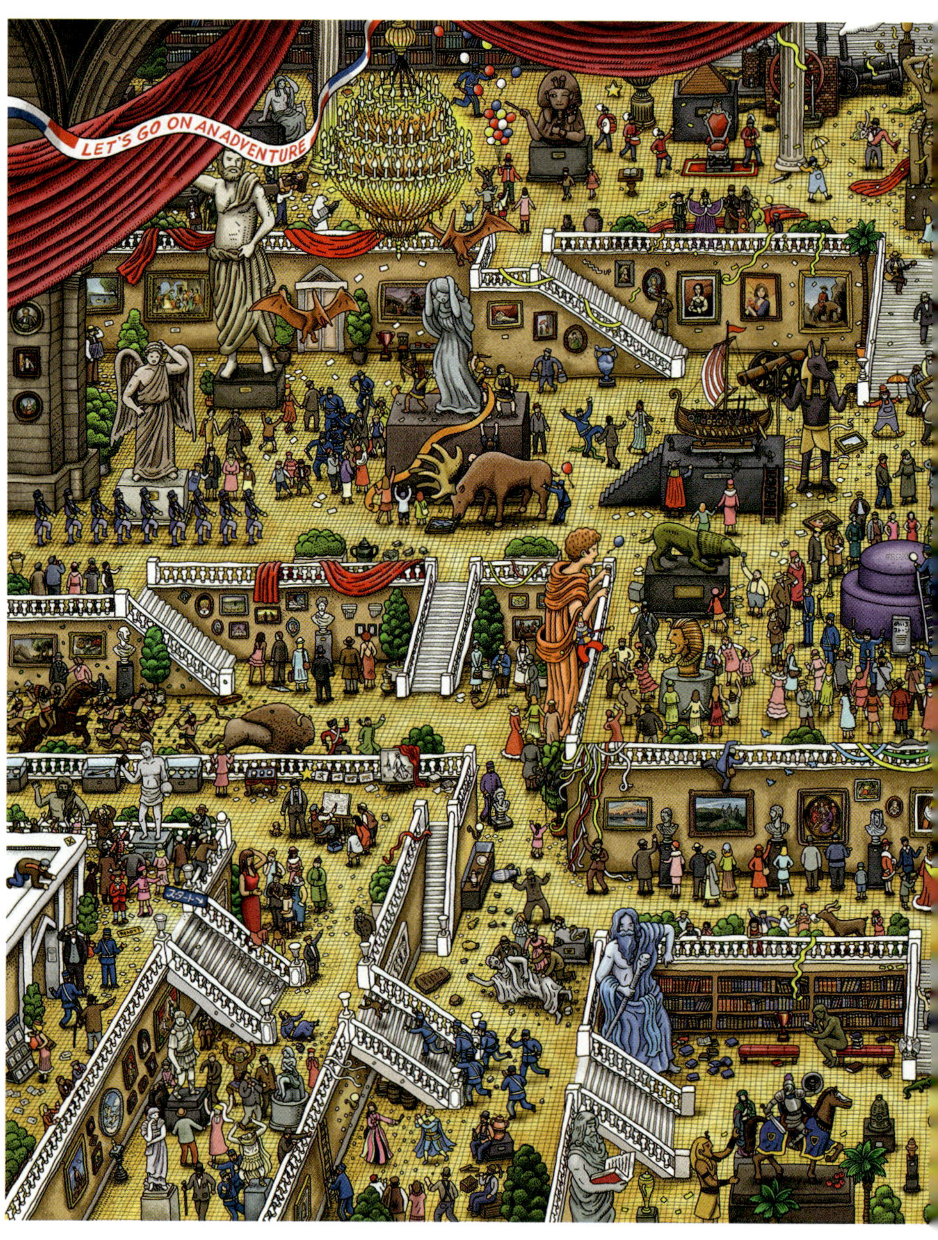
LET'S GO ON AN ADVENTURE
スタート

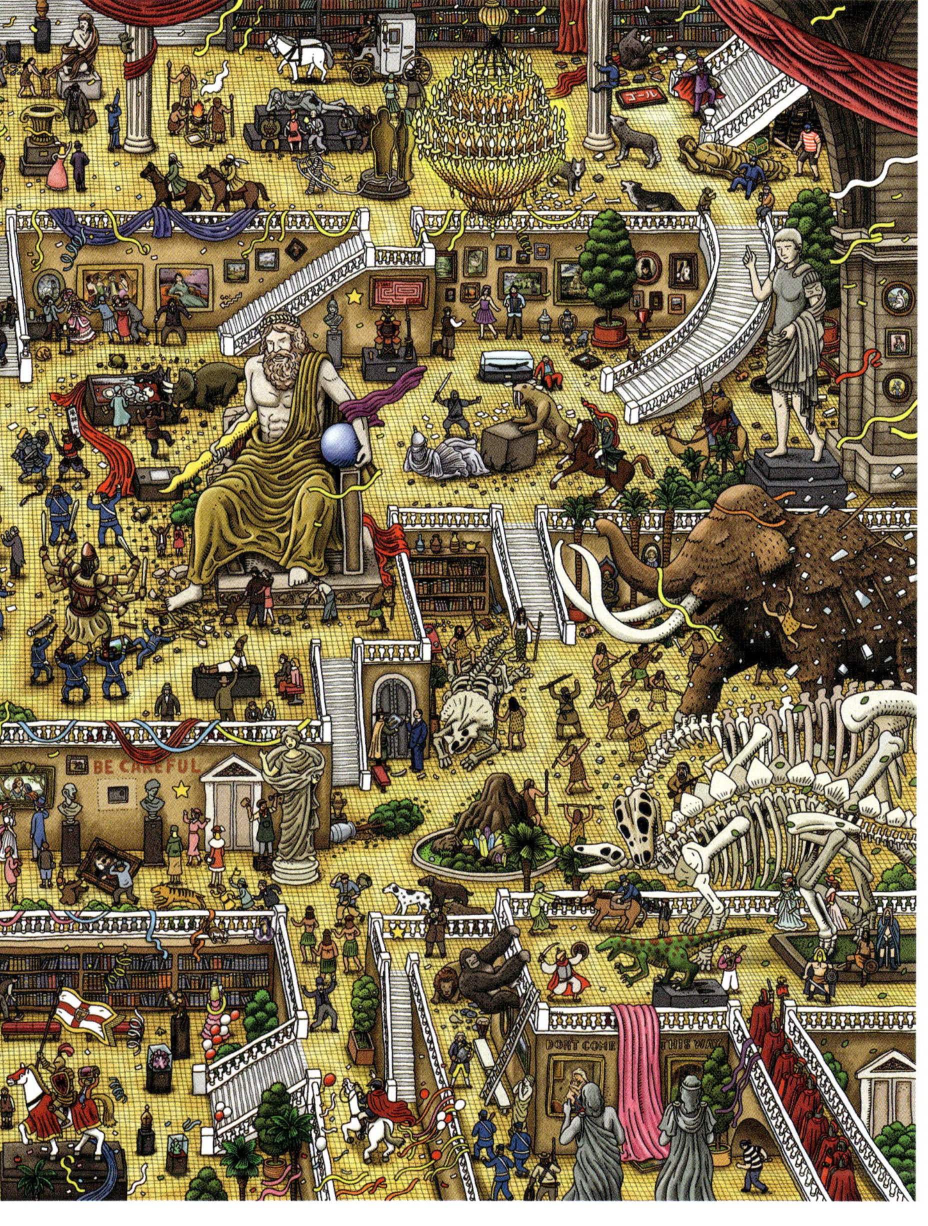
BE CAREFUL
DON'T COME THIS WAY

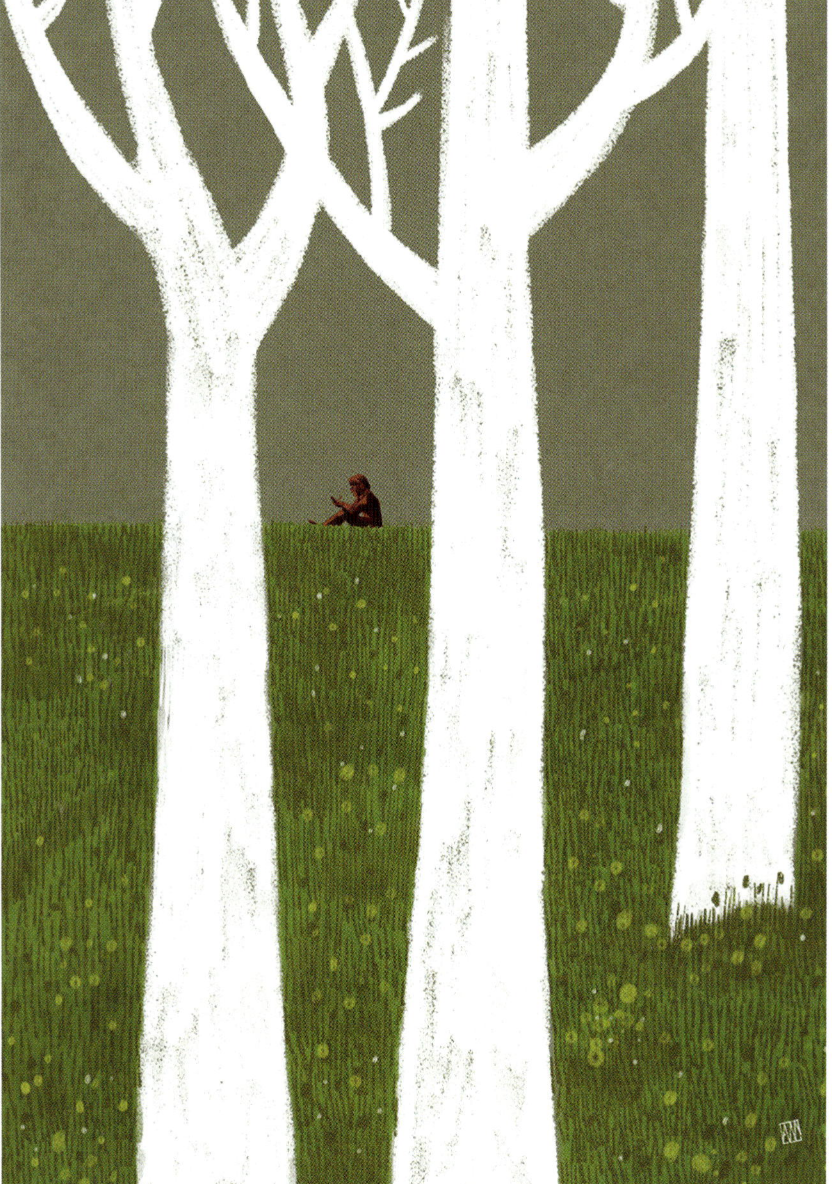

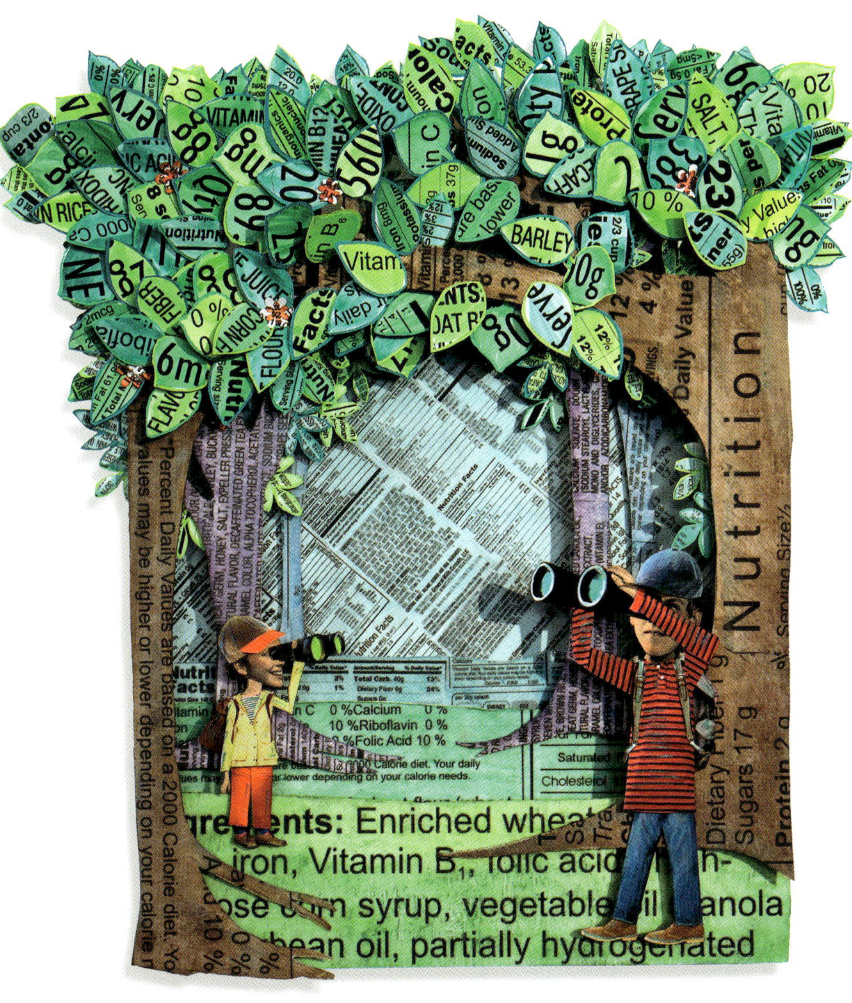

Megan Berkheiser *www.pushart.com*

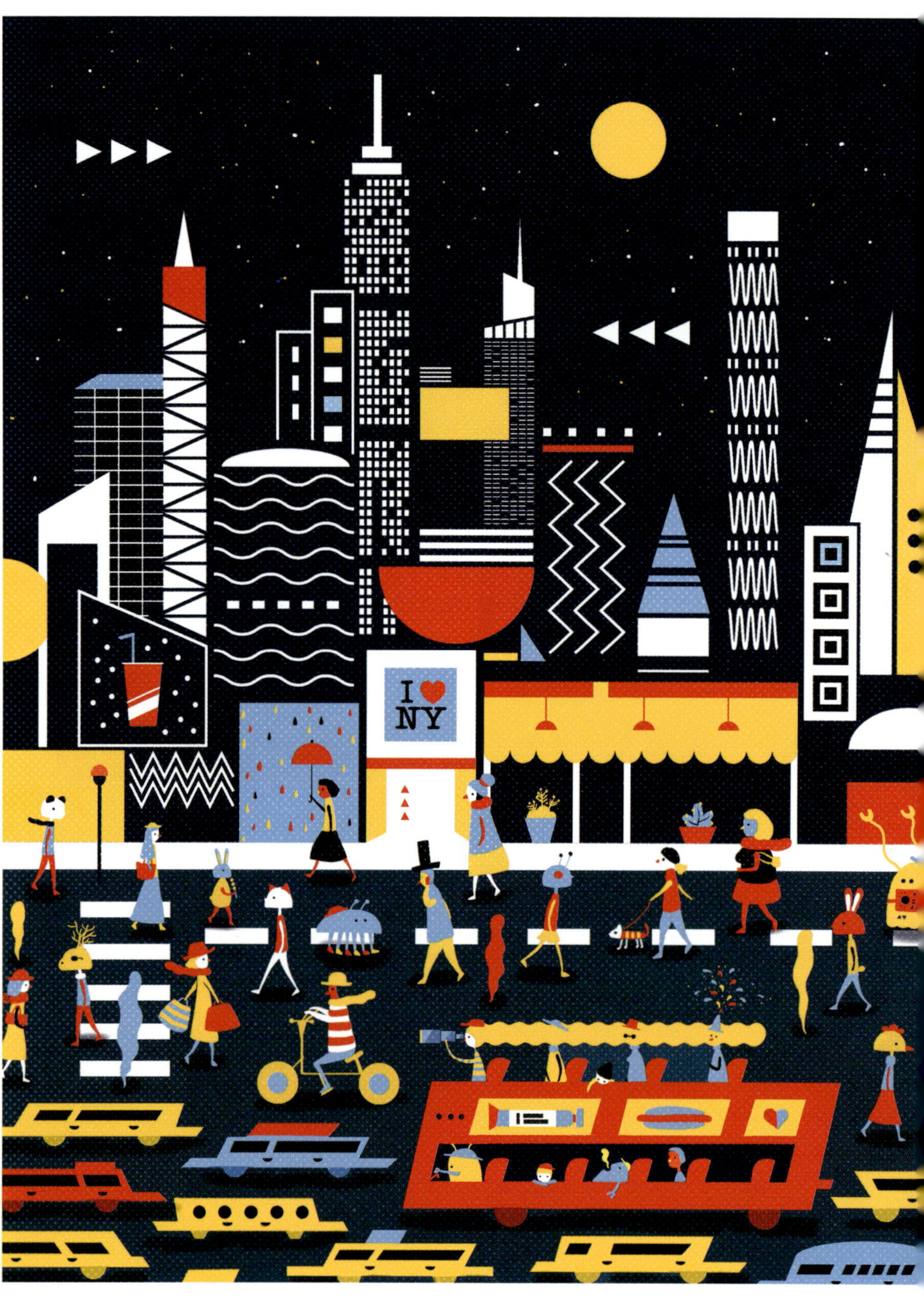

Yao Yu *www.yaoyu.work*

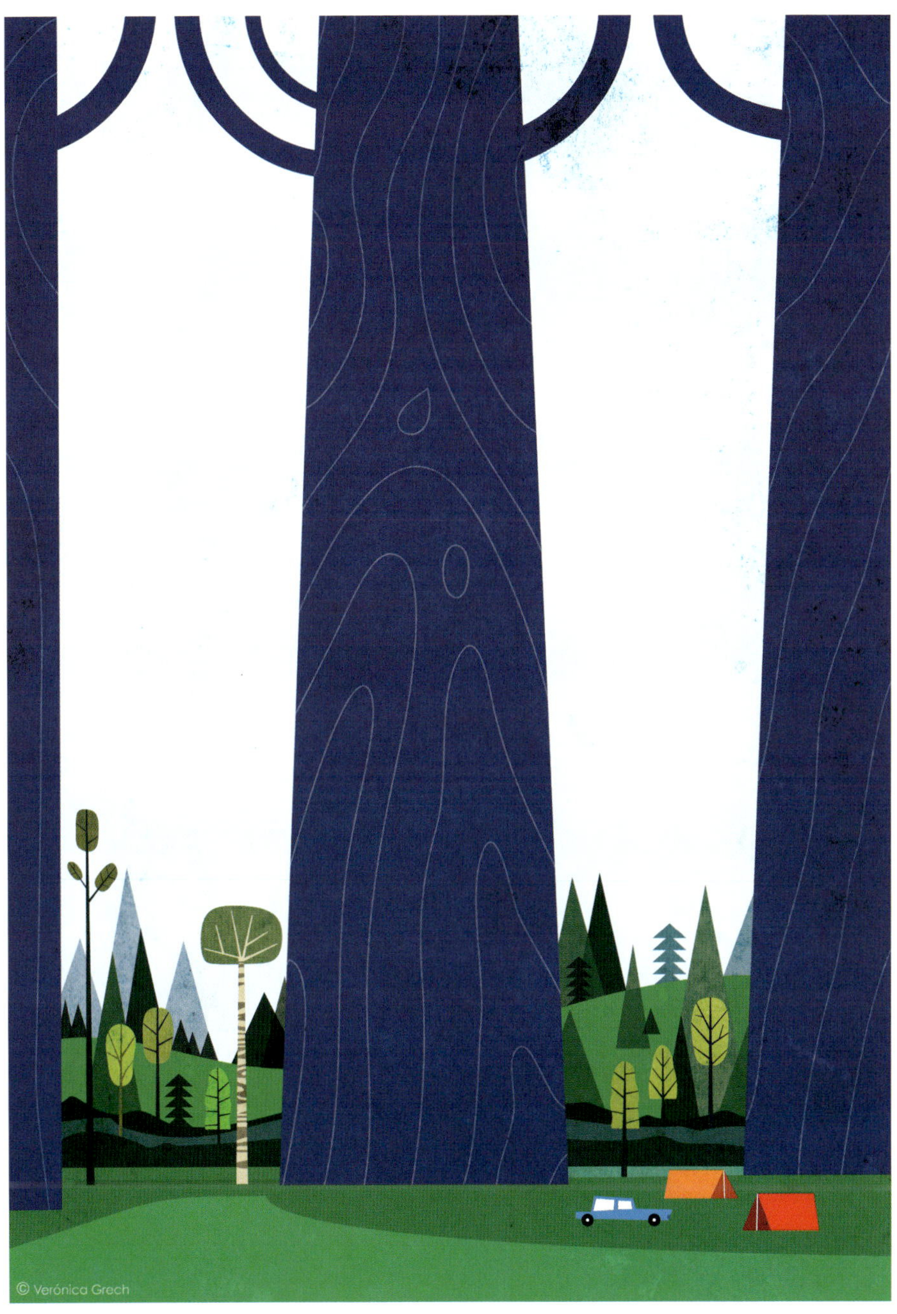

Verónica Grech *www.veronicagrech.com*

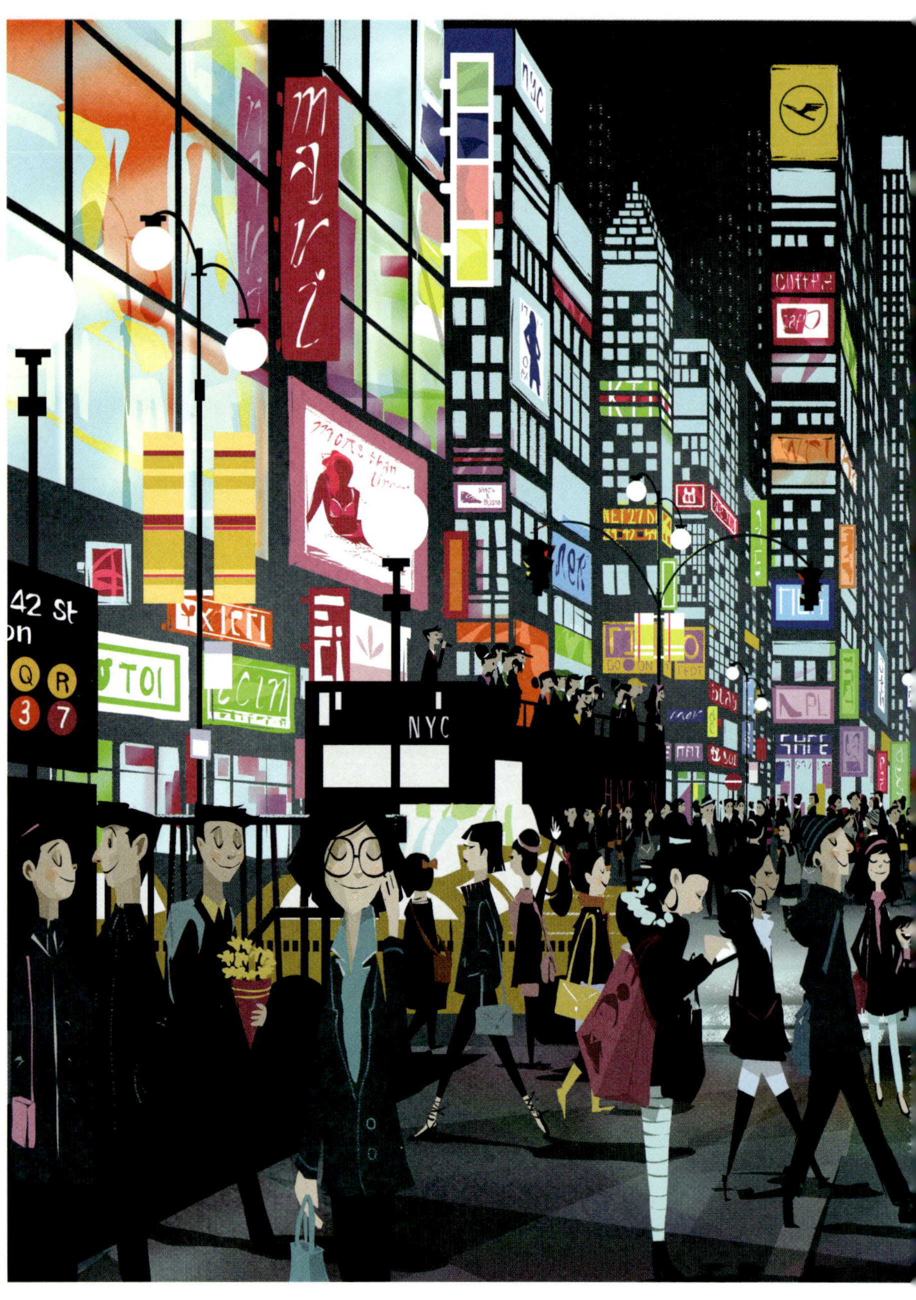

Eda Kaban *www.shannonassociates.com*

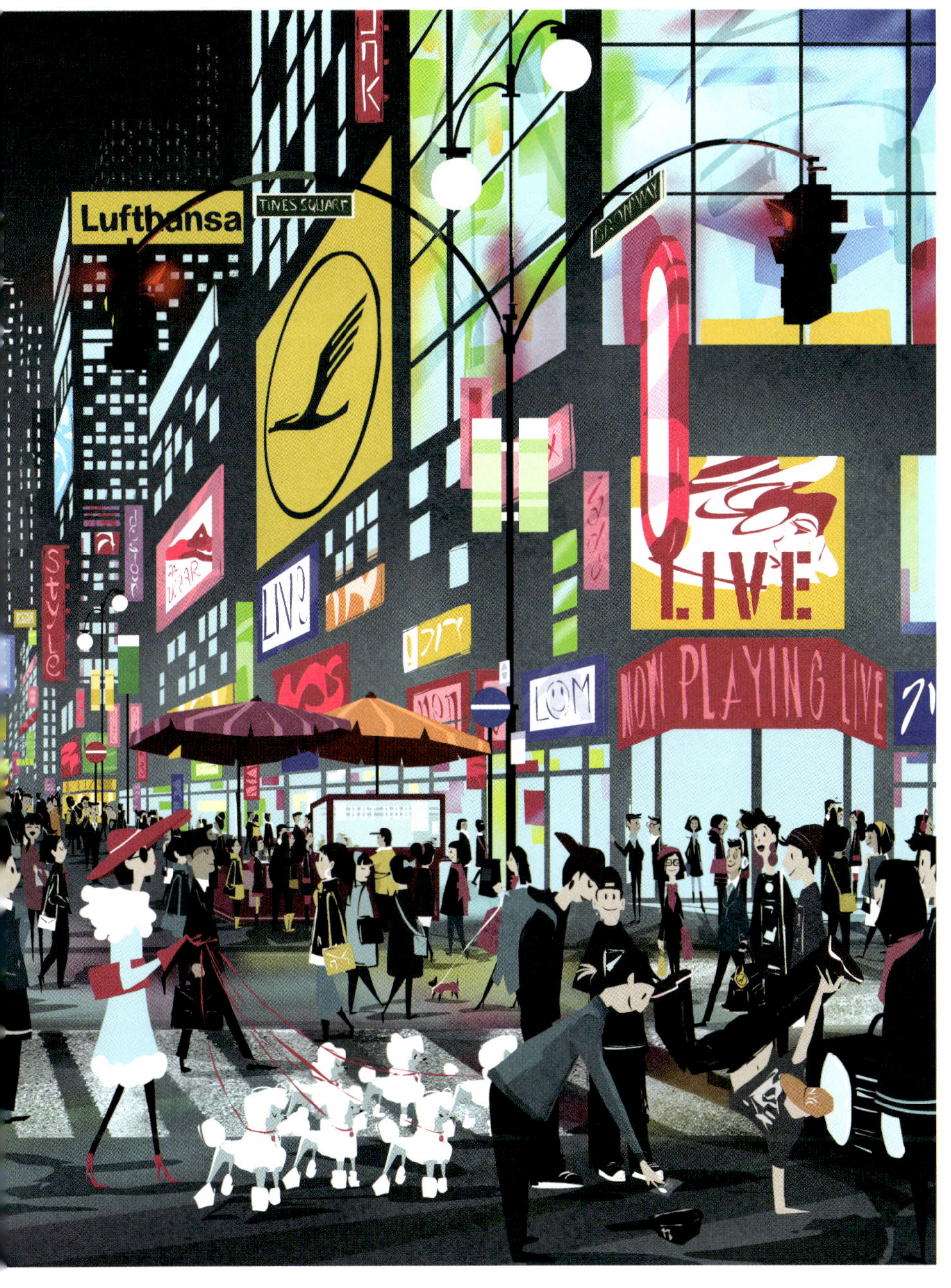
Lufthansa
TIMES SQUARE
BROADWAY
LIVE
LIVE
NOW PLAYING LIVE
Style
LOM

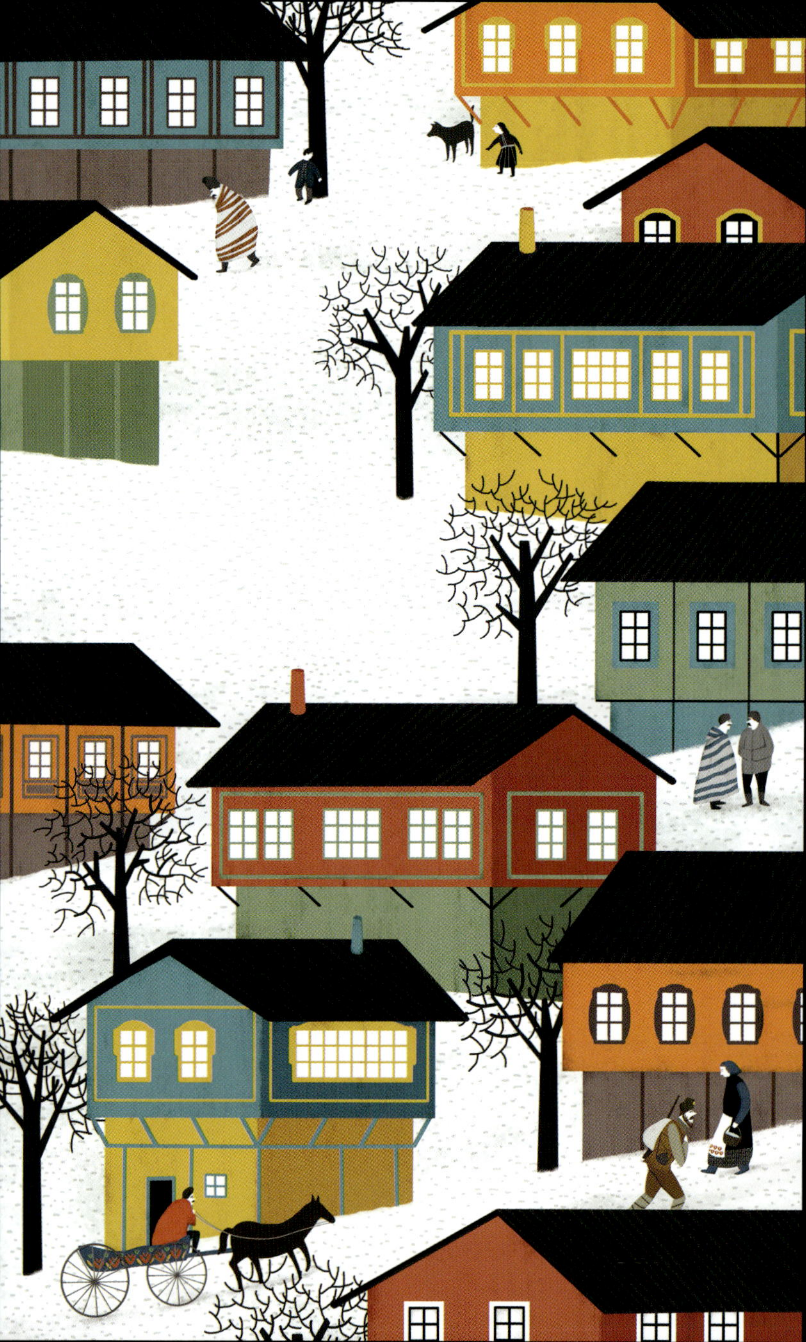

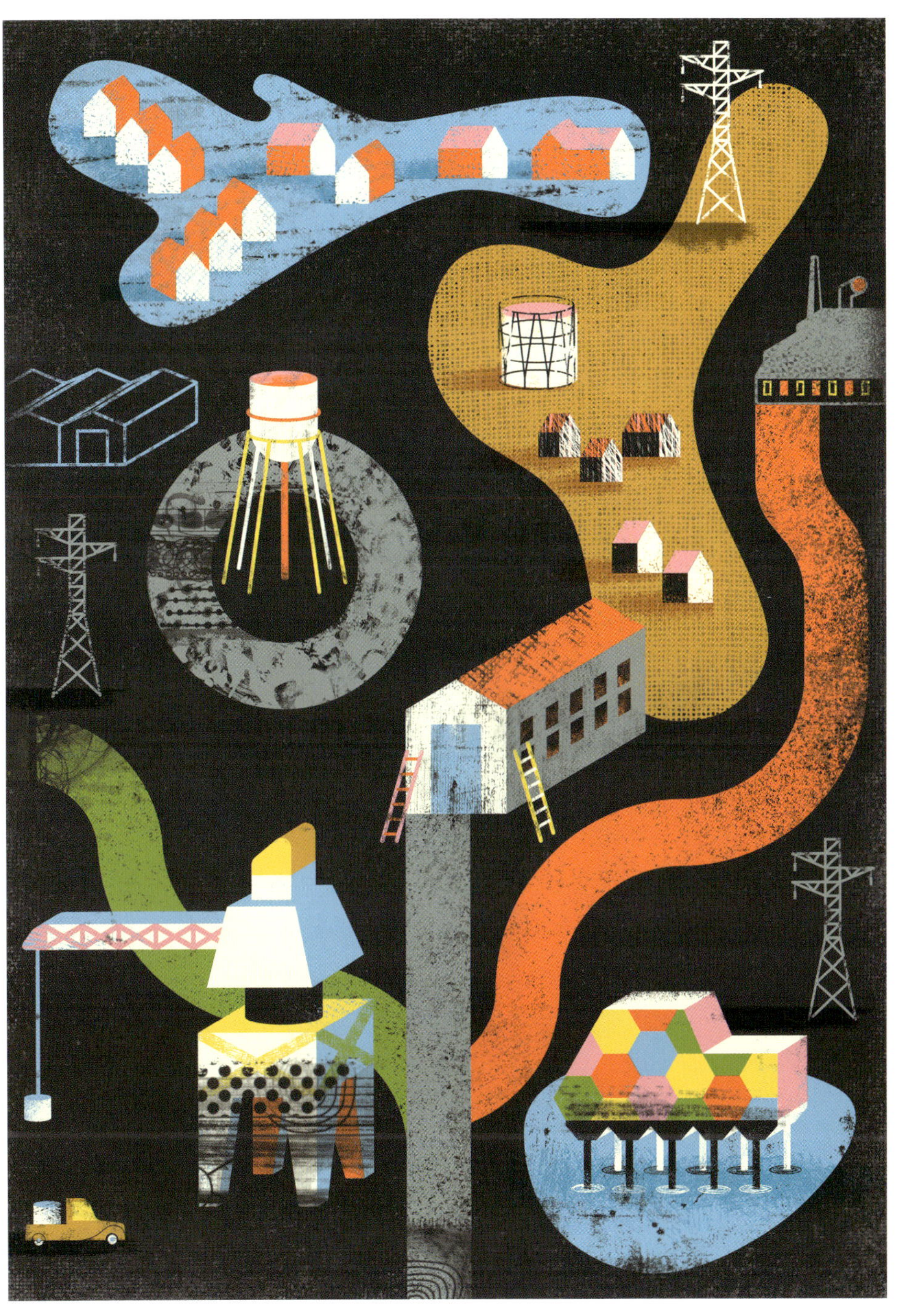

Ian Murray *www.mrmurray.co.uk*

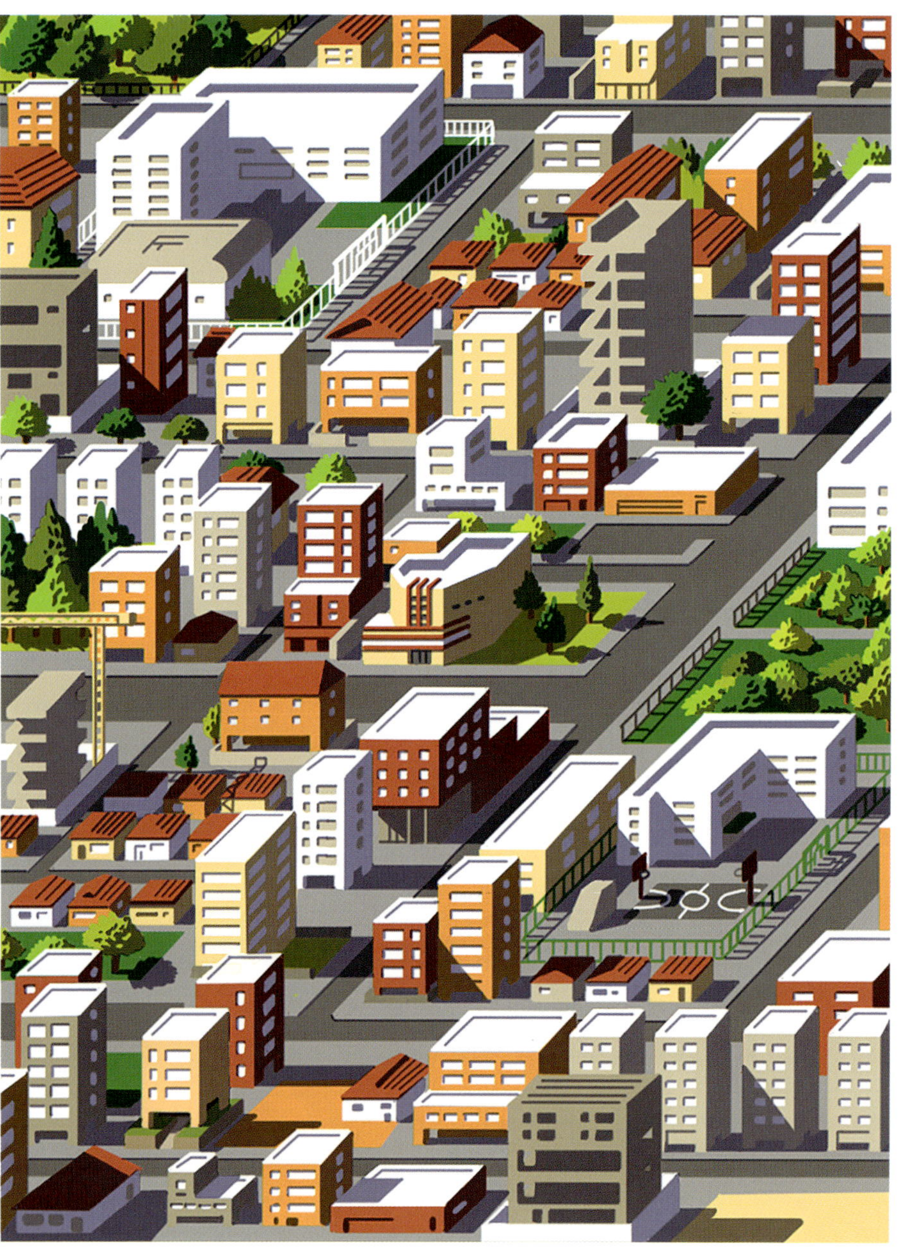

Tom Engler *www.flickr.com/tomengler*

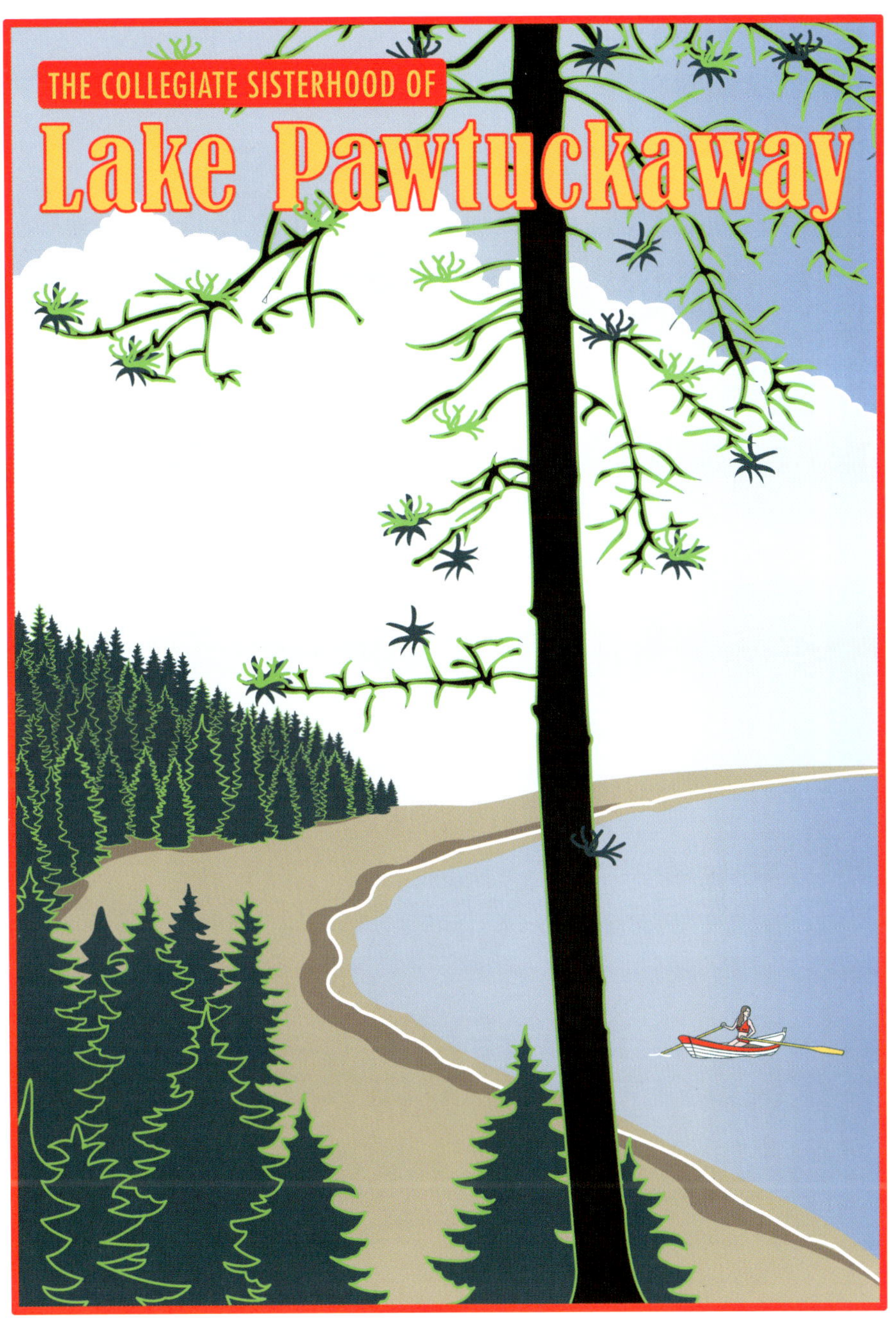

Toni Damkoehler *www.tonidamkoehler.com*

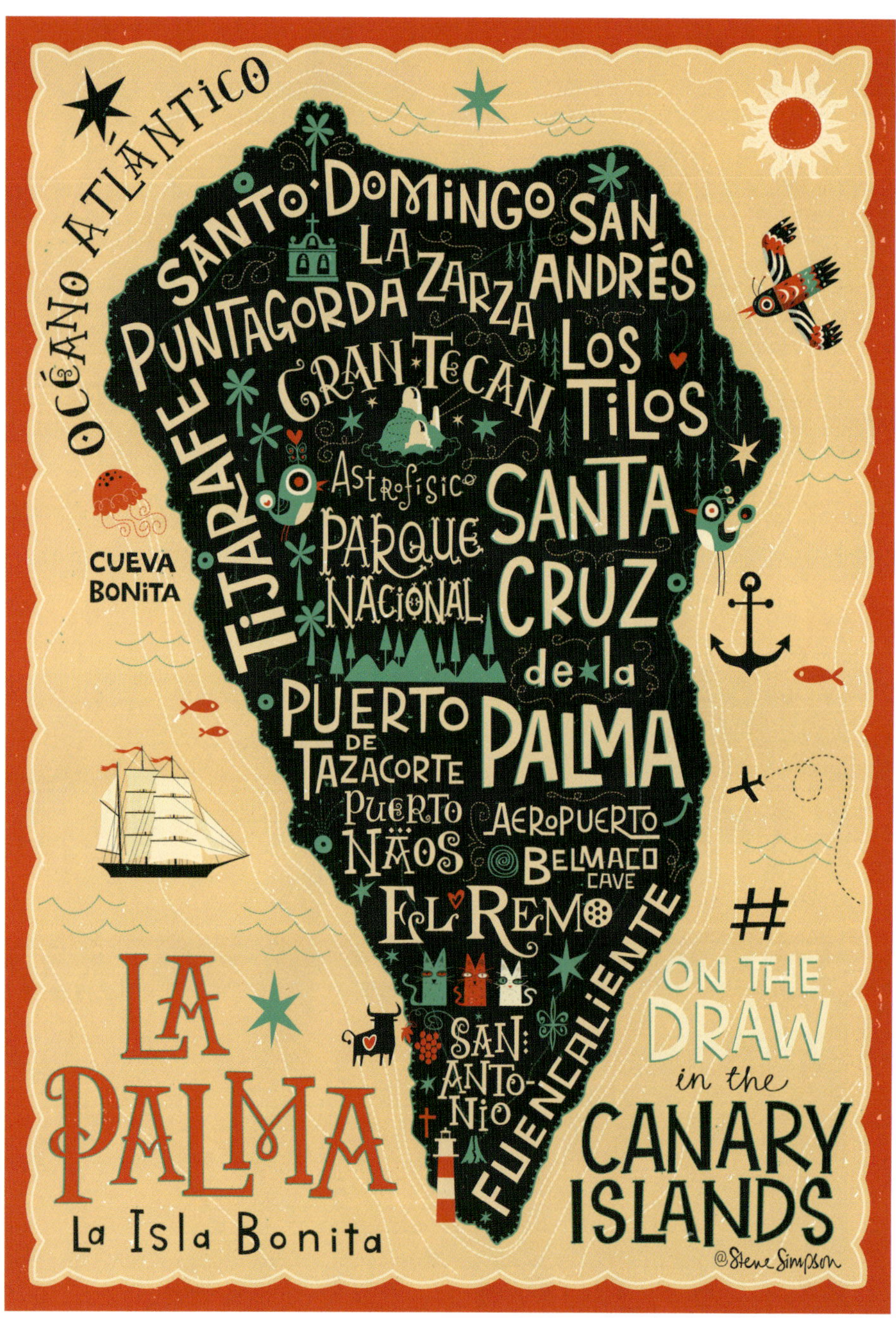

Steve Simpson *www.stevesimpson.com*

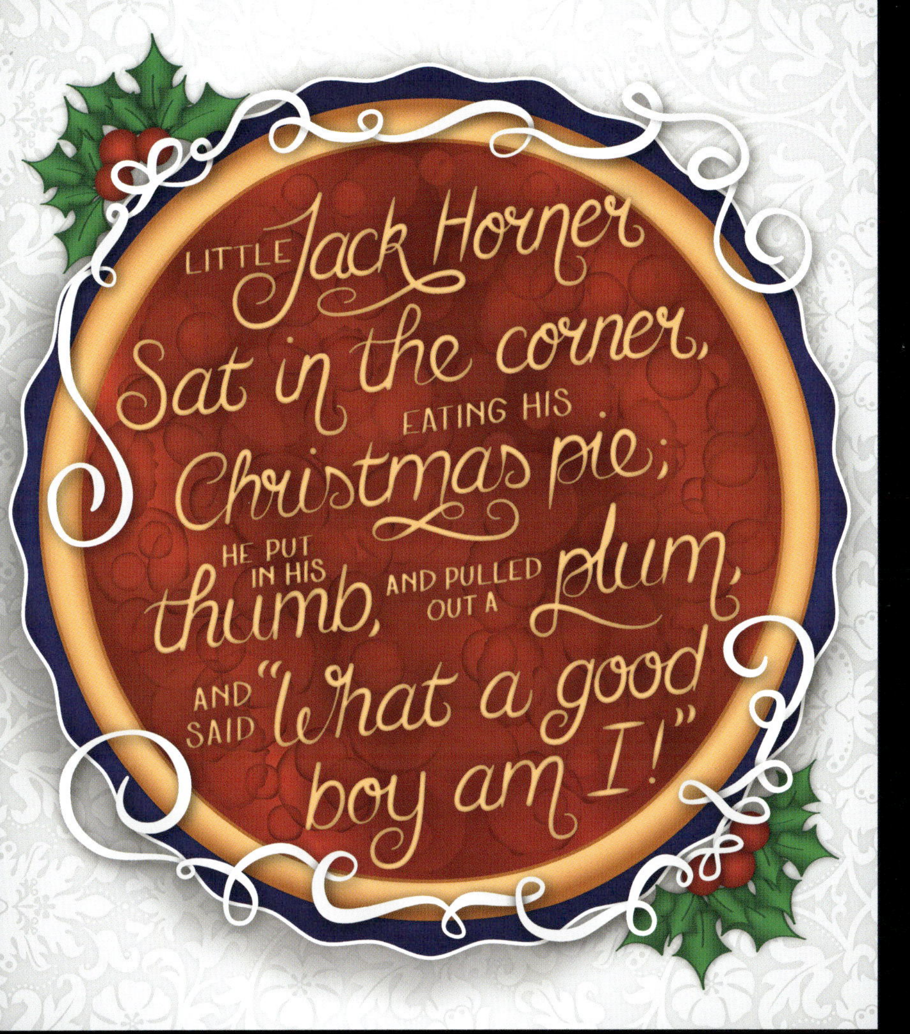

LITTLE Jack Horner
Sat in the corner,
EATING HIS
Christmas pie;
HE PUT IN HIS thumb, AND PULLED OUT A plum,
AND SAID "What a good boy am I!"

140

Smile O voluptuous Coolbreathed earth! earth of the slumbering Liquid Trees! earth of departed sunset! earth of the mountains Misty-topt! earth of the vitreous pour of the full moon just tinged with blue! the river! of shine and dark mottling the tide EARTH of the limpid gray of clouds brighter and clearer for my sake!

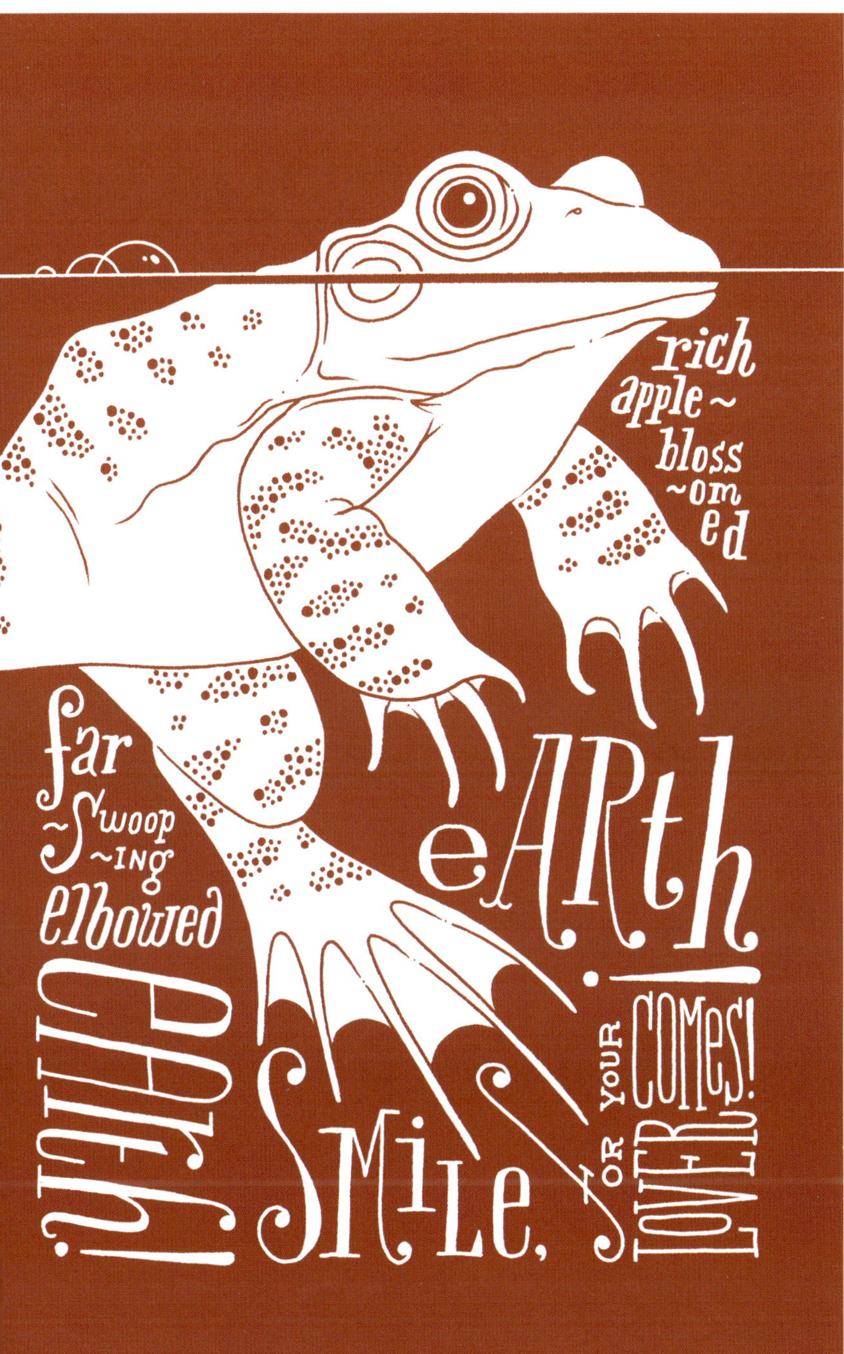
rich apple~ bloss ~om ed
far ~Swoop ~ing elbowed
eARth
SMiLe,
for your
comes!
LOVER!

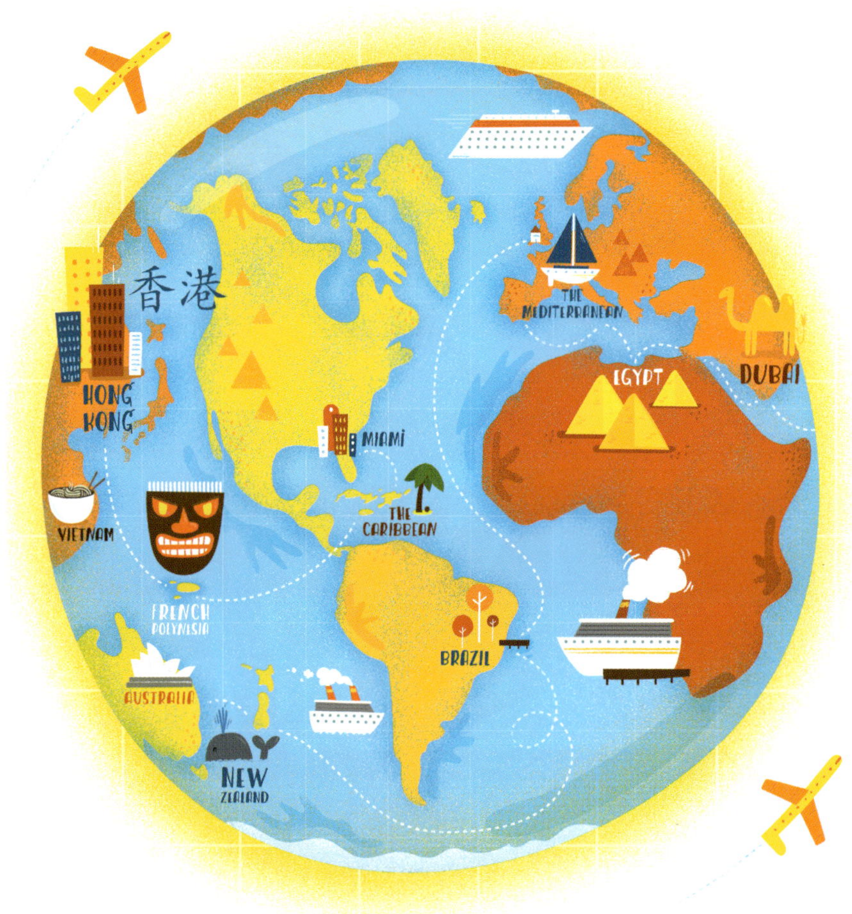

Shaw Nielsen *www.shawnielsen.com*

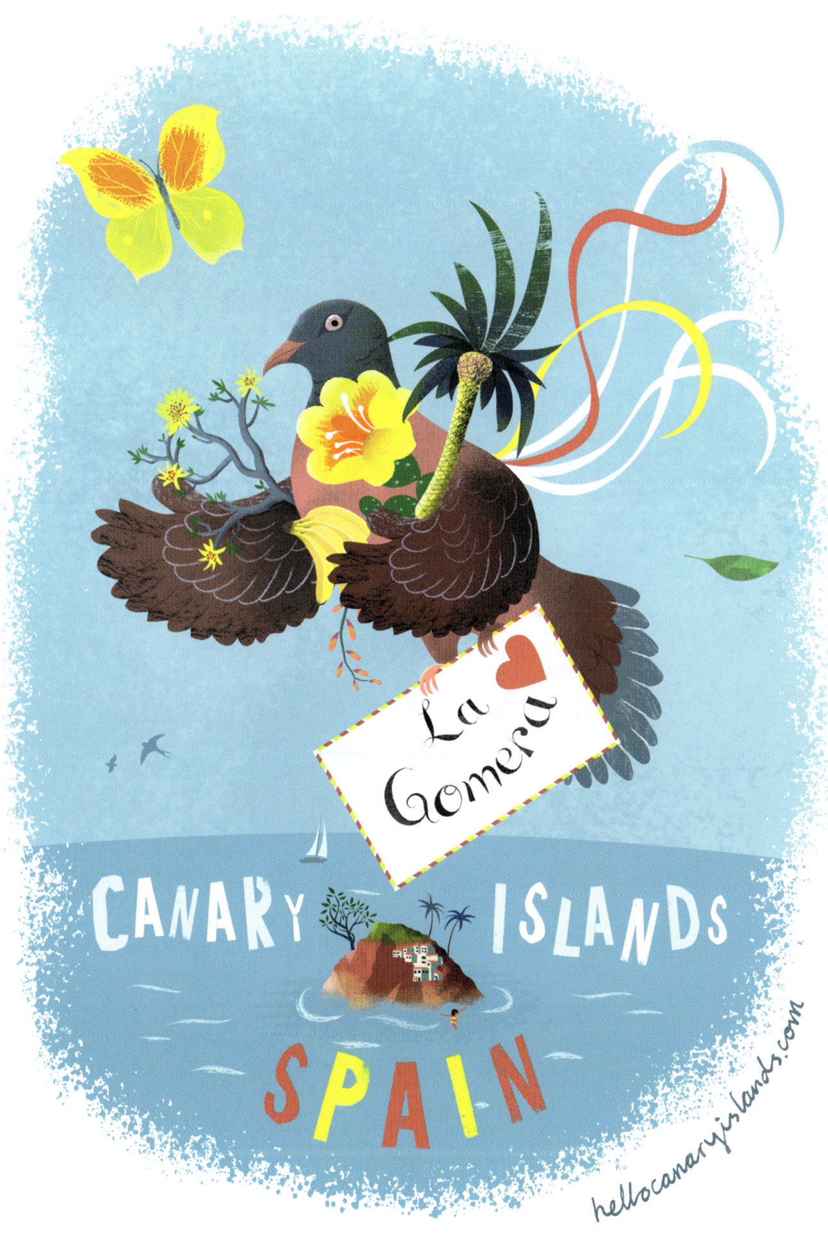

Jens Magnusson *www.jensjens.com*

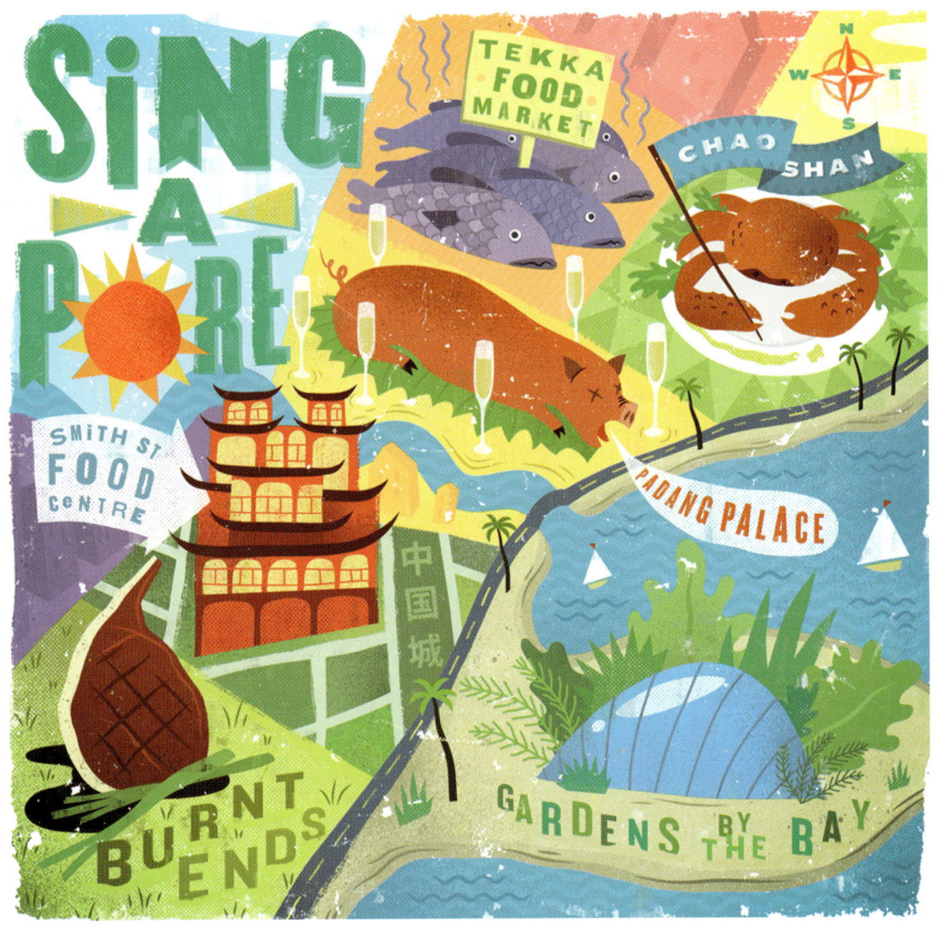

Tyler Gross *www.grossillustration.com*

144

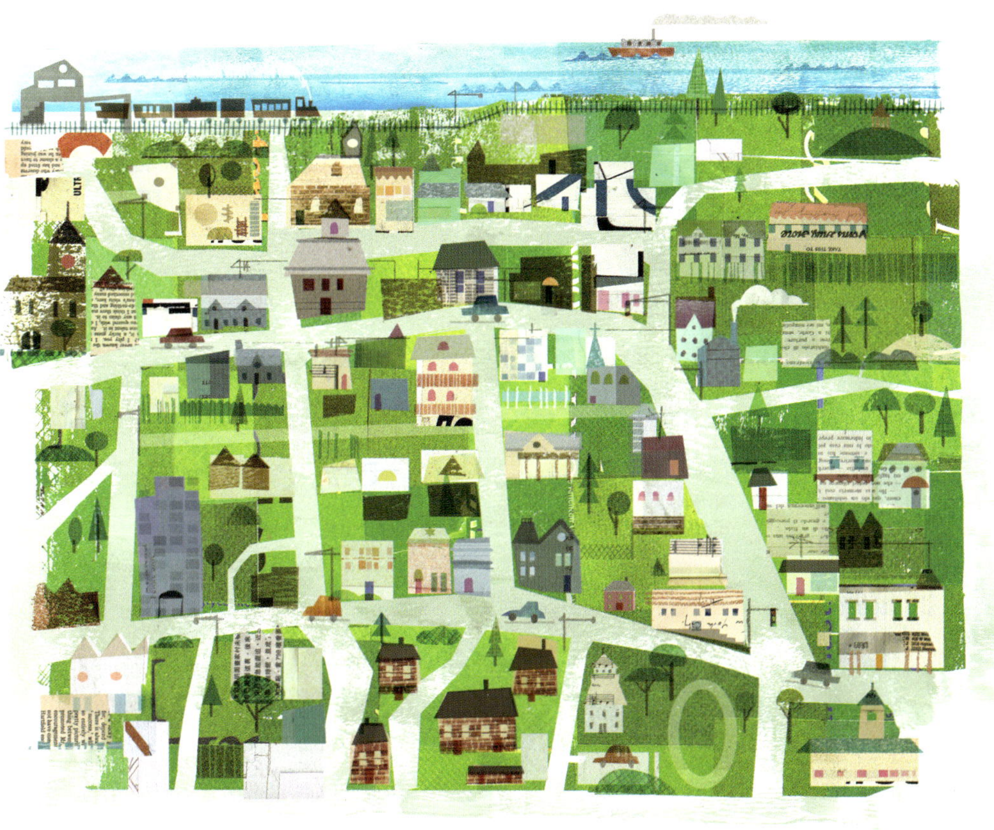

Maria Carluccio *www.mariacarluccio.com*

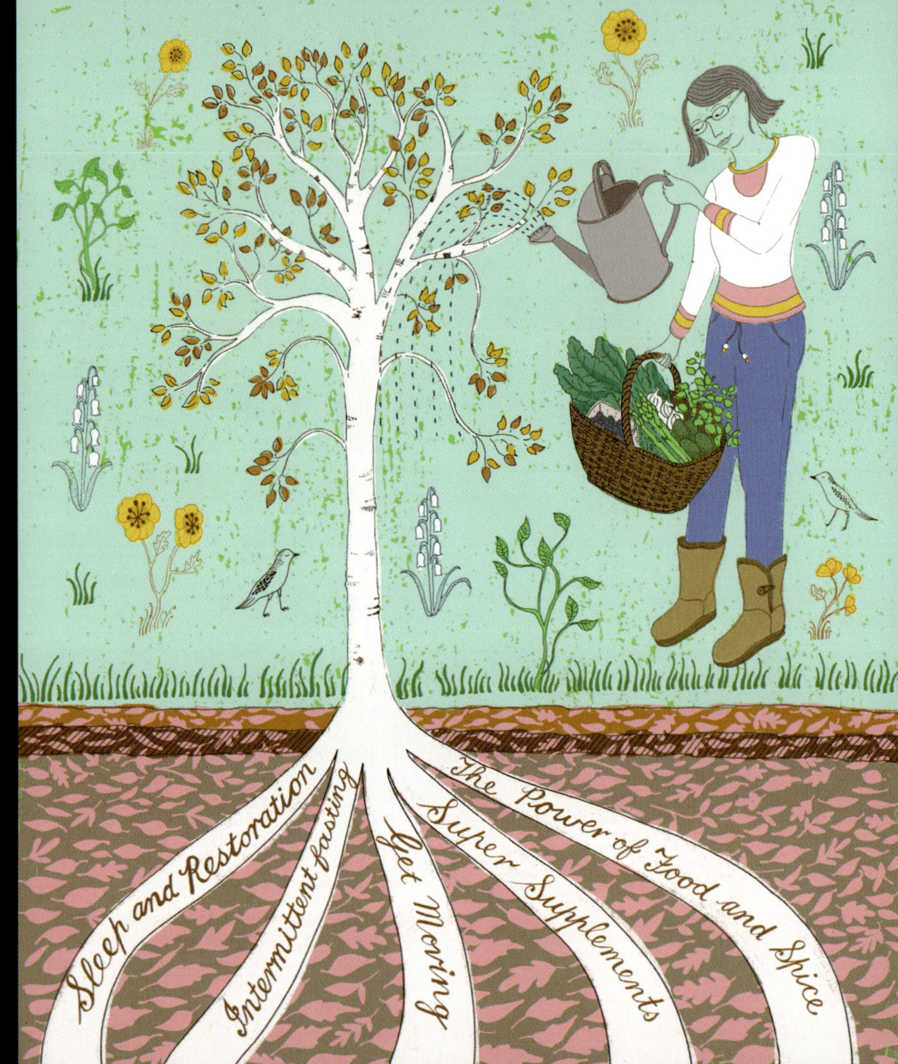

Sleep and Restoration
Intermittent fasting
Get Moving
Super Supplements
The Power of Food and Spice

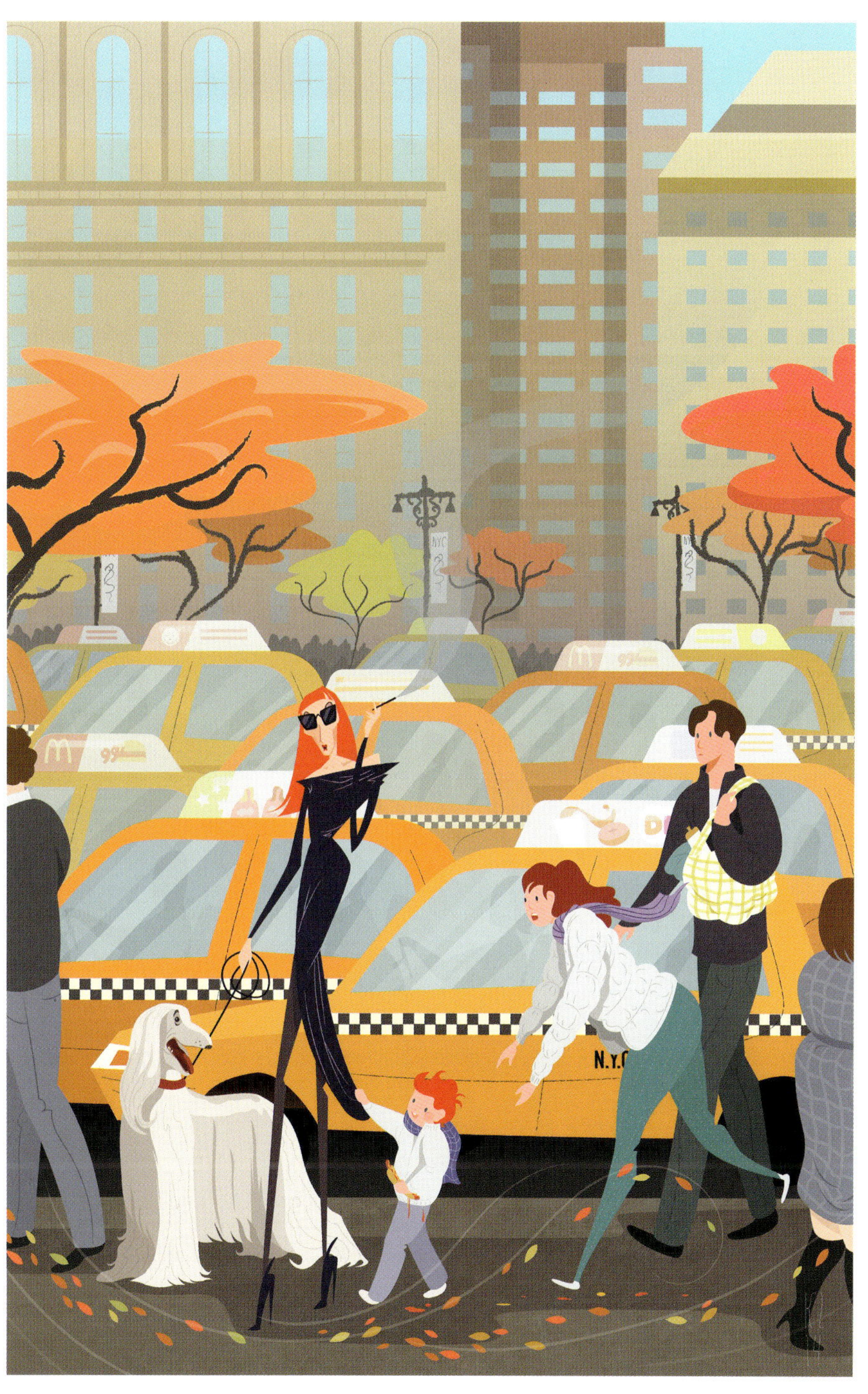

Krystal Lauk *www.krystallauk.com*

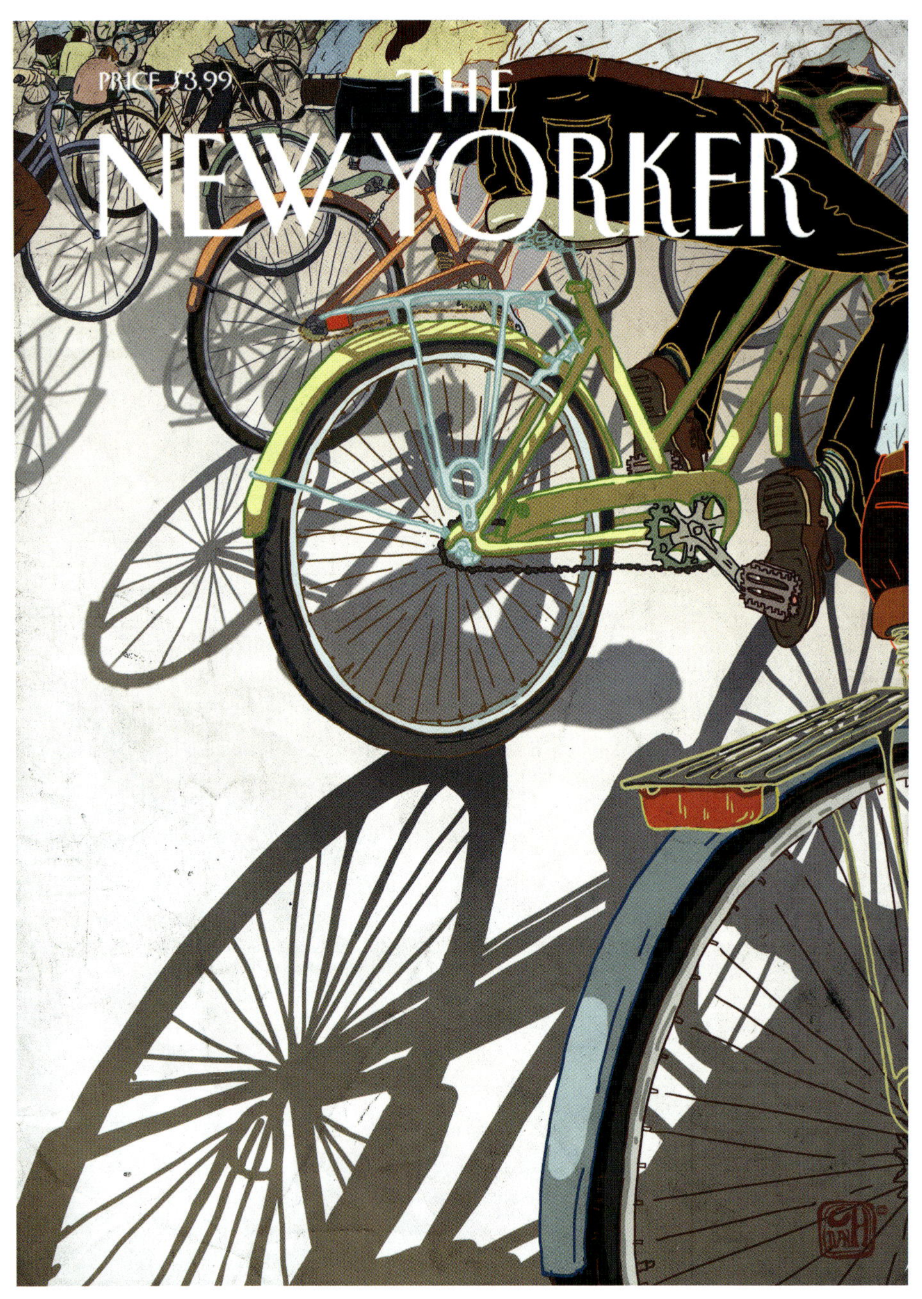

Hong Chen *www.hongillu.com*

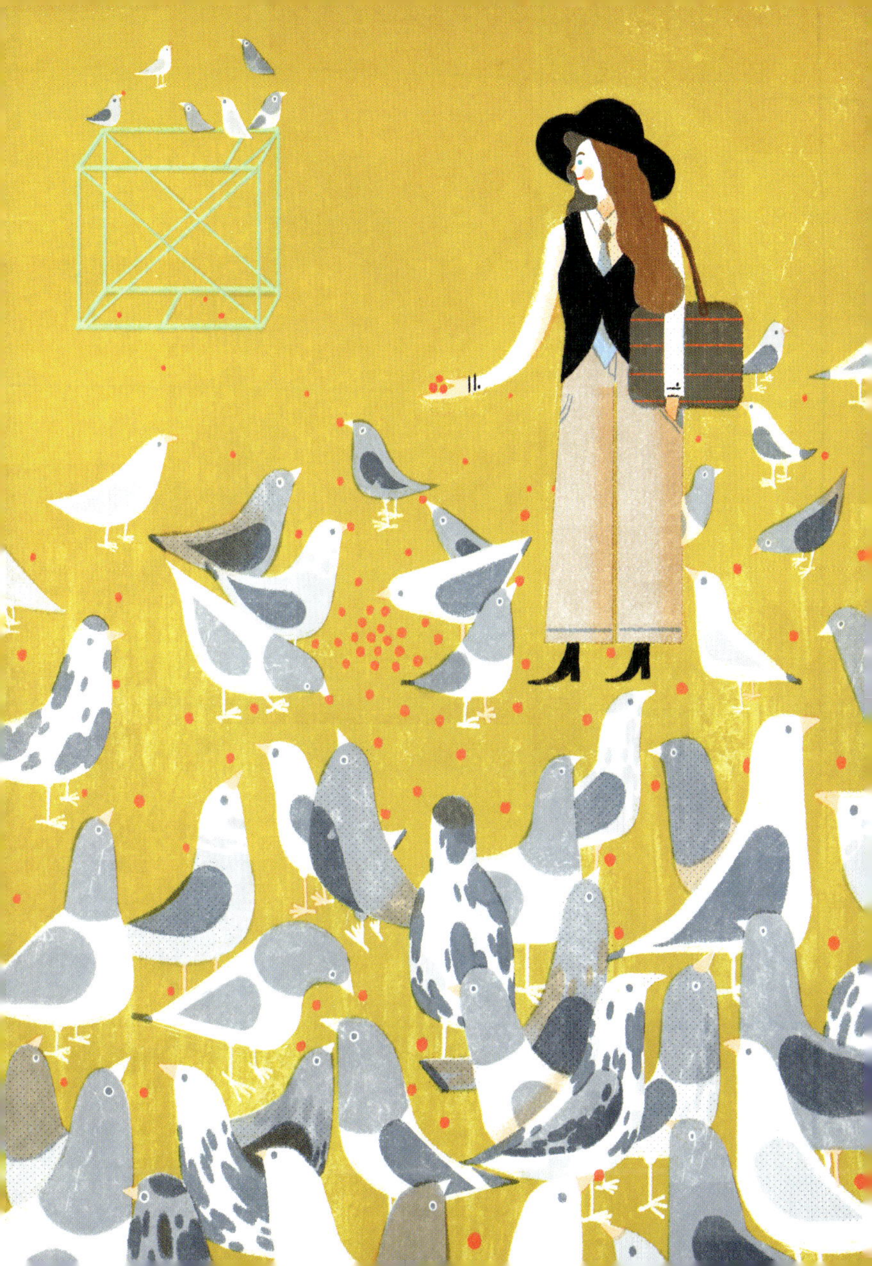

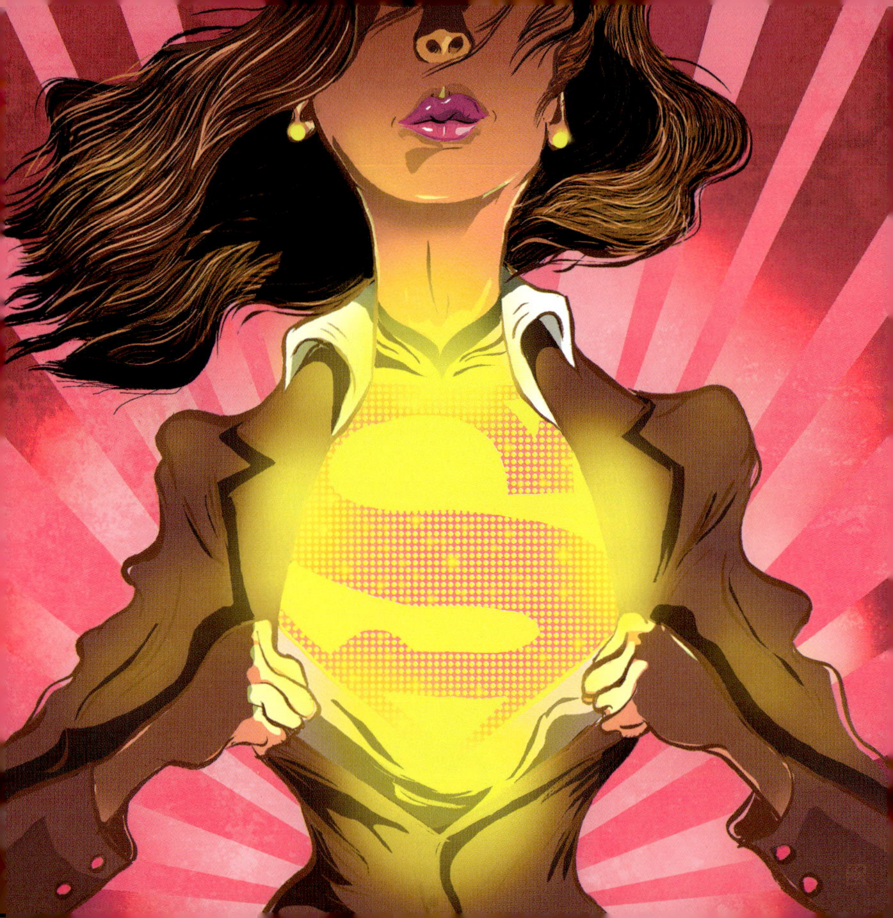

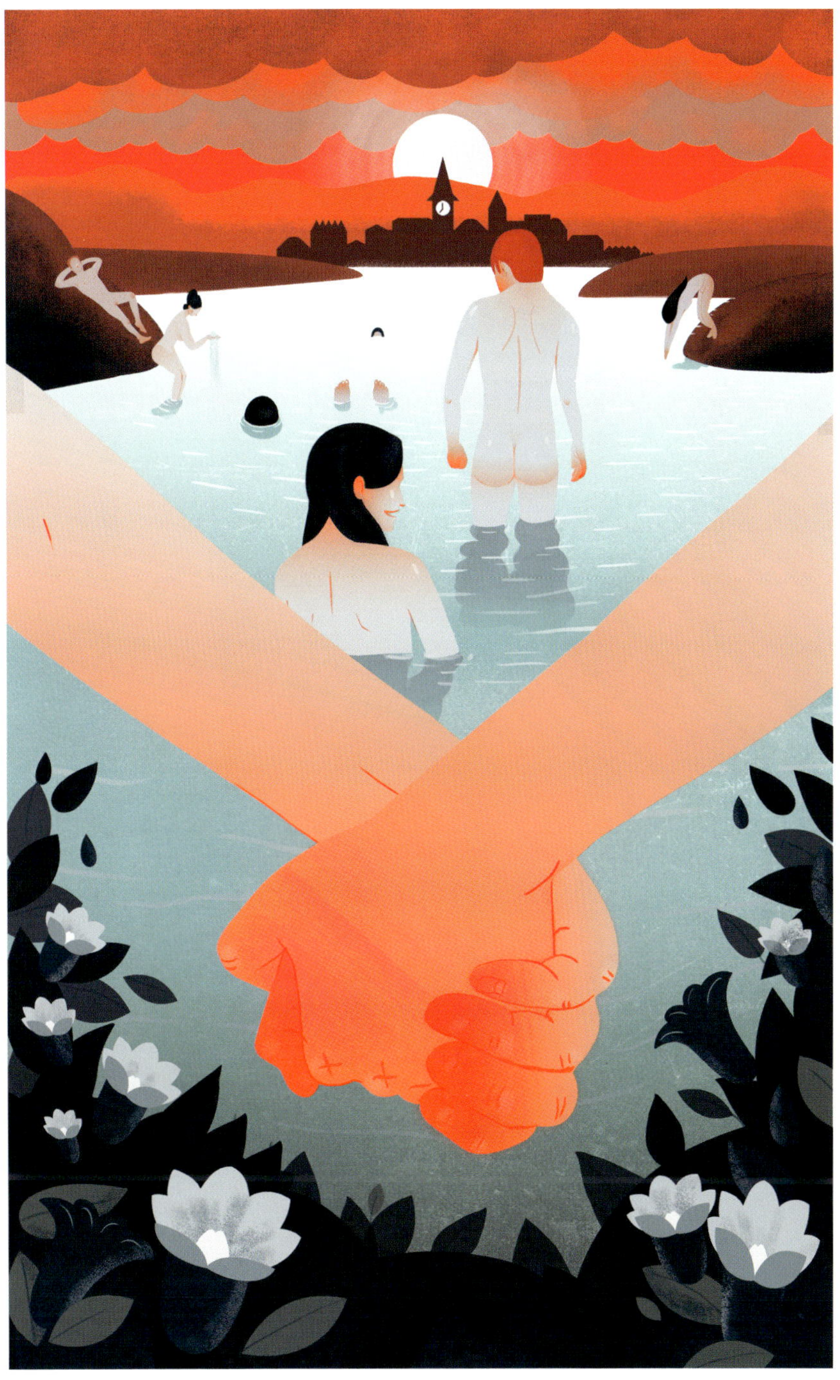

Elyse Salazar *www.elysesalazar.com*

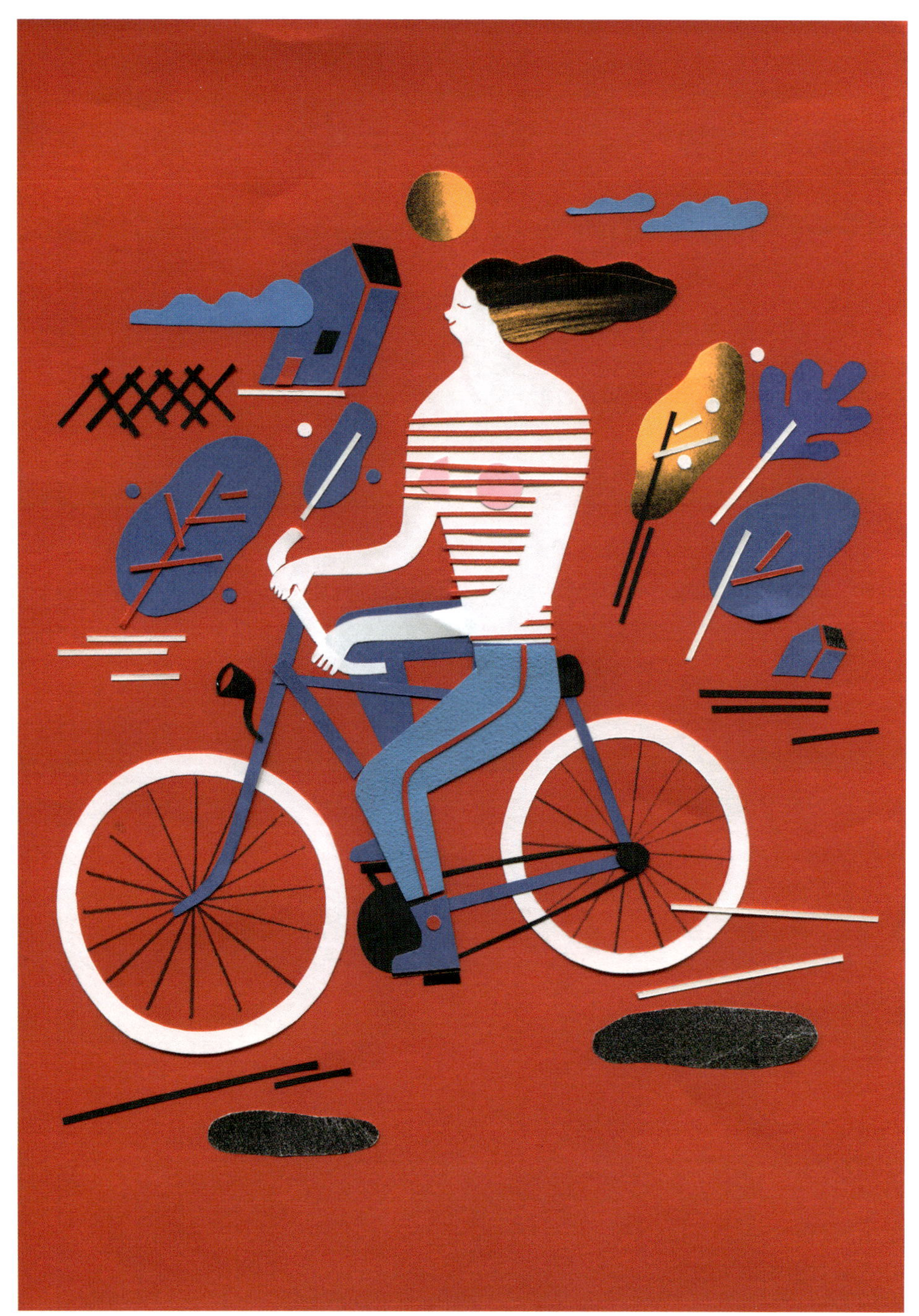

Stephanie Wunderlich *www.wunderlich-illustration.de*

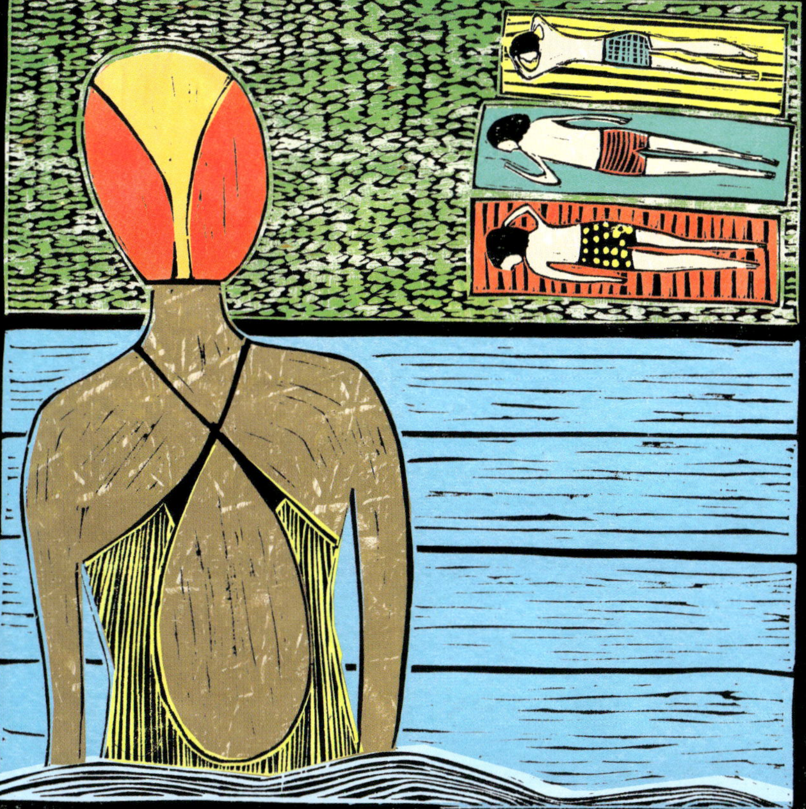

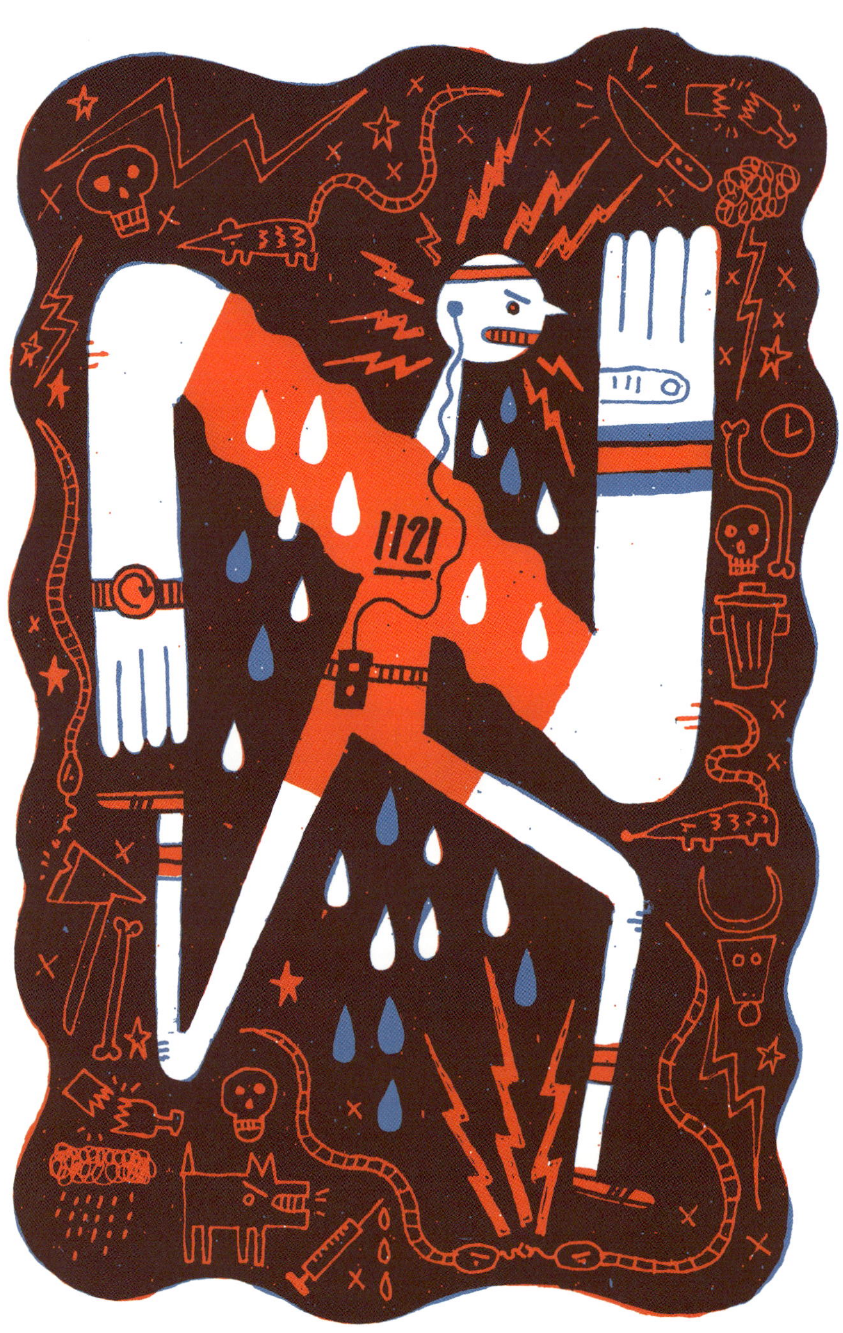

Benoit Tardif *www.bentardif.com*

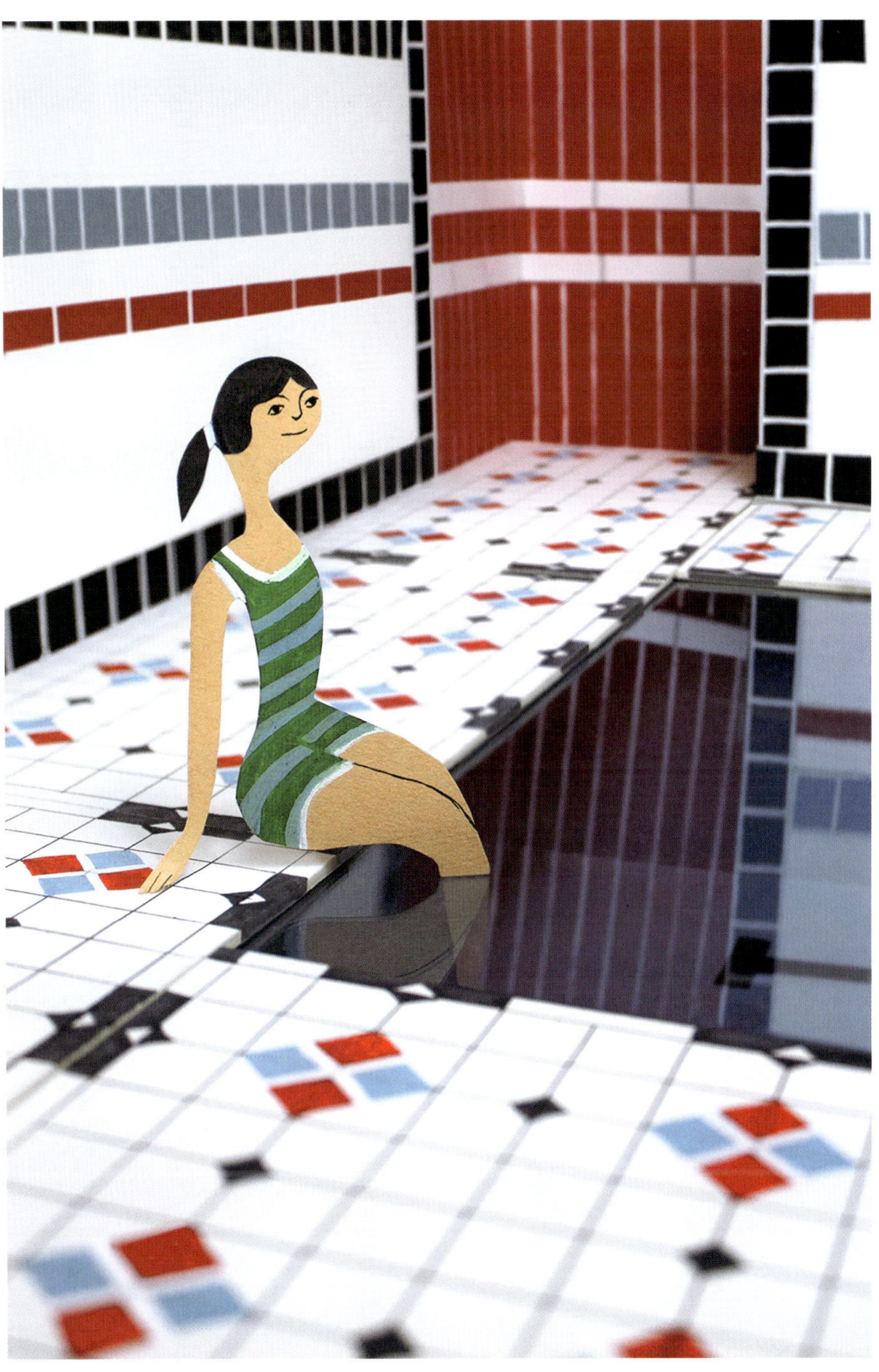

Angela Rio *www.angelario.com*

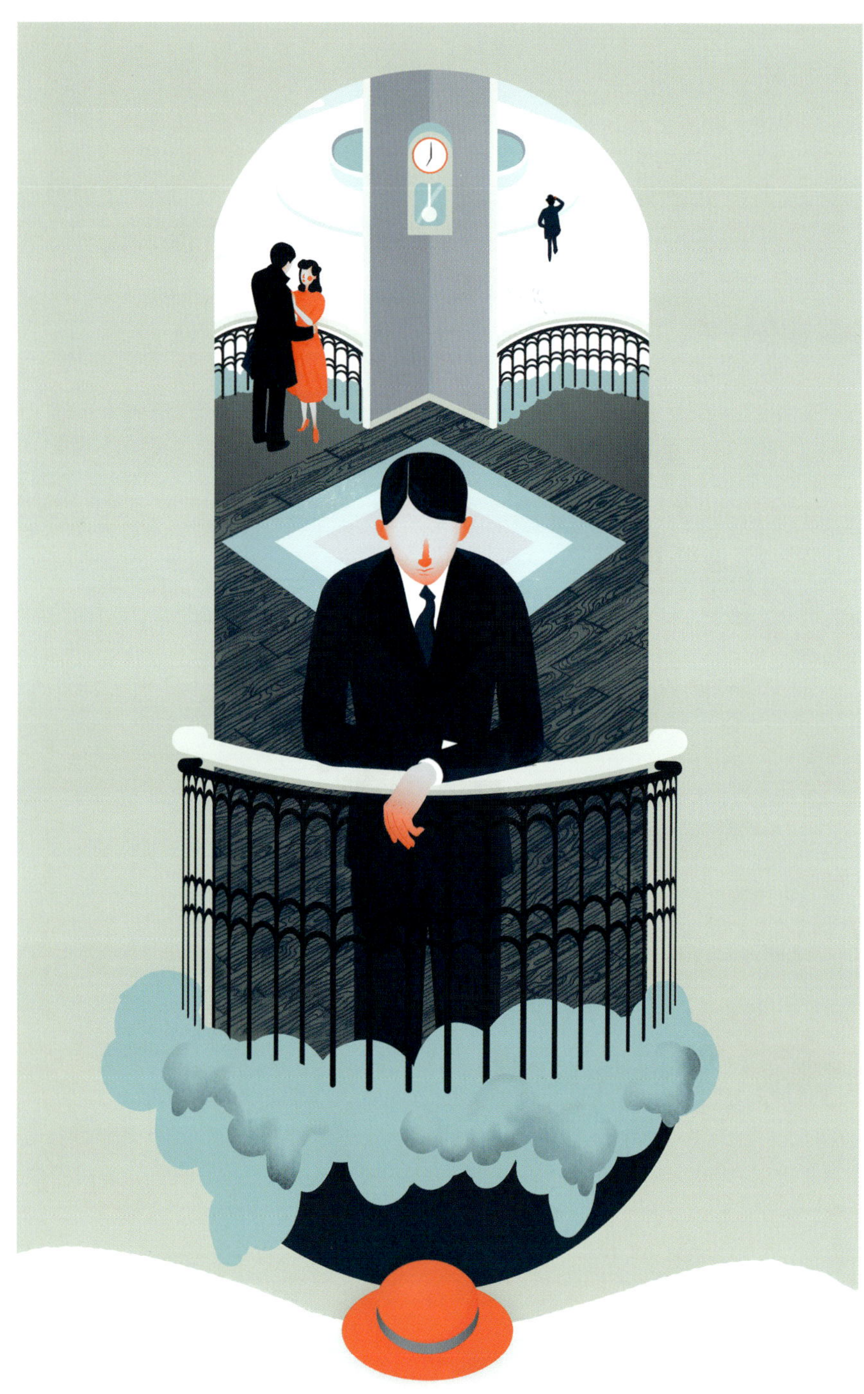

Elyse Salazar *www.elysesalazar.com*

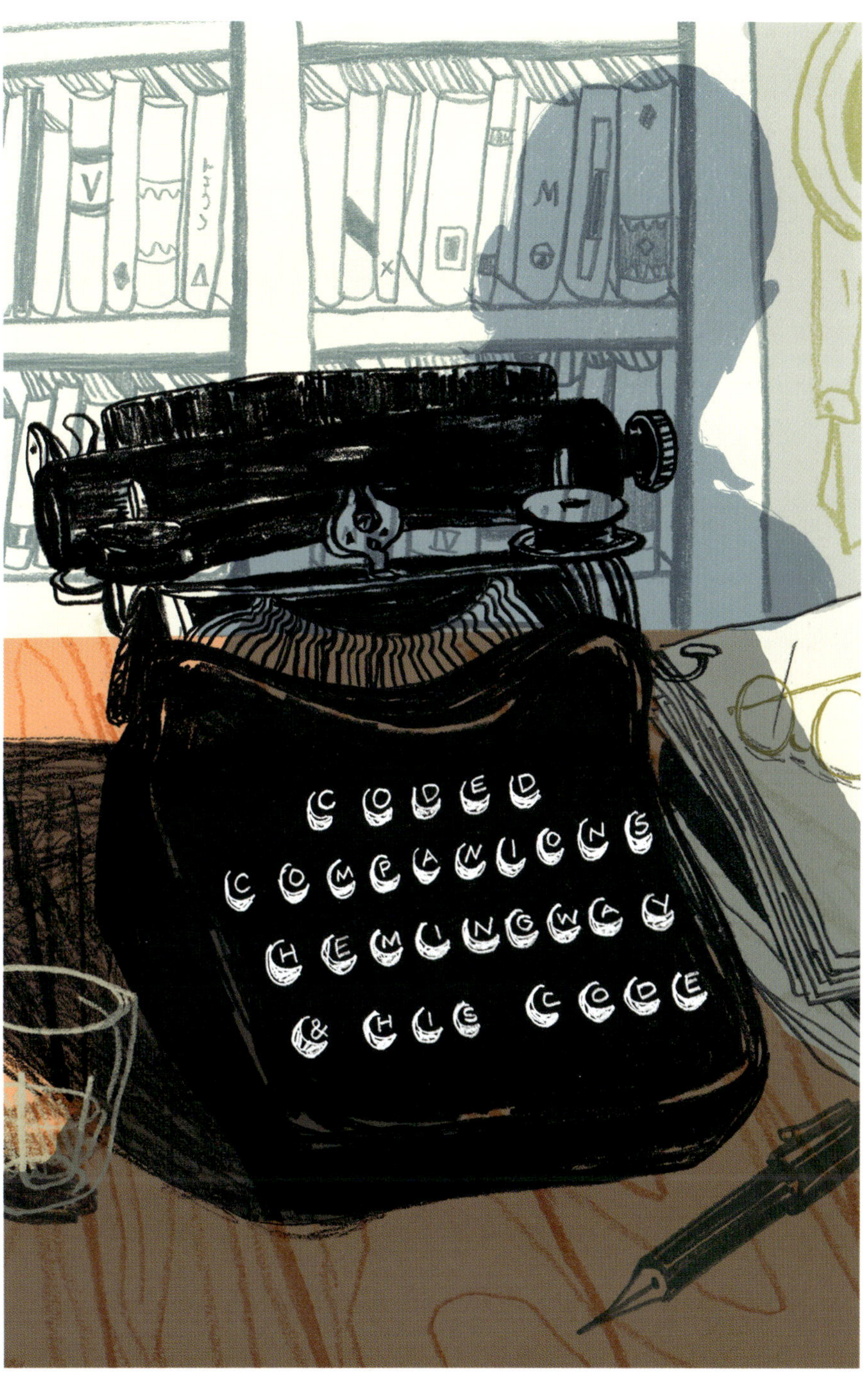

Molly Snee *www.mollysnee.com*

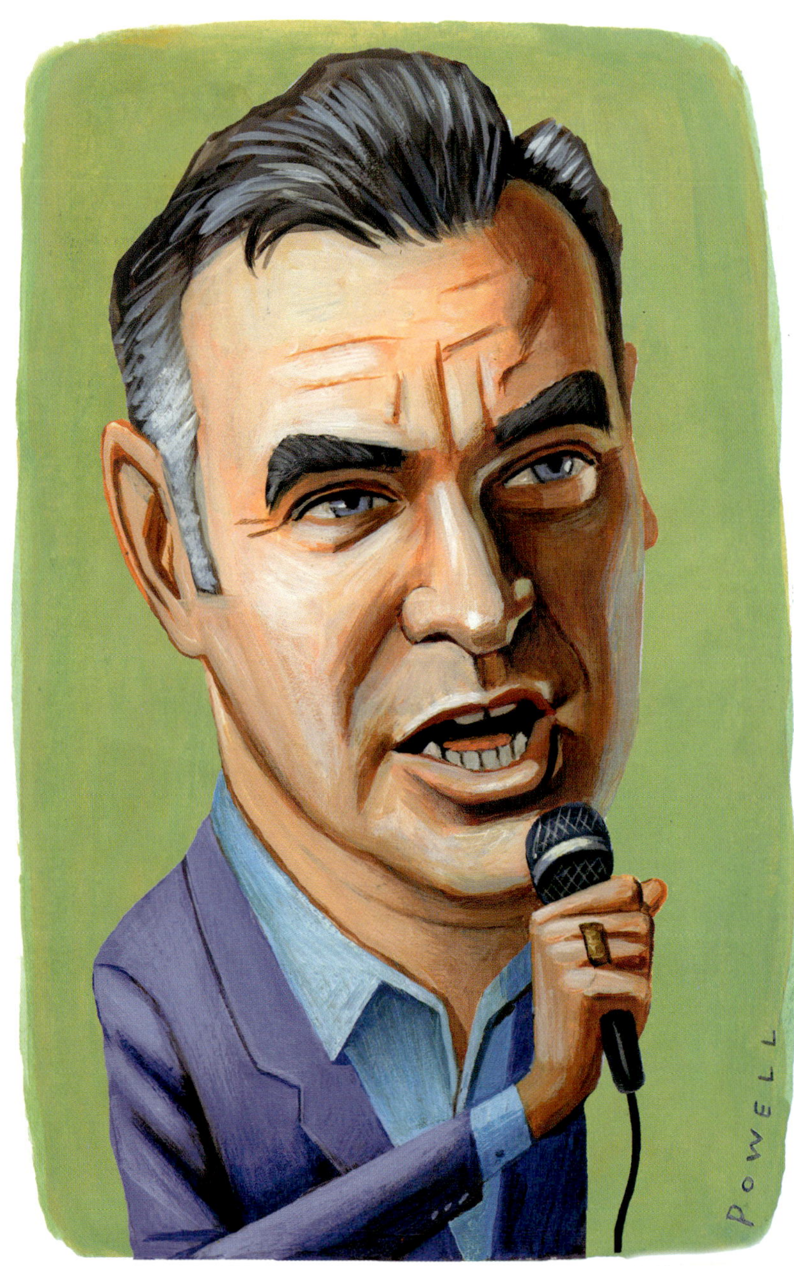

Charlie Powell *www.charliepowell.net*

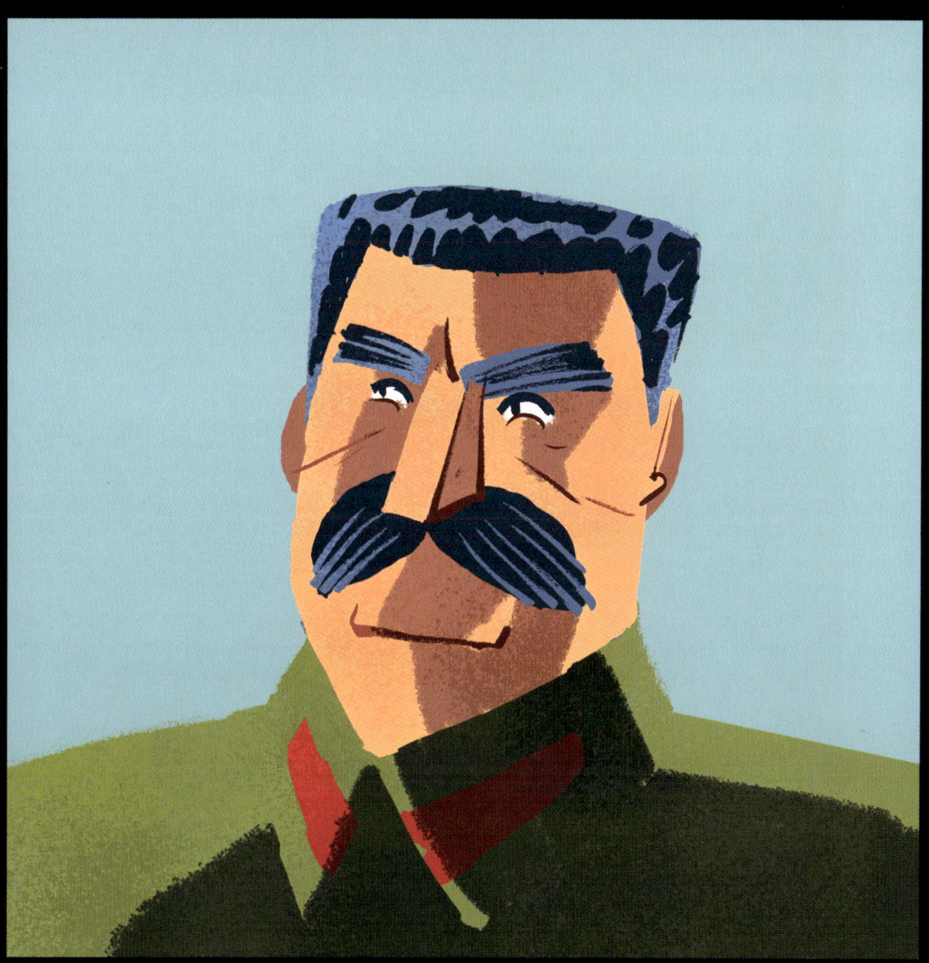

Jan Bielecki *www.janbielecki.com*

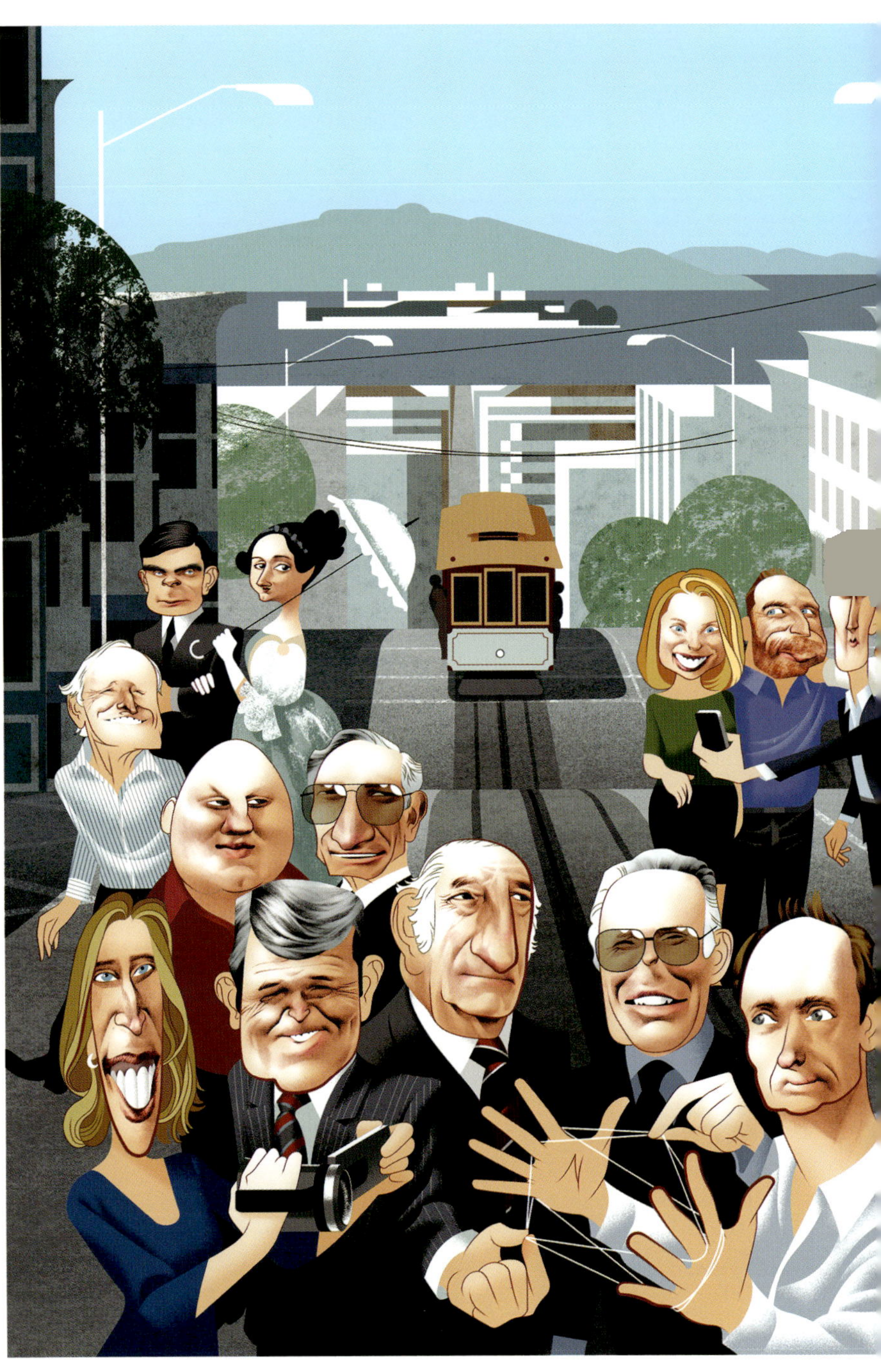

Andre Carrilho *www.andrecarrilho.com*

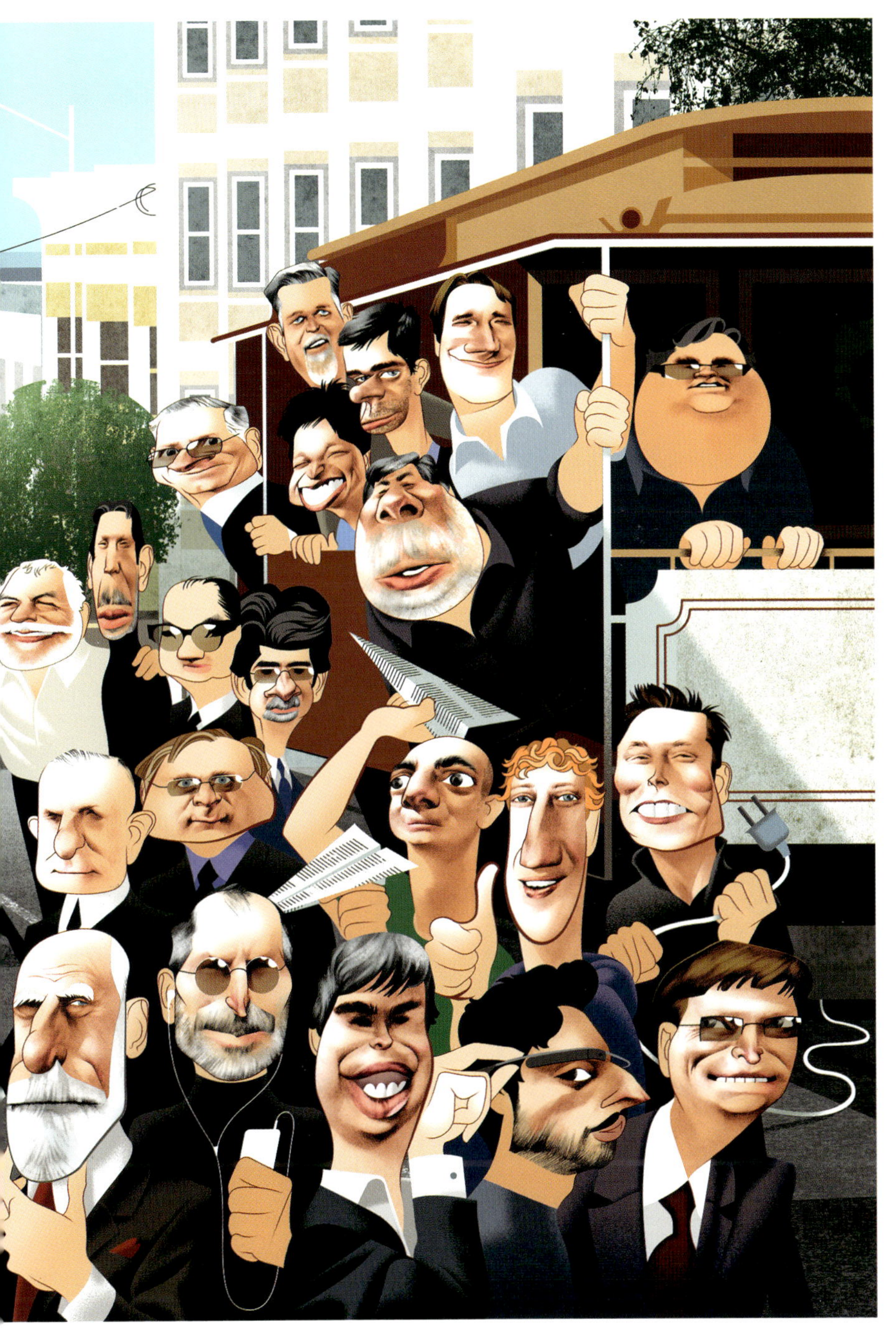

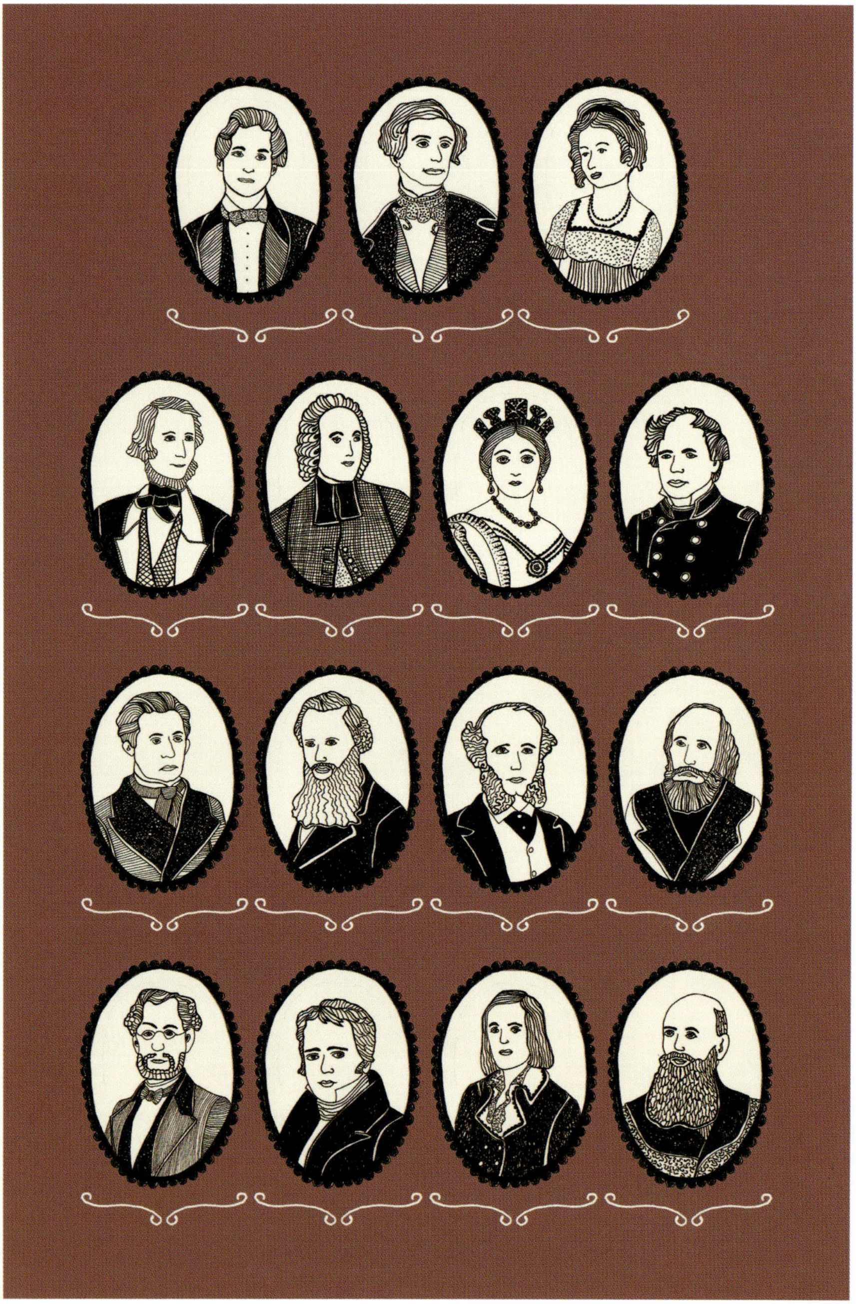

Sonja Kislinger *www.sanni.net*

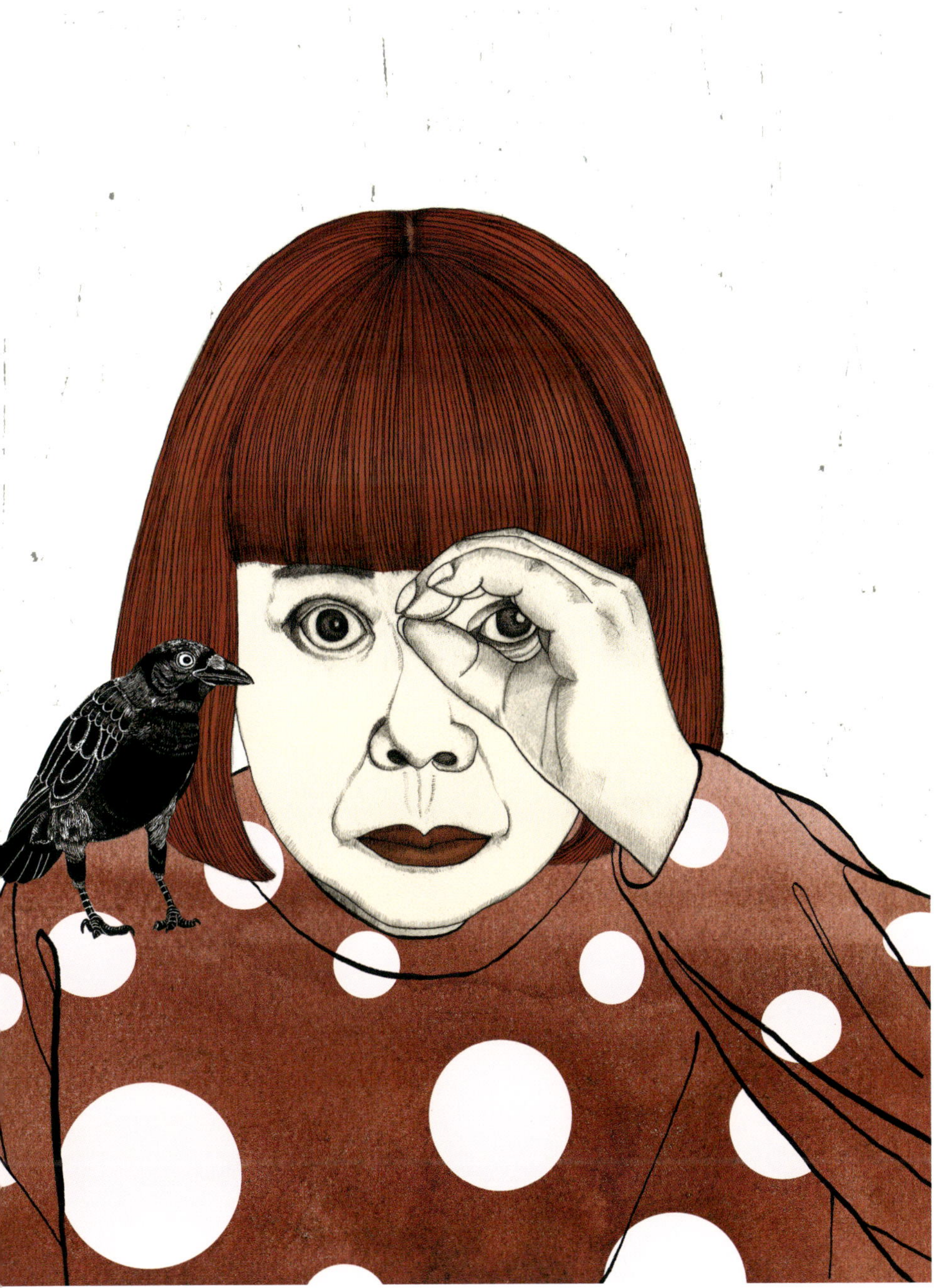

Jing Li *www.jingliwaa.tumblr.com*

163

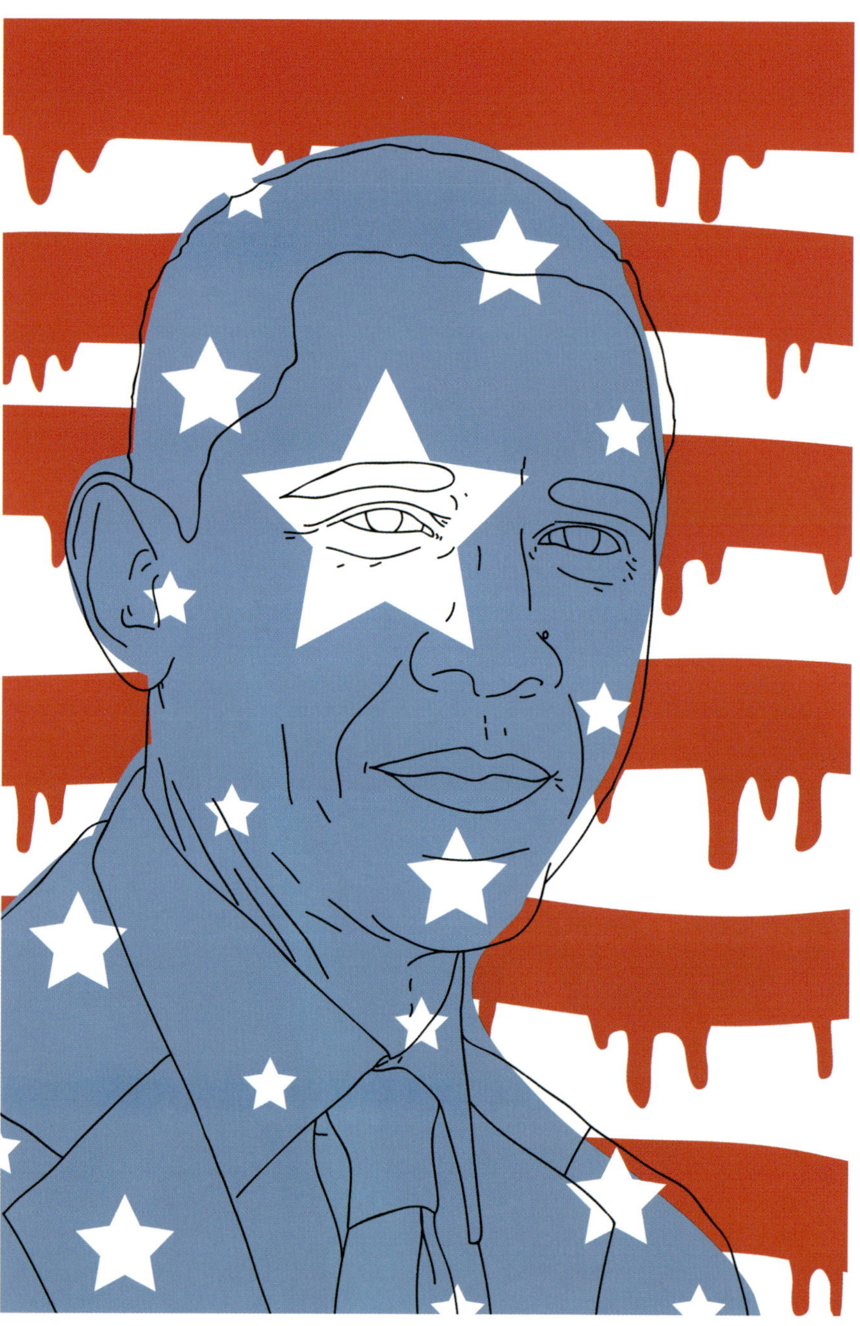

Federico Gastaldi *www.federicogastaldi.com*

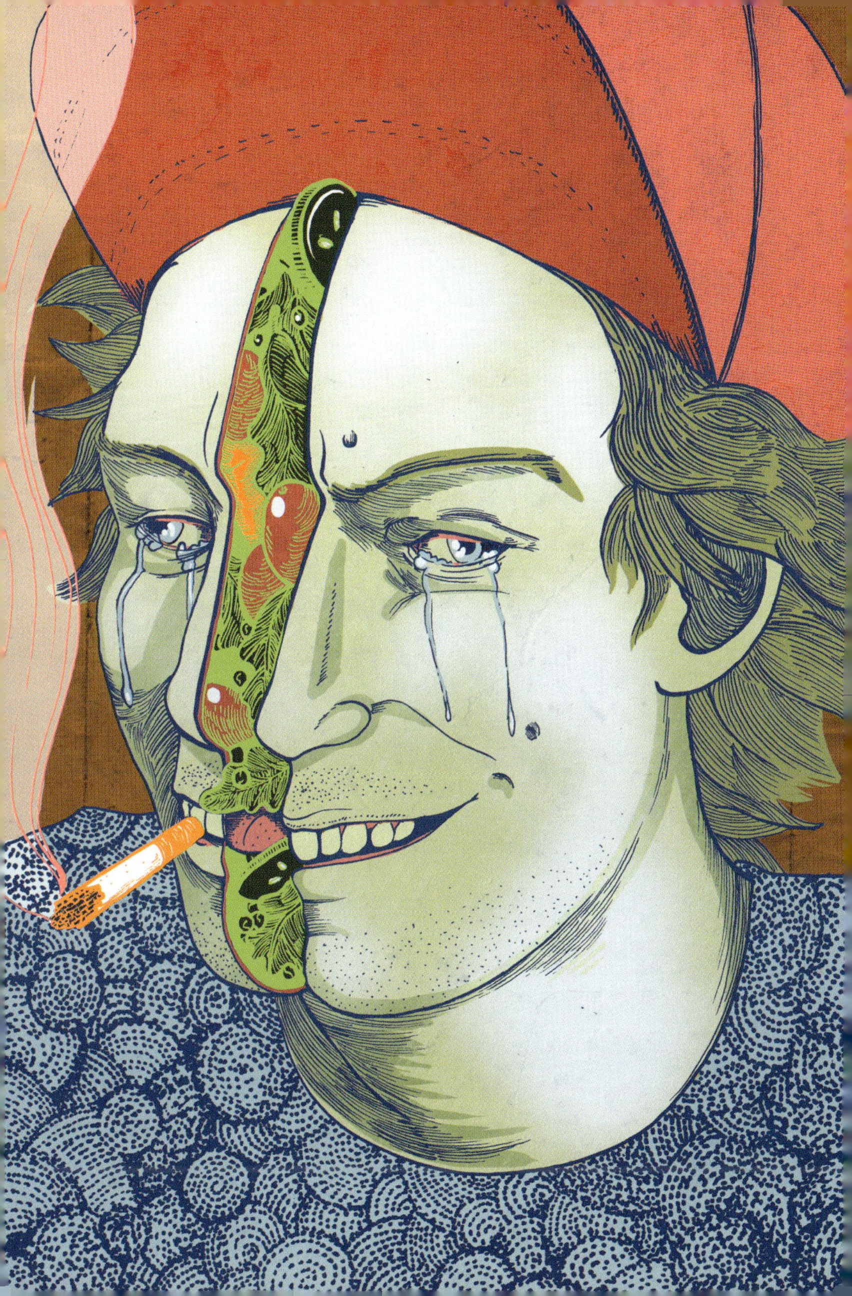

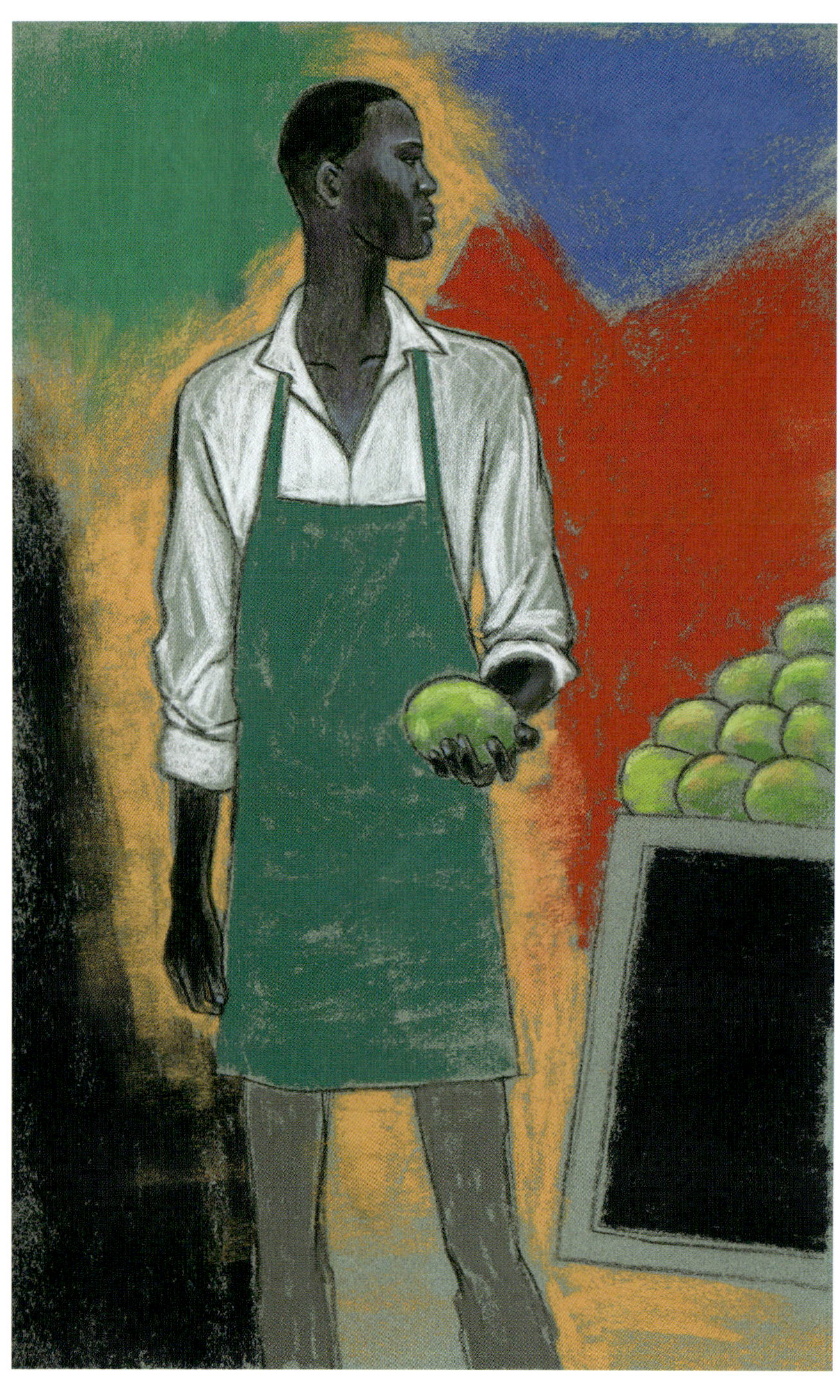

Jamie Hogan *www.jamiehogan.com*

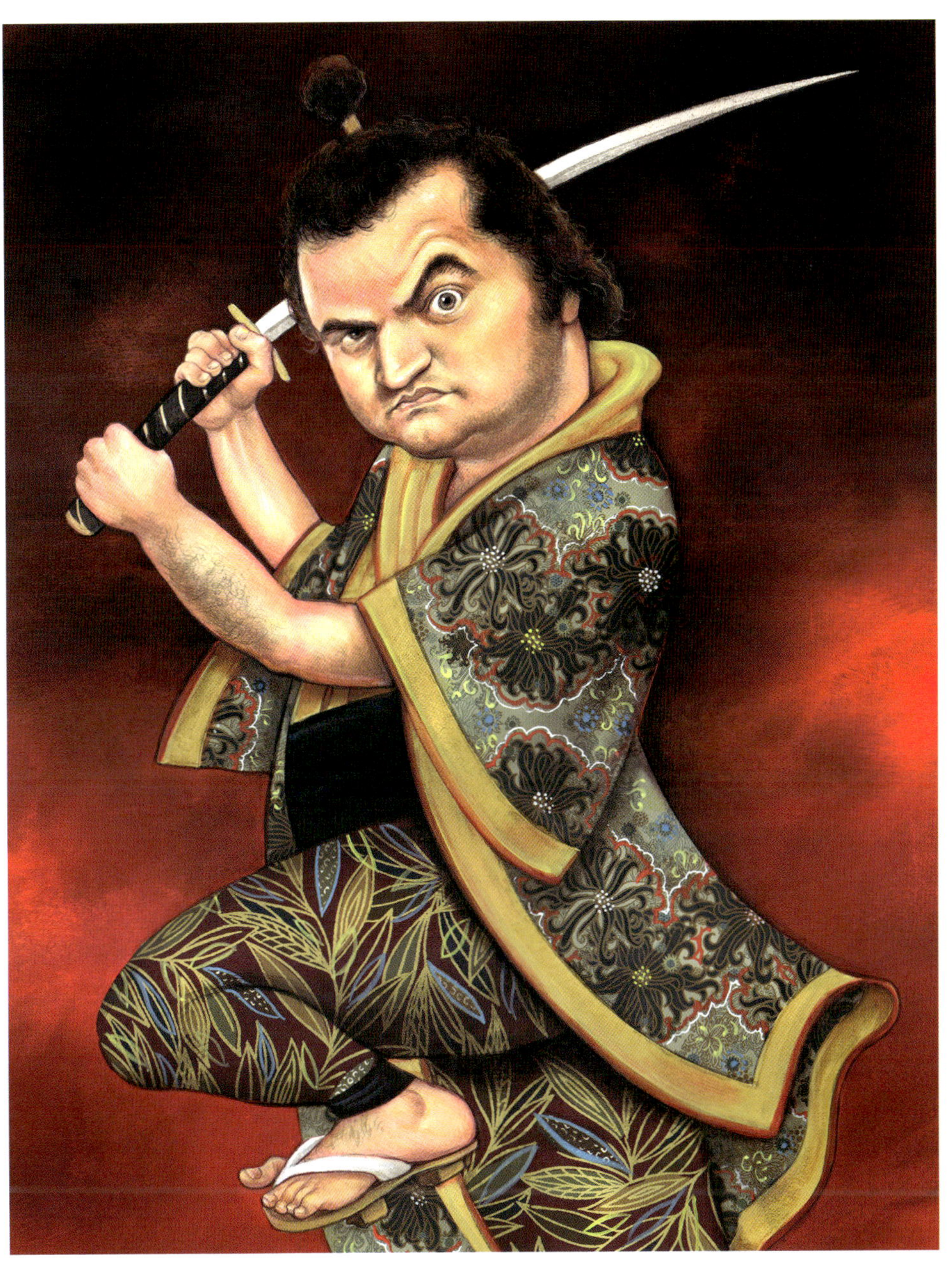

Anita Kunz *www.anitakunz.com*

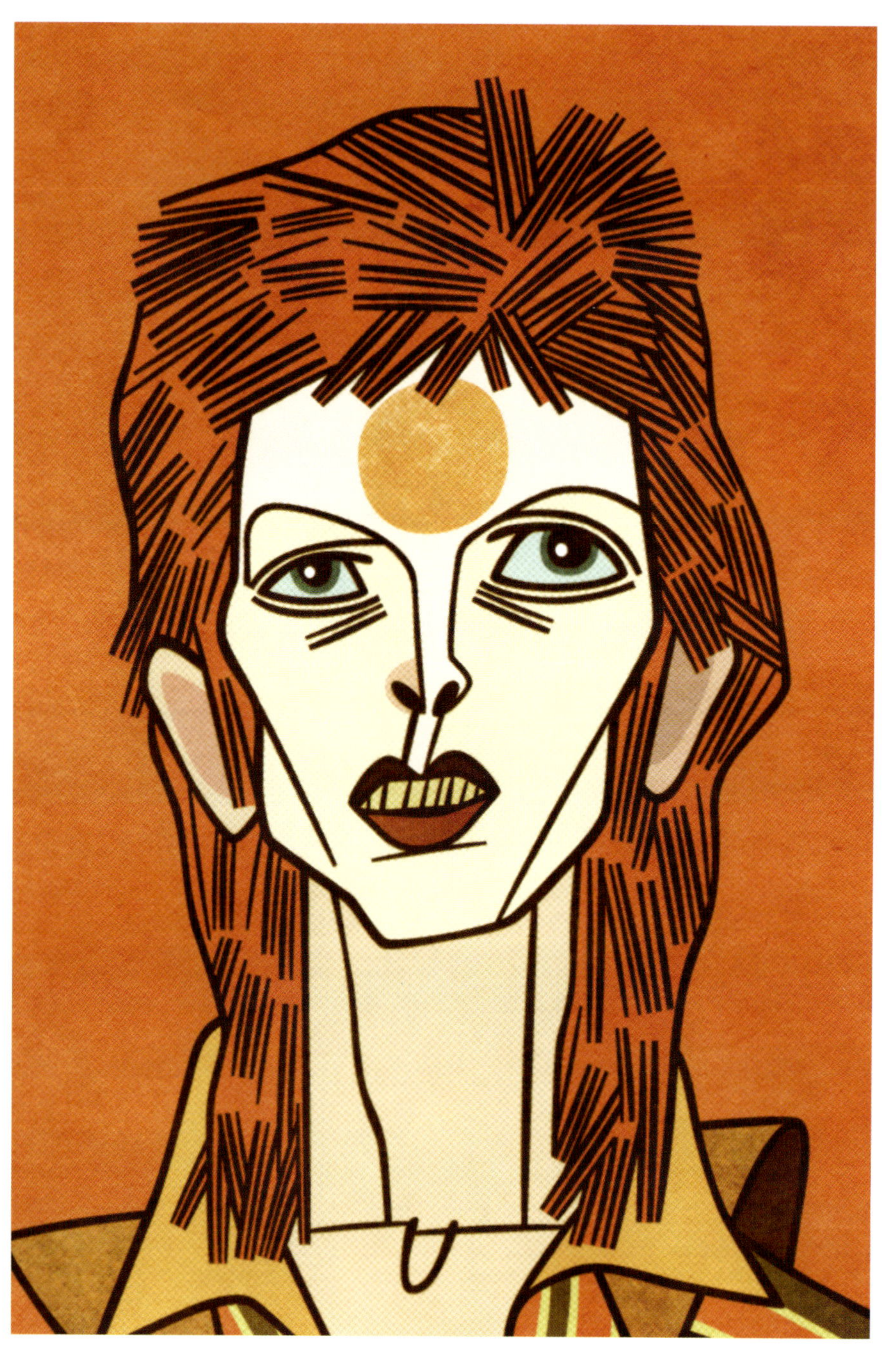

Toby Thane Neighbors *www.tobythaneneighbors.com*

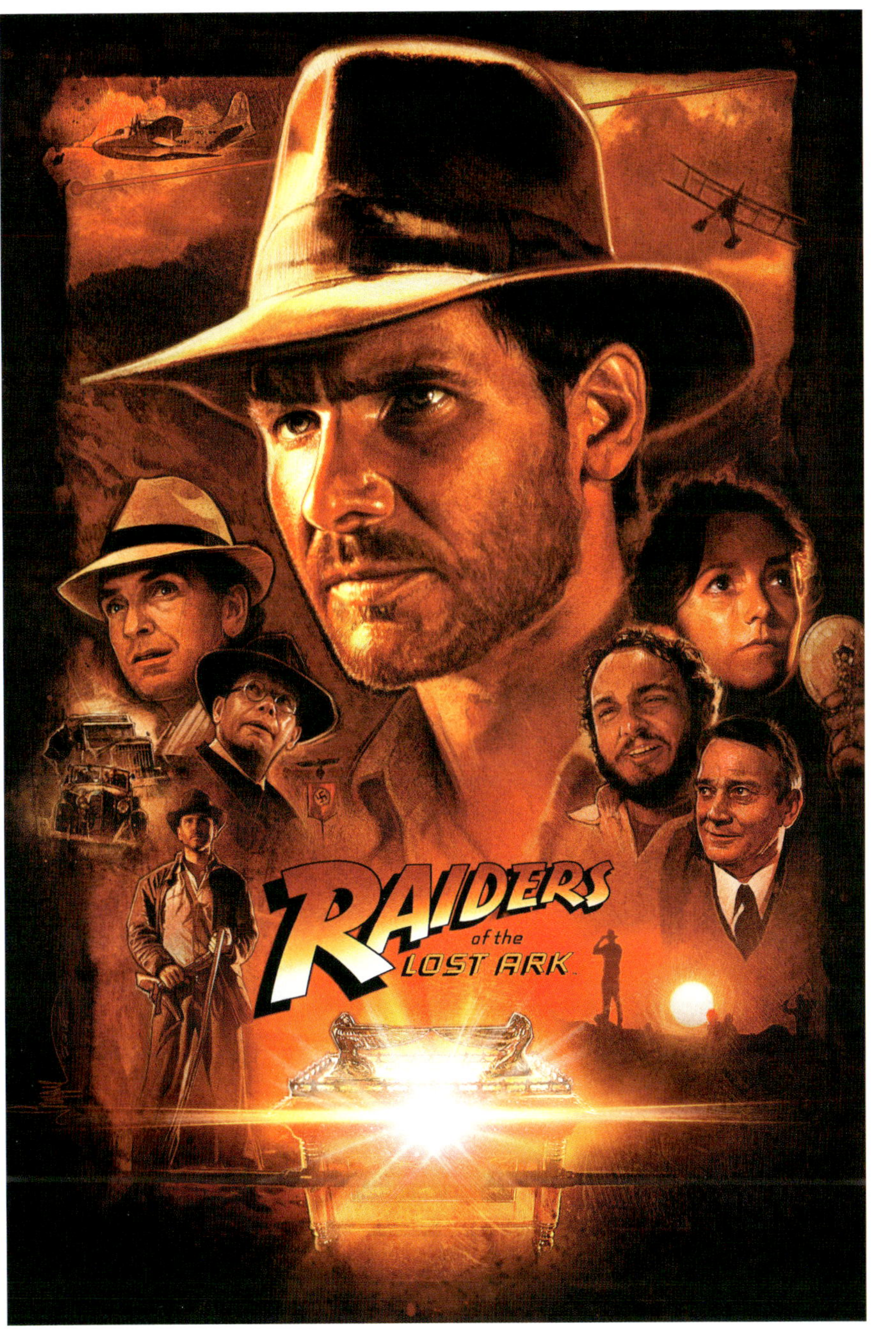

169

Paul Shipper *www.paulshipperstudio.com*

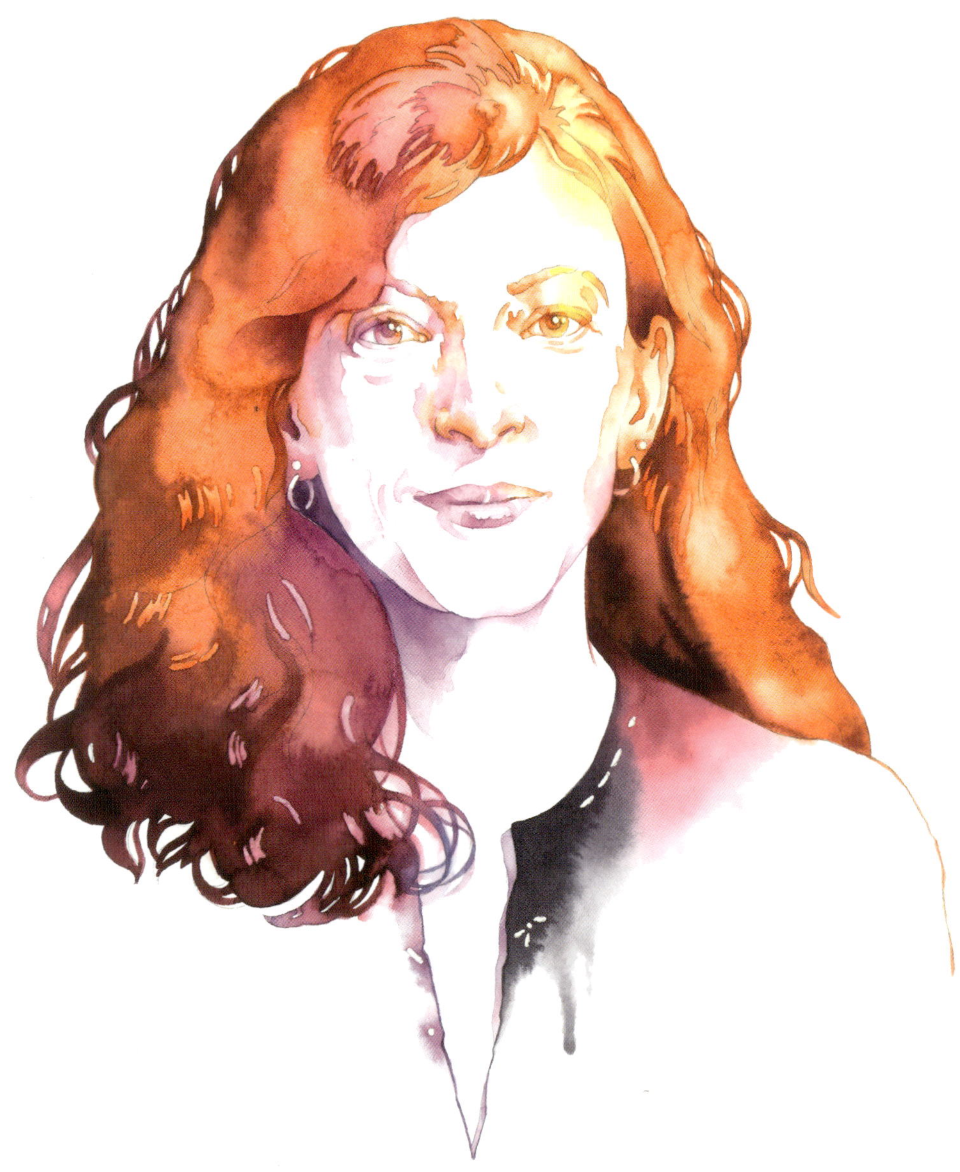

Cheryl Chalmers *www.cherylchalmers.com*

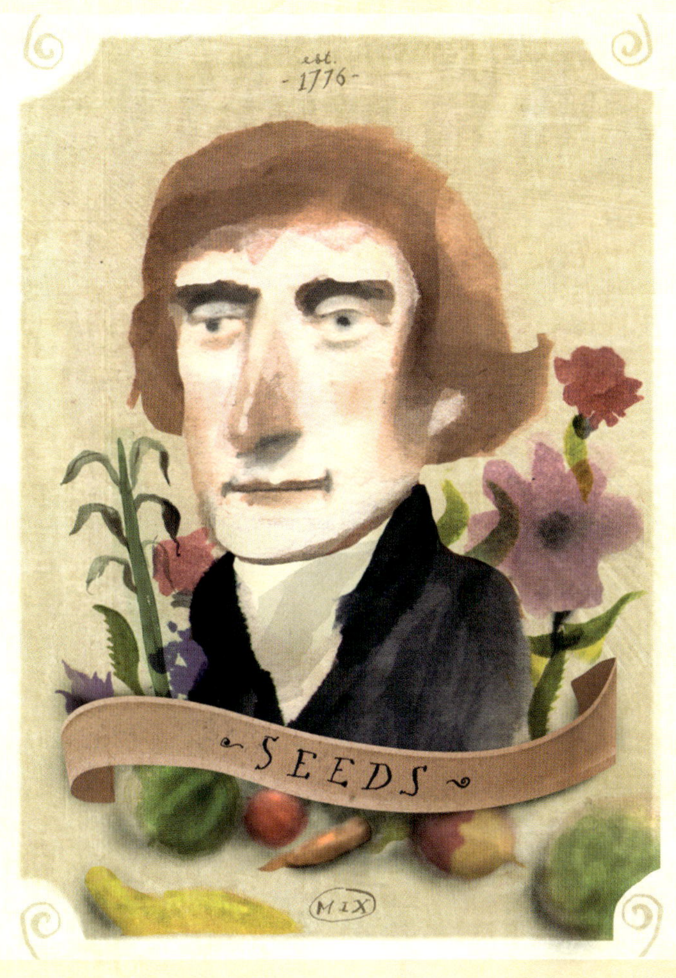

est.
- 1776 -
SEEDS
MIX

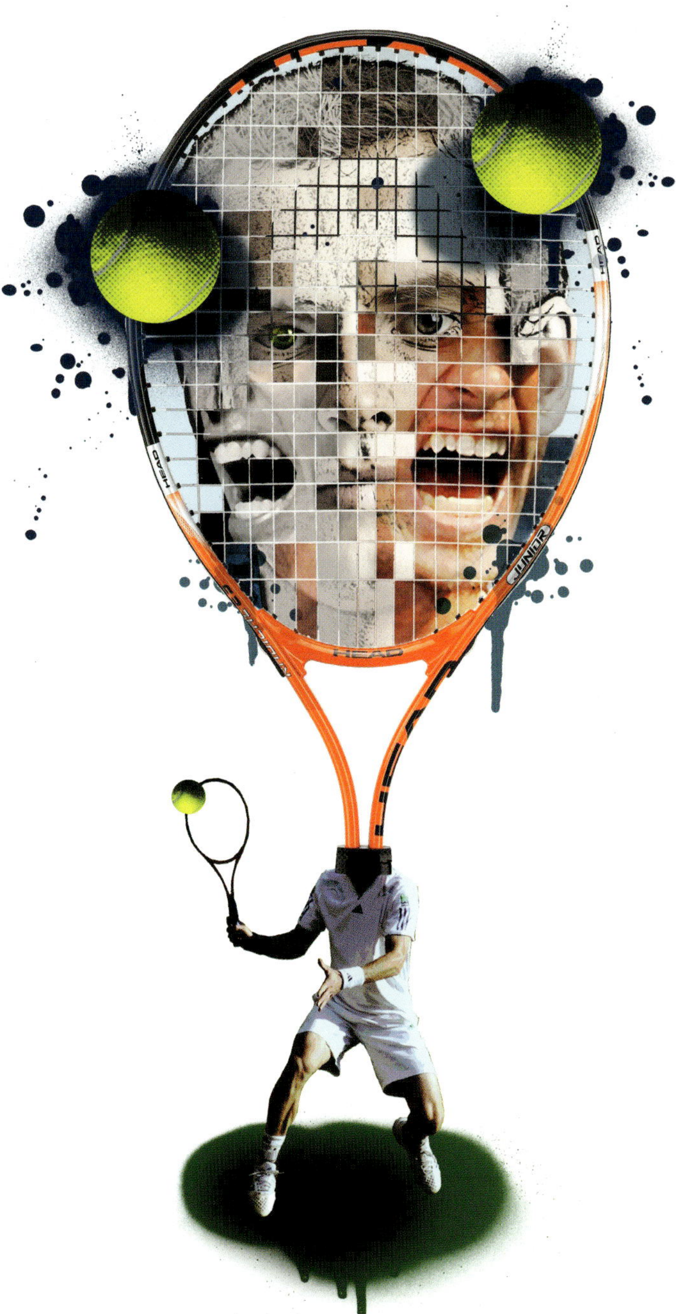

172

Paul Bateman *www.paulbateman.co.uk*

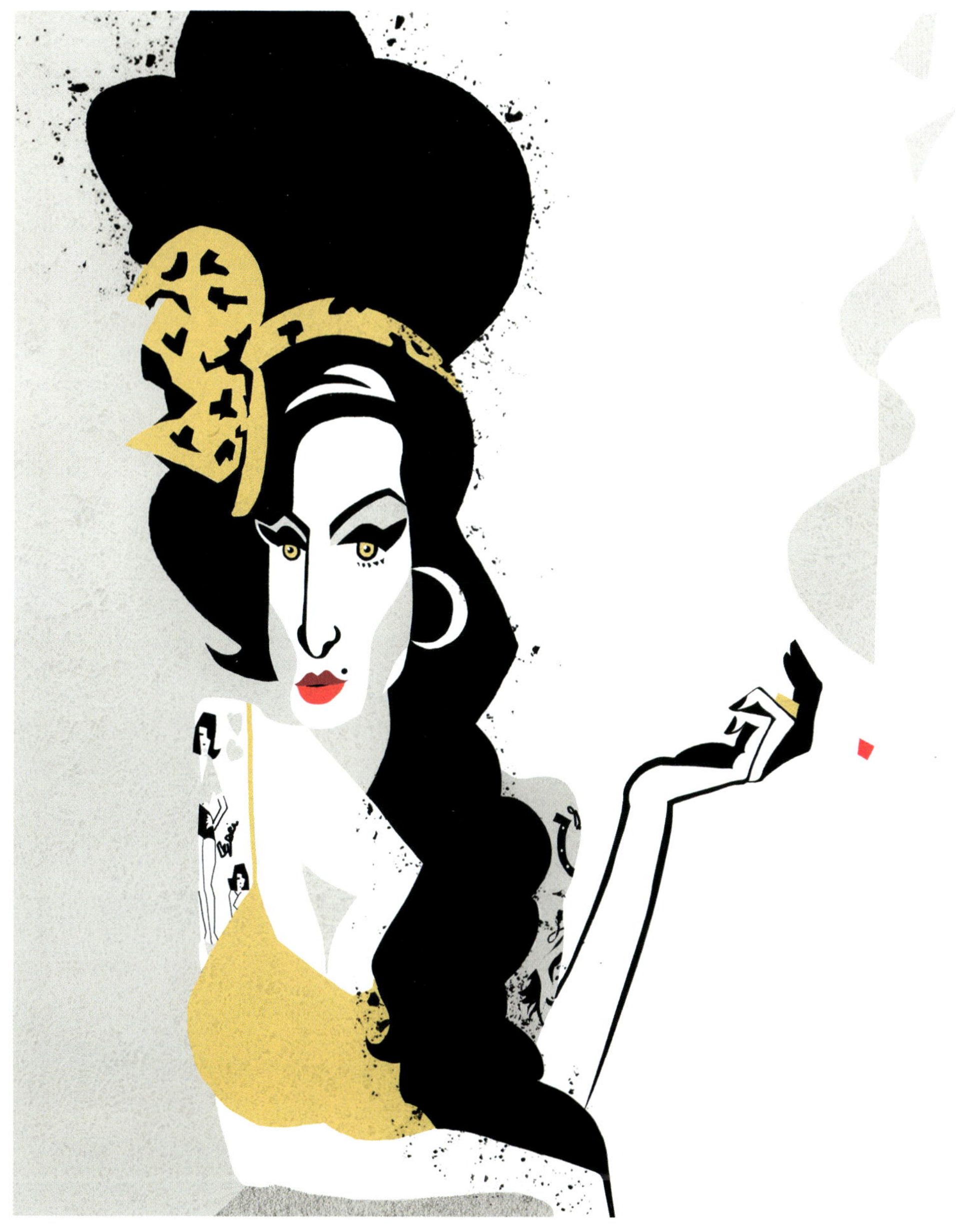

Igor Gnedo *www.igorgnedo.com*

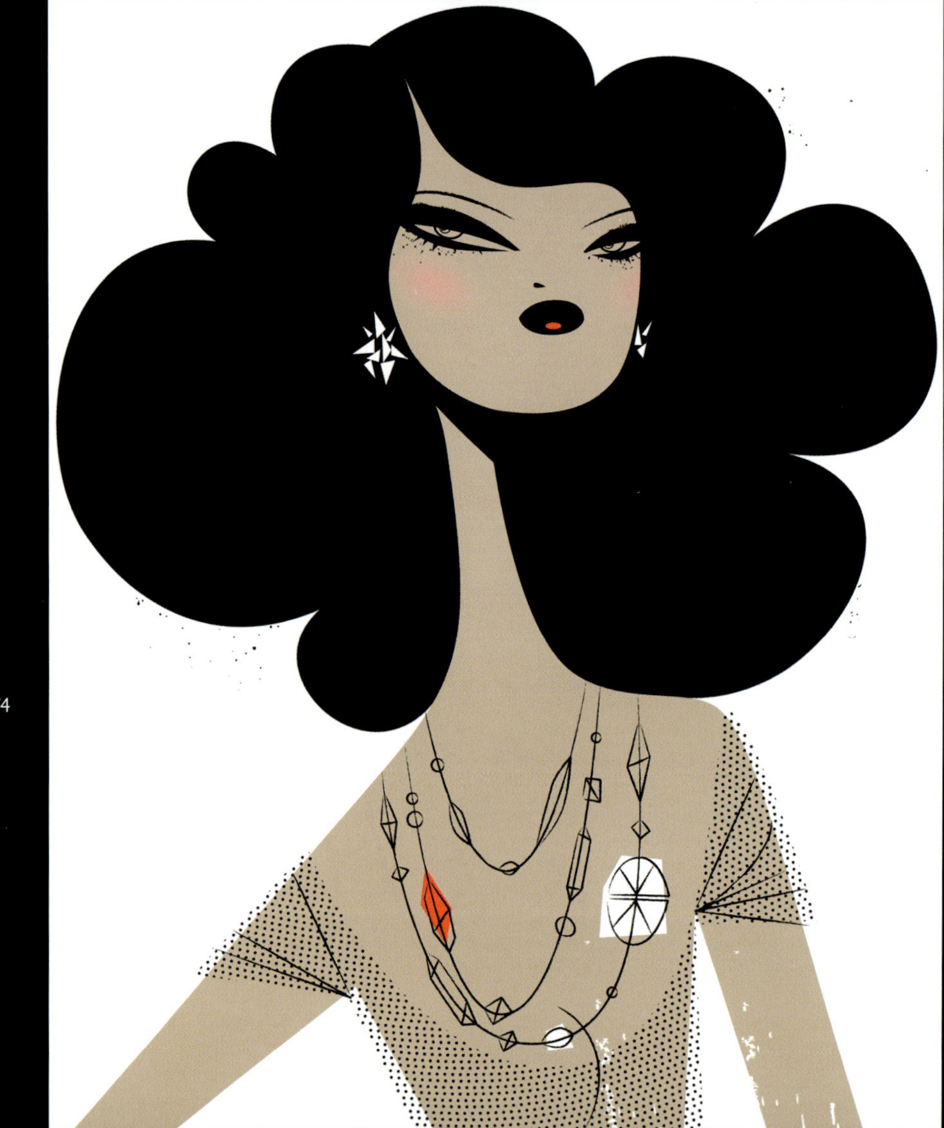

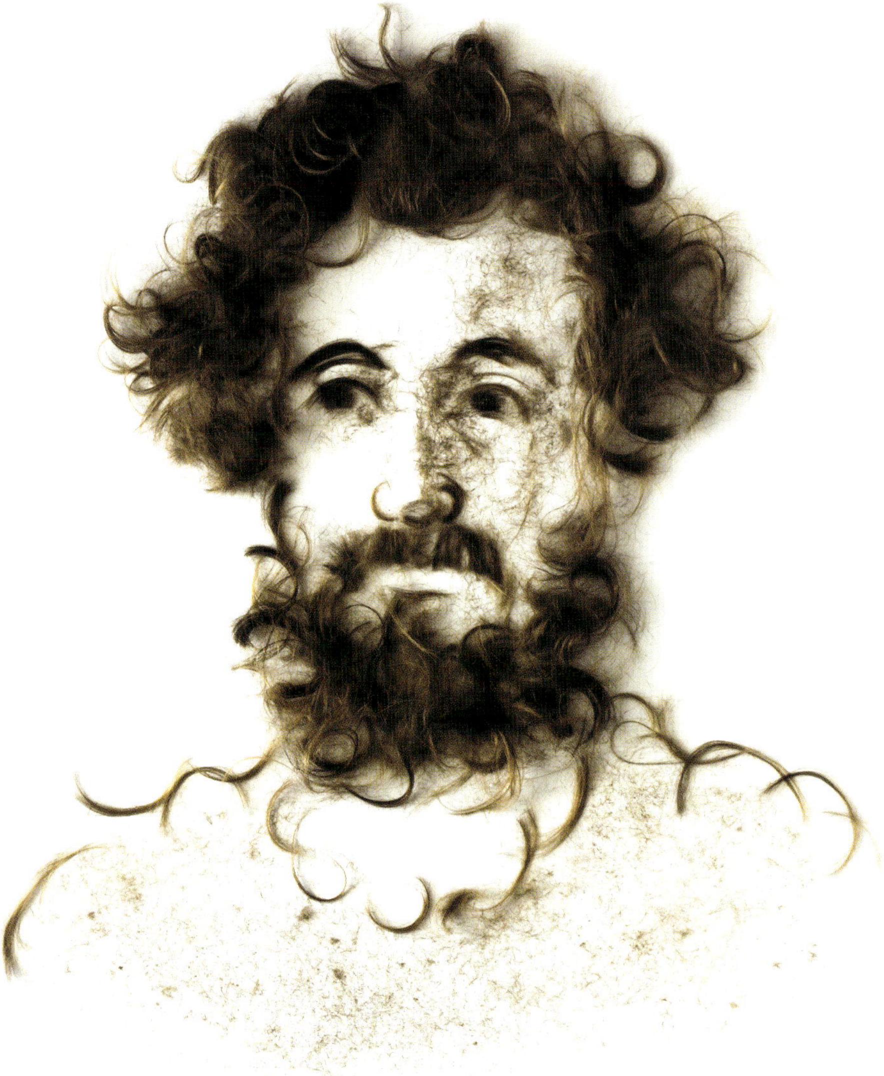

175

Filip Peraić *www.peraic.com*

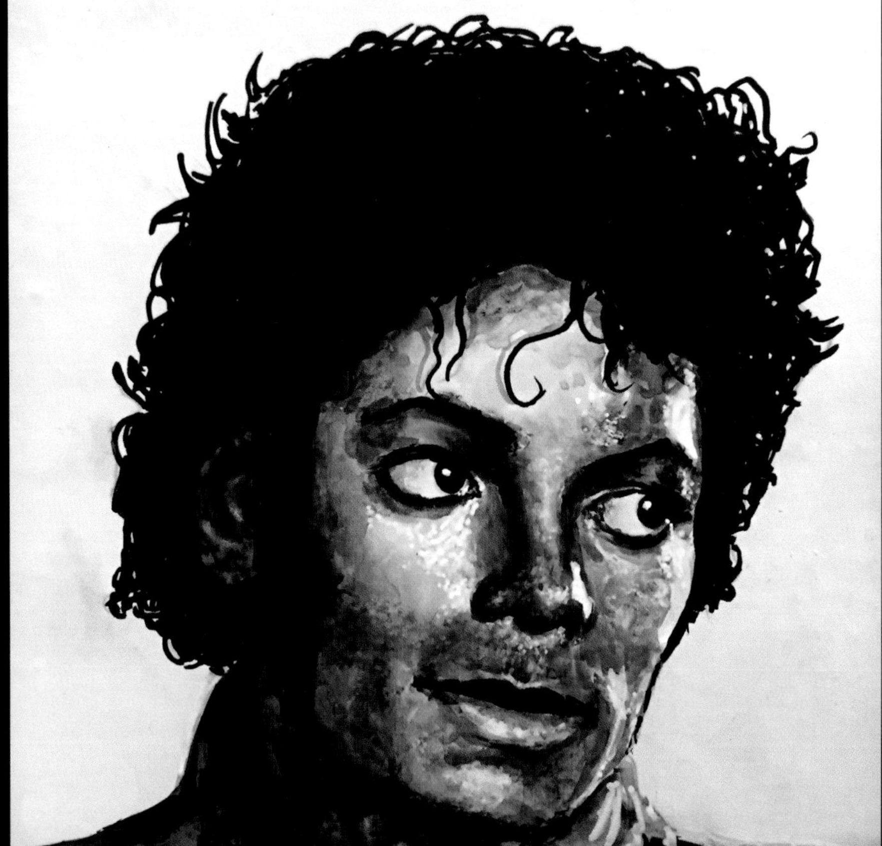

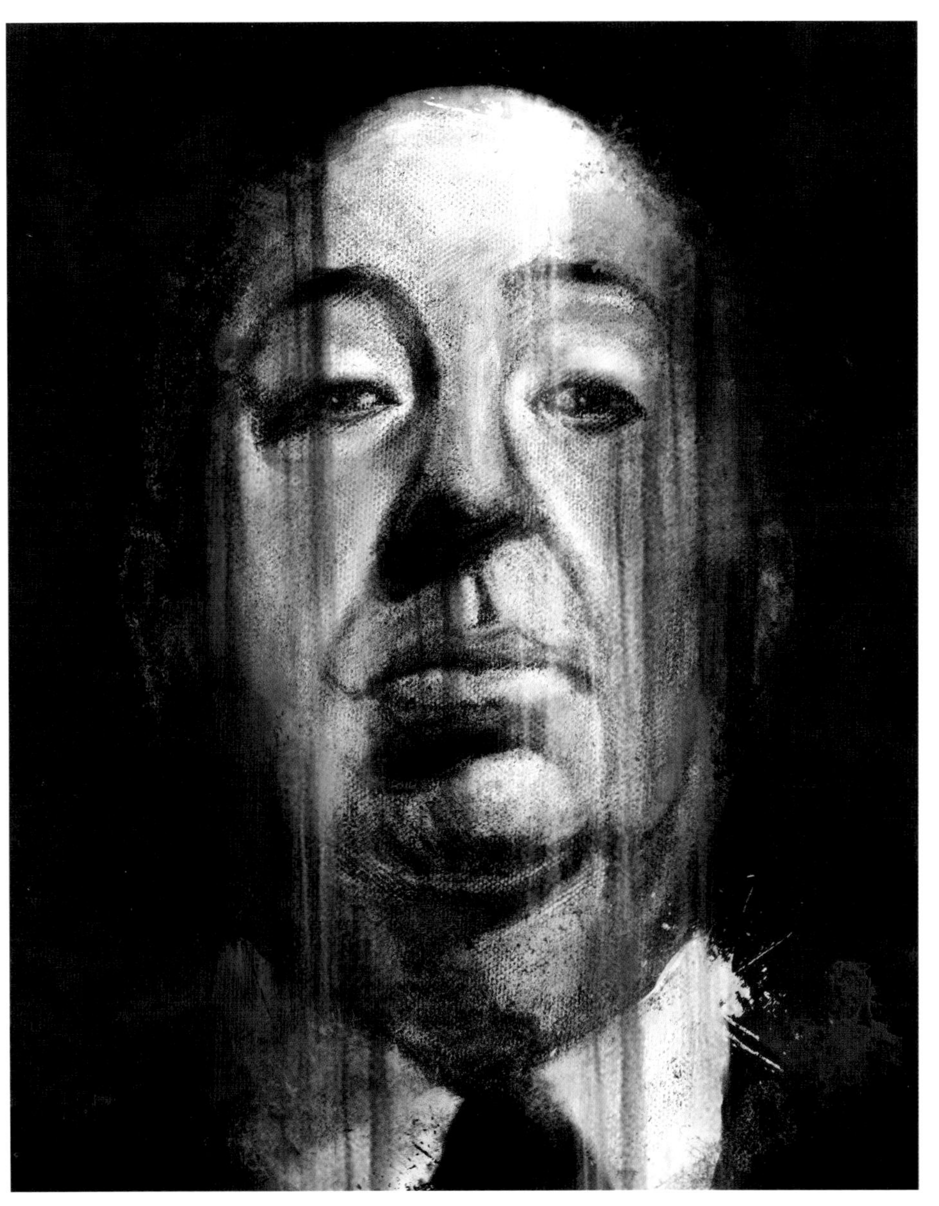

Somya Raju *www.somyaraju.com*

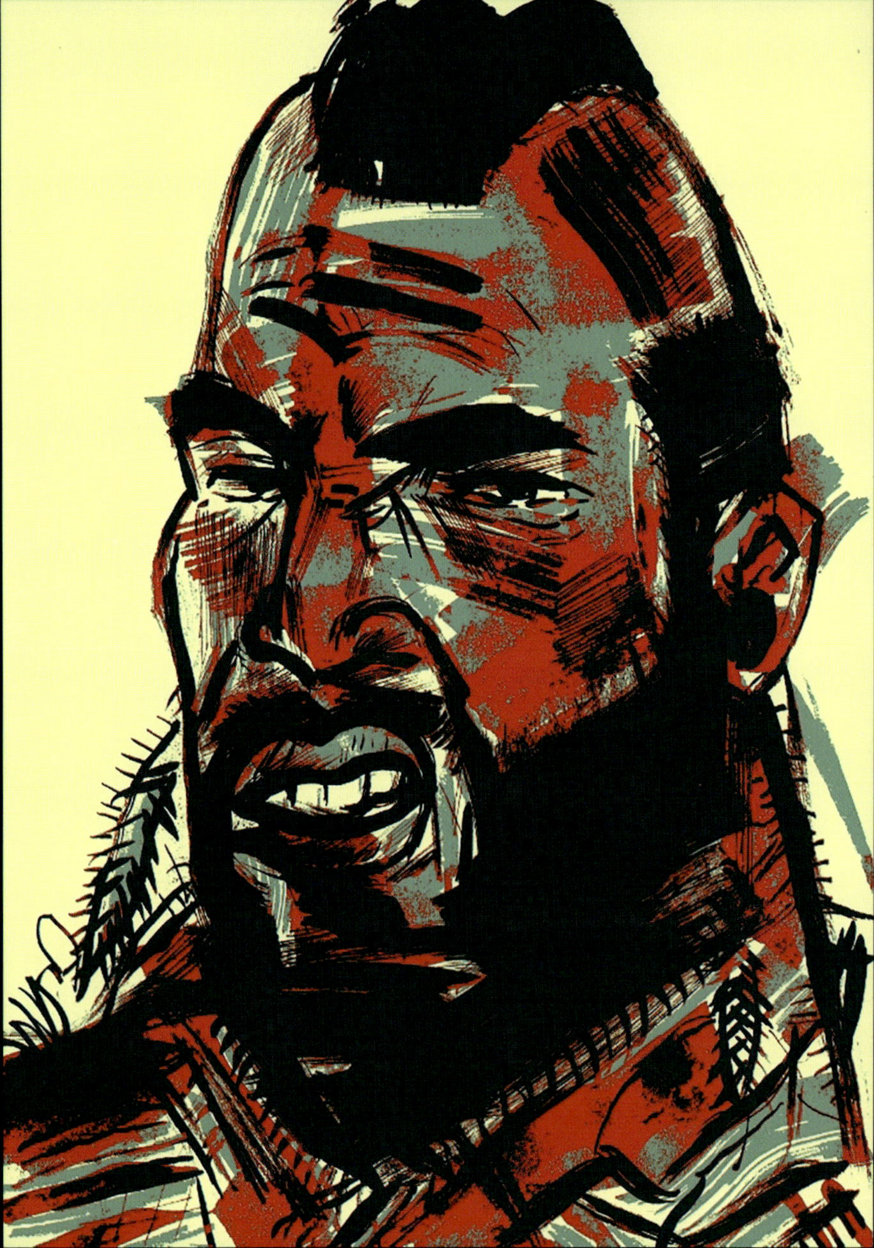

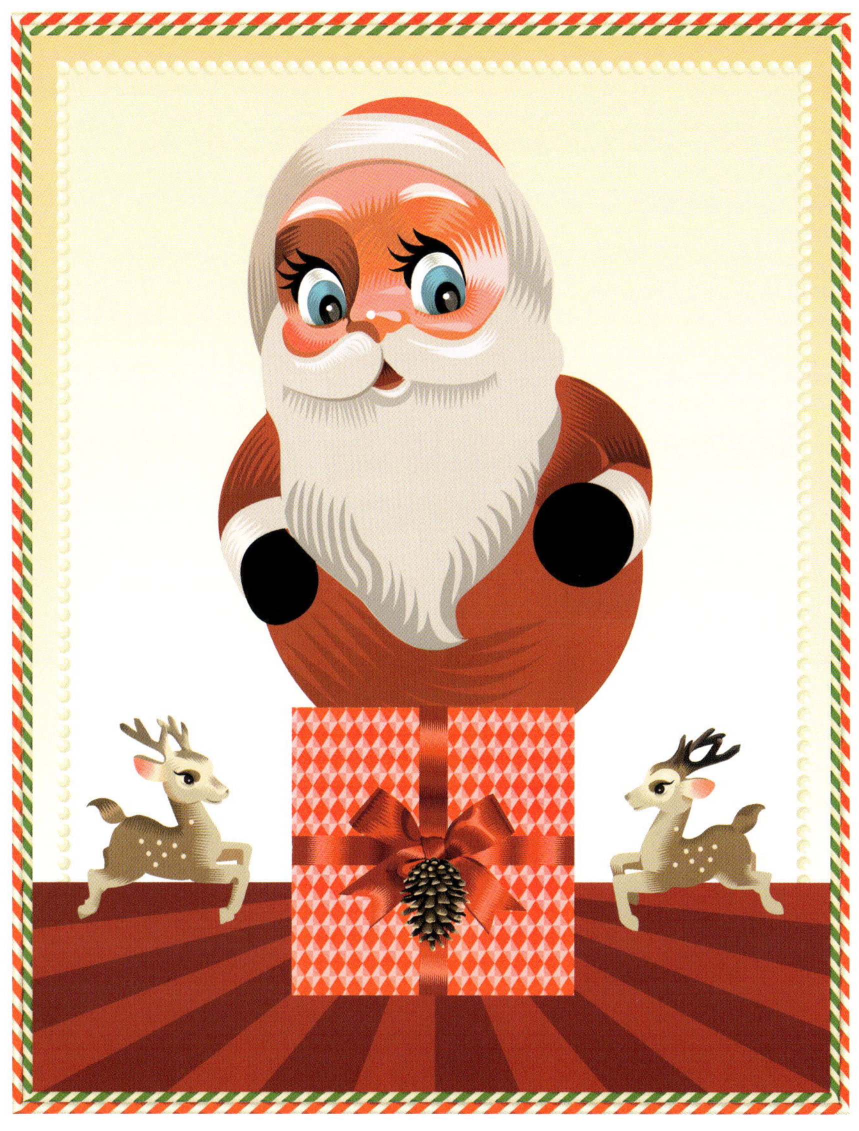

Q. Cassetti *www.qcassetti.com*

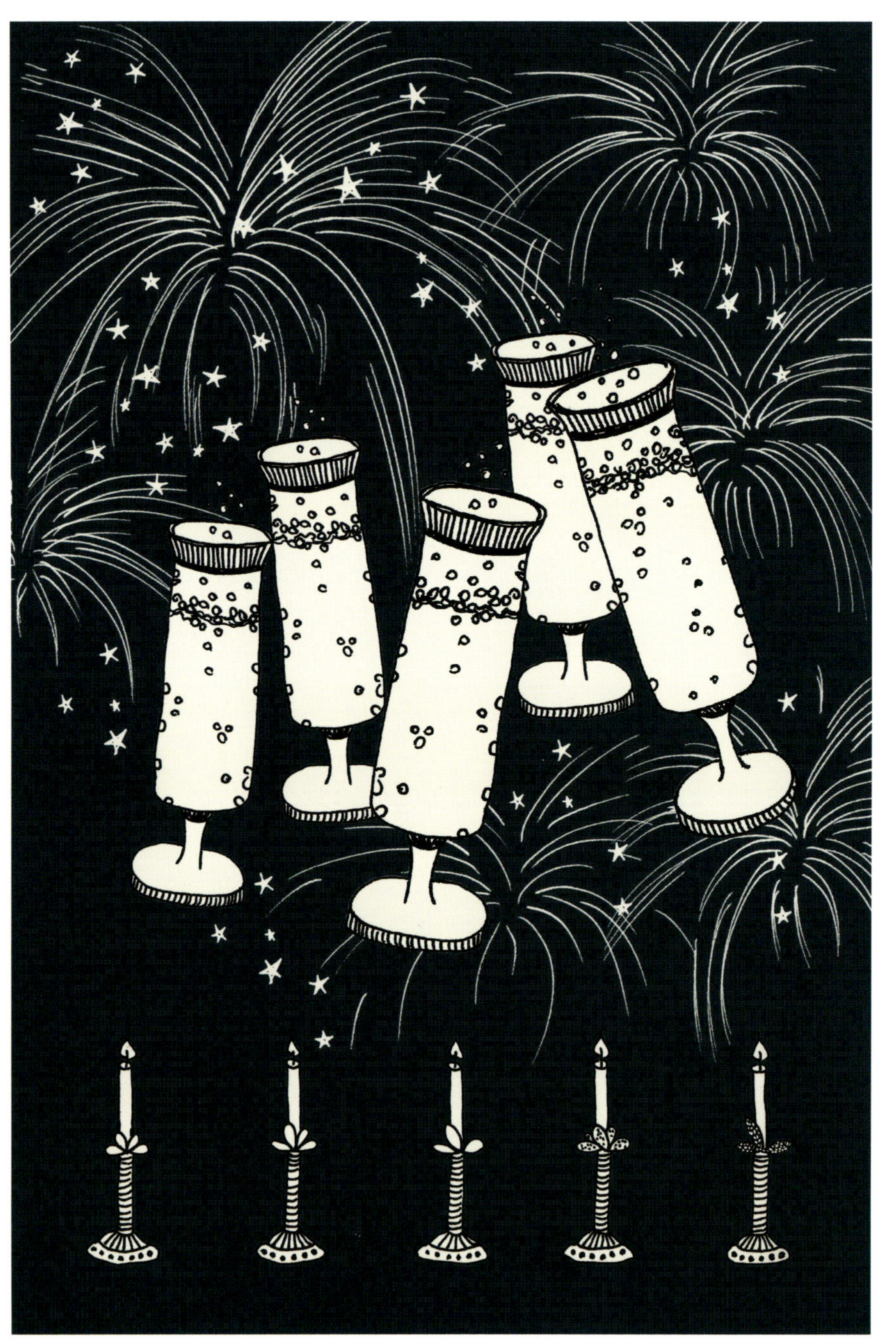

Sonja Kislinger *www.sanni.net*

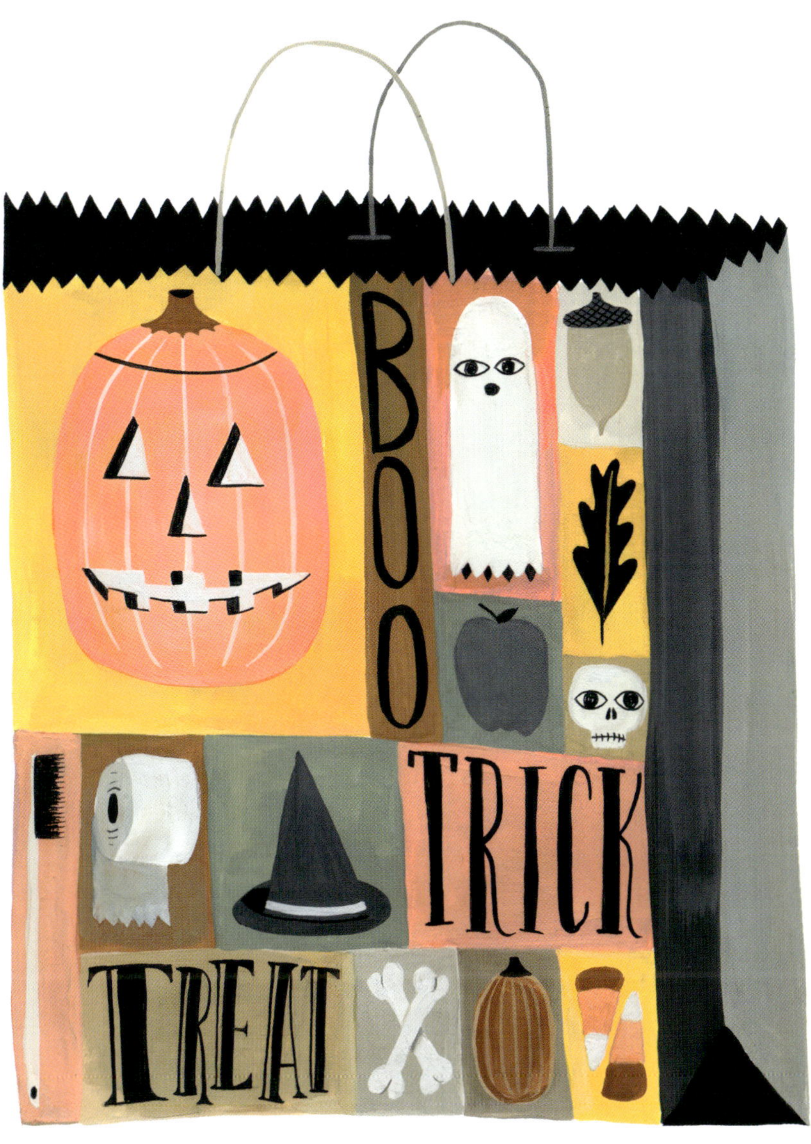

Mark Hoffmann *www.studiohoffmann.com*

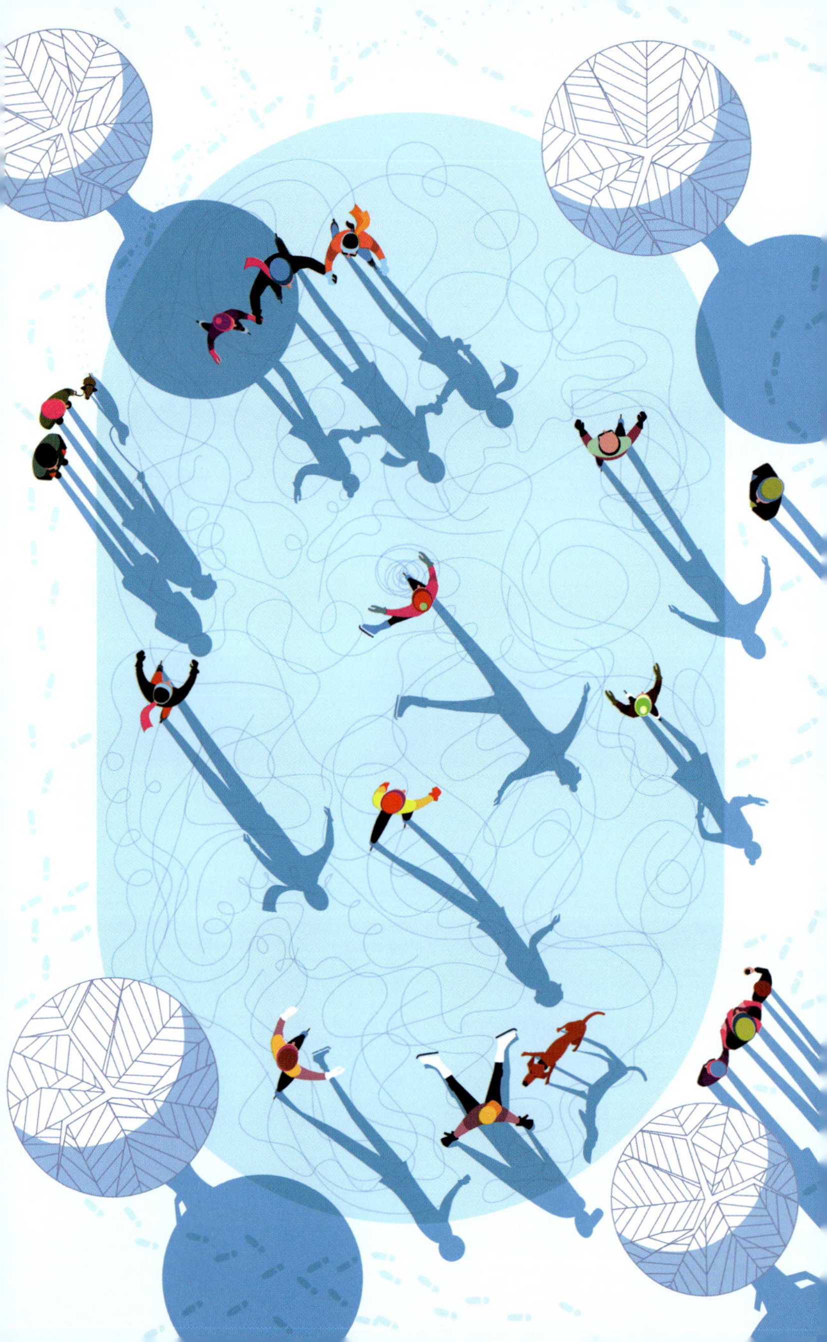

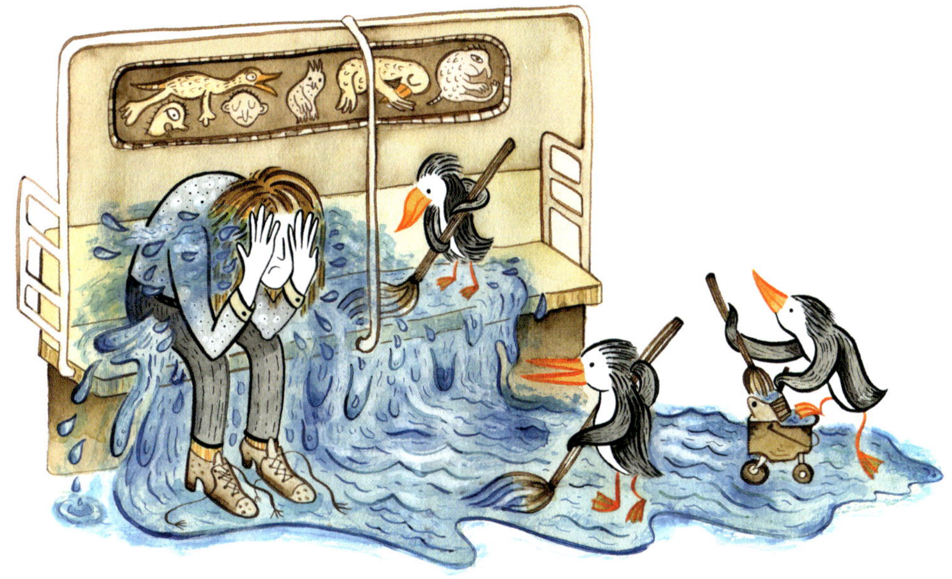

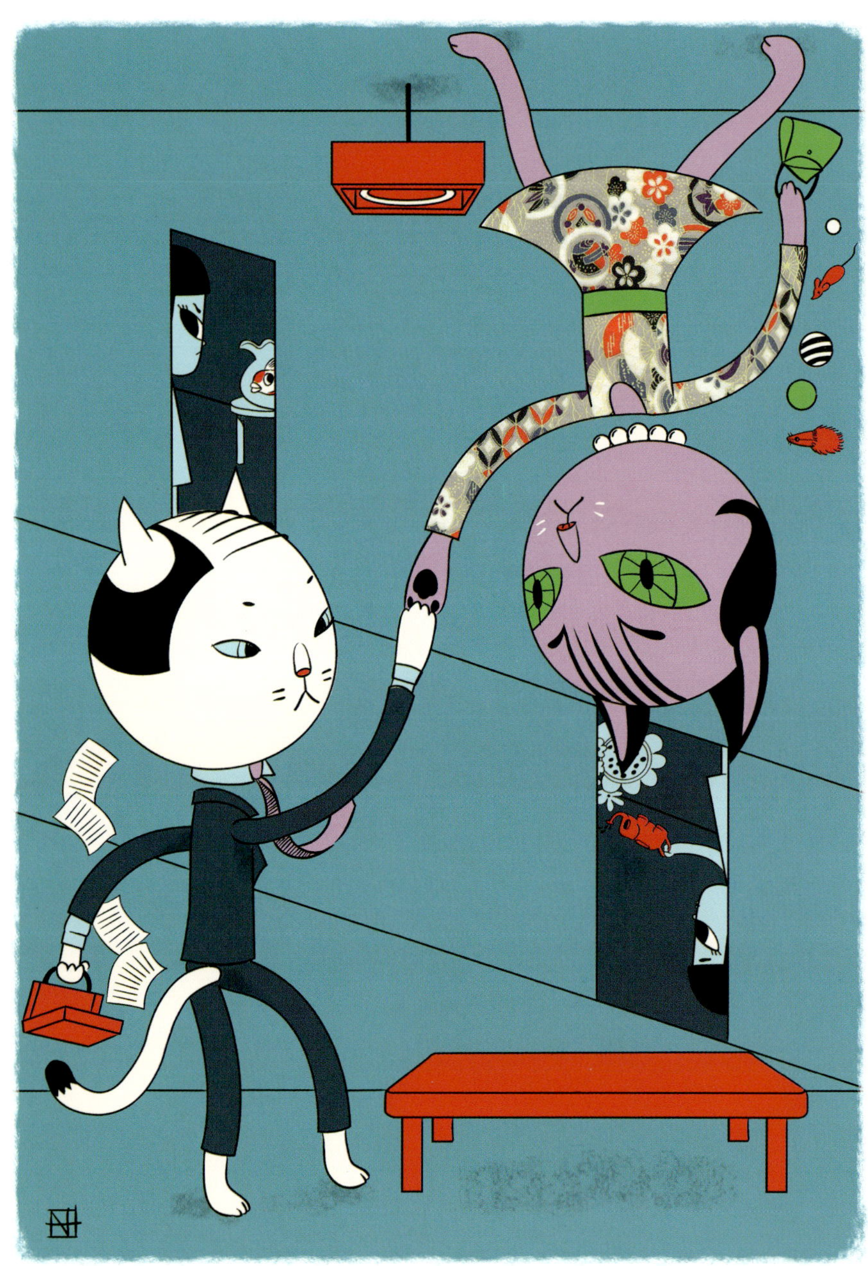

184

Andrea Innocent *www.otoshimono.org*

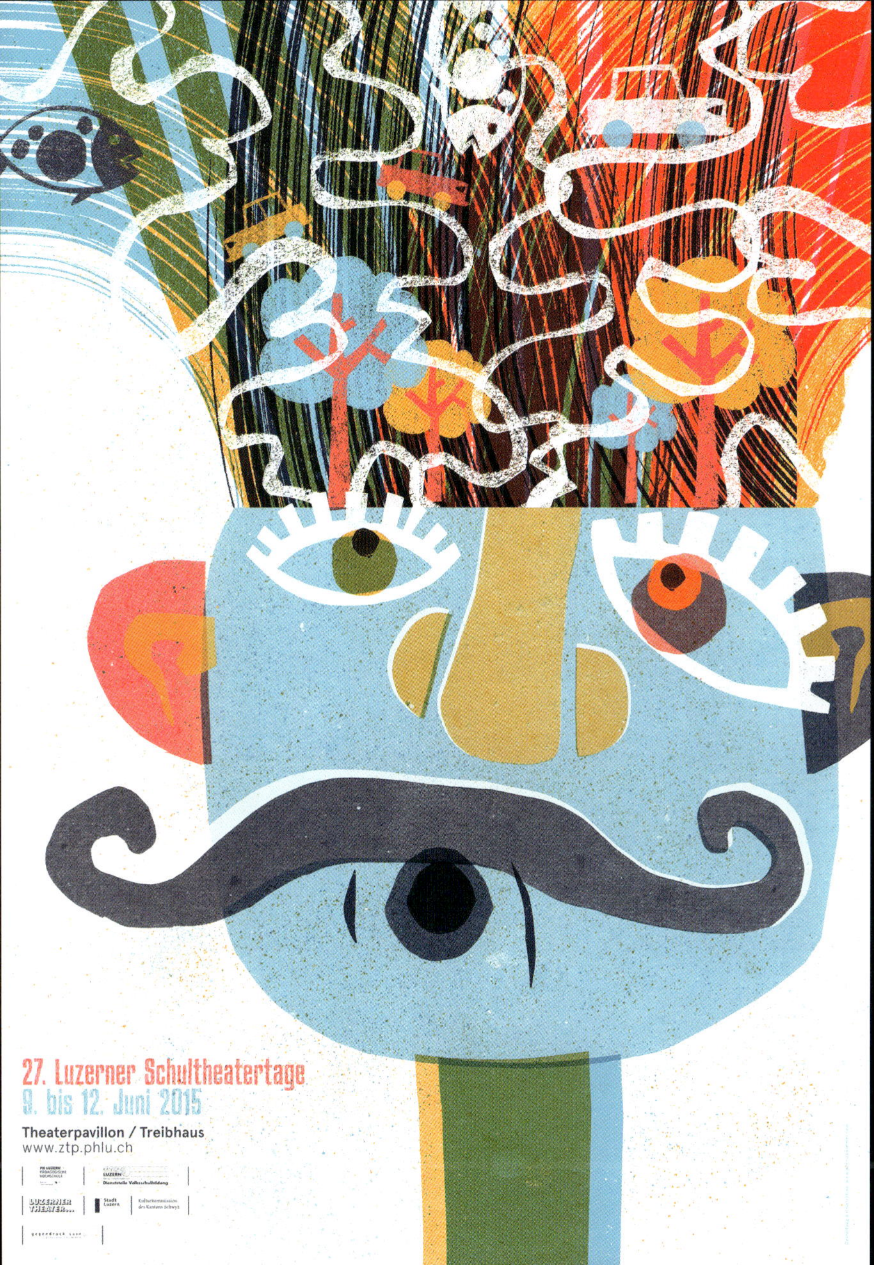

27. Luzerner Schultheatertage
9. bis 12. Juni 2015
Theaterpavillon / Treibhaus
www.ztp.phlu.ch

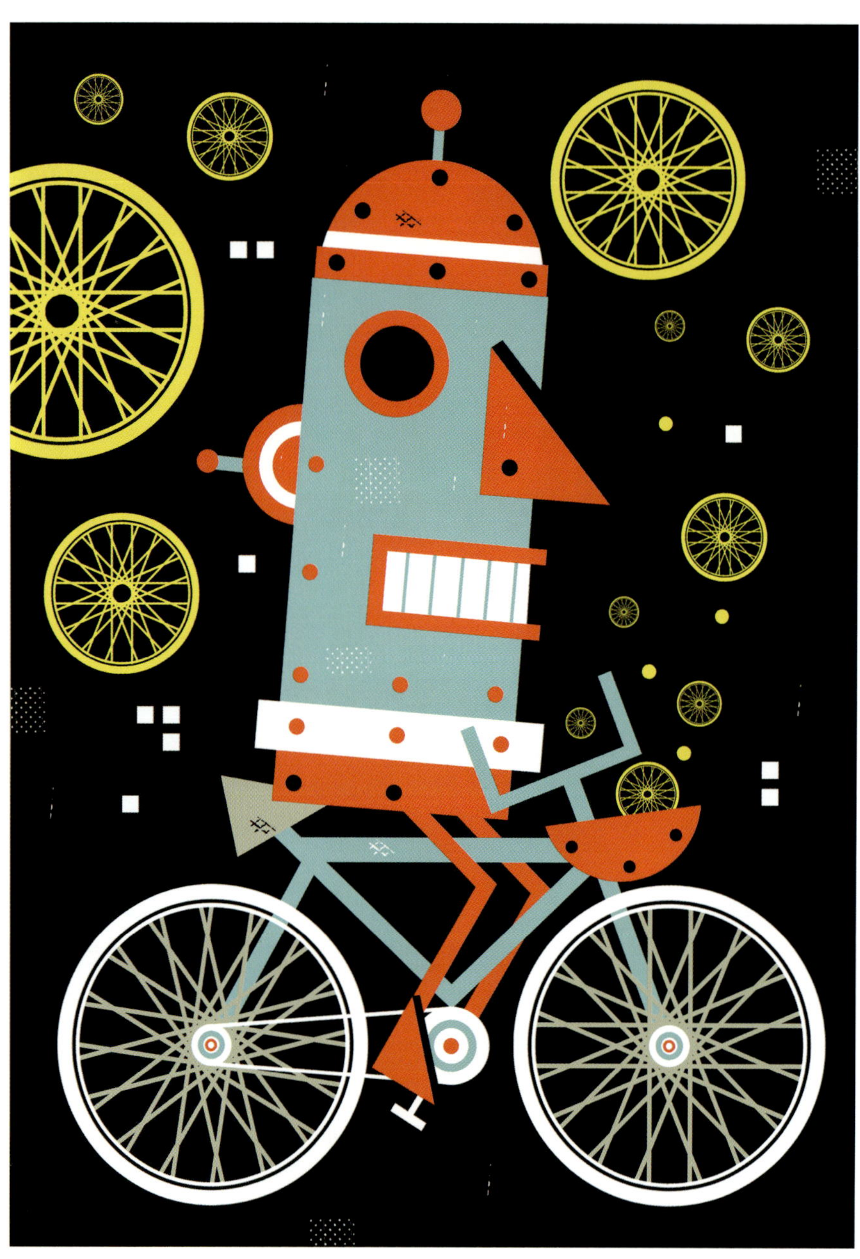

Daniel Bueno *www.buenozine.com.br*

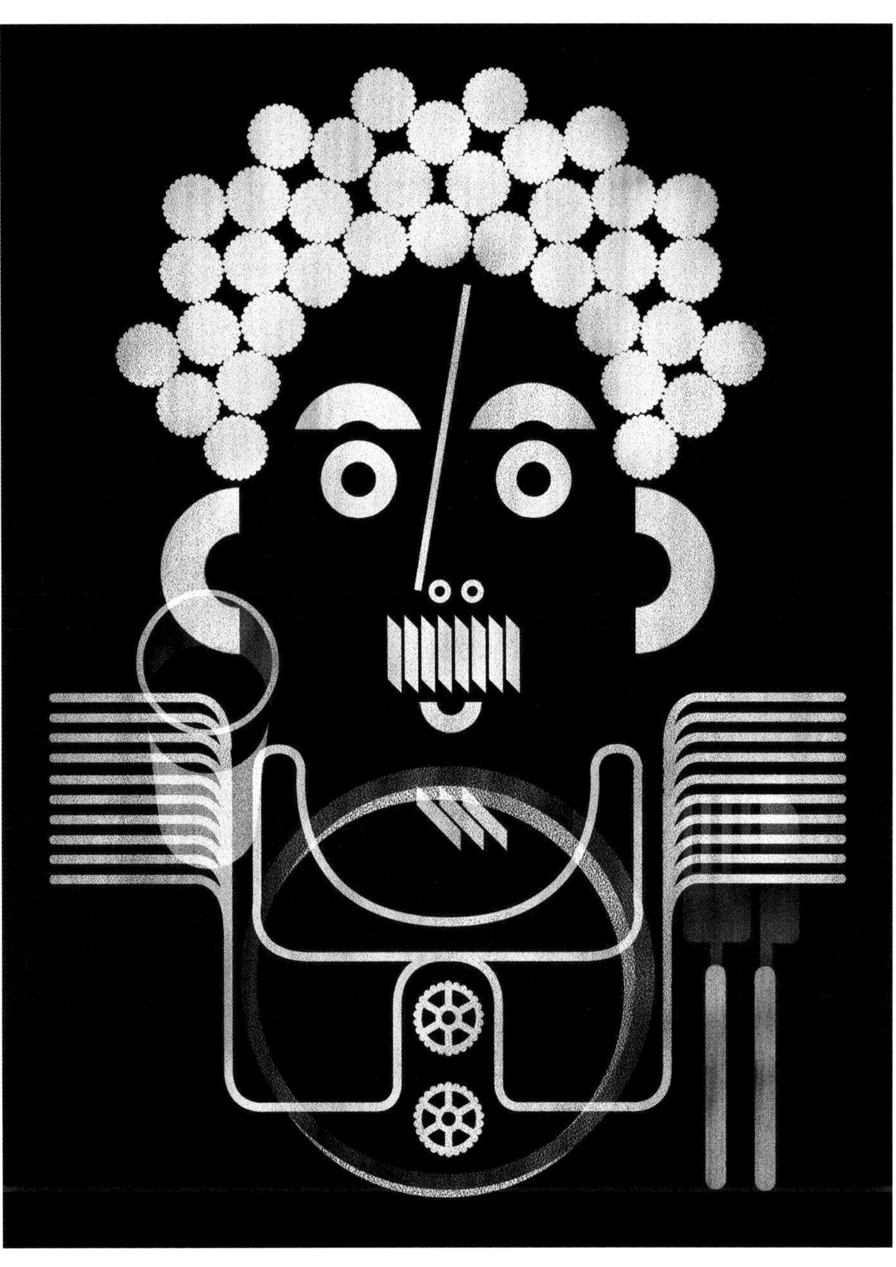

Giulio Bonasera *www.giuliobonasera.com*

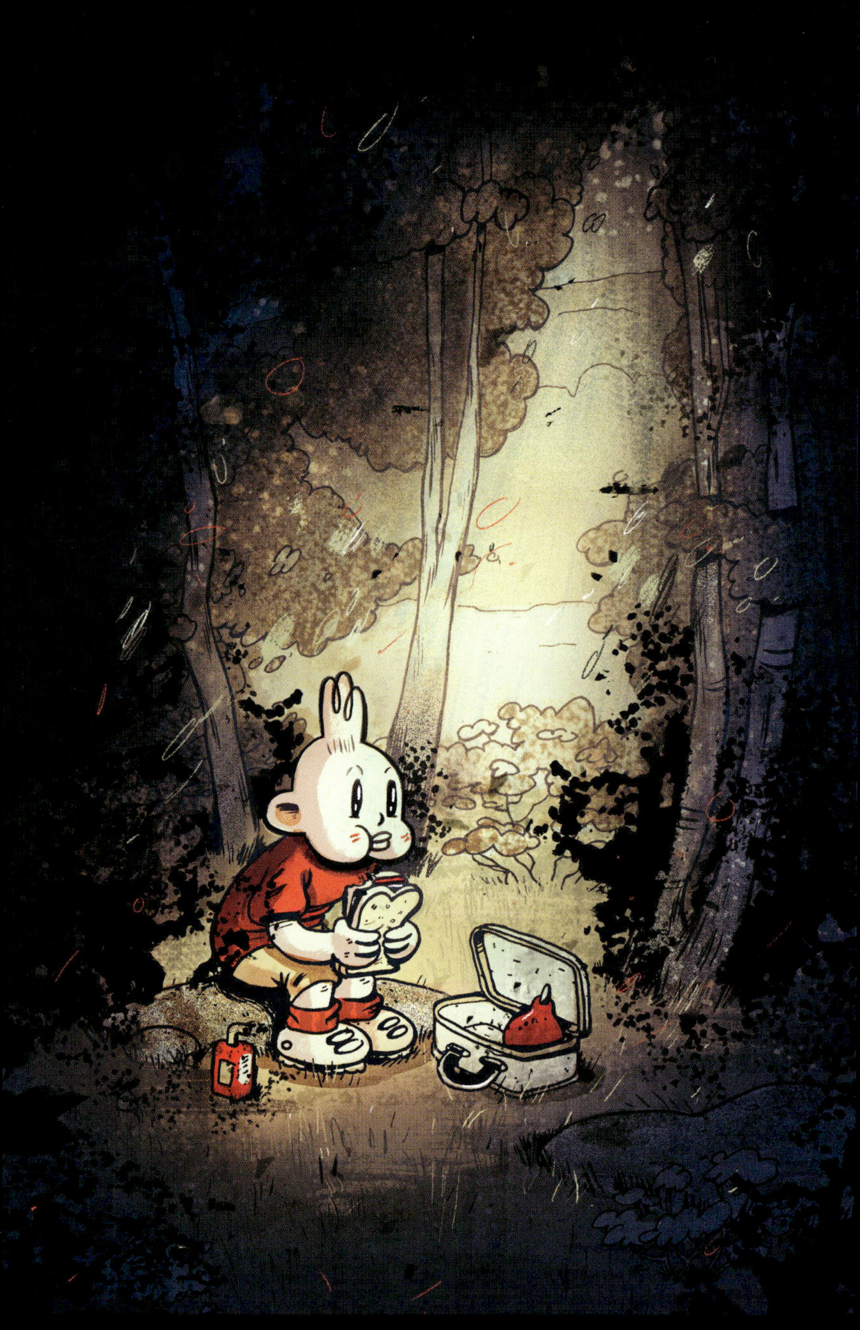

Jackie Ferrentino *www.jackierent.com*

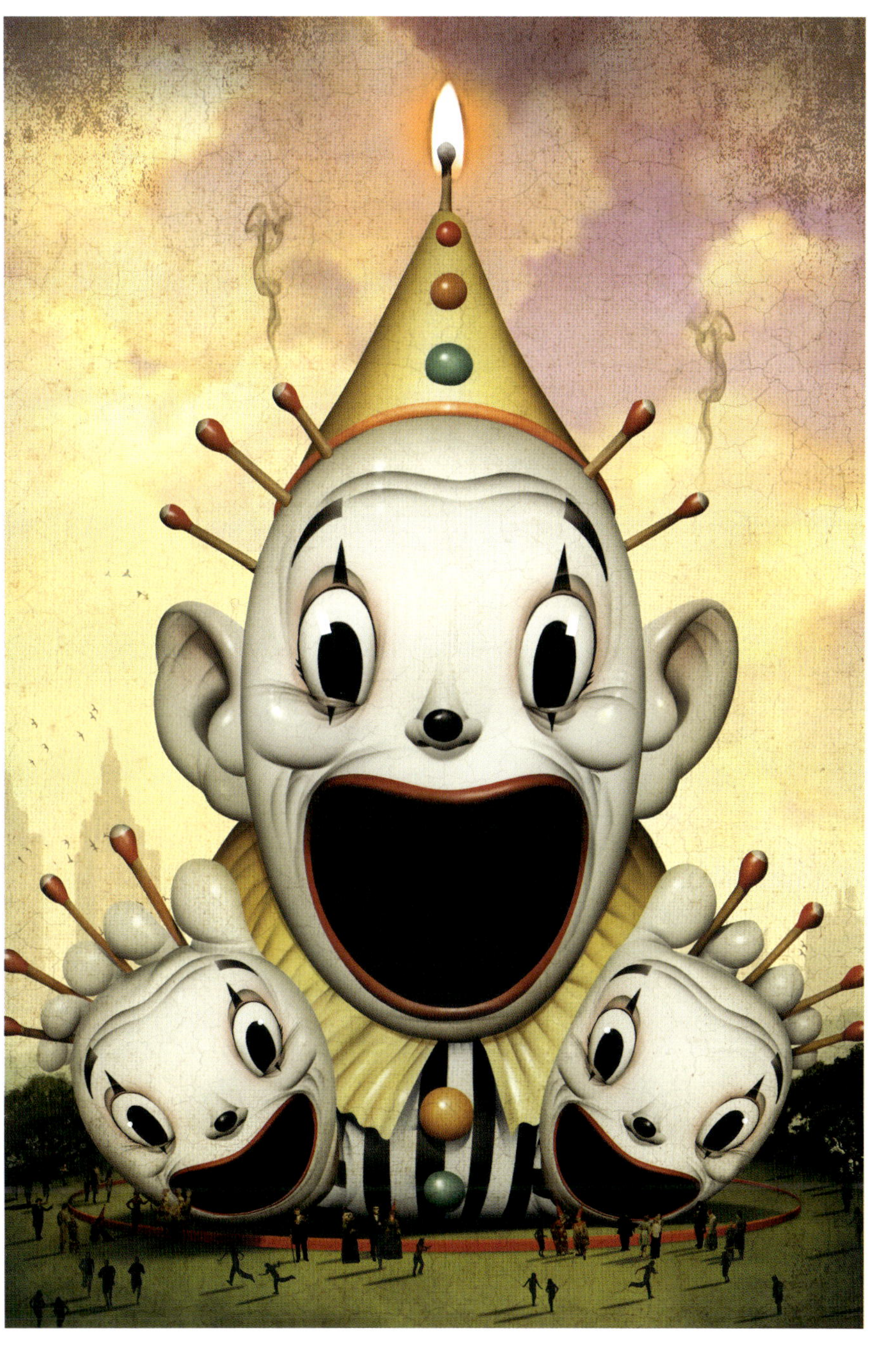

Bill Mayer *www.thebillmayer.com*

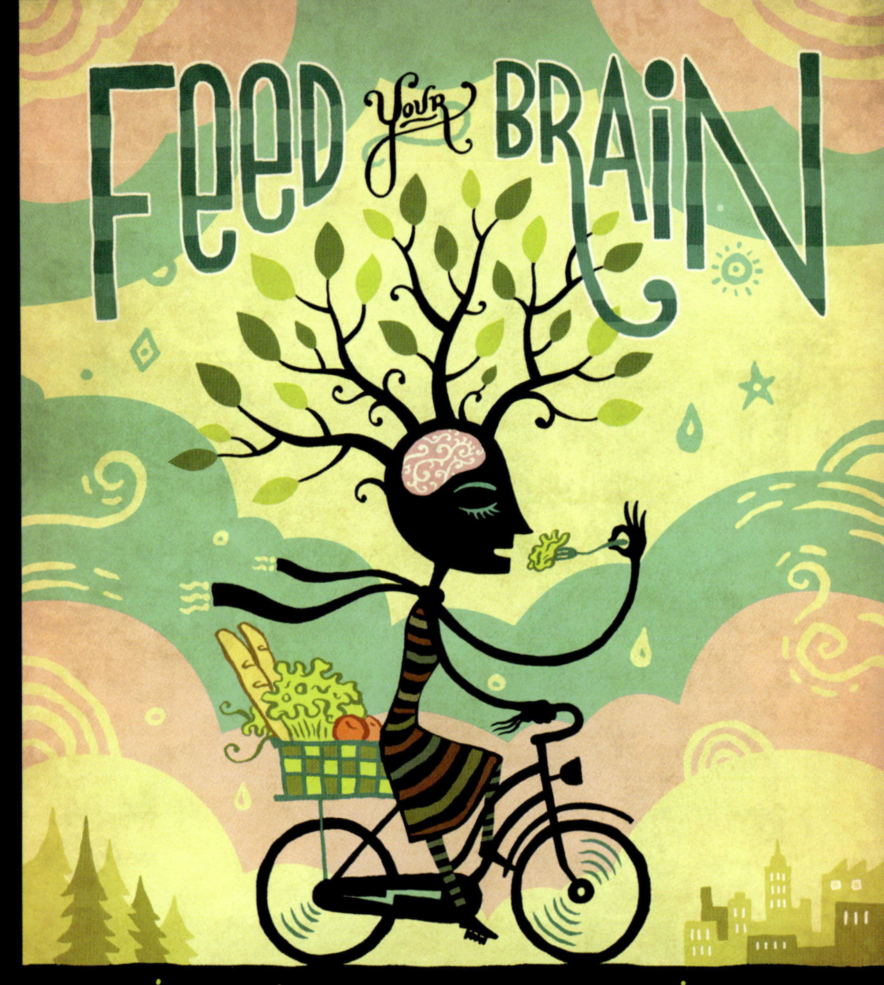
FEED YOUR BRAIN

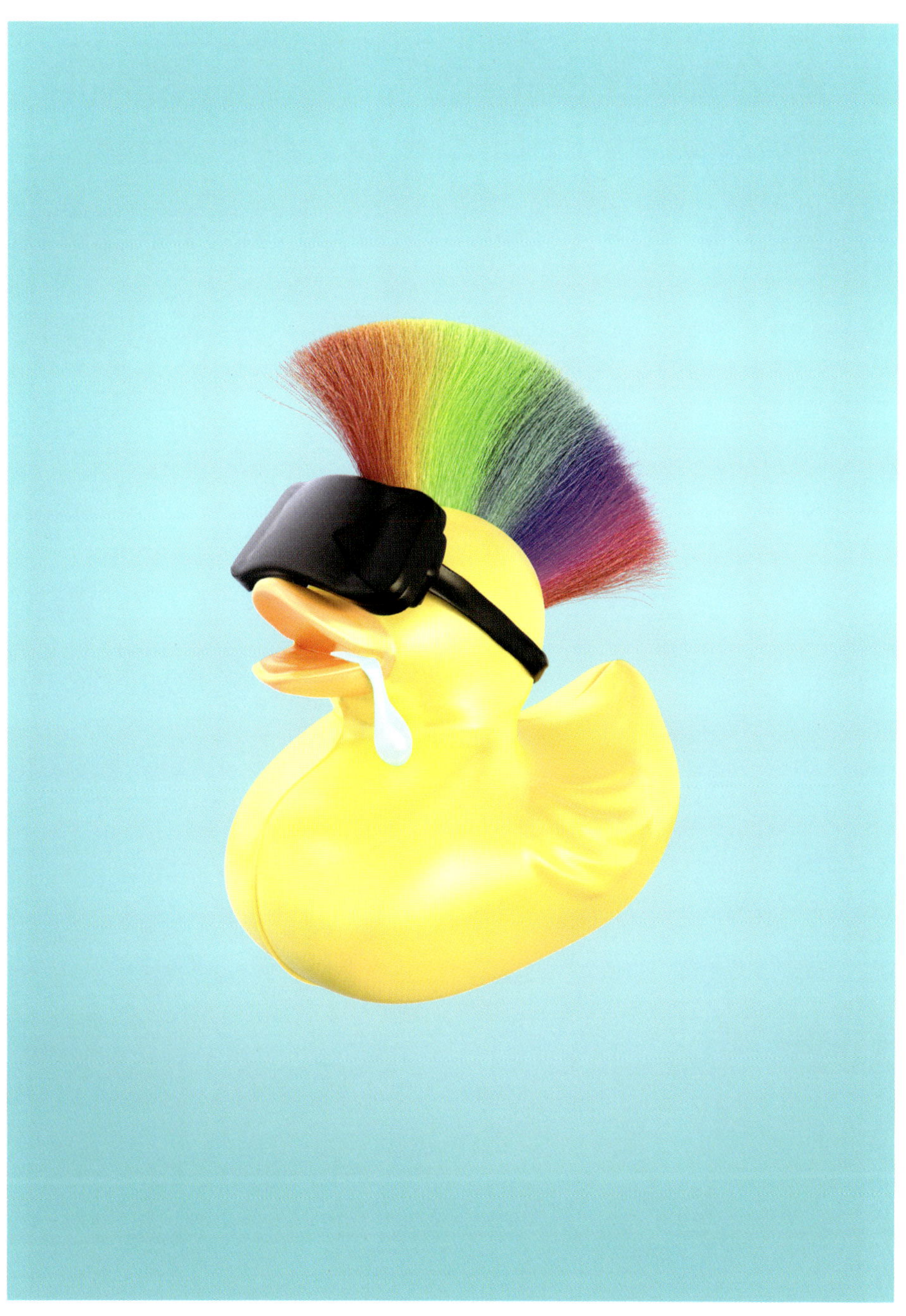

Kathrin Roedl *www.katenastudios.com*

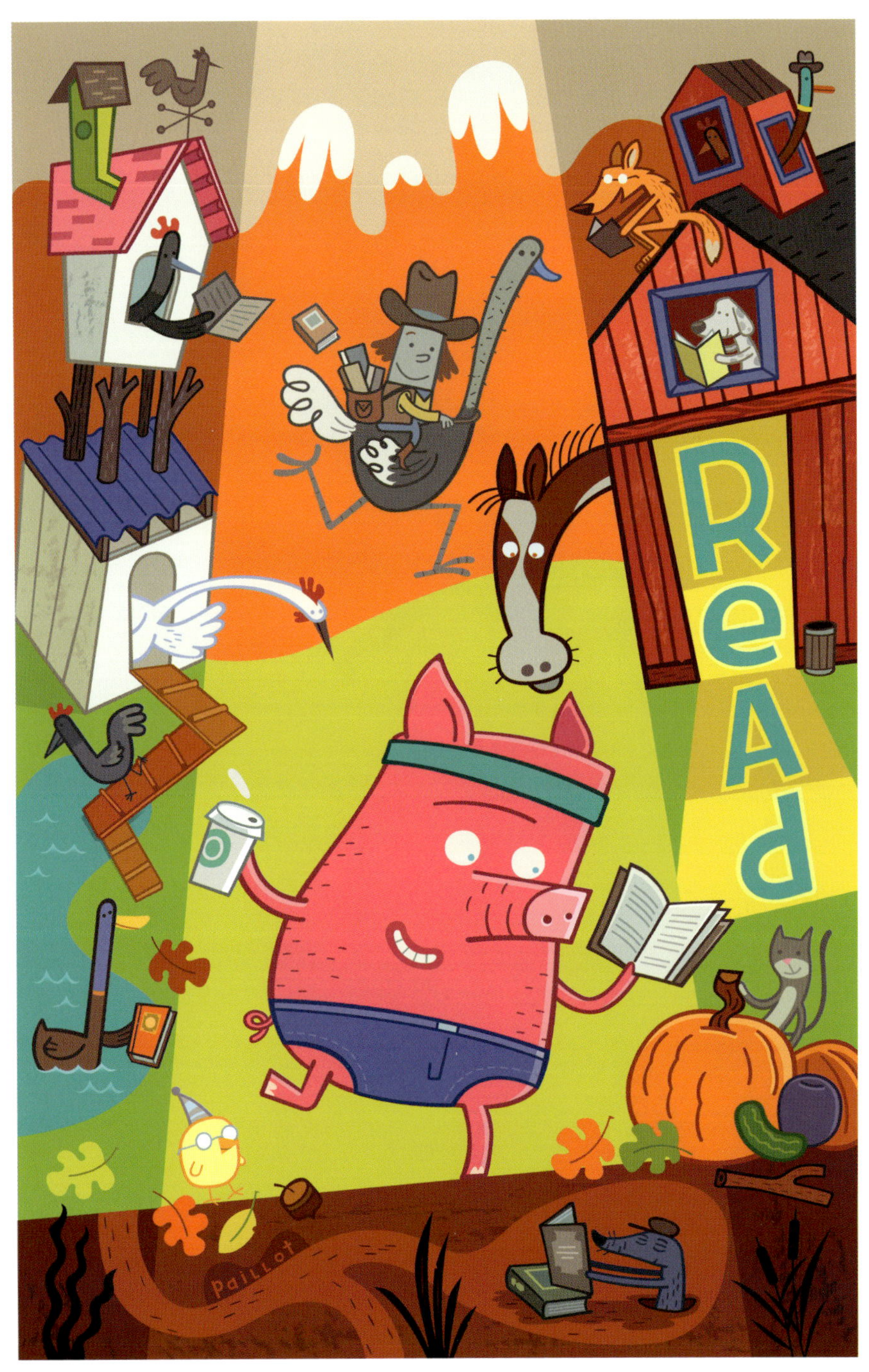

Jim Paillot *www.jimpaillot.com*

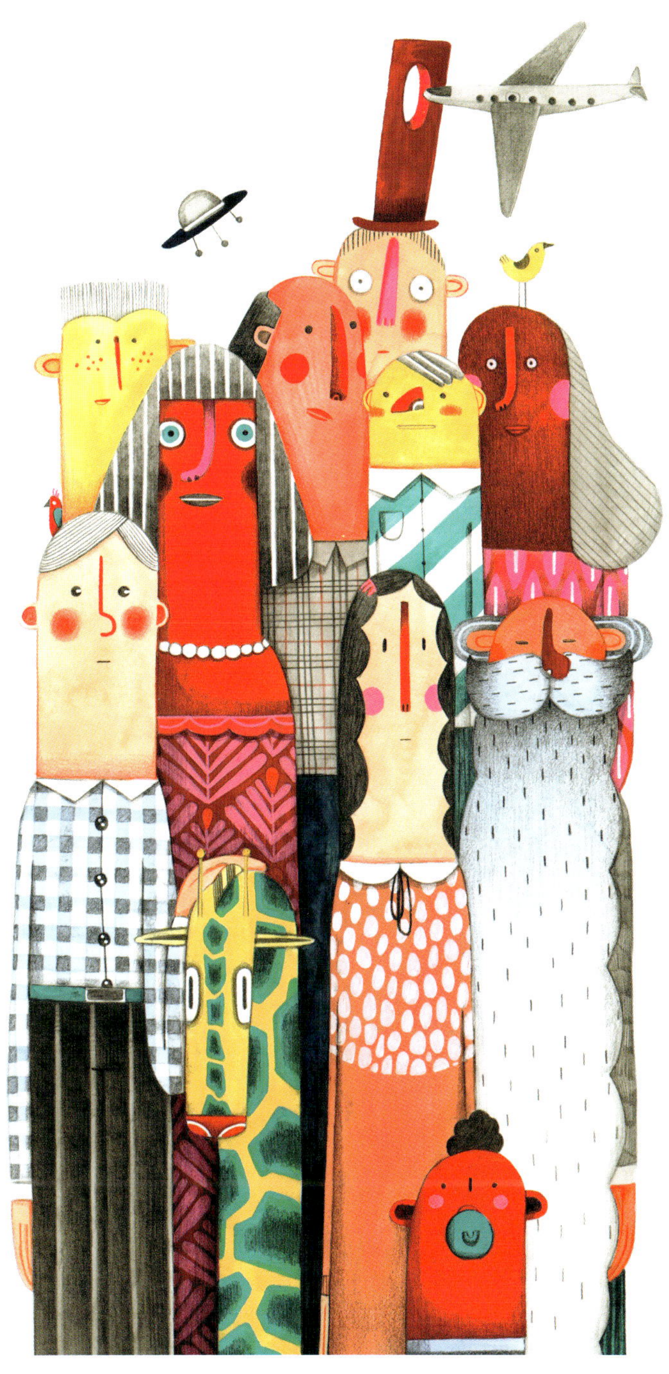

Marion Arbona *www.marionarbona.com*

194

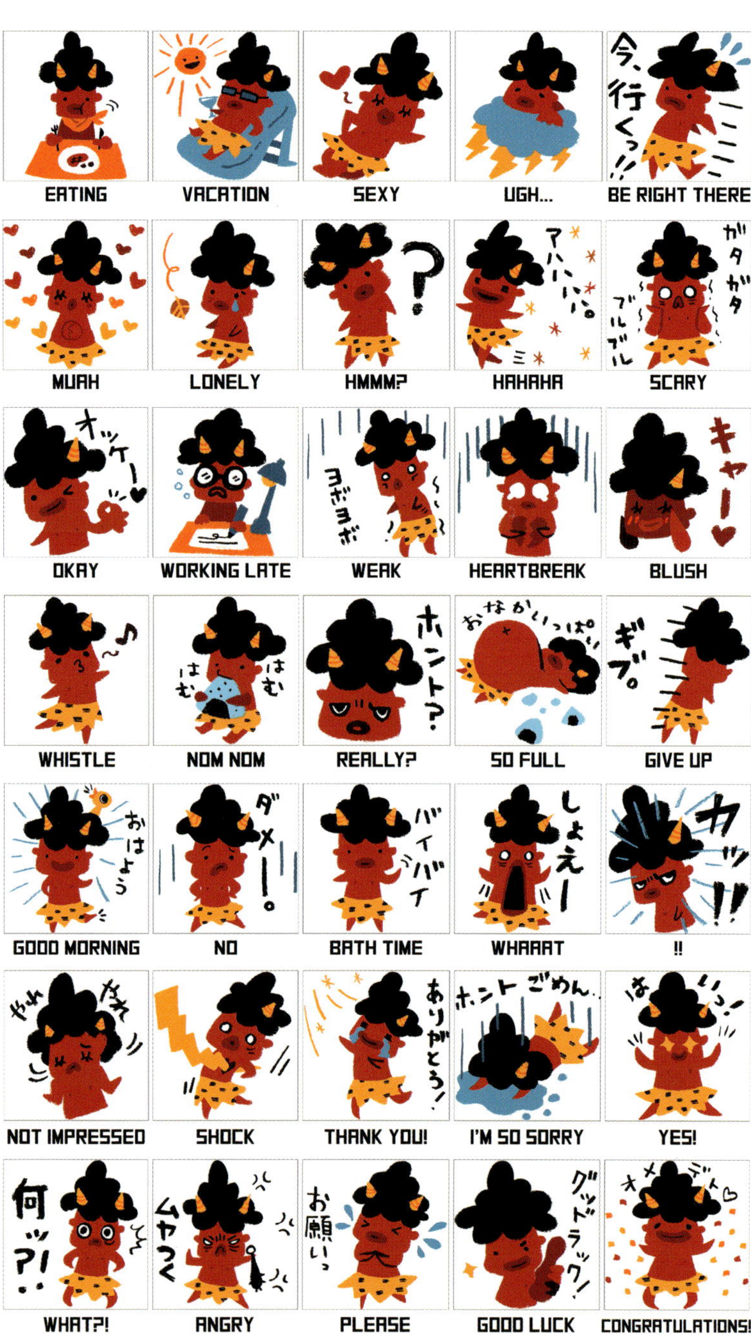

Shiho Pate *www.shihopate.com*

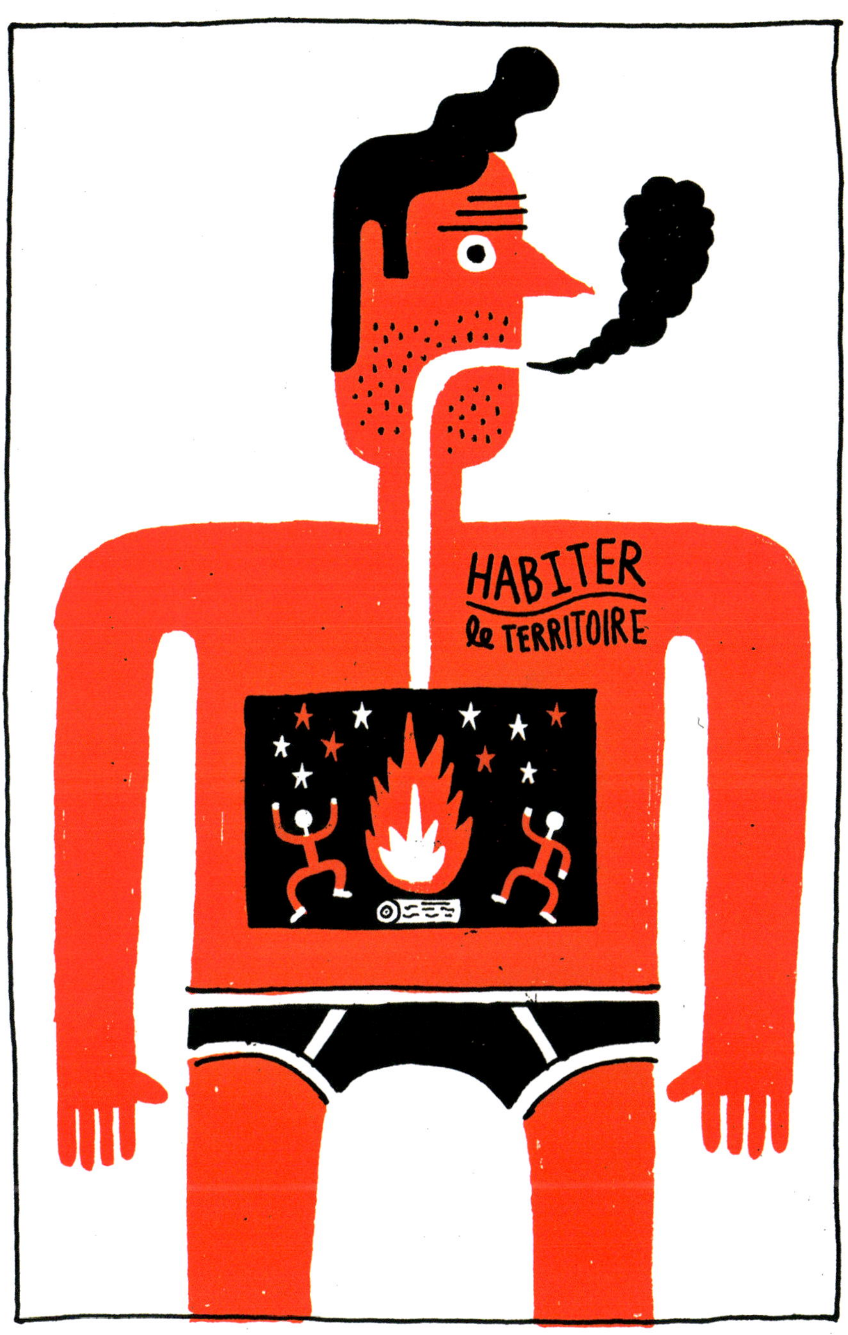

Emmanuel Polanco *www.colagene.com*

196

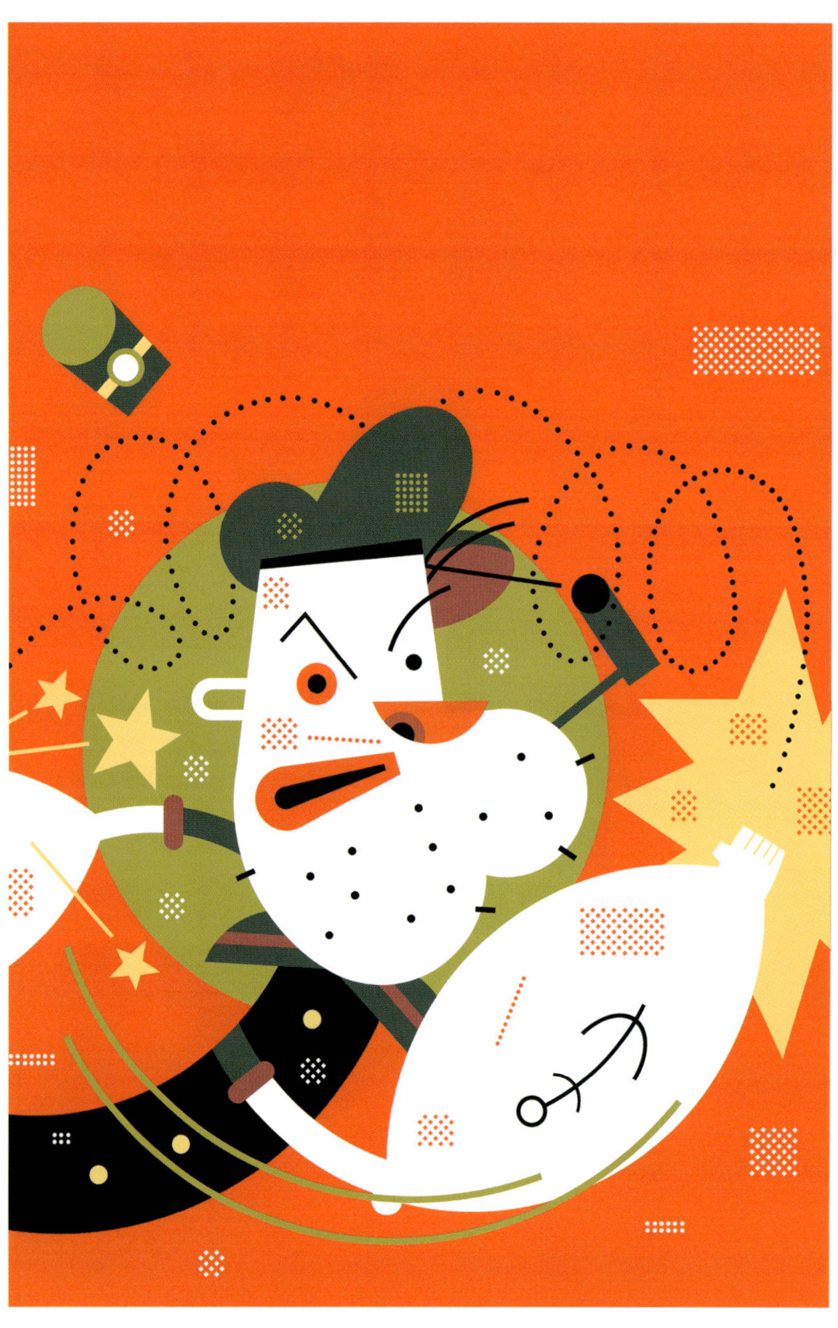

Daniel Bueno *www.buenozine.com.br*

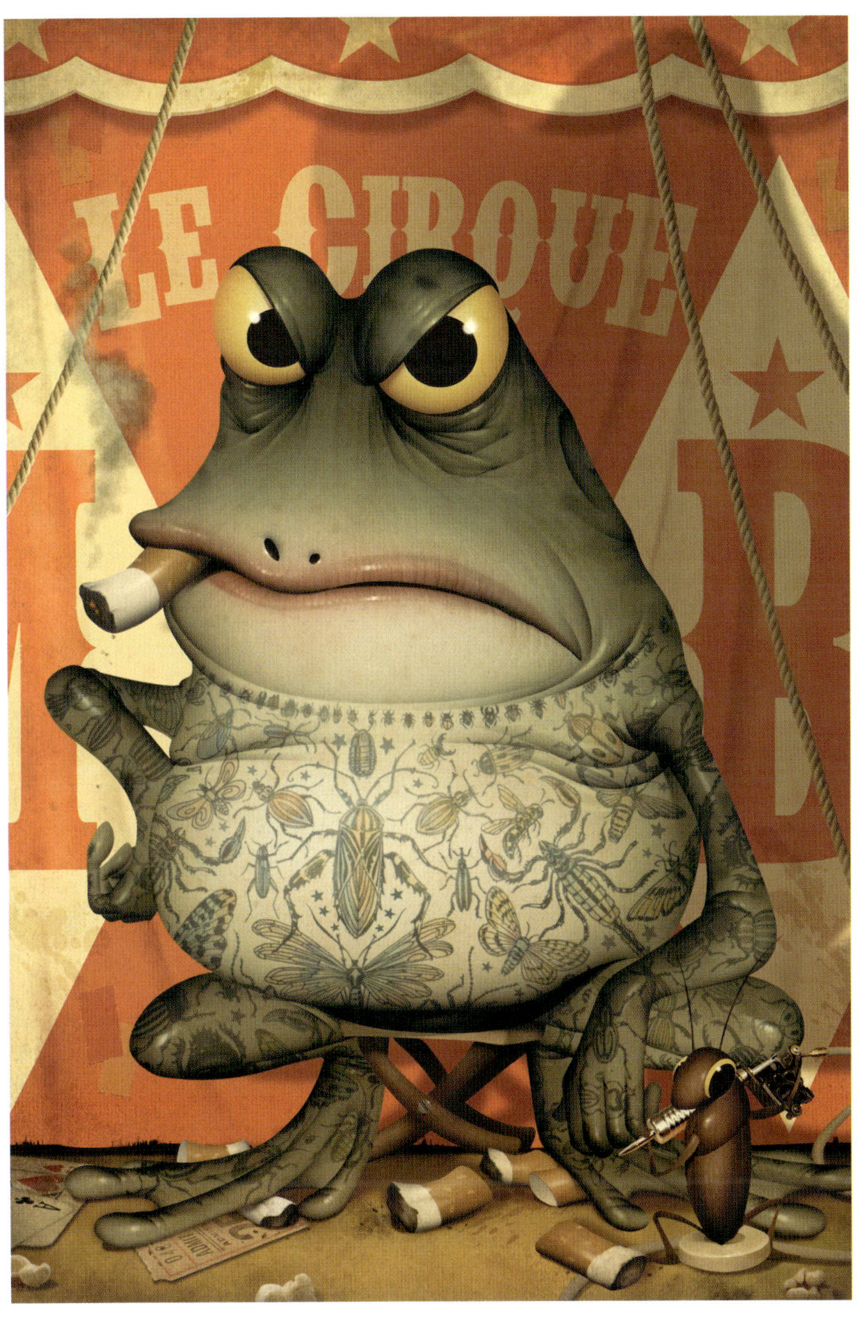

Bill Mayer *www.thebillmayer.com*

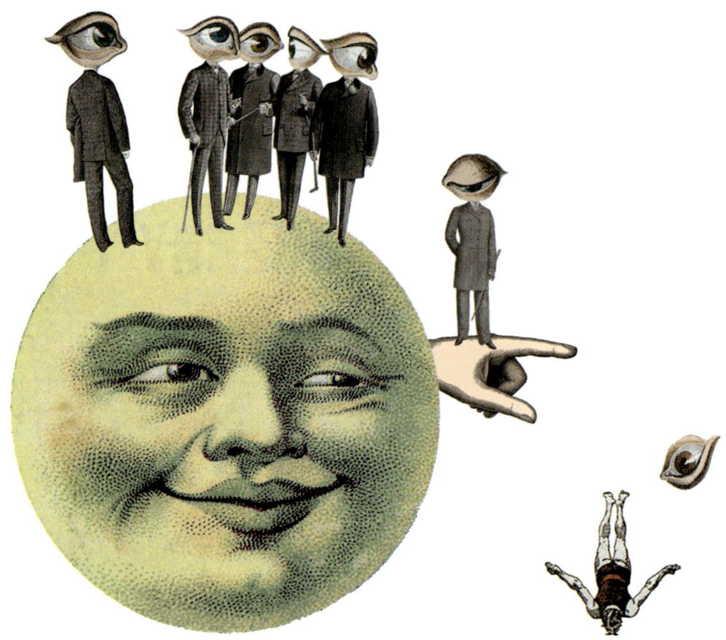
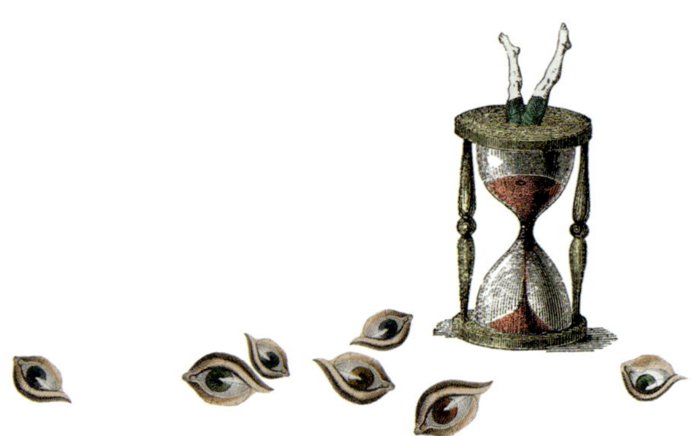

Xiangdi Nie *www.beibeinie.com*

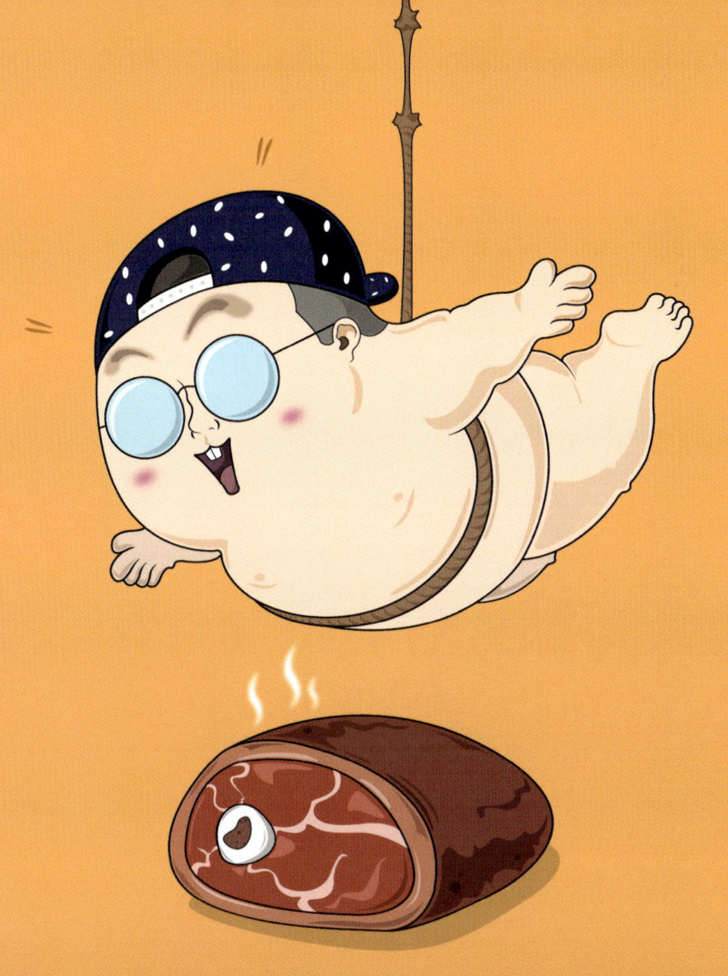

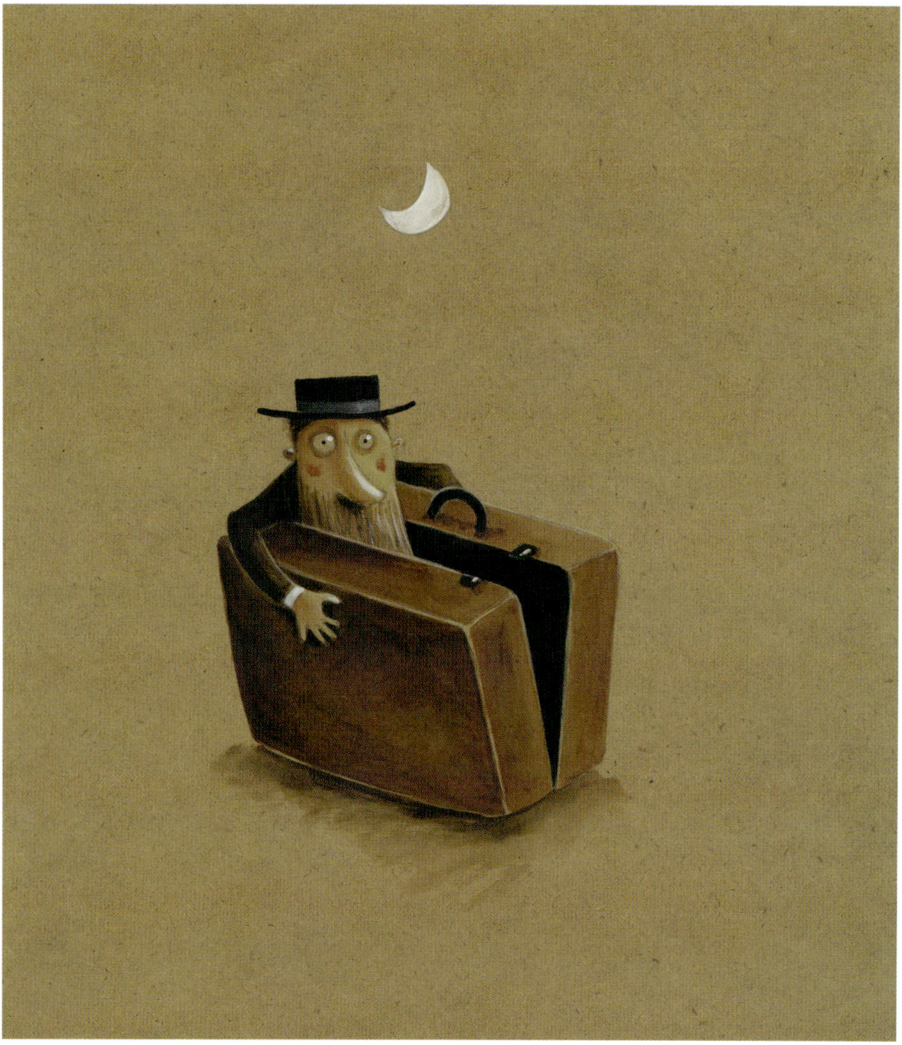

João Vaz de Carvalho *www.jvazcarvalho.com*

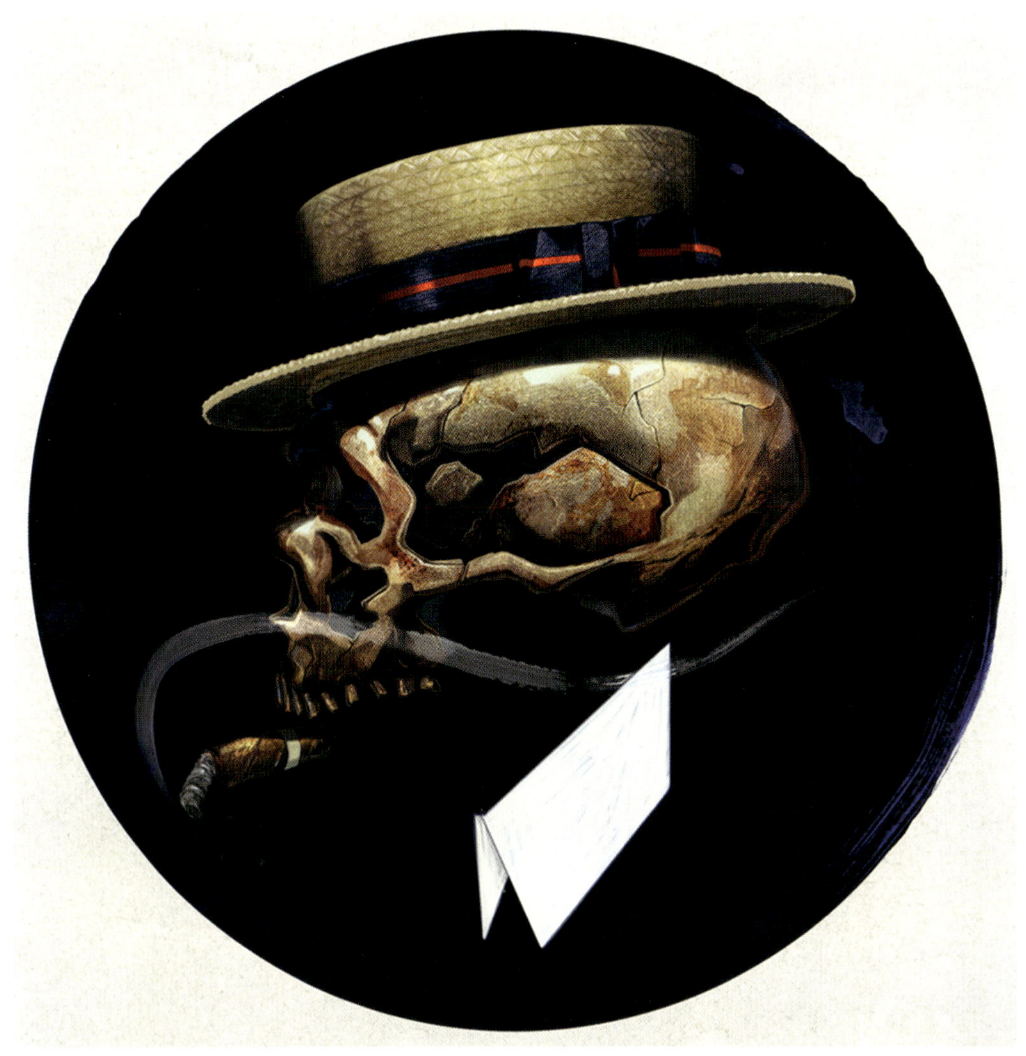

Jonathan Bartlett *www.bartlettstudio.com*

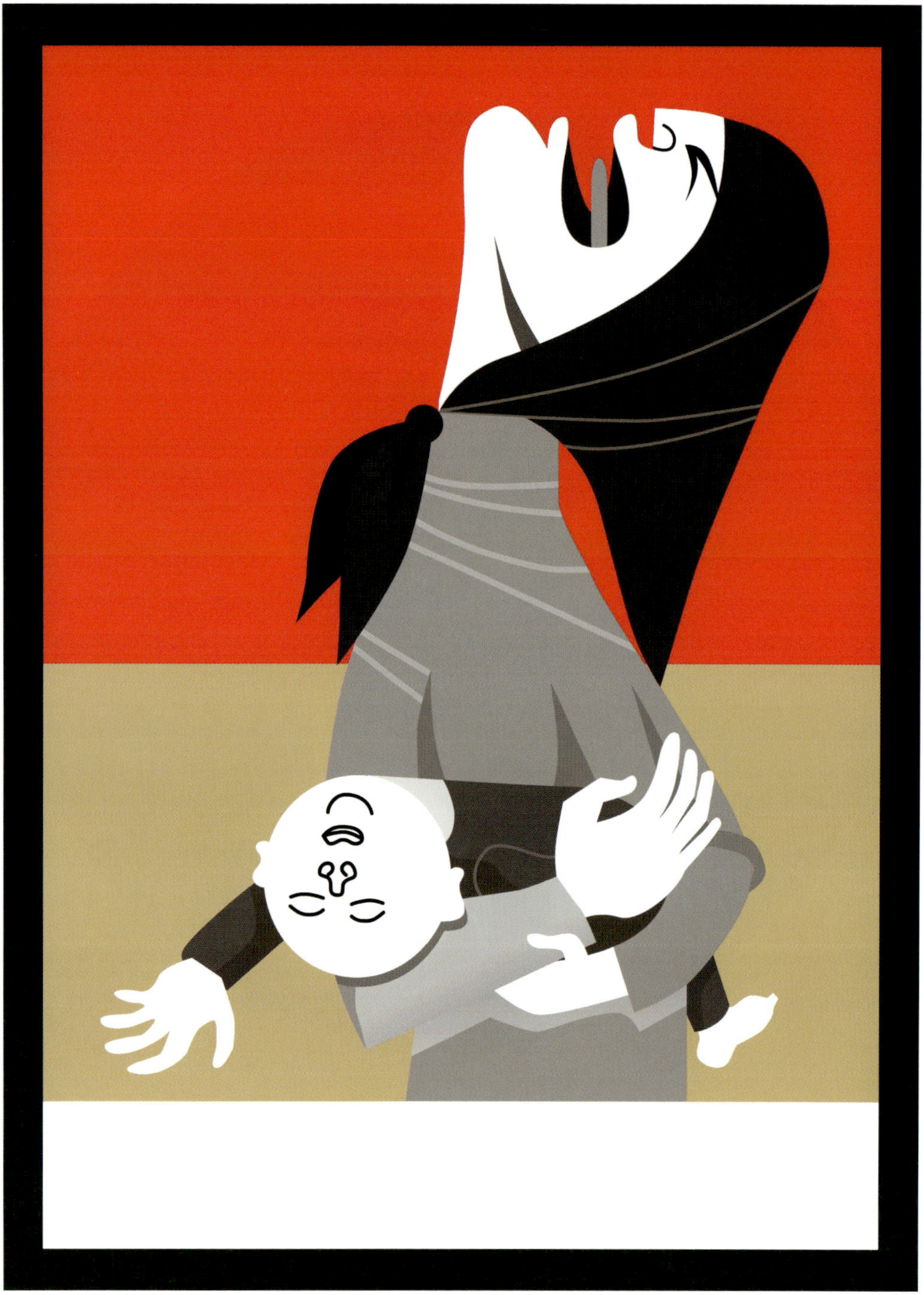

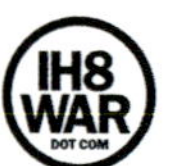

"Stop Killing" David Smith, United Kingdom

Artists and Designers Against War...or whatever they call it.

ILLO 16 INDEX

GARY AAGAARD 84
520.395.0565
aagz@msn.com
www.garyaagaard.com

LIISA AALTIO 98
647.997.1895
liisa.aaltio@gmail.com
www.liisaaaltio.com

CAMERON AITKENHEAD 43
+61 456.198.807
cam.aitkenhead@gmail.com
www.camaitkenhead.gallery

A.RICHARD ALLEN 124
+44 120.252.5181
info@arichardallen.com
www.arichardallen.com

MARION ARBONA 12, 38, 193
514.276.3909
marion.arbona@gmail.com
www.marionarbona.com

ANNA & ELENA BALBUSSO 66
+39 027.010.8739
apiue@balbusso.com
www.balbusso.com

BARRY BARNES 112
712.885.2321
bb@trainedeyegraphics.com
www.trainedeyegraphics.com

JONATHAN BARTLETT 108, 201
336.345.0369
jb@bartlettstudio.com
www.bartlettstudio.com

PAUL BATEMAN 71, 172
+44 771.682.3046
paul@paulbateman.co.uk
www.paulbateman.co.uk

MEGAN BERKHEISER 129
212.615.6707
meganberkheiser@pushart.com
www.pushart.com

JAN BIELECKI 159
hello@janbielecki.com
www.janbielecki.com

SILVIA BONANNI 46
348.003.1978
silvia@silviabonanni.it
www.silviabonanni.it

GIULIO BONASERA 88, 187
+39 066.449.1705
giuliobonasera@gmail.com
www.giuliobonasera.com

DAVIDE BONAZZI 80
212.997.0115
bonazzi@salzmanart.com
bonazzi.salzint.com

JANETTE BORNMARKER 105
+46 733.307.398
hello@janettebornmarker.se
www.janettebornmarker.se

DANIEL BUENO 186, 196
+55 113.881.8418
buenozine.com.br@gmail.com
www.buenozine.com.br

MARIA CARLUCCIO 21, 145
914.231.5012
mariacarluccio@verizon.net
www.mariacarluccio.com

ANDRÉ CARRILHO 160
+35 191.405.7936
mail@andrecarrilho.com
www.andrecarrilho.com

Q. CASSETTI 179
607.387.5424
q@theluckystone.com
www.qcassetti.com

CHERYL CHALMERS 170
607.387.4133
cherchalmers@yahoo.com
www.cherylchalmers.com

HONG CHEN 148
ivanhongchen@hotmail.com
www.hongillu.com

JULIEN CHUNG 36
514.377.2846
info@julienchung.com
www.julienchung.com

DAVID COOPER 150
917.518.5911
david@davidcooperart.com
www.davidcooperart.com

ALAIN CORBEL 116
alacorbel@gmail.com
www.alaincorbel-cos.blogspot.pt

SARA CORBETT 11
347.268.3118
beakulon@gmail.com
www.saracorbett.com

CAMERON COTTRILL 82, 86
727.729.2607
camcottrill@gmail.com
www.camcottrill.com

ALLEN CRAWFORD 140
609.784.8055
allen@allencrawford.net
www.allencrawfordillustration.com

MIRKO CRESTA 79
+41 765.124.832
mirkocresta@gmail.com
www.mirkocresta.info

BENEDETTO CRISTOFANI 62
212.997.0115
cristofani@salzmanart.com
cristofani.salzint.com

MIKE CURATO 31
212.206.5600
mikecurato@gmail.com
www.mikecurato.com

HUGH D'ANDRADE 190
415.513.3444
hugh@hughillustration.com
www.hughillustration.com

ANDREA D'AQUINO 107
646.361.7036
andrea@andreadaquino.com
www.andreadaquino.com

GIOVANNI DA RE 53
+39 339.534.4974
info@giovannidare.com
www.giovannidare.com

TRINA DALZIEL 146
+44 790.963.7236
trina.dalziel@mail.com
www.trinadalziel.com

TONI DAMKOEHLER 137
920.217.2195
damkoeht@uwgb.edu
www.tonidamkoehler.com

MAI LY DEGNAN 99
mdegnan20@student.scad.edu
www.mailydegnan.com

PENELOPE DULLAGHAN 52
937.433.8383
scott@scotthull.com
www.scotthull.com/artists/penelope-
dullaghan

ROB DUNLAVEY 34
508.651.7503
rob@robd.com
www.robd.com

JEAN-MANUEL DUVIVIER 111
322.648.0512
jmduvivier@skynet.be
www.jmduvivier.com

NICHOLAS ELIAS 104
516.640.0542
nick@eliasartstudio.com
www.eliasartstudio.com

TOM ENGLER 136
tom.engler1@gmail.com
www.flickr.com/tomengler

LISK FENG 149
liskfeng@gmail.com
www.liskfeng.com

JACKIE FERRENTINO 188
908.644.2036
www.jackierent.com

PAUL GARLAND 106
+44 776.113.6314
paul@paul-garland.com
www.paul-garland.com

FEDERICO GASTALDI 164
federicogastaldi1@gmail.com
www.federicogastaldi.com

MICHAEL GLENWOOD 91
703.502.3400

FEDERICO GASTALDI 164
federicogastaldi1@gmail.com
www.federicogastaldi.com

MICHAEL GLENWOOD 91
703.502.3400
michael@mglenwood.com
www.mglenwood.com

IGOR GNEDO 173
igorgnedo@gmail.com
www.igorgnedo.com

AAD GOUDAPPEL 95
+31 615.303.587
aad@aadgoudappel.com
www.aadgoudappel.com

VERÓNICA GRECH 131
+34 655.44.98.70
veronicagrech@gmail.com
www.veronicagrech.com

PETER GREENWOOD 182
773.459.3448
peter@brighton.co.uk
www.peter-mac.com

TYLER GROSS 144
314.606.9598
tyler@grossillustration.com
www.grossillustration.com

JOEY GUIDONE 63
+39 328.906.8497
guidone@salzmanart.com
guidone.salzint.com

HEATHER HECKEL 10, 176
239.272.4312
heather.heckel@gmail.com
www.heatherheckel.com

JAKOB HINRICHS 28
+49 176.963.655.32
mail@jakobhinrichs.com
www.jakobhinrichs.com

MARK HOFFMANN 181
781.771.5733
mh@studiohoffmann.com
www.studiohoffmann.com

JAMIE HOGAN 166
207.766.9726
jamiehogan58@gmail.com
www.jamiehogan.com

TED HWANG 199
+82 109.272.7532
tedhwang93@naver.com
www.instagram.com/hwangted93

IC4DESIGN 126
+81 822.431.999
info@ic4design.com
www.ic4design.com

STACY INNERST 171
412.805.1305
info@stacyinnerst.com
www.stacyinnerst.com

ANDREA INNOCENT 184
+61 417.339.896
innocentgirl@otoshimono.org
www.otoshimono.org

TOM JELLETT 42
+61 297.984.909
tom@tomjellett.com
www.tomjellett.com

EDA KABAN 132
212.333.2551
edakaban@gmail.com
www.shannonassociates.com/artist/
edakaban

JAIME KIM 33
jaimeillustration@gmail.com
www.jaimekim.com

LUNA KIRSCHE 123
geral@mariadasideias.com
www.mariadasideias.com

SONJA KISLINGER 162, 180
+49 306.950.5604
sonja@sanni.net
www.sanni.net

URS J. KNOBEL 103
+41 41.781.2550
info@ursjknobel-art.ch
www.ursjknobel-art.ch

VIKTOR KOEN 81
212.254.3159
viktor@viktorkoen.com
www.viktorkoen.com

KATRINA KOPELOFF 183
720.352.3791
katrina@katrinakopeloff.com
www.katrinakopeloff.com

JON KRAUSE 77, 90
215.338.1531
jk@jonkrause.com
www.jonkrause.com

JIALE KUANG 67
912.441.9977
kuangjiale@gmail.com
www.lokkuang.com

ANITA KUNZ 167
416.364.3846
akunz@anitakunz.com
www.anitakunz.com

KRYSTAL LAUK 147
415.940.9499
krystal.lauk@gmail.com
www.krystallauk.com

JING LI 163
912.507.9946
jingli132@gmail.com
www.jingliwaa.tumblr.com

ANSON LIAW 92
416.738.8896
ansonliawillustration@rogers.com
www.illoz.com/liaw

MIKE LOWERY 101
703.362.4450
mike@argyleacademy.com
www.argyleacademy.com

HOLLY MACDONALD 102
holly_mac17@hotmail.co.uk
www.hollymacdonald.co.uk

ROSS MACDONALD 55, 56
203.270.6438
brightworkpress@gmail.com
www.ross-macdonald.com

JENS MAGNUSSON 143
+46 709.182.672
jens@jensjens.com
www.jensjens.com

MAGOZ 59
+34 661.065.286
magoz@magoz.is
www.magoz.is

LAUREN MARRIOTT 19
www.ralphiillustration.com

JESSICA MATTHEWS 139
+61 422.565.888
jess@jessmatthewsdesign.com
www.jessmatthewsdesign.com

BILL MAYER 189, 197
404.378.0686
bill@thebillmayer.com
www.thebillmayer.com

MARK MCGINNIS 73
773.368.4045
mistermcginnis@gmail.com
www.mistermcginnis.com

MARCO MELGRATI 89
+39 334.373.1854
melgrati@salzmanart.com
melgrati.salzint.com

JOSE ALÉ MERCADO 128
+353 86.172.3751
info@alemercado.com
www.alemercado.com

RENÉ MILOT 14
416.425.7726
renemilot@renemilot.com
www.renemilot.com

JULIA MINAMATA 109
416.399.8795
julia@juliaminamata.com
www.juliaminamata.com

IAN MURRAY 135
779.175.4195
ian@mrmurray.co.uk
www.mrmurray.co.uk

ALEX NABAUM 87
435.654.8501
alex@alexnabaum.com
www.alexnabaum.com

GARY NEILL 74
514.482.0488
gary@garyneill.com
www.agoodson.com

ROBERT NEUBECKER 93
435.729.0049
robert@neubecker.com
www.neubecker.com

LAUREN NEWBURG 16
lmlnewburg@gmail.com
www.newburgart.com

XIANGDI NIE 198
+44 758.018.2601
beibei@beibeinie.com
www.beibeinie.com

SHAW NIELSEN 27, 142
303.517.8065
shaw@shawnielsen.com
www.shawnielsen.com

CHELSEA O'BYRNE 122
778.237.9759
chelsea.obyrne@gmail.com
www.chelseaobyrne.com

MELDA ONCU YILDIZ 39
+90 505.669.6167
meldaoncu@gmail.com
www.meldaoncu.com

JIM PAILLOT 40, 192
480.633.2485
jim@jimpaillot.com
www.jimpaillot.com

KATIE PAK 49
647.388.9519
info@katiepak.com
www.katiepak.com

CURTIS PARKER 76
937.433.8383
scott@scotthull.com
www.scotthull.com/artists/curtis-parker

DARON PARTON 35
daron@watermarkltd.com
www.watermarkltd.com/artists/daron-
parton

SHIHO PATE 194
256.503.2916
hello@shihopate.com
www.shihopate.com

FILIP PERAIC 175
filip@peraic.com
www.peraic.com

VALERIA PETRONE 44
212.475.044
valeria@valeriapetrone.com
www.valeriapetrone.com

DENISE PLAUCHE 17
678.458.5316
denise@deniseplauche.com
www.deniseplauche.com

EMMANUEL POLANCO 29, 195
514.845.4730
apham@colagene.com
www.colagene.com/en/illustration/
emmanuel-polanco

EMILIANO PONZI 61
+39 349.052.6205
info@emilianoponzi.com
www.emilianoponzi.com

ANDY POTTS 113
+44 078.171.59049
info@andy-potts.com
www.andy-potts.com

CHARLIE POWELL 158
831.457.9470
cpowell@cruzio.com
www.charliepowell.net

SOMYA RAJU 177
somyaraju@gmail.com
www.somyaraju.com

FATINHA RAMOS 18
+32 495.991.554
design@fatinha.com
www.fatinha.com

JACOB REEVES 165
440.251.4221
jake.reeves.art@gmail.com
www.jakereevesart.com

ANGELA RIO 155
215.939.6685
oh.angelario@gmail.com
www.angelario.com

LUISA RIVERA 20
luisa@luisarivera.cl
www.luisarivera.cl

KATHRIN ROEDL 191
+49 179.654.3314
hello@kathrinroedl.de
www.katenastudios.com

ELYSE SALAZAR 151, 156
404.630.3907
elyse@elysesalazar.com
www.elysesalazar.com

STEPHAN SCHMITZ 54, 69, 70
+41 449.407.356
stephan.schmitz@gmx.ch
www.stephan-schmitz.ch

RICK SEALOCK 115
519.744.2412
sealock@rogers.com
www.ricksealock.com

BORIS SÉMÉNIAKO 65
+33 617.324.468
bs@borissemeniako.fr
www.borissemeniako.fr

PAUL SHIPPER 169
+44 771.316.5684
hello@paulshipperstudio.com
www.paulshipperstudio.com

STEVE SIMPSON 138
+353 872.659.641
mail@stevesimpson.com
www.stevesimpson.com

LASSE SKARBÖVIK 60
+46 707.228.567
lasse@stockholmillustration.com
www.lasseskarbovik.com

MARK SMITH 72
212.997.0115
smith@salzmanart.com
smith.salzint.com

MOLLY SNEE 157
703.408.3615
sneemolly@gmail.com
www.mollysnee.com

DAVE SZALAY 48
330.972.8202
dms@szalaydesign.com
www.szalaydesign.com

KEN TACKETT 75
603.724.7995
kentackett@suddenlink.net
www.kentackettart.com

BENOIT TARDIF 154
514.845.4730
illustration@colagene.com
www.bentardif.com

DARIA THEODORA 15, 114
daria@xintheodora.com
www.xintheodora.com

BRENNA THUMMLER 32
814.573.2299
brennathummler@gmail.com
www.brennathummler.com

SUE TODD 125
416.784.5313
sustodd@rogers.com
www.suetodd.com

MAN-TSUN TSANG 118
+852 9726.1951
hitme@manxtsun.com
www.manxtsun.com

JEAN TUTTLE 96
303.388.3333
jean@jeantuttlestudio.com
www.jeantuttle.com

KIRSTEN ULVE 174
212.533.1105
kirsten@kirstenulve.com
www.kirstenulve.com

TIM VAN DEN BROECK 24
+32 485.625.092
welcome@timvandenbroeck.com
www.timvandenbroeck.com

JOÃO VAZ DE CARVALHO 200
+351 964.131.349
contacto@jvazcarvalho.com
www.jvazcarvalho.com

ALEXEI VELLA 57
212.997.0115
vella@salzmanart.com
vella.salzint.com

GARY VENN 50
+64 211.241.759
gary@garyvennillustration.com
www.garyvennillustration.com

KLAAS VERPLANCKE 25, 26, 94
+32 499.269.964
mail@klaas.be
www.klaas.be

MICHAEL WARAKSA 30
414.347.4055
michaelwaraksa@att.net
www.michaelwaraksa.com

LAURA WEISZER 58
215.776.7155
laweiszer@gmail.com
www.lauraweiszer.com

TAYLOR WESSLING 119
949.375.2635
taylor@taylorwessling.com
www.taylorwessling.com

IAN WHADCOCK 23, 78
+44 796.711.9058
i.whadcock@gmail.com
www.ianwhadcock.com

PATRICK WIDMER 185
+49 892.189.0535
hallo@patrickwidmer.com
www.patrickwidmer.com

OLI WINWARD 83
707.822.5500
winward@salzmanart.com
winward.salzint.com

GARY WRIGHT 110, 178
supera4illustration@gmail.com
www.supera4illustration.dunked.com

STEPHANIE WUNDERLICH 152
+49 173.272.4695
info@wunderlich-illustration.de
www.wunderlich-illustration.de

JAMES YANG 22, 64
212.807.6627
james@jamesyang.com
www.jamesyang.com

XIAOHUA YANG 117
612.351.7862
yangxiaohuaart@gmail.com
www.yxhart.me

MORAN YOGEV 153
yogevmoran@gmail.com
www.behance.net/moranyo

HEIDI YOUNGER 51, 100
631.356.5176
heidi@heidiyounger.com
www.heidiyounger.com

YAO YU 130
eileenyuyao@gmail.com
www.yaoyu.work

NATALYA ZAHN 97
617.301.0494
natalya@natalya.com
www.natalya.com

NATALIA ZARATIEGUI 134
+34 609.494.87
nataliazaratiegui@gmail.com
www.nataliazaratiegui.com

TINA ZELLMER 120
+49 177.779.5921
info@tinazellmer.com
www.tinazellmer.com

FRANCESCO ZORZI 45, 68
+39 335.721.8367
me@francescozorzi.it
www.francescozorzi.it

PUBLISHER'S NOTE
Every effort has been made to
ensure that the credits and contact
information complies with the
information provided us. 3x3 is not
responsible for missing information.
We apologize for any omissions or
spelling errors that may have been
carried through from the original
submission of materials.

WE HOPE YOU HAVE ENJOYED OUR ANNUAL DIRECTORY *AND* WE'D LOVE TO HEAR

ANY SUGGESTIONS TO IMPROVE OUR BOOK.

IF WE'VE EXCITED *YOU* ABOUT THE PROSPECT OF USING ILLUSTRATION THEN WE'VE

ACCOMPLISHED *OUR* FIRST GOAL.

AND WE'RE CERTAIN YOU'LL HAVE A WONDERFUL EXPERIENCE USING *ANY* AND *ALL* OF

THE ILLUSTRATORS WE HAVE PRESENTED.

AND DON'T FORGET YOU ALSO HAVE ACCESS TO *ALL* OUR ARTISTS ONLINE AT

3X3DIRECTORY.COM *AND* IN OUR FREE *EBOOK*.

THERE YOU'LL HAVE DIRECT LINKS *TO* EACH ARTIST'S WEBSITE ALONG WITH THEIR

DETAILED CONTACT INFORMATION.

AND WE'D ENCOURAGE YOU TO *ADD* OUR 3X3 INTERNATIONAL ILLUSTRATION ANNUAL

TO YOUR COLLECTION *OF* REFERENCE MATERIALS.

OUR 420-PAGE PAPERBACK ANNUAL IS AVAILABLE *AT* SELECTED BOOKSTORES

ACROSS THE COUNTRY *OR* DIRECT FROM OUR ONLINE STORE.

GO *TO* WWW.3X3MAG.COM FOR DETAILS.

HAVE QUESTIONS OR COMMENTS? CONTACT US AT INFO@3X3DIRECTORY.COM